Do It Yourself

Visual Basic®

... or Borland's DELPHI,
if u want something better!

Do It Yourself

Visual Basic®

William J. Orvis

SAMS

A Division of Prentice Hall Computer Publishing
11711 North College, Carmel, Indiana 46032 USA

To Julie, who fought off the kids, took care of Cub Scouts, bussed kids to school, coached soccer, represented GATE, bussed kids from school, secretaried PTA, doctored the animals, bussed kids to school, doctored Dad's animals, bussed kids from school, and even managed to do the laundry once in a while. Thank You.

International Standard Book Number: 0-672-27382-9
Library of Congress Catalog No.: 92-67C53

Composed in Carmel, Indiana by Prentice Hall Computer Publishing
Printed in the United States of America

Publisher
Richard K. Swadley

Publishing Manager
Joseph B. Wikert

Managing Editor
Neweleen A. Trebnik

Acquisitions
Linda Sanning

Development Editor
Jennifer Flynn

Production Editor
Kezia Endsley

Editors
Lori Cates
Cheri Clark
Jodi Jensen
Christine Pfeiffer

Technical Editor
Jeffery Hsu

Editorial Assistants
San Dee Phillips
Rosemarie Graham

Production Analyst
Mary Beth Wakefield

Book Design
Michele Laseau

Cover Art
Dan Armstrong

Production
Jeff Baker, Claudia Bell, Scott
Boucher, Brad Chinn, Michelle
Cleary, Mark Enochs, Brook
Farling, Phil Kitchel, Anne
Owen, Kevin Spear, Allan
Wimmer, Phil Worthington,
Christine Young

Index
Susan Vandewalle

About the Author

William Orvis is an electronic engineer at the University of California's Lawrence Livermore National Laboratory, where he is involved in the large scale numerical modeling of solid state devices, development of micron-sized vacuum microelectronic devices, and computer security research. (He describes himself as being a computer virus smasher.) Orvis received both B.S. and M.S. Degrees in Physics and Astronomy at the University of Denver in Colorado. He is the author of : *ABC's of GW-BASIC* (Sybex 1990), *Excel Instant Reference* (Sybex 1989), *1-2-3 for Scientists and Engineers* (Sybex 1987, 2nd ed. 1991), and *Electrical Overstress Protection for Electronic Devices*, (Noyes Data Corporation, 1986). His books have been translated into Japanese, Italian, and Greek. He also has written for *Computers in Physics*, and *IEEE Circuits and Devices Magazine*.

Overview

Contents

2   Learning the Visual Basic Environment   15

Part II: Opening Up Visual Basic

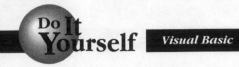

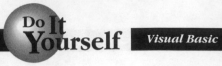

16 Properties   **537**

18 Objects 615

Part IV: Appendixes

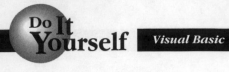

Acknowledgments

I want to thank Joe Wikert and Jennifer Flynn from SAMS Corporation, who kept the pressure on to get this work done, and of course, all of the others at SAMS who got this book from manuscript to print. Without them, you wouldn't be looking at anything now. I also want to thank Danny and Tien at Today Computers in Plesanton, California for all the help straightening out some new hardware.

I want to thank BJ, Skye and Sierra for not being too upset as I shut myself away to learn Visual Basic and do this book; we start on your projects tomorrow. Even Shane gets thanked this time, for not helping too much. Lastly, I want to thank Julie for keeping everything else going, and holding the house together while I worked on this book.

Trademark Acknowledgments

SAMS has made every attempt to supply trademark information about company names, products, and services mentioned in this book. Trademarks indicated below were derived from various sources. SAMS Corporation cannot attest to the accuracy of this information.

Microsoft BASIC is a registered trademark of Microsoft Corporation.

IBM is a registered trademark of International Business Machines Corporation.

Pac-Man licensed to Atari by Namco-America, Inc.

Microsoft, MS-DOS, GW-BASIC, BASICA, and Excel, are registered trademarks of Microsoft Corporation

QuickBASIC, Visual Basic, and Windows are trademarks of Microsoft Corporation

OS/2 is a registered trademark licensed to Microsoft Corporation

Apple, Macintosh are registered trademarks of Apple Computer, Inc.

Preface

When Howard SAMS Computer Publishing approached me to write a book about Microsoft's new Visual Basic, I was interested, but I hadn't seen the software yet. It had just come into Beta test, so little was available in the press about it. I only heard it was supposed to be something really interesting. Beta test copies soon arrived in the mail and I started to experiment. As with any new language, before you can use it, you have to try everything out and see how it compares to other languages you have used. Then, you can transfer your experience with other languages to the new language and figure out how best to apply it. I have written several hundred thousand lines of code in numerous versions of BASIC, and it usually only takes a day or two to figure out a new version and start doing useful work with it. Well, no such luck with Visual Basic. Visual Basic is such a total departure from traditional BASIC, that much of the prior knowledge went right out the door. It's not that Visual Basic doesn't run codes written in other versions of BASIC; it does, and it's not that the commands and statements are different, they aren't. The difference is how new programs are created and structured.

To say that I am enthusiastic about Visual Basic is to understate my feelings. Visual Basic is one of the most significant new developments in computer languages to come along in many years. And this development didn't come in a "hard" language like C or Pascal, that only real programmers understand, it came in BASIC, which everyone can use and understand.

I'm used to writing many lines of code to create the visual interface of a program—to define what it looks like on the screen and how it receives and responds to commands. Visual Basic takes much of that work into its own hands, and lets you draw the visual interface with a mouse. No longer do I have to guess where a button goes, I draw it exactly where I want it. No longer do I have to write code to determine when an event has occurred, I only have to write code to handle the events themselves. (An event is something that happens to a program, such as the user clicking a button with the mouse or pressing a key at the keyboard.) Everything else is taken care of by Visual Basic.

Thus began a frantic process of discovery to determine how best to create applications in this new implementation of an old language. In addition, I had a whole lot of fun. It's really an ego boost to create a polished Windows application in a couple of hours. Too soon though, I had to stop playing and get to work, because my publisher wanted to know where the current chapter was, and how soon she could expect to see the next one. Ah well, the writing is over now, so I can get back to playing. That is, if I can get my computer back from my nine-year-old son, B.J. Luckily, I'm in line with my two year old, Shane, and he still lets me help.

William J. Orvis
Livermore, California

Introduction

Microsoft Visual Basic is a considerable branch in the development of BASIC computer languages—and all computer languages. Computer languages and the programs they create are essentially text files. The program is text, the results are text, and most of the output is text. Even on the Macintosh, where the Graphical User Interface (GUI) is a well-defined art, programs created with the BASIC interpreters and compilers are still text files that write or draw on a window rather than the whole screen. With Windows, as with the Macintosh operating system, you can create GUI applications, but the process is long and painful. Mountains of code must be written to create and draw windows on the screen, draw buttons and other controls on the windows, and track the keyboard and mouse.

Visual Basic, on the other hand, includes the GUI interface from the beginning. You start with a window (called a Form) and draw buttons or controls on it, and Visual Basic generates the code to create them on the screen, and to track the interactions of the mouse and keyboard with them. In fact, you never see any of that code; it is all handled in the background by Visual Basic. When something happens to a Form or control (an event), Visual Basic passes control of a program to you, the programmer. For example, if you press a button by clicking it with the mouse, you don't have to worry about determining whether the button has been pressed or writing code to show the button being pressed. You just write the code that tells the computer what to do after the button is pressed.

In the past, up to 90 percent of the code written for a large application dealt with the user interface, with only 10 percent going to the meat of the application. So switching to a programming environment that handles most of the user interface for me (I still have to create the interface and draw it) results in a major change in my program development time. Now, in minutes, I can create a professional-looking Windows application, complete with windowed interface, buttons, Check boxes and graphics windows. Rather than spending my time figuring out how to make the user interface work, I spend it making the meat of the program work, and work efficiently.

If you have programmed before, I think you will find this an exhilarating experience. If you have never programmed before, may you never have to find out what it's like not to have a Visual Basic-like environment.

In This Book

This book teaches the novice programmer the elements of the Visual Basic environment, the BASIC language, programming conventions and methods, and the development of a Graphical User Interface. Using the different GUI (Graphical User Interface) controls as a vehicle, this book guides the reader through the conventional BASIC language, and the Visual Basic enhancements. With each control, I develop a significant programming example both to show off the control, and to provide the user with a useful application. I hope that as you develop each application, you learn how to modify it to suit your particular needs. Throughout this particular book, I inserted sidebars called FYI-Ideas (set off with a light-bulb icon) to point you toward more advanced versions of the applications.

Many books develop simple trivial examples to demonstrate programming and the language. These examples are fine for demonstrating a piece of the language, but they don't show how larger applications work, and they aren't useful later on. The example programs used in this book are not only vehicles for learning the language, but are meant to be usable additions to your programming library. Some of them are slightly longer than you might be used to seeing in a book on a programming language. However, I think the increased functionality of the programs is well worth it.

Part I is an introduction to Windows, Windows programming, and Visual Basic programming. This part explains how to use the Windows environment and the basics of Windows programming. The Visual Basic programming environment is then examined, along with an overview of program development process.

Part II is a tutorial on Visual Basic programming. In Part II, each Visual Basic object introduced in Part I is examined in more detail. Visual Basic objects are the Forms, Buttons, and Text boxes that make up the visual interface of a Visual Basic program. In addition, as the part progresses through the objects, the BASIC programming language (which ties all these objects together), is also developed.

Part III is a complete Visual Basic reference. Parts II and III complement each other, with Part II supplying the common usage of the language elements and objects, and Part III supplying the details. In Part III, each of the functions, statements, and methods that comprise the Visual Basic language is explained, along with its syntax, and an example showing its usage. In addition to the language elements, each object has properties that control how it looks and how it works. Each of these properties is explained in detail, with a description of what part of an object's character a property controls, and how to change that property. Messages are passed from the objects to a program using events. Each object has a specific set of events that it handles and passes on to a program. Each of these events is examined in Part III.

Part IV is an Appendix to Visual Basic, containing installation instructions, a table of the ASCII (ANSI) character codes, and a table of the keycodes. The ASCII character codes are the standard encoding used to store strings of characters in a BASIC program, and the keycodes are used to identify the specific keys on the keyboard.

Who Can Use this Book?

This book is for the novice computer programmer who wants to learn Visual Basic programming in the Windows environment, and for the advanced or not-so-advanced computer user who wants to learn programming. It's also for the programmer who wants to learn about programming in the Windows environment, without the mass of code needed in other languages that tends to obscure an understanding of the environment. Advanced programmers will probably find this book too slow for them, but if they glance at the language syntax in each chapter and work through the examples, they will get a useful understanding of the language, and of programming in the Windows environment.

The direction of this book is toward the home and small business computer user, though large business and technical computer users will have no problem applying the techniques to their work. The problems are all somewhat generic in their application, so they can readily be adapted to a particular situation. I often indicate extensions to a problem, and point the reader in the direction needed to achieve them.

What You Must Know

You must be familiar with using Windows and Windows methods. I don't expect you to be an expert, but you must at least be able to launch Windows, launch a program under Windows, maximize and minimize windows, and switch between applications. If you have never used Windows before, play with it for an hour or two. Run a word processor or a spreadsheet program and move the windows around, resize them, and try the commands and controls. The Windows package contains lots of good information and examples to help you learn it quickly.

What You Must Have

Visual Basic requires some specific hardware and software. You must have a computer with at least a 286 processor and one megabyte (1M) of memory. To efficiently use Windows, 2M of memory or more is better, and considering the current price of memory, I think you will find it well worth the cost. You need a graphics monitor and card such as the CGA, EGA, VGA, 8514, Hercules, or compatible. I wouldn't recommend anything less than an EGA system in order to use the full capabilities of Windows or Visual Basic. You need a hard disk drive with approximately 5M free for the complete Visual Basic package. You can get away with about 2.5M if you leave out the icon library, the examples, and the tutorial. You also need a mouse. I know the Windows documentation says you don't need a mouse, and perhaps you can operate everything without one, but get a mouse anyway. Using Windows without a mouse is like driving a boat without a rudder. You probably can make it turn with a lot of hard work, but a rudder makes things much simpler and smoother. The same goes for a mouse and Windows.

For software, you need DOS 3.1 or later and Windows 3.0 or later. If Windows isn't installed on your machine, you must install it first, before trying to install Visual Basic. Follow the directions in the Windows package, and maybe you will get lucky the first time. Windows sometimes needs some experimentation before it works properly. After Windows is installed and running, then install Visual Basic. A description of the installation process is in Appendix A, "Installing Visual Basic," of this book. Installing Visual Basic is easy after installing Windows.

I made the mistake of upgrading my hardware and installing Windows at the same time, and it took a while to get all the right drivers and memory managers in place and working together. Then I ran into an incompatibility between my disk manager software and Windows. It turned out that I needed to change only a simple software switch, but it took a while to find it. Much thanks to Danny and Tien at Today Computers in Plesanton, California who helped me straighten everything out.

What Conventions Do You Use?

As I develop the language elements, I often resort to syntax statements to describe the syntax of that element. In Part III of this book, every function, statement, and method includes a syntax statement. A syntax statement is an expression of the grammar of the computer language, showing where the commas go and how the words are spelled. The format of a syntax statement is as follows.

- Words and symbols that must be typed exactly as they are shown in the syntax statement are in `monospace bold`.

- Placeholders for variable names or constant values are in *`monospace italic`*, and where appropriate, are followed by the variable type suffix characters. The variable type suffix characters indicate the type of variable or number that is expected at this location. The types are, % (Integer), & (Long integer), ! (Single precision floating point), # (Double precision floating point), @ (Currency), and $ (String). These types will be explained in more detail later.

- Alternate entries (where you must make a choice) are separated with vertical bars (|) and surrounded by braces ({ }).

- Repeated clauses are followed by an ellipsis (...).

- Optional entries are surrounded by square brackets([ ]).

    For example,

```
On [Local] Error {GoTo line¦Resume Next¦GoTo 0}
```

In the example, the key words `On`, `Local`, `Error`, `GoTo`, `Resume`, and `Next` must be typed exactly as shown so they are in monospace bold. The words `On` and `Error` are required, but [`Local`] is optional, so it is surrounded

by square brackets. At the end of the statement are three clauses, from which you must select one, so they are surrounded with braces and separated by vertical bars. The word *line* is a placeholder for a variable or a constant value so it is in monospace italic.

A second example is

```
MsgBox(msg$[,type%[,title$]])
```

In this example, the keyword **MsgBox**, the two parentheses, and the two commas must be typed exactly as shown, so they are bold. The first argument, *msg$*, is a placeholder for a string. The argument *type%* is a placeholder for an integer and *title$* is a placeholder for another string. The first argument is required, but the second two are optional. The bracket-within-bracket arrangement indicates that if the third argument, *title$,* is used, the second argument, *type%,* must also be included.

Outside of the syntax statements, the following conventions are used to highlight different items.

- Words, such as the code in programming examples, that the reader must type exactly as they are written are in `monospace bold`.

- The access keys ("hot" keys) for keyboard access to menu items and buttons are underlined on the computer but are bold in the text of this book (the **F**ile menu, for example).

- Some keyboards have Return keys and others have Enter. I use Enter in this text, but these keys are interchangeable, so use the one on your keyboard whenever I use Enter.

- Visual Basic keywords, variable names, methods, procedures, functions, events, properties, and objects are in computer font, such as `End`, `Open`, `MsgBox`, and `Form1`.

- Visual Basic buttons, such as **View Code**, **Insert**, and **OK** are in **bold**.

- In the step-by-step programming examples, Visual Basic's drawing tools are used to create the various buttons and boxes that make up the visual interface of the example. Whenever a drawing tool is needed to complete a step described in this book, an icon representing the particular tool appears next to the step.

 For example, the icon for a Picture box is at the beginning of this paragraph. Use these icons to insure that you are using the correct tool. The Toolbox window is described in Chapter 2, "Learning the Visual Basic Environment."

- The length of a line in Visual Basic is occasionally longer than can be printed in the book. Visual Basic statements cannot be arbitrarily split into two lines, because the program will not continue working. Therefore, when a line must be split in this book, it is prefaced with the character ⤺. Note that when you type a line followed by one that is started with this character, the two lines must be joined for the program to work. For example, in the following procedure, the first and second lines must be typed as a single line in a Visual Basic program, or you receive a syntax error.

```
Sub LeftArrow_MouseDown (Button As Integer,
    Shift As Integer, X As Single, Y As Single)
LeftArrow.BackColor = BLACK
End Sub
```

Where You Can Find the Examples

If you don't feel like typing all the examples in this book, they are available on disk directly from the author for $20. In addition to the examples from this book, the disk includes some simple applications and pieces of test code for the advanced methods not covered in this book, such as Dynamic Data Exchange and Dynamic Link Libraries. To get the disk, use the coupon at the end of this book. Note that Prentice Hall Computer Publishing is not involved in the sale of this disk, and makes no warranty for it.

Boxed Notes

Occasionally, a piece of information or advice does not fit within the current tutorial. Notes of this type are separated from the rest of the text of the chapter in a boxed note, as shown here.

> This is an example of a boxed note.

Programming tips and shortcuts also are separated from the examples in a tip, as shown here.

Holding down the Ctrl, Alt, Shift, and CapsLock key with the right hand while pressing Shift, Enter and Backspace with the left hand is guaranteed to get you strange looks.

Tips and notes that warn of problems or possibly unwanted results are inserted as cautions.

If you try the last tip, you may look dumb.

Finally, all the examples represent fairly basic applications that can be expanded and modified to show a lot more functionality. In these cases, I describe some of the possible changes that can be made and briefly point you in the right direction to make those changes in a FYI-Idea box.

Wow!! I just had a great idea and I want to share it with you!!

Where Are You Going?

You are going on a wonderful trip, where you create your own worlds, travel among friends or enemies, win battles, and become the master of your computer. You are going to teach this machine who is boss, and make it politely carry out your wishes.

Part I

Visual Basic Basics

Windows Programming

Early versions of high-level computer languages, such as BASIC and FORTRAN, were largely text oriented. The program was a text file typed on cards or at a Teletype, and the results were printed on a line printer, or Teletype. With the help of special libraries and graphical output devices such as plotters and film recorders, they could do graphics, but the graphics were not real-time. They usually arrived on a roll of microfilm an hour or two after the program had completed running.

With the advent of glass-fronted terminals (terminals with the output on a CRT rather than on paper), programmers started drawing graphics on the terminals. However, the graphics were still a part of the output, they only got to you faster than microfilm.

The Graphical User Interface (GUI) actually started at the Xerox Palo Alto Research Center (Xerox PARC), where engineers developed a graphical interface complete with icons and a mouse. Unfortunately, that project was not a commercial success, and largely disappeared. On the other hand, a visit to Xerox PARC by Steve Jobes, one of the founders of Apple

Computer, provided the inspiration for the Macintosh's GUI. Because of the popularity of the Macintosh interface, Microsoft developed Windows, and Microsoft and IBM developed OS/2 for the PC and PC-compatible computers.

One of the basic tenets of the modern operating systems is the use of reusable blocks of code, and the even more modern concept of a code object. An *object* is an abstraction of the world of subroutines and code to the real world of physical things. Objects consist of such things as windows, buttons, and menus, and are much more than reusable blocks of code. An object is a combination of the data that comprises the object and the code that manipulates that data. For example, a button consists of the drawing of the button on the screen, several parameters describing where and how large to make the button, and the code that draws the button on the screen and initiates the action of the button when it is pressed.

Much of a modern operating system comprises large libraries of these reusable objects, the use of which significantly reduce the amount of time needed to develop a new application. When you want a button on your application, you no longer have to spend several days coding it from scratch, instead you spend a few minutes attaching a button object to your program and passing it the information about where and how big you want the button. The button object actually draws the button on the screen and changes the image of the button to simulate a pressed button.

In This Chapter

This chapter gives you some background on Windows, and the Object-Oriented Programming (OOP) methods used in Visual Basic. This is not a detailed discussion of Windows' methods or Object-Oriented Programming, but a brief overview of these two topics. This chapter covers

- Using Windows.
- The Windows Environment.
- Object-Oriented Programming.
- Object-Oriented Programming with Visual Basic.

Using Windows

A window in Windows 3.0 contains several distinct parts—see Figure 1.1. Along the top is a Title bar. The title in the center of the Title bar can be several different things. The usual choices are the name of the running application or the file name of the document the application is working on. On the right side of the window are two buttons. The left button is the **Minimize** button. The right one is the **Maximize/Restore** button, which is a **Maximize** button when a window is normal size, and a **Restore** button when a window is maximized. A **Maximize** button has a single vertical arrow on it and a **Restore** button has a vertical double arrow on it.

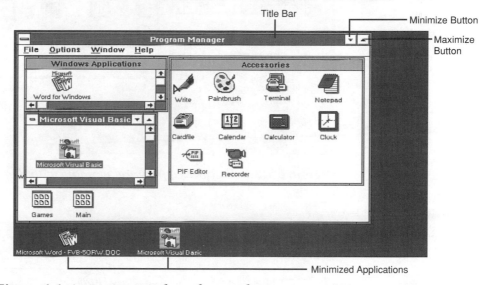

Figure 1.1. A program window of normal size.

On the left side of the Title bar is the **Control** button that opens the Control menu, as shown in Figure 1.2. To open the Control menu, click the button with the mouse, or press Alt-spacebar (for a program window), or Alt-hyphen (for a document Window). You can also press Alt and use the left and right arrow keys to move the focus to the button, then press Enter.

The Control menu contains the **R**estore, **M**ove, **S**ize, Mi**n**imize, Ma**x**imize, and **C**lose commands. Program windows also have the **S**witch To command on the Control menu. The primary use of these commands

5

is for running windows without a mouse. To select a command without a mouse, press the underlined letter (the hot key) or move the focus with the arrow keys and press Enter when the command is selected. To select a command with the mouse, click the command. Table 1.1 describes the operation of the buttons on the title bar and the commands on the Control menu.

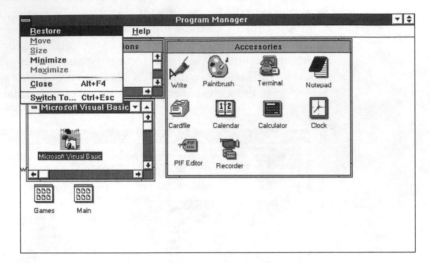

Figure 1.2. *A Maximized program window with the Command menu open.*

Table 1.1. Operation of the Windows controls on the Control menu.

Command	Function
Restore	Returns a maximized or minimized window to its initial size. To restore a maximized window with the mouse, click the **Restore** button, double-click the Title bar, or click the **Restore** command on the Control menu. To restore a minimized application, double-click the minimized application's icon.

Command	Function
Move	Moves the window with the arrow keys. Press Enter when you have the window where you want it. To move the window with the mouse, place the mouse pointer on the Title bar, press down on the left mouse button, and drag the window to its destination.
Size	Resizes the window with the arrow keys. To resize the window using the mouse, place it on the border of the window (pointer should change to double-ended arrow), then press the left mouse button and drag the border to the new position.
Minimize	Reduces the window to an icon, such as those along the bottom of Figure 1.1. To minimize the application with the mouse, click the **Minimize** button.
Maximize	Expands the window to fill the screen, such as Figure 1.2. To maximize the window with the mouse, click the **Maximize** button, or double-click the Title bar.
Close	Closes the window; this action ends the application if the window is an application window. To close the window with the mouse, double-click the button that opens the Command menu.
Switch To	Brings up a list so you can switch to another running application. To change applications with the mouse, click the applications window.

The Windows Environment

The Windows environment maintains the visual interface of a Windows program. It also keeps track of which code is running, and what resources that code needs. As it is currently implemented, Windows is a shell over the DOS operating system. Windows also provides a large library of functions to make developing a Windows program much simpler. All the functions to create and manage windows are available in the system, so a programmer does not have to develop these functions on his or her own. These libraries not only make programming easier, but make programs more consistent with each other so you have less to learn in order to use a new program.

A Shell Over DOS

The Windows environment is a shell over the DOS operating system that provides the control and capability to run multiple applications in a graphical, "windowed," user interface. A shell is a program that forms an interface between DOS and the user. It accepts user commands, and issues the respective DOS commands. In Windows, multiple applications can run simultaneously, with each given one or more windows on the screen to draw on and a piece of memory to run in. The Windows operating system manages the visual interface, allocates the memory to different programs, records which program is running, and provides access to the disk drives.

Memory and Screen Management

Each running application appears in one or more windows on the screen, with the active application's windows in front. Applications also can have document windows within their program windows to contain documents. Each application must stay in its assigned window and block of memory, otherwise bad things can happen. In a 286 machine, any application that uses memory outside of its assigned area causes problems by destroying the other application in the area it used. In 386 and later machines with

Windows running in 386 enhanced mode, the hardware prevents an application from moving out of its assigned area by not allowing any memory accesses outside of that area.

Because not all computers are 386 machines, the Windows programmer must insure that his or her code does not access memory outside of its assigned memory blocks. The operating system does take care of assigning and managing those blocks, however.

Multitasking

In addition to managing memory, the Windows operating system manages task-switching between multiple running applications. In most cases, the application in the foreground is using most the CPU time; however, the system, and other applications can also run in the background when the foreground application isn't busy. The Multitasking method used in Windows is not preemptive, meaning it does not interrupt a running application to run another, but depends on the benevolence of the running application to yield time to the system. If a windows application does not occasionally yield the CPU to the system, background jobs won't run, and the system won't update windows or handle the peripheral devices such as the printer.

The Windows programmer must insure that his or her program regularly yields control to the system. The system will then take care of its tasks, and pass control to one of the programs running in the background. When the background program passes control back to the system, the system will then activate the foreground job again.

Libraries Of Windows Functions

The Windows operating system contains a large library of functions, available for any application to use. There are functions to create the visual environment, such as windows and menus, functions to manage memory, functions to communicate with other applications, functions to communicate with system resources such as the printer and the disk drives, and general functions to facilitate drawing pictures.

These functions are stored in Dynamic Link Libraries, which are accessible by any running program. They are called Dynamic Link Libraries, because they don't have to be attached to a program to be used, but are dynamically linked to it as needed at run time. All these functions significantly reduce the amount of coding a programmer must do, by providing most of the standard functions in a ready-to-use format.

Device Independence

One of the biggest headaches found when creating an application on a DOS machine is the large number of different peripheral devices that you, the programmer, must be prepared to handle. It's not uncommon for an application program to come with a hundred device drivers to handle all the different types of monitors and printers that could possibly be on a system. With Windows, the operating system communicates with all the devices and provides a standard interface for all programs to use. Thus, a Windows programmer no longer has to worry about what monitor or printer is attached to a system, she or he simply prints on the assigned window or to the standard printer.

Language Types

There are basically two different types of languages available on a computer, Interpreted and Compiled. The difference between these two is how a program is executed, and not in the physical structure of the language. When a code is first written, it resides essentially in a file in text form. An interpreter reads each line of that code, converts the line into machine language commands and then executes them. The machine language commands are the numeric codes that the CPU understands. When the code for one line has run, the interpreter moves to the next line, and converts and executes it. The benefits of an interpreted language are almost immediate execution of a code after a change, modification of a running application, and simplified error detection and correction.

A compiler, on the other hand, first converts a whole program into machine language codes then stores those codes in a file. That file is now an executable program that can be run directly without further interpretation. The benefits of a compiled code are increased speed over an interpreted code, and stand-alone execution. A compiled code runs faster because the lines of code are already in machine language form and don't have to be reinterpreted each time they are executed. The increase in speed can be a factor of 100 or more over interpreted codes. An interpreted code must have the interpreter in memory as well as the code. After compilation, the compiler is no longer needed and the code can run by itself.

Visual Basic is both an interpreter and a compiler. The interpreter is used to speed code development, and the compiler is used to increase the speed of the code after development is complete.

Object-Oriented Programming

Object-oriented programming is the current development in programming methodology. This method bundles code and data into somewhat autonomous objects. The idea is that when you create an object to do something, you no longer have to know how it works, you simply pass it messages. That way, an object created in one program can be reused easily in another.

Objects

With the introduction of Visual Basic, Microsoft has made a large advance in the field of Object-Oriented Programming (OOP). Not only does Visual Basic have objects, but the objects are real, touchable things like buttons and boxes. Other object-oriented languages create objects with an object command of some sort that defines a block of code and data as an object. You are then supposed to imagine that object as a "thing" with features you can use. Visual Basic makes it easier by making the object a visible thing rather than a coding abstraction.

The main object in a Visual Basic program is the Form. A Form is a window that you build an application on. On the Form you attach Controls, such as Command buttons, Option buttons, Check boxes, Text boxes, Labels, and Scroll bars. Each of these is a Visual Basic object. To attach an object to a Form, you draw it with the mouse. The whole visual interface of a Visual Basic program is drawn rather than coded.

Events

Objects communicate with each other, with the system, and with the program using events. Events are actions that an object might want to respond to. When the mouse is moved and a mouse button is clicked, the system keeps track of where the mouse pointer is, and what object was under it when it was clicked. If the object was a button, the system sends a `Click` event to the button object. The button object visually simulates a pressed button, and passes a `button_click` event to the program. If the programmer writes a procedure to handle `button_click` events, that procedure gets control and carries out its function. When that function is complete, control passes back to the system to wait for the next event.

As a programmer, you have the option to respond to numerous events passed to you by the objects that make up your program. These events include things like clicking or double-clicking an object, or pressing a key while the object has the focus. Chapter 17, "Events," in Part III of this book lists all the events you can respond to. To respond to an event, you create an event procedure with the name

```
object_event
```

which is then executed whenever the object passes on that event.

Objects don't pass all events to the program; many events are handled by the object or by the Windows operating system. For example, if you drag the edge of a window, you can change the size of a window. Resizing the window is handled by the operating system; you, the programmer don't have to do anything, though you will be passed a `Resize` event by the window (called a Form in Visual Basic), to inform you that a change has taken place.

Methods

Objects are not simply bundled code blocks, but a bundling of data and the code that manipulates it. Every object contains code to manipulate its own data, known as methods. To invoke a method, type the object name, a dot, then the method name. Following the method name are any arguments the method needs. For example,

```
Form.PrintForm
```

This is a statement executing the Form's `PrintForm` method. The `PrintForm` method prints the contents of a Form (a Visual Basic window) on the printer. Another example follows.

```
Form.Print "Good Morning"
```

Here, `Print` is another method contained in the Form object that prints on a Form. In this case, it prints the text `"Good Morning"` on the Form.

Properties

The data contained in an object is stored in its properties. Properties not only contain the data stored in an object, such as the text to be printed in the `Printer` object, but also the object's dimensions, color, and numeric codes that specify its capabilities. For example, going back to the Form object, which has a property called `BorderStyle`. Setting the `BorderStyle` property to `1 - Fixed Single` prevents a Form from being resized by dragging its borders. Changing `BorderStyle` to `2 - Sizable`, makes it possible to change the size of the object by dragging its borders. Chapter 16, "Properties," in Part III of this book lists all the properties of the different objects.

Inheritance

Inheritance is the property of OOP where an object inherits the methods of the objects from which it is made. When you draw a Label on a Form, the Form inherits the Label's properties. For example, the `Caption` property of a Label contains the text printed on the Label. If the Label is named `Label1` (all objects have names), and it is drawn on `Form1`, then `Form1` inherits the `Caption` property, which is accessed as follows.

```
Form1.Label1.Caption
```

All the properties of objects drawn on a Form are accessed in this way.

Forms also inherit the methods of the objects, so when a Form has a Picture box drawn on it, the Form inherits the Picture box's `Print` method. The Form can now print on a Picture box.

Visual Basic, the Next Step

Visual Basic represents the next step in Object-Oriented Programming. In Visual Basic, not only is code and data encapsulated, it even looks like the object it represents. In most object-oriented languages, you access a button object and tell it its location and size with lines of code. Only after you run your program can you actually see what it looks like. In Visual Basic, button objects look like buttons rather than lines of code. No longer do you have to imagine what it will look like, you draw it on a Form with a button drawing tool. Check boxes, Option buttons, and all the standard Windows objects look like the object they represent.

What You Have Learned

This chapter presented a brief overview of the Windows environment, and the use of Object-Oriented Programming in Visual Basic. The intent here is to give you a feeling for the methods and procedures discussed in this book. For more information on Windows methods, see the Microsoft Windows User's Guide included in your Windows package. For more information on programming with Visual Basic, read on; an adventure begins.

Learning the
Visual Basic Environment

Visual Basic is more than a programming language—it's a complete environment for developing Windows applications. This environment includes a program editor to create and modify the code you write, an interpreter to execute an application within the environment, a compiler to turn an application into stand-alone code that runs in the Windows environment, and a debugger to determine why an application does not work. Visual basic is unique in that only a few lines of code are needed to create a complete, working Windows application. In most programming languages, it takes a hundred or so lines of code simply to open a window, let alone create anything with it.

In This Chapter

In this chapter, you learn the application and operation of all the different commands and windows of the Visual Basic environment. The purpose of this chapter is to give you the flavors of the Visual Basic environment, and teach you how to develop programs in that environment. If you are concerned when you find that many of the descriptions are superficial, don't be; the next few chapters cover the individual parts more completely. For now, get a feel for the overall structure of Visual Basic, and how the windows and commands work together to make a program. Specifically, this chapter shows you how to

- Use the Visual Basic windows.

- Use the menu commands.

- Use tools from the Tool window to create controls.

- Create a Windows application.

- Save and retrieve an application.

- Compile an application.

Starting Visual Basic

Like most Windows applications, Visual Basic is extremely simple to start. First, find the Visual Basic icon in one of the Program Manager's Group windows. When you install Visual Basic with the Setup program, it usually places the icon in a special Microsoft Visual Basic Group window by itself. When you find the icon, simply double-click it. Visual Basic opens to the environment shown in Figure 2.1.

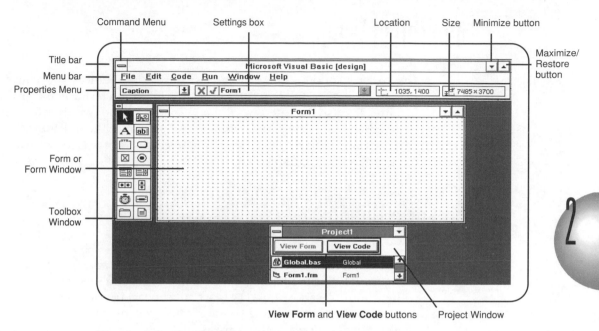

Figure 2.1. The Visual Basic screen at startup.

Negotiating the Windows

The first things you see when Visual Basic opens are three windows: the Form window (Form1), the Project window (Project1), and on the left side, the Toolbox window. Along the top, just below the Menu bar, is the Properties bar. Three other windows are opened as you need them: the Code window, the Color Palette window, and the Menu Design window. You can access hidden or closed windows from either the Windows menu on the menu bar or from the Project window. A seventh window, the Immediate window, can be opened only when a running program has been stopped with a Stop statement or a Break command.

The Project Window

The Project window is home for the Visual Basic application. The names of all the files and modules that comprise an application reside in the Project window. It's also the gateway to an application's windows. By selecting a Form or module in the Project window and pressing either the **View Form** or **View Code** button, you can bring the selected Form or Code window to the front so that you can edit it.

The Form Window

The Form window, or Form, lies above and to the left of the Project window in Figure 2.1. It is the foundation of your application's user interface. All your buttons, Text boxes, and Lists are attached to a Form, which becomes the application window that you see when you run your program. The simplest application usually consists of at least one Form, although an application can contain as many Forms as are necessary to complete the application. Although all Forms are visible when you are designing your application, Forms can be made visible or invisible by a running code. Consequently, only the Forms that have to be seen are visible on-screen when your application runs.

The Toolbox Window

The Toolbox window contains all the *objects* that can be placed on a Form. An object is a programming abstraction relating a physical object and the code attached to it. That is, an object is something that has physical presence on the screen, or at least corresponds to a physical presence in a computer application, such as a Timer. The following list of icons shows all the objects on the Toolbox window that can be attached to a Form.

Picture box—Displays a picture.

Label—Displays text Labels that the user cannot edit.

Text box—Displays or inputs text that the user can edit.

Frame—Provides a visual frame for combining controls.

Command button—A button that causes the application to take a particular action.

Check box—A button for setting nonexclusive options.

Option button—A button for setting mutually exclusive options.

Combo box—A combined Text box and List box.

List box—A box containing a list of items.

Horizontal Scroll bar—An input device for setting a value visually with a horizontal scale.

Vertical Scroll bar—An input device for setting a value visually with a vertical scale.

Timer—An alarm clock that causes an event to take place at a certain time.

Drive List box—A List box that contains all the disk drives available.

Directory List box—A List box that contains all the subdirectories in the current directory.

File List box—A List box that contains all the files in the current directory.

To attach an object, select it on the Toolbox window by clicking it with the mouse. Move the cursor to where you want the object's upper-left corner to be positioned. Hold down the left mouse button, move the mouse pointer to the lower-right corner of the object, and release the mouse button.

To reshape an object, select it and place the pointer on one of the black selection rectangles that surround the object. Press the left mouse button, and drag the rectangle until the object is the desired shape.

To move an object, select it by clicking it with the mouse, then hold down the left mouse button and drag the object to the desired location. Go ahead and create a few controls on Form1 and experiment with them a little. You can't hurt anything by doing so.

The Code Window

Associated with each Form is a Code window, shown in Figure 2.2, that contains the BASIC code for the Form and for all the objects attached to it. You access the Code window from the Project window by selecting the Form and pressing the **View Code** button. You also can access the Code window by double-clicking the interior of the Form or any control on the Form. Actual BASIC code resides in the Code windows of a Visual Basic program. Code windows are attached also to modules (discussed later), which are places to store code not associated with any specific Form or control.

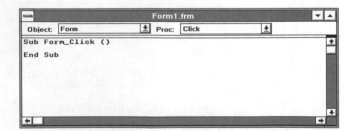

Figure 2.2. A Visual Basic Code window.

The two drop-down menus at the top of the window in Figure 2.2 are for creating a code template to use with the Form. On the left, the Object menu lists all the objects (buttons, Text boxes, and so on) attached to the

Form, including the Form itself. On the right, the Procedure menu lists all the events (mouse click, keystroke, and so forth) associated with the currently selected object. When you select an Object and an Event, Visual Basic automatically inserts the correct procedure header and footer in the Code window. You could type the header and footer in the window, but by using the menus you ensure that the format and spelling are correct.

The Color Palette Window

The Color Palette window, which is shown in Figure 2.3, is used to select colors visually. The Color Palette window normally is not visible, so you must activate it with the Color Palette command in the Window menu. Colors and patterns are defined in Visual Basic with large, unintuitive hexadecimal numbers (base 16). The Color Palette window makes selecting a color much more straightforward.

The Color Palette window changes the colors of the front-most Form, or the colors of the active object on the front-most Form. The Color Palette window is activated also by the Settings box on the Properties bar when a color property is being set. (You read about the Properties bar later in this chapter.)

Figure 2.3. The Color Palette window.

The two squares on the left side of the Color Palette window control where your color selection is applied. If you click the small inner square, your next color selection becomes the foreground color. The foreground of a window is usually any text or objects drawn on the Form. If you click the large, outer square, the next color selection becomes the background color of the selected object. Experiment with the Color Palette window all you want. Select Form1 or one of the controls you placed on Form1. Then select the Color Palette window and change the colors. Any foreground or background change immediately appears on that Form or object.

The Menu Design Window

The Menu Design window is hidden also. Activate it by clicking the **Menu** Design command on the **W**indows menu. The Menu Design window attaches one or more menus to the front-most Form, as shown in Figure 2.4. You can experiment with the Menu Design window if you want, but it's not as simple to figure out as the Color Palette window. You will learn about it in more detail in Chapter 7, "Using Custom Menus."

The Immediate Window

The Immediate window appears only when an application is running. It is a simple window, like a blank Form, on which messages from a running code are printed. You can use it also to execute one-line BASIC commands and statements when a program is paused with a `Stop` statement or the Brea**k** command on the **R**un menu.

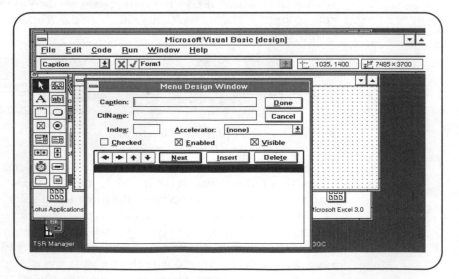

Figure 2.4. *A Menu Design window.*

Understanding Modules

Forms and modules are similar because they are both objects that have code attached to them. However, Forms are visible objects that contain control objects and interact with the user. Modules are invisible objects used for storing procedures not attached to a Form or control. Although you can store unattached procedures on a Form, it is a good programming practice to "modularize" a code by placing the unattached procedures in a module, especially if you have several of them.

Procedures on modules are available for use by all other modules and Forms, whereas procedures on a Form are available only to the other procedures on the same Form. For example, a procedure that clears all printed text from a Form could be attached to the Form it clears, but a procedure to convert text strings into binary numbers would go into a Module where it could be used by any other procedure. Note that these locations are not absolute; they depend on your particular application.

Unattached procedures stored in a module or Form are reusable. If several parts of your program have to execute identical procedures, you can store one copy of each procedure in a module and access it time and time again. This not only saves space, but it also makes maintaining your code easier because you only have to make corrections to the one copy in the module.

The Global module is automatically a part of every Visual Basic program. The Global module is the place where global definitions and declarations are placed. A *definition* is a name that is assigned a constant value. For example, the name True is usually defined as –1, the value of a logical True. The name True can then be used in a program rather than –1, making the program much more readable. A declaration defines the type of value that can be stored in a variable. For example, the phrase Index As Integer in a Dim or Global statement declares the variable Index as the numeric type Integer. More on definitions and declarations in Chapter 4, "Using Strings and Text Boxes," and Chapter 5, "Using Numbers and Control Structures."

Definitions and declarations placed in the Global module are available everywhere in your application. The file CONSTANT.TXT has a large list of useful definitions that you can load into the Global module and use in your application. Note that you can put only definitions and declarations, not code, in the Global module.

Using the Menus

Visual Basic uses six menus: **File**, **Edit**, **Code**, **Run**, Window, and **Help**. If you have used other Windows applications, you probably are familiar with the **File**, **Edit**, and **Help** menus.

File, Edit, and Help are available in some form on most Windows applications. The Code menu contains commands for working with Code windows. As you might expect, the **Run** menu contains commands for running an application. **Run** also contains the commands for debugging. You already used the **Window** menu to open or select closed or hidden windows.

The File Menu

As with most Visual Basic applications, the **File** menu (see Figure 2.5) is used to open and close files. The first command is New Project, which clears the screen of all old Forms and modules and creates a new Form and project window. If you haven't saved the old project, Visual Basic gives you one last chance to do so before deleting the project.

```
File
New Project
Open Project...
Save Project
Save Project As...

New Form
New Module
Add File...          Ctrl+F12
Remove File
Save File            Shift+F12
Save File As...      F12

Print...

Make EXE File...

Exit
```

Figure 2.5. *The File menu.*

24

Visual Basic programs actually are stored in several files that are brought together in the Project window. The contents of the Project window are stored in a .MAK file. Forms are stored in .FRM files, including any code attached to the Form or its controls. Modules are stored in .BAS files.

If you are familiar with other languages and operating systems such as UNIX, you will notice that the .MAK files are similar in function to makefiles. A makefile contains all the information necessary to recreate a compiled program. When a program is compiled, the Make program examines the makefile to determine what files to compile and combine to create the final application. Visual Basic uses a similar process in that the Project file contains the names of all the files that are necessary to recreate an application.

You use the Open Project, Save Project, and Save Project As commands to open or save all the files in a project. When you open a project, you only have to open the .MAK file. Loading the .MAK file automatically opens the rest of the .FRM and .BAS files that make up the project. The Save Project As command allows you to save the current Project file (the .MAK file) with a new name or in a different directory.

To change the name of every file in a project, or to save them in a different directory, select each file in the Project window, then use the Save File As command on the File menu. Once all the files are saved, use the Save Project As command to save the project description shown in the Project window.

The New Form and New Module commands add either a new blank Form or a new blank module to the list of files in the Project window. The Add File command adds a Form or module file existing on disk to the current Project window. The Save File and Save File As commands copy a current Form or module to a disk file. Thus, you can share useful pieces of code between different programs by simply attaching previously written Forms and modules.

The Remove File command deletes a Form or module from the Project window and removes the Form or module from your application. Note that Remove File removes a Form or module only from the current project. It does not delete the file from the disk. You must use the File Manager to do that. The Print command lets you print the contents of the active Form or module.

The Make .EXE File command compiles the current project into a stand-alone, executable Windows application. Once compiled, a program is independent of the Visual Basic program and only requires the VBRUN100.DLL run-time library file in order to run. Your Windows directory is a good place to store the run-time library file.

The last command on the File menu is the Exit command, which quits the Visual Basic application. As with the New Project command, you have another chance to save the current project before Visual Basic quits.

The Edit Menu

The Edit menu, shown in Figure 2.6, is standard among Windows applications. It contains the Undo, Cut, Copy, and Paste commands. In addition, the Visual Basic Edit menu contains the Paste Link, Delete, Grid Settings, and Align to Grid commands.

Edit	
Undo	Alt+Backspace
Cut	Shift+Del
Copy	Ctrl+Ins
Paste	Shift+Ins
Paste Link	
Delete	Del
Grid Settings...	
Align to Grid	

Figure 2.6. The Edit menu.

The Undo command, as its name suggests, undoes or reverses your previous change. Because Undo applies only to the last change you made, execute it immediately if you have to reverse some action; otherwise you won't be able to do so.

The Cut, Copy, and Paste commands move data between the clipboard and your Visual Basic project. After you copy something to the clipboard, you can save it, paste it to another location in your project, or paste it to a completely different application (such as a word processor).

To cut or copy data, select it with the cursor and execute the Cut or Copy command. The Copy command places a copy of the selected text or object on the clipboard without deleting it from its original location. The Cut command removes the selected text or object from its original location and places it on the clipboard. The Paste command inserts the contents of the clipboard at the cursor if it is text, or on the current Form if it's a control. The Paste Link command also pastes the contents of the clipboard to the current project. In addition, it establishes a link between Visual Basic and the source application from which the data was copied (assuming that application supports a link). Once linked, every data change made in the source application also is made to the linked application. The **D**elete command erases the currently selected control or text.

The last two commands on the **E**dit menu control the grid on the current Form. The **G**rid Settings command calls a dialog box that allows you to change the grid spacing, visibility, and grid snap on the current Form. When grid snap is on (when the **A**lign to Grid box is checked), new controls drawn on a Form are automatically aligned to the grid. The **A**lign To Grid command causes the selected objects on a Form to align themselves to the closest grid point on the Form.

The Code Menu

The **C**ode menu, shown in Figure 2.7, contains the commands for manipulating the Code window. The first command, View Co**d**e, opens the Code window associated with the currently selected object. You can open a Code window also with the **View Code** button in the Project window, or by simply double-clicking the object. The **L**oad Text and **S**ave Text commands either load the contents of a text file into the Code window or save the contents of the Code window in a text file. You can create or edit text files with most word processing programs, although they have to be saved in the word processing applications as plain text files, without any formatting information.

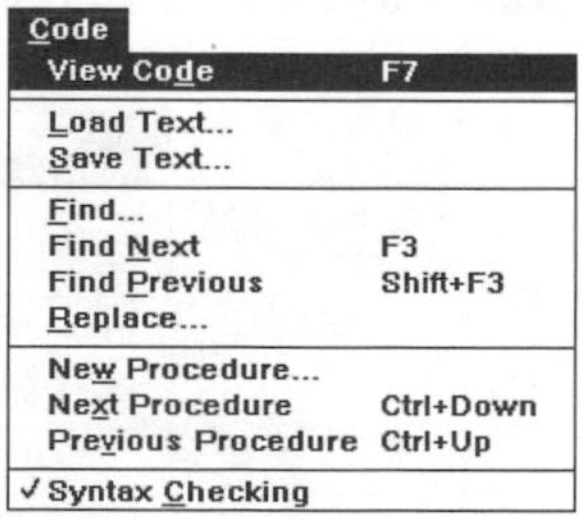

```
Code
 View Code              F7
 Load Text...
 Save Text...
 Find...
 Find Next             F3
 Find Previous         Shift+F3
 Replace...
 New Procedure...
 Next Procedure        Ctrl+Down
 Previous Procedure    Ctrl+Up
 √ Syntax Checking
```

Figure 2.7. The Code menu.

The Find, Find Next, and Find Previous commands locate specific strings of text in the Code window. First, use the Find command first to set the string to be located. Then use the Find Next and Find Previous commands to find the next and previous locations of that string. To find and replace a string, use the Replace command.

The New Procedure command creates a new function or subroutine template on the active Code window. If the procedure is going to be attached to a control, use the Object drop-down menu at the top of the Code window instead of the New Procedure command. The Next Procedure and Previous Procedure commands move forward and backward through the different procedures stored on a Form.

When the Syntax Checking command is checked, Visual Basic looks for syntax errors in each line of code as you type it. If Syntax Checking is unchecked, Visual Basic won't check for syntax errors until you run the program.

The Run Menu

The Run menu, shown in Figure 2.8, contains the commands for running, stopping, and debugging a project. The Start and End commands start and stop the current program. When a program is running, the Start command changes into Break, which pauses a running program so that you can examine the variables and make minor changes if necessary. The Ctrl-Break keyboard command has the same effect. When a program is paused, Break changes into Continue. Use the Continue or Restart commands to resume execution after executing a Break. The Continue command continues execution from where it was stopped. The Restart command starts everything over as if you executed End and then Start.

```
Run   Window   Help
Start              F5
End
Restart            Shift+F5
Single Step        F8
Procedure Step     Shift+F8
Set Next Statement
Show Next Statement
Toggle Breakpoint  F9
Clear All Breakpoints
Set Startup Form...
Modify Command$...
```

Figure 2.8. The Run menu.

The rest of the commands on this menu are for debugging code. You use the Single Step and Procedure Step commands to step through a program that has been stopped with a Break command, a Stop statement, or a breakpoint set with a Toggle Breakpoint command. The Single Step command steps through every statement in a program, whereas the Procedure Step command single-steps only in the current procedure. If the current procedure calls another procedure, that procedure is executed in its entirety before the program halts at the next statement in the current procedure. That is, stepping occurs only in the current procedure and not in any external procedures.

The Set Next Statement command changes the execution order of a program that has been paused with the Break command or a Stop statement or a breakpoint. Normally, when you use the Continue command or one of the Step commands, Visual Basic executes the next executable statement. The Set Next Statement command is used to start execution at a different statement. In a paused program, place the cursor in the place in the statement where you want execution to continue, then execute the Set Next Statement command.

When you execute Continue or one of the Step commands, execution continues at that statement. Use it to run the same piece of code repeatedly to see the effect of changes. You can use the Show Next Statement command to display the next statement to be executed, without actually executing it.

If you know approximately where a code is having problems, insert either a Stop statement or a breakpoint directly before the problem code. You insert and remove breakpoints with the Toggle Breakpoint command. When the execution of a code reaches a breakpoint, it halts execution and pauses as if you had executed the Break command. The Clear All Breakpoints command is used to remove all breakpoints that were inserted with the Toggle Breakpoint command. Breakpoints also disappear when you close a Project. You must edit the program to remove the Stop statements.

Normally, execution of a program starts with the first Form that is defined. To change the Form executed first when Start is executed, select the Form and execute the Set Startup Form command.

Some programs are designed to use command lines when you run them. For example, when starting a word processing program, if you follow the program name with the name of a file, the program starts and automatically opens that file for editing. The Modify Command$ command is used to modify the contents of the command line with the current Visual

Basic program. Use it to test a program with different command lines. After a program is compiled, the command line is set in the normal way, by following the program name with the command line.

The Window Menu

The Window menu, shown in Figure 2.9, activates the different windows listed in the menu. In a windowed environment, it is easy to "lose" a window behind other windows. Executing any of the Window menu commands brings the window to the screen if it already is open, or opens it if it is not yet open. The windows that can be opened are the Color Palette window, the Immediate window, the Menu Design window, the Project window, and the Toolbox window.

Figure 2.9. The Window menu.

The Help Menu

The Help menu, shown in Figure 2.10, contains the standard help commands: Index, Keyboard, Tutorial, Using Help, and About. The Index command opens the help index for Visual Basic. The Keyboard command lists the key combinations that can be used to select commands from the keyboard rather than using the mouse. The Tutorial command starts the Visual Basic tutorial. The Using Help command describes how to use the on-line help. The About command gives the current version, copyright notice, licensing information, serial number, windows mode, and memory available for Visual Basic.

Figure 2.10. *The Help menu.*

Understanding the Properties Bar

The Properties bar is a feature unique to Visual Basic. All the Forms and controls have properties such as color, size, and location. With the Properties bar, you select a property and change its value. The Properties bar consists of two List boxes: the Properties list, and the Settings box. When you pull down the Properties list by clicking the arrow, you see a list of all the properties of the currently selected Form or control that can be set at this time. Figure 2.11 shows the Properties bar with the Properties list for Form1 dropped down.

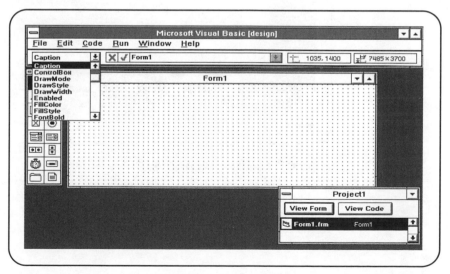

Figure 2.11. *The Properties bar with the Properties list dropped down.*

For example, start Visual Basic (if it isn't running already) and click Form1. Figure 2.11 shows the Properties list with the Form's Caption property selected. The Caption of a Form is the title in the title bar at the top of the Form. When a property is selected, its current value is displayed in the Settings box. If a property has a fixed set of allowed values, you can drop down a list from the Settings box and select the value from it. Otherwise you must type the value of the property. In Figure 2.11, the value of the Caption property is Form1. Because this property is a title, it can have any value you desire, but must by typed in the Settings box.

Select FontName from the Properties List box and click the arrow to the right of the Settings box. You see a list like the one in Figure 2.12, which shows all the Fonts available on your system. Your list might be different, depending on the fonts you have installed.

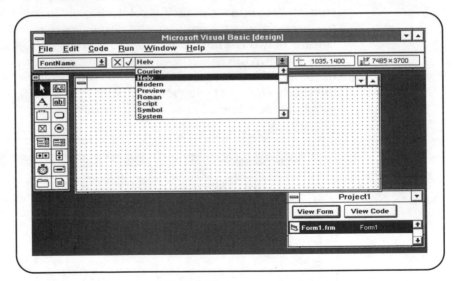

Figure 2.12. Using the Settings box.

To change the font used for printed text, simply select the new font from the list and click the box with the checkmark in it (the box that falls to the left of the Settings box). The box containing an X is a cancel box. If clicked, it returns the Property to its original value.

The properties listed in the Properties bar are only those properties that can be set at design time, that is, when you are writing your program. Forms and controls also have other properties that can only be set at run time by your computer. A Visual Basic program can set or change most of the properties at run-time. This topic is discussed in more detail in Chapter 3, "Understanding Forms."

Understanding the Running Modes

Before I go on, a short discussion of the Visual Basic running modes is necessary. As you switch between editing a program and running it, Visual Basic switches its mode of operation and behaves differently toward user interaction.

Design Mode

When you first start Visual Basic, it is in Design mode, which is where you create your application. Everything you have done so far has been in Design mode. In Design mode, you can

Create files

Open projects

Close projects

Save projects

Copy code

Cut code

Paste code

In short, you can make just about any changes you want to your project.

Interpreted Running Mode

When you select the **Start** command from the **R**un menu, the Visual Basic interpreter takes over and begins running your program. First, all the Form and Project windows you used to create your application are closed. Next, the interpreter displays the first Form and control that you have defined. Then the interpreter executes your program one line at a time. The interpreter also opens the Immediate window.

The interpreter reads a line of code, *converts* (interprets or compiles) it into microprocessor commands (*machine codes*), and executes those commands. Machine codes are numbers that your microprocessor interprets as commands to do something. Because the microprocessor commands are not saved, each time a line of code is executed it must be interpreted again. A benefit of this process is that you can make a change and run your program immediately without having to compile it. Unfortunately, the program runs more slowly than a compiled code because each statement must be interpreted before it can be executed.

While your program is running, you cannot make changes to your code, open project files, or save project files. For the most part, the only commands available (other than those you defined in your program) are those on the **R**un menu: **E**nd, Brea**k**, **R**estart, and the debugging commands. When you execute Brea**k**, Visual Basic returns to a semi-Design mode state. You can edit the code in this state, then restart it from where it stopped. Visual Basic goes back to Design mode if you execute the **E**nd command, or if your code finishes executing.

Compiled Running Mode

Compiled mode isn't actually a Visual Basic mode, although it is a different state of operation for your program. When you compile a program, Visual Basic reads the statements in your program, interprets them, converts them into microprocessor commands, and stores the commands in an .EXE file (an executable program file). The increase in speed originates at this point. Because all your code already has been interpreted and converted into microprocessor commands, the statements do not have to be interpreted each time they are executed, which saves a step.

When you execute the .EXE file, your processor reads and executes the microprocessor commands independently of Visual Basic. (Well, the execution is *almost* totally independent. The VBRUN100.DLL Visual Basic run-time library must be accessible by your program.) At this point, the only commands available are those that you built into your program.

Building a First Program

Now that you have a basic idea of how the Visual Basic environment works, you can go through the steps to build a program. This program doesn't do much; however, when you create it, you use many of the commands and procedures discussed in this chapter. It also uses some language elements that have not been discussed so far. Don't worry about the new language elements now. You learn about them in more detail later in this book.

The Good Morning Program

The Good Morning program, MYONE.EXE, displays a window with two Text boxes and two buttons. You type your name in one box. Good Morning appears in the second box, followed by the name you typed in the first box. Also, Good Morning changes to Good Afternoon or Good Evening, depending on the time of day. MYONE.EXE isn't an exciting program, but it does exercise many of the options in Visual Basic. As you make your changes, use Figure 2.13 as a guide.

1. Start Visual Basic or execute the New Project command on the File menu to get new Project and Form windows.

   First change the caption of the Form1 Form window. The Caption property is the name displayed at the top of the Form. The current caption is Form1. That's not terribly informative, so change it to My First Program.

2. Click the Form to select it. The Properties List box should show the Caption property. If not, click the arrow to the right of the box and select Caption from the list.

3. In the Settings box, select the text Form1 and type **My First Program** in its place. Press Enter or click the Check box to make the change in the Caption property.

   Now that you have a blank Form, put the Controls and Text boxes on it.

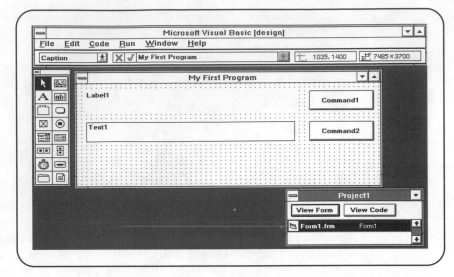

Figure 2.13. *The* My First Program *Form layout.*

 4. In the Toolbox window, select the Label tool (the icon shown in the outside margin) and draw a Label on the Form. Make the Label about 3/4 of an inch tall and 5 inches wide.

 The two boxes on the right side of the Properties bar contain the location of the upper-left corner of the selected object and the current width and height measured in *twips*. A twip is 1/1440 of an inch and 5 by 3 inches is 7200 by 1080 twips.

 5. In the Toolbox window, select the Text box icon (the icon shown in the outside margin) and draw a Text box of about the same size as the Label. Place it directly below the Label.

 6. In the Toolbox window, select the Command button tool (the icon shown in the outside margin) and draw a button to the right of the Label. Select the Command button tool again and draw a second button below the first.

The next step is to change the properties of the boxes and buttons you just drew on the Form. Change the Caption properties of the buttons to reflect their use. Change the CtrlName properties to make your program more readable. The Caption property of a button is the text displayed on top of the button. The Caption property of a Label is the text displayed in the Label. The CtrlName property is the name that the object is referred to in the code.

7. Select the first button (marked **Command1**) and change its Caption property to OK. Change its CtrlName property to OKButton.

8. Select the second button (marked **Command2**) and change its Caption property to Quit and its CtrlName property to QuitButton. Your Form now should look like Figure 2.14.

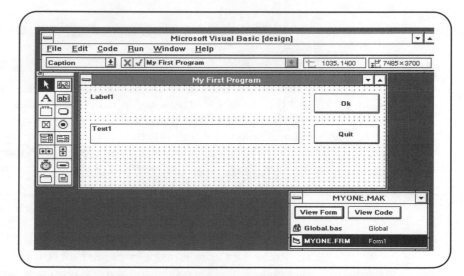

Figure 2.14. *The* My First *Program Form (edited).*

The next step is to attach code to the different objects on the screen. Attach code to the **Quit** button first. When the **Quit** button is pressed you want the code to end. When you open the Code window, it already has a template in it for the selected object, and for the most probable event. To change either of these, select the object and event from the Object and Procedure List boxes at the top of the Code window.

9. Double-click the **Quit** button to open the Code window associated with it. The code template already should be set for the QuitButton object and the Click event. If not, select QuitButton from the Object list and Click from the Proc list. The Code window now should show the header and footer for a QuitButton_Click event. That is, the code in this Procedure is executed whenever you click

the button marked **Quit**. Type a Stop or End statement between the procedure header and footer. Your Code window now should look like Figure 2.15.

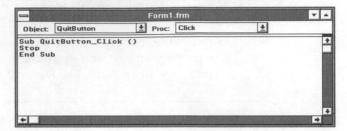

Figure 2.15. *The* QuitButton_Click *procedure.*

When the program starts up, you want the contents of the Label and the List box to have some initial values. You could set these values at design time, as you did for the Caption properties of the Command buttons, or you could do it in code that is executed when the application starts. A good place to put startup code is in the Form_Load procedure, which is executed when the Form is loaded (right before it is displayed).

In the Label, put the instructions to the user, such as

Please type your name below.

To access the Caption property of the Label1 Label, combine the CtrlName (Label1) and the property (Caption) separated with a period (Label1.Caption). All properties are accessed in this way. The visible text in a Text box is contained in the Text property rather than in the Caption property, as it is with the Label and Command buttons. You want the Text box to be blank, so set its Text property to the empty string.

10. In the Object list, select Form. The Code window changes to the Form window. In the Proc list, select the Load event. Type the following code between the Form1_Load header and footer:

```
Label1.Caption = "Please type your name below."
Text1.Text = ""
```

Your Code window now should look like Figure 2.16.

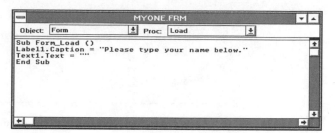

Figure 2.16. *The* Form1_Load *procedure.*

The code that does all the work in this program is attached to the **OK** button. When that button is pressed, you want the code to check the time of day to see if it is morning, afternoon or evening. Then the code should combine the text Good Morning, Good After-noon, or Good Evening with what the user typed in the Text box, displaying the result in the Label.

11. Select OKButton from the Object list. Select Click from the Proc list. Type the following code between the OKButton_Click header and footer (notice the space after the text "Good Morning ", "Good Afternoon ", and "Good Evening "):

```
If Val(Time$) > 0 And Val(Time$) < 12 Then
   Label1.Caption = "Good Morning " + Text1.Text
ElseIf Val(Time$) >= 12 And Val(Time$) < 18 Then
   Label1.Caption = "Good Afternoon " + Text1.Text
Else
   Label1.Caption = "Good Evening " + Text1.Text
End If
```

Your Code window now should look like Figure 2.17. The Time$ function gets the time of day. It returns a string of text that con-tains the current time. The format of that string is "hh:mm:ss," in which hh is the hour, mm is the minute, and ss is the seconds. Applying the Val() function to this string returns the first number in the string, which is the current hour (on a 24-hour clock).

To test the hour to see what time it is, use the If Then Else statement. The first If statement checks to see if the time is between 0 and 12 (Midnight and Noon). If it is, the next statement is executed, which combines the text "Good Morning " with the contents of the Text box (Text1.Text). The result is assigned to the Caption of the Label (Label1.Caption). If the time isn't between 0 and 12, the ElseIf statement checks to see if it is between 12 and 18 (Noon and 6 p.m.). If it is, "Good Afternoon " is used rather

39

than `"Good Morning "`. If the time isn't between 0 and 12 or 12 and 18, the statement following the `Else` statement is executed, which uses `"Good Evening "` rather than `"Good Morning "` or `"Good Afternoon "`.

Actually, you can have fun with this program by making changes to it. You can add more `ElseIf` statements between the `If` statement and the `EndIf` statement to test for different ranges in the time and to print an appropriate message. For example, you could test for the range 9 a.m. to 10 a.m. and display a rude comment about being late. Or you could test for 6 p.m. to 7 p.m. and display `Go Home, it's dinner time`. When you complete this chapter, come back to this point and experiment a little.

Running Your Program

Your program is ready to be run in interpreted mode, so select **Start** from the **Run** menu. If you made no typing errors, your screen looks like Figure 2.18. Your Form window waits for you to use it.

Figure 2.17. The `OKButton_Click` procedure.

Type your name in the Text box and click the **OK** button to see your message appear in the Label, as in Figure 2.19. If you made a typing mistake somewhere, Visual Basic probably will give you a syntax error and show you the offending statement. Fix it, and try to run your program again.

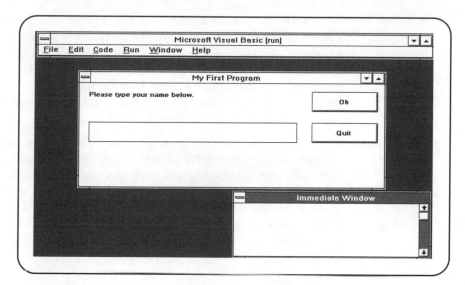

Figure 2.18. *The* My First Program *after startup.*

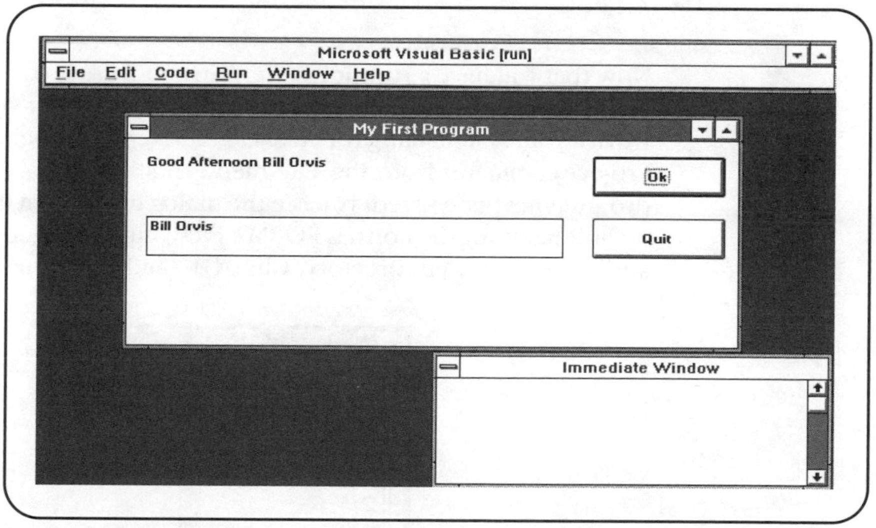

Figure 2.19. *The* My First Program *after pressing the* **OK** *button.*

You may have noticed the Immediate window hanging around the Form window. The Immediate window appears whenever a program is being run in interpreted mode. Its primary use to debug programs—see Chapter 13, "Debugging," for more information.

To test your code for different times of day, run the code and execute the **B**reak command in the **R**un menu. Open the Immediate window, type `time$="9:00"`, and press Enter. This sequence changes the setting of your system clock to 9 a.m. Also, you could type `print time$` and press Enter to see what the current time is. Select the **C**ontinue command under the **R**un menu to make your program start running again. See what it prints when you type your name and press the **OK** button.

If it works, break the program once more, change the system clock to a different time, and run the program again. You can continue changing the time and testing the program until you are satisfied that it works. Don't forget to reset the system clock to the correct time when you are done. If your program runs but doesn't do what it is supposed to do, execute the **E**nd command on the **R**un menu and check your code and properties settings until you find the error.

Saving Your Work

Now that you have a running code, you should save it. When you work on longer programs, save them frequently so you don't risk losing all your work if your system hangs or crashes. To save your program, select the Save Project command from the **F**ile menu. Because this is the first time this program has been saved, you see the dialog box shown in Figure 2.20. The default name for the Form is FORM1.FRM, but I changed it to MYONE.FRM and selected the VB directory. Click **OK**, and the Form is saved.

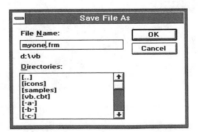

Figure 2.20. *The save dialog box for the Form.*

Next, the dialog box in Figure 2.21 appears for you to save the Project file. Again, I changed the default name from PROJECT1.MAK to MYONE.MAK and clicked **OK**. If your code has more Forms or modules, a dialog box appears for each one. The second time you save your work, these dialog boxes won't appear. Visual Basic knows where to store your work, and what names to use. To save your code in a different directory, or with a different name, use the Save Project As and the Save File As commands in the File menu. If you change the file names, don't change the .MAK or .FRM extensions to the file names. Because we have not used the Global module, the file Global.BAS isn't saved for this program. The Global module is stored in the Global.BAS file.

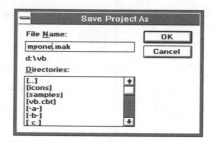

Figure 2.21. *The save dialog box for the project.*

Retrieving Your Work

Retrieving your work is easier than saving it. You have to retrieve only the project file; all the other files are retrieved automatically. Right now, your program is still in memory. Delete it with the New Project command in the File menu. Select the Open Project dialog from the File menu and a file open dialog box appears. Set the directory by double-clicking the disk letters and directory names until you get into the directory that contains the MYONE.MAK file. Click the MYONE.MAK file and click the OK button. Your program is loaded back into memory.

Compiling Your Program

The last step is to compile your program into a stand-alone application. With your program in memory, select the Make .EXE File command from

the File menu. The dialog box shown in Figure 2.22 appears for you to select the directory and name for your application. As you can see in the figure, the VB directory is on my D: drive. When you click **OK**, your program is compiled and stored on disk. Note that the library file, VBRUN100.DLL, included with Visual Basic must be accessible by the running program.

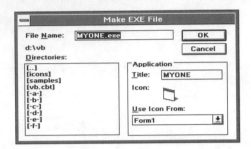

Figure 2.22. The Make .EXE File dialog box.

To run your program, switch to the File Manager, open the VB directory, and double-click MYONE.EXE. Alternatively, open the Microsoft Visual Basic Group window under the Program Manager and the VB directory under the File Manager. Drag the icon of the MYONE.EXE application from the directory window to the Group window. This installs MYONE.EXE in the Microsoft Visual Basic Group (see Figure 2.23). You then can close the File Manager and execute MYONE by double-clicking its icon in the Group window.

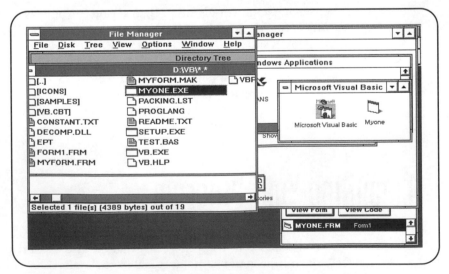

Figure 2.23. Copying your program to a File Group window.

This completes all the steps necessary to create and compile a Visual Basic program. If you want, go back now and try to change some of the properties of the Form, buttons, and Text boxes. Try changing the font with the FontName property, or the size of the text with the FontSize property. Or you could experiment with the colors of the Form and controls with the ForeColor and BackColor properties. Go ahead and experiment with the code. Have some fun with it.

> The Iconwrks example program is used to create custom icons, and is included with Visual Basic (see Plate II). Use it to create a custom icon for your first program. Once you have the icon stored in a file, attach it to the program using the **Properties** command on the **File** menu of the Program Manager.

What You Have Learned

In this chapter, you examined the Visual Basic environment and its capabilities, including the commands, menus, controls, and windows. You also built your first windows application, performing all the steps from designing it to compiling it into a stand-alone application. Specifically, you examined

- The Project window.
- The Form window.
- The Toolbox window.
- Code windows.
- The Color palette window.
- The Immediate window.
- The **File** menu.
- The **Edit** menu.
- The **Code** menu.

- The **R**un menu.

- The **W**indow menu.

- The **H**elp menu.

- The Properties bar.

- The running modes of operation.

- Creating and running a first application.

- Compiling an application.

- Saving and retrieving a program.

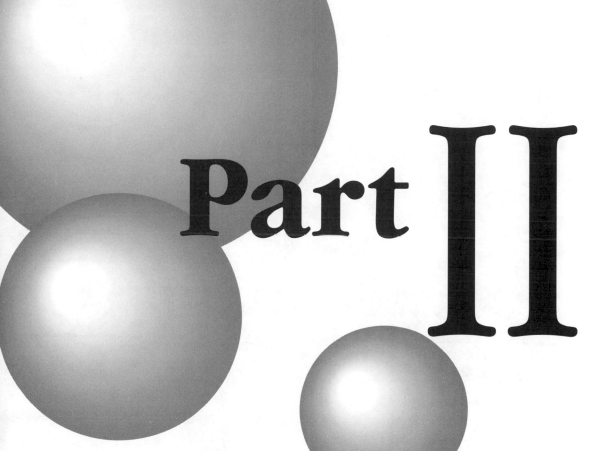

Part II

Opening Up
Visual Basic

Understanding Forms

In This Chapter

This chapter discusses Forms. Pay close attention to Forms, because they are the foundation of most Visual Basic programs. This chapter shows you how to

- Create a Form.
- Change the appearance of a Form.
- Print on a Form.
- Print to a printer.
- Draw objects on a Form.
- Create custom printed Forms.
- Print a Form to a printer.

Creating a Form

Forms are the visual background for all the controls and boxes that make up an application. When you first create a Form, it appears as a standard, blank Windows window. It has a title bar showing its name, and draggable borders to change its size and shape. The Form also has a Control menu in the upper-left corner and **Maximize** and **Minimize** buttons in the upper-right corner.

A Form is like an adjustable drawing board on which you draw objects (such as buttons and labels) to form the visual interface of a project. Everything you want to see when your application is running is attached to a Form. In addition to being the place where the visual parts of objects are attached, Forms also contain objects attached to the Form. Nearly every project has at least one Form attached to it. Although you can create projects with a visual interface without using Forms, it is much more difficult.

You can attach as many Forms to a project as you want to create your application. I suspect there is a limit to the number of Forms you can attach to a single project; however, I haven't run into it yet. To avoid cluttering the screen, you can hide Forms that are not being used and make them visible when you want them.

The first Form in a project is created automatically when you execute the New Project command on the **F**ile menu. If the Form is hidden by other windows, bring it to the front by clicking a corner, or select it on the Project window and press the **View Form** button. To add Forms to a project, execute the New **F**orm command on the **F**ile menu. A new Form appears on the Project window and the screen.

Printing on a Form with the Print Method

In addition to drawing buttons and boxes on a Form, you can print on a Form using the `Print` method. Text printed on a Form starts in the upper-left corner and continues down the Form with each successive `Print` statement.

Printing on a Form in this manner is similar to printing on the screen in other versions of BASIC, with one important difference: A Form does not scroll when your printed text goes off the screen. It simply disappears off the bottom as your application continues printing. If you continue printing off the bottom of the Form, an overflow error results after approximately 100 lines. To print onto a scrollable window, add the new text to the Text property of the Text box. You also can print on the Immediate window when a program is running, by using the Debug object with the Print method. See Chapter 13, "Debugging and Error Trapping," for more details.

The Print method prints text on Forms, on picture boxes, to the printer, and on the Immediate window. Its syntax is

```
[Object.]Print [Expression][{;|,}]
```

in which *Object* is the name of the object to print on and *Expression* is the text you want printed. Ending the method with a comma, a semicolon, or nothing controls where the cursor is left after *Expression* is printed. The cursor position determines where printing starts the next time you execute Print. Appending nothing to the end of a Print method causes the insertion point to move down one line and left to the margin. A comma moves the insertion point to the next print field (every 14 spaces). A semicolon leaves the insertion point at the end of *Expression*. For example, print a few lines on a Form.

1. Start with a new project by opening Visual Basic. If Visual Basic already is open, execute the New Project command on the **File** menu.

2. Select Form1 and open its Code window by double-clicking the Form, by clicking the **View Code** button on the Project window, or by selecting the View Code command in the **Code** menu.

3. The Click event should be selected. If not, select it from the Procedure list.

4. Add one line of code to the procedure template so it reads

```
Sub Form_Click ()
Print "Hello "
End Sub
```

5. Execute the **Start** command on the **Run** menu. A blank Form appears.

6. Click the Form to execute the procedure. "Hello" is printed on the Form, as shown in Figure 3.1.

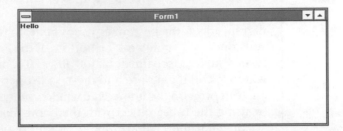

Figure 3.1. *Printing a single line on a Form.*

7. Click several times on the Form. "Hello" is repeated as shown in Figure 3.2. If you continue to click the Form, the text eventually runs off the bottom.

Figure 3.2. *Printing several times on a Form.*

8. Execute the **E**nd command on the **R**un menu to quit the program and go back to Design mode.

Try printing other text on the Form. Also try placing a comma or semicolon after the expression and see what happens.

Don't delete this program yet, because you use it again later to examine some of a Form's properties.

Changing the Appearance of Forms

The appearance of a Form (its size, shape, color, text style, and so forth) is controlled by its properties. In addition, properties control how a Form reacts to certain events, such as the redrawing of a Form's contents when it's uncovered. Three different classes of properties are associated with objects: those that can be changed only at design time, those that can be changed only at run time, and those that can be changed at any time. The majority of a Form's properties can be changed at any time. Most design-time-only properties are readable at run time, even though they can't be changed. Table 3.1 lists some of the more commonly used properties of a Form. See Chapter 15, "Command Reference," for a complete list.

Table 3.1. Commonly used properties of a Form.

Run-time and Design-time Properties

Property	*Description*
BackColor	The background color
Caption	The title displayed at the top of the Form
FontBold	Make the next text printed on the Form bold (True or False)
FontItalic	Make the next text printed on the Form italic (True or False)
FontName	The name of the font used for text printed on the Form
FontSize	Set the point size of the next text printed on the Form
FontUnderline	Underline the next text printed on the Form (True or False)
ForeColor	The foreground color
Height	The height of the Form (in twips—one-twentieth of a point)

continues

Table 3.1. continued.

Run-time and Design-time Properties

Property	Description
Left	The distance from the left side of the Form to the left side of the screen (in twips)
Top	The distance from the top of the Form to the top of the screen (in twips)
Visible	Is the Form visible at run time? (True or False)
Width	The width of the Form (in twips)

Design-time-only Properties

Property	Description
BorderStyle	The thickness of the Form's border
ControlBox	Does the Form have a Control box? (True or False)
FormName	The name used internally for the Form in the Code window
MaxButton	Does the Form have a **Maximize** button? (True or False)
MinButton	Does the Form have a **Minimize** button? (True or False)

The Properties Bar

To change a Form's properties at design time, select the Form and change its properties with the Properties bar. The Properties bar contains two List boxes and four numbers. The first List box on the left is the properties list.

It contains all properties that can be changed at design time. It does not contain any properties that can be changed *only* at run time. To the right of the properties list is the Settings box, which contains the value of the current setting for the property displayed in the Properties bar—see Figure 3.3.

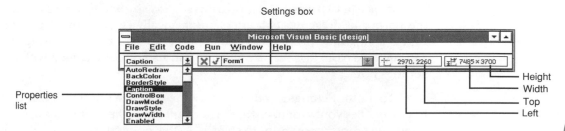

Figure 3.3. The Properties bar with the properties list dropped down.

Four numbers in two groups of two appear on the right side of the Properties bar. The two numbers on the left show the location of the upper-left corner of the currently selected object. The position is measured down and to the right of the upper-left corner of the screen if the object is a Form. The position is measured down and to the right of the upper-left corner of the drawing area of the Form if the object is on the Form. The drawing area of a Form is everything below the title bar. The right pair of numbers displays the width and height of the current object.

By default, both the location and the size of an object are measured in twips (which, as you recall from Chapter 2, "Learning the Visual Basic Environment," are equal to 1/1440 of an inch). Although the twip might seem to be an odd unit of measure, it is 1/20 of a *point,* which is a printer's unit of measure. Most older versions of BASIC use *pixels* as the unit of measure on the screen. A pixel is the smallest point that can be drawn on a screen; however, the size of a pixel is dependent on the video adapter and monitor used. Thus, an object with its size defined in pixels is different sizes on different monitors. An object with its size defined in twips is the same size on any monitor. The scale used can be changed to inches, centimeters, millimeters, or to some user-defined unit using the Scale Mode property—see Chapter 12, "Drawing with Visual Basic."

$$20 \text{ twips} = 1 \text{ point} = 1/72^{th} \text{ of an inch} \quad \boxed{So\ 72\ pts \equiv 1\ inch} \\ \boxed{\&\ 1,440\ twips = 1\ inch}$$

Changing Properties with the Settings Box

To change the appearance of a Form (or any object on a Form), you must change the value of its properties. At design time, the values of properties are changed in two ways. For properties such as size and location, moving the Form and dragging its borders automatically changes the Top, Left, Width, and Height properties. Other properties are changed using the Settings box. Note that the size and location also can be changed with the Settings box.

To use the Settings box on the Properties bar, first select the Form that has properties you want to change. Then pull down the properties list and select the property you want to change. At this point, the current value of the property is displayed in the Settings box. To change a property, type a new value in the Settings box. Some properties have a fixed list of possible values (for example, True or False). If this is the case, the Settings box becomes a List box. You change the property by pulling down the list of settings (click the down arrow on the right side of the Settings box). Then select the value from the list of settings. For color properties, the down arrow changes into an ellipsis (...). Clicking the points displays the Color Palette window. When you select a color in the Color Palette window, the numeric code for that color is inserted in the Settings box.

You can return to the earlier example and change some properties.

1. You should be in Design mode. If you aren't, execute the **End** command on the **Run** menu. If you made any changes in the procedure you created in the earlier example, remove them before continuing.

2. Select Form1. Then select the FontSize property on the Properties bar.

3. Pull down the Settings list. Select the largest point size available. I chose 24 points; however, your sizes might be different from mine, depending on which fonts you have installed on your system, what kind of printer you have, and the video adapter you have.

4. Run the program and click the Form a few times. It should look like Figure 3.4.

5. Quit the program with the **End** command on the **Run** menu.

Figure 3.4. *Printing on a Form with the* FontSize *property set to 24 points.*

> Try changing some of the other properties of the Form (such as ForeColor or BackColor), or some of the text attributes (such as FontUnderline and FontName), and run the example again. Don't be afraid to experiment with the properties or code. Although the manual might tell you what will happen, it could be ambiguous or wrong. The only way to see exactly what a property or code segment does is to try it.

Dynamically Changing Properties in a Running Application

You can change properties in a running application with a statement of the following format:

```
[object.]property = value
```

in which *object* is the name of the object having the property to be changed (the Form name in this case), *property* is the name of the property, and *value* is a new value for that property. If object is omitted, the attached form is assumed to be the value. If the construction [*object.*]*property* is used on the right side of a formula rather than on the left side, it returns the current value of that property. For example, the following code changes the foreground color to &HFF, where &HFF is the hexadecimal number for red.

```
ForeColor = &HFF&
```

57

For example, add a line to the print example to turn the FontStrikethru property on and off each time the Form is clicked. The FontStrikethru property can be either True or False, so use the Not function, which switches True to False or False to True. The value of Form1.FontStrikethru on the right side of the formula provides the old value of the property. The Not function reverses the property's value. The equals sign assigns the new value back to Form1.FontStrikethru on the left side of the formula.

1. Continue with the preceding example. You should be in Design mode. If you aren't, execute the **End** command on the **Run** menu. If you have made any changes in the procedure that was created in the earlier example, remove them before continuing.

2. Change the code in the Form_Click procedure so it reads

```
Sub Form_Click ()
Form1.FontStrikethru = Not Form1.FontStrikethru
Print "Hello "
End Sub
```

3. Run the program and click the Form a few times. It should look like Figure 3.5.

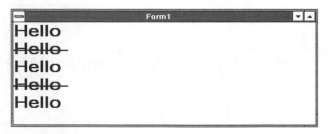

Figure 3.5. *Setting properties with code.*

Printing to the Printer

In addition to printing on Forms, you can print to the printer by using Printer as the object in the Print method. For example, change the Form-printing example so it prints to the printer rather than on the Form.

1. In Design mode, select the Form, open its Code window, and select the Click process.

2. Change the object in the `Print` method to the `Printer` object so that the procedure reads

```
Sub Form_Click ()
Form1.FontStrikethru = Not Form1.FontStrikethru
Printer.Print "Hello "
End Sub
```

3. Run the program and click the Form.

   The program doesn't seem to be doing anything. However, if you check on the desktop of your Windows environment, the Print Manager has appeared. The Print Manager actually is storing the text to be printed to the printer until you either quit the application or issue the `Printer.EndDoc` method.

4. End the program.

   The Print Manager now sends the text to the printer. The Print Manager prints one `Hello` to the printer for every time you clicked the Form. But what's this? The font has changed back to the small 12-point size, and `FontStrikethru` doesn't seem to be working. The problem is that the second line of the procedure still refers to the Form and not the `Printer` object. Also, at design time you cannot set any of the printer properties. You must set them with code, so go back and change the `Form1_Click` procedure.

5. Open the code window and select the `Click` procedure. Change the object to `Printer` where you change the `FontStrikethru` property. Add a line to set the name of the printed font. Then add another line to change the font's point size. The procedure now should read

```
Sub Form_Click ()
Printer.FontName = "Tms Rmn"
Printer.FontSize = 24
Printer.FontStrikethru = Not Printer.FontStrikethru
Printer.Print "Hello "
End Sub
```

6. Run the program and click the Form a few times. Then end the program. This time the printed output looks much like the printing in Figure 3.5.

> Unlike other versions of BASIC, Visual Basic has no LPRINT statement. The LPRINT statement is replaced with the Printer.Print method; however, the text is not printed until you quit the program or execute the Printer.EndDoc method. Also, you cannot insert a Printer.EndDoc statement after every Printer.Print statement, because Printer.EndDoc also issues a page feed after the last printed text.

Printing on a Text Box

Often you have to print a list of items on the screen, and you want them to be in a scrollable box. Word processors and telecommunication programs are examples of programs that have to write on scrollable lists. Do this by adding text to the Text property of a large Text box.

First you need a large Text box on a Form. Clear any text already on the box, and set the Multiline property to True. If Multiline is False, only one line of text is printed on the Text box. Turn on the Vertical Scroll bar with the ScrollVertical property.

1. Clear the old project by executing the **New Project** command on the **File** menu (save the old project first if you want to keep it and name it whatever you want to).

2. Select the Text box tool in the Toolbox window, and draw a List box that is nearly as large as the interior part of the Form. Leave a little space at the top so a small amount of the Form is showing to click.

3. With the Text box selected, select the Multiline property in the Properties list. Set its value to True in the Settings box.

4. Select the Text property and delete the contents of the Settings box. This clears the text inside the window.

5. Select the ScrollBars property and set it to 2-Vertical.

   In the Form_Click procedure, append the new text to the text currently in the Text box. Also append a carriage return and a line feed.

6. Open the Code window. Select the Form object and the Click procedure. Then insert a line to add the text Hello to the contents of the Text box. The procedure should look like the following:

```
Sub Form_Click ()
Text1.Text = Text1.Text + "Hello " + Chr$(13) + Chr$(10)
End Sub
```

7. Run the program and click several times on the Form where it isn't covered by the Text box. Your Form now looks like Figure 3.6.

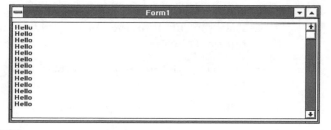

Figure 3.6. Printing in a Text box.

Drawing Your User Interface

Forms are most commonly used as backgrounds for the user interface to your application. As you did in Chapter 2, "Learning the Visual Basic Environment," you draw the different controls and boxes on your Form to create the interface you want. The Toolbox window is the source of the drawing tools for creating your interface. All the tools work in the same manner.

- Select a tool in the Toolbox window.

- Move to where you want the upper-left corner of your object.

- Hold down the left mouse button (or the right button if you are left-handed and have used the Windows Setup program or the Control Panel to switch the buttons).

- Drag down to the lower-right corner of your object, and release the mouse button. The object appears where you drew it. Its location, height, and width appear on the right side of the Properties bar.

Some objects, such as the Timer, have a fixed size. No matter how large you draw them, they always appear the same size. Other objects (such as the Label box and the Text box) are the size you drew them. If an object you've drawn is the wrong size or in the wrong location, you can adjust it.

- To move an object, select it and do one of the following:

  Edit the object's Top and Left properties.

  Place the cursor on the object, and hold down the left mouse button. Drag the object to its new location, and release the button.

- To change the size of an existing object, you can do one of the following:

  Edit the Height and Width properties.

  Select the object and drag one of the small black squares that appear around it until it is the shape you want.

Editing an object's size and location properties also is useful when grid snap is turned on and you want a size or location that isn't on a grid point. When grid snap is turned on, the screen is covered with an array of equally spaced points. When you move or size an object, the mouse pointer jumps from one grid point to the next, skipping the points in between. You could turn grid snap off by unchecking the Snap to Grid check box in the **Grid** Settings dialog box on the **Edit** menu. Then you could move or resize the object, and then turn on grid snap again. Or you could simply edit the object's properties.

Creating a Custom Form

In business situations, you often have to either fill out or create a Form. You can buy a Form-generation program, or you simply can use Visual Basic to create an on-line Form you can fill out on the screen. The Form's contents are either printed or stored on a disk for use by another program.

A few evenings ago, my wife ran up to me and said she was out of vaccination certificates (she's a veterinarian). She had just vaccinated a dog (Jessie) we were giving away in the morning, and she needed a blank certificate. Her suppliers take a week or two to get forms to her; however, she needed a form right away so the new owners would have the correct paperwork when they picked up Jessie.

Using Visual Basic, I created the following vaccination certificate as a stand-alone application. You run the application, fill in the form, and press a button to print it. Creating the custom Form took only about an hour. Of course, to be able to legally sign it takes about eight years of college and a license, so don't try to use this form for your own pets (unless you are a veterinarian too).

The first step is to design the Form. Sketch the different fields and labels you want so you have a rough idea where they go. The ordering of the fields is not terribly important.

Frames have to go behind any objects that are on them. The first time I created the Form described here, I forgot to put a frame around the outside. I tried to put it on at the end, but it covered everything else, rather than being in the background. Because the physical ordering of objects on the Form cannot be changed, I had to redo the Form from scratch.

Something else to consider at this time is the tab ordering of the Text boxes. When you are filling out the Form, you can press Tab to move from object to object. The order in which the objects are selected is determined by the order in which they are drawn on the Form. However, that ordering can be changed by changing the `TabIndex` property. The `TabIndex` property,

which is incremented each time a new object is drawn on a Form, determines the tab order. If you change the value of the `TabIndex` property of an object, it moves to that position in the tab order. All the `TabIndex` properties of the other objects on the Form are adjusted to make room for it. In this example, you want to tab from one Text box to the next. So you need to put all the Text boxes on the Form first.

I give you the exact positions and sizes of all the objects on this Form so you can create a Form identical to the one in Figure 3.7. Alternatively, you can look at the figure and draw the objects to make your Form similar to mine. It might not be identical, but you will see how to create a custom Form.

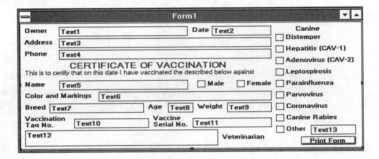

Figure 3.7. The vaccination Form in progress.

1. Start with a blank Form by either starting Visual Basic or executing the **New** Project command on the **File** menu.

2. Enlarge the Form until it is 8475 twips wide by 4500 twips high.

3. Select the Frame tool and draw a frame that is about the same size as the Form. Set the following properties of the frame:

```
Top = -80        Left = 5
Width = 8340     Height = 4060
Caption = ""
```

4. Table 3.2 lists 13 Text boxes and their properties. Look at Figure 3.7 and draw the boxes first. Then adjust their properties to match those in the table. Set the `Text` property for each Text box to a blank.

It's easiest to draw all the boxes on the Form first in roughly the right location and size. Then you select one property and adjust it on all the boxes, rather than setting all the properties for a single box before going on to the next. To do this, select the first box and select the property to be adjusted. Change the property and press Enter to accept the change. Then press Tab to move to the next box. Using this procedure, you can go down the list of boxes, then change to the next property and do it again. Continue this process for all the properties that have to be adjusted.

Table 3.2. Text box properties for the custom Form.

CtlName	Left	Top	Width	Height
Text1	960	220	3135	300
Text2	4680	220	1455	300
Text3	960	580	5175	300
Text4	960	940	5175	300
Text5	960	1900	3135	300
Text6	1920	2260	4215	300
Text7	720	2620	2295	300
Text8	3600	2620	615	300
Text9	5040	2620	1095	300
Text10	1320	3100	1815	300
Text11	4200	3100	1935	300
Text12	120	3460	4695	500
Text13	7080	3340	1095	300

5. There are 15 Labels on the Form. Using Figure 3.7 and Table 3.3, attach them to the Form.

Table 3.3. Label box properties of the custom Form.

CtlName	Left	Top	Width	Height	Caption
Label1	120	220	735	260	Owner
Label2	4200	220	495	260	Date
Label3	120	580	855	260	Address
Label4	120	940	855	260	Phone
Label5	120	1300	6015	260	CERTIFICATE OF VACCINA-TION *(see note)
Label6	120	1540	6135	260	This is to certify that on this date I have vacci-nated the described below against **(see note)
Label7	120	1900	615	260	Name
Label8	120	2260	1815	260	Color and Markings
Label9	120	2620	615	260	Breed
Label10	3120	2620	495	260	Age
Label11	4320	2620	735	260	Weight
Label12	120	2980	1095	380	Vaccination Tag No.
Label13	3240	2980	975	380	Vaccine Serial No.
Label14	4920	3580	1215	260	Veterinarian
Label15	6720	200	975	260	Canine

Notes:

    * For Label5, set these additional properties: FontSize = 12, Alignment = 2 - Center.

    ** For Label6, set this additional property: FontBold = False.

6. Place 11 Check boxes on the Form using Figure 3.7 and Table 3.4 as guides. Draw the smallest box that shows the entire check box.

Table 3.4. Check-box properties of the custom Form.

CtlName	Left	Top	Width	Heigth	Caption
Check1	4320	1920	735	260	Male
Check2	5280	1920	975	260	Female
Check3	6240	480	2055	260	Distemper
Check4	6240	840	2055	260	Hepatitis (CAV-1)
Check5	6240	1200	2055	260	Adenovirus (CAV-2)
Check6	6240	1540	2055	260	Lepto-spirosis
Check7	6240	1900	2055	260	Parainflu-enza
Check8	6240	2260	2055	260	Parvovirus
Check9	6240	2620	2055	260	Coronavirus
Check10	6240	2980	2055	260	Canine Rabies
Check11	6240	3360	2855	260	Other

7. Using the Command button tool, insert a button on the lower-right corner of the Form. Give the button the following properties:

```
Left = 6840   Top = 3700    Width = 1335   Height = 260
Caption = Print Form   CtlName = PrintIt
```

Your Form should now look like Figure 3.8. All that remains is to add some code to automatically fill in the current date and to print the Form when the user presses the Command button.

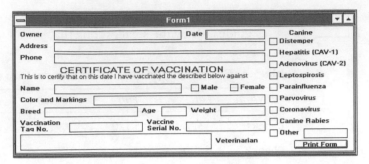

***Figure 3.8.** The user interface for the vaccination certificate custom Form.*

The PrintForm Method

Rather than having to draw the contents of the Form on the Printer object, you can use a special method. The Print.Form method prints a Form to the printer as it appears on the screen. The format of this method is

```
[Form.]PrintForm
```

If you leave out the Form argument, it prints the current Form.

1. Open the code window for the Form, and select the PrintIt object and the Click procedure. Insert code into the procedure template until it appears as the following:

```
Sub PrintIt_Click ()
PrintIt.Visible = 0
PrintForm
PrintIt.Visible = -1
End Sub
```

Setting the PrintIt.Visible property of the Command button to 0 (False) makes the button disappear before printing the Form with the PrintForm method. After the Form is printed, setting PrintIt.Visible equal to -1 (True) makes the button visible again.

2. Select the Form object and the Load procedure, and insert the following code:

```
Sub Form_Load ()
Text2.Text = Date$
End Sub
```

The date$ function always returns a string containing the current date. Setting the Text property of the Text2 Text box with the DATE$ function causes the current date to be inserted in the box at the time the Form is loaded. The box is editable, so the date can be changed by the user if necessary.

3. Save the program with the name VETFRM (in files VETFRM.FRM and VETFRM.MAK).

4. Run the program with the **Start** command on the **Run** menu.

If you were a veterinarian, you would type the dog owner's name and a description of the dog. You also would click the check boxes to select the vaccines you gave to the dog. When the form is filled out, click the **Print It** button. The form is printed to the printer.

If everything works correctly, you now can compile the custom Form into an .EXE file that can be given to anyone who needs to create the Form.

In addition to printing the Form, the data could be written to a file that could be read by a database program to keep a record of what animal has received what vaccinations—see Chapter 9, "Using Sequential Files." An accounting program also could read the file and print a bill for the patient's owner. I'm sure you can imagine many other uses for custom Forms developed in this way.

To print on a preprinted Form takes much trial and error. To do so, create a custom Form that has the Text box fields in the same place as the fields on the preprinted Form. In the PrintIt_Click procedure, make all the field descriptions invisible (the Label boxes in this example) during printing, in the same manner as was done with the **Print It** button. Then fill out the Form with dummy text and print it. If it doesn't fit the preprinted Form, move things around and print it again. Continue this trial-and-error procedure until you are satisfied with the result.

What You Have Learned

In this chapter you learned about Forms, which are the foundation of most Visual Basic programs.

- You created new Forms with the New Project and New **Form** commands.

- You printed text on a Form and to the printer using the `Print` method.

- You changed the appearance of a Form and the text printed on it by changing its properties both in Design mode and dynamically in a running program.

- You created a custom Form-filling program.

- You printed the contents of a Form to the printer using the `PrintForm` method.

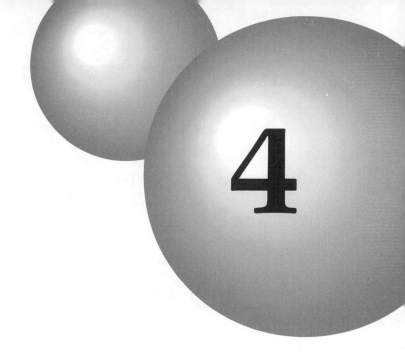

Using Strings

The primary method of communication with Visual Basic objects and with the user of a Visual Basic program are strings of text. While numbers are used internally for calculations, indices, and counters, they must be converted to strings before they can be displayed in a Text box or Label. Thus, manipulating strings and converting numbers to strings are important aspects of any Visual Basic program.

In This Chapter

Most of what you've read so far in this book has dealt with strings of text. List boxes and Label boxes display text on the screen. Many object properties are defined as strings of text. This chapter formally defines strings and string formulas and expands on the details of using strings in programs. This chapter shows you how to

- Define variables and determine their scope.

- Define strings.

- Create string formulas.

- Manipulate strings with string functions.

- Create an envelope-addressing program.

The Variable

Before discussing strings and string formulas, you have to consider the concept of variables and their scope, because variables are where you store information in a computer program. Later, you will learn about strings and how to manipulate them.

A *variable* is a descriptive name used to store information and the results of calculations. Actually, the information is stored in the computer's memory, and the variable name points to that location. Whenever a variable name is used in a program, it is replaced by the contents of that memory location. A variable name is an abstraction that makes computer programs more readable. For example, `Label1.Caption` is a string variable that names the location of the string of text used for the caption of `Label1`. If I used an address such as `9FC80` for that location rather than the variable name, no one, including me, would have any idea what the program was doing. Using variable names makes reading a computer program understandable.

A variable name can contain up to 40 characters, including letters, numbers, and the underscore (_). The first character of a variable name must be a letter, and you cannot use a reserved word such as `Print` as a variable. However, a reserved word can be contained within a variable name, as in the variable `PrintIt`. Although you are allowed 40 characters for a variable name, I recommend that you not use that many characters. Use enough characters to make it obvious what the variable is, but not so many that you spend all day typing 40-character variable names. A good rule of thumb is to imagine that you must give your program to someone else (your mother, for example), and she must be able to read your program and understand what it is doing. When you come back to your program in a year or so, the odds are good that you still will understand it.

The Scope of Variables

The scope of a variable is a description of where in a program the variable can be accessed—see Figure 4.1. The variables associated with the properties of objects, such as Label1.FontName, are predefined and available to any code attached to the Form containing that object. User variables (those that you define for your own use) are defined either by using them in a procedure, or with the Dim (or Global in the Global module) statement.

At the highest level is the Global module, which contains only definitions. Any variable defined in the Global module is available anywhere in a program. To define variables in the Global module, use the Global statement as

Global MyName As String

which defines MyName as a global string variable.

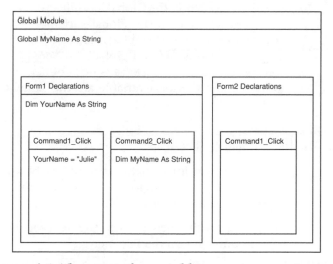

Figure 4.1. *The scope of a variable.*

On the next level below the Global module are variables defined in the (declarations) sections of forms or modules. Variables defined there are available in any procedure in that particular Form or module, but not in any other Form or module. In other words, they are defined only in the Form or module in which they are defined. With the Dim statement, variables are defined in the (declarations) section of a Form or module,

which has exactly the same format as a Global statement. Here, YourName is defined as a string variable:

```
Dim YourName As String
```

At the lowest level are the local variables that are defined or used in an individual procedure. Local variables are available only in the procedure in which they are used or defined, and nowhere else. When the procedure ends, the local variables go away, and their old values are unavailable the next time the procedure is called. To make local variables survive the ending of a procedure, define them in the procedure with the Static statement. Variables defined with the Static statement persist until the next time the procedure is called. The Static statement also has exactly the same syntax as the Global statement. The following code defines OurName as a static string variable.

```
Static OurName As String
```

The declaration of a local variable always overrides the global declaration of a variable with the same name (see Figure 4.1, in which MyName is defined globally in the Global module but also is defined as a local variable in Command2_Click). The global variable and the local variable are two different variables. Changing one has no effect on the other. The variable YourName also is defined globally in Form1 and used in Command1_Click. However, because YourName is not defined in Command1_Click, the global variable and the local variable are the same. Changing one changes the other.

The Variable Scope Example

Try experimenting with the scope of variables, using an example set up like Figure 4.1. Create two forms. Define MyName in the Global module and in Command2. Click on Form1.

1. Start with a new project. Create a second Form with the New **Form** command on the **File** menu.

2. Draw two Command buttons on Form1 and one Command button on Form2.

3. Select the Global module in the Project window, open its Code window, and type **Global MyName as String**.

4. Select Form1 in the Project Window and press the **View Code** button.

5. Select the Form_Click procedure for Form1 and type

74

```
Sub Form_Click()
Print MyName
End Sub
```

6. Select the `Form_Load` procedure and type

```
Sub Form_Load()
MyName = "Bill"
Form2.Show
End Sub
```

The `Form2.Show` method is needed to make the second Form appear on the screen when the program is run.

7. Select the `Command2_Click` procedure and type

```
Sub Command2_Click()
Dim MyName As String
Print MyName
End Sub
```

8. Select the `Command1 Click` procedure and type

```
Sub Command1_Click ()
Print MyName
End Sub
```

9. Select `Form2`. Open its Code window, select the `Command1_Click` procedure, and type

```
Sub Command1_Click()
Print MyName
End Sub
```

Now by clicking the buttons or the Form, you see the values of the three variables. You first work with `MyName`, which is defined globally and given a value in `Form_Click` on `Form1`. Note that when you run this program, `Form2` may not be hiding behind `Form1`, so move `Form1` over a little to see `Form2`.

10. Run the program and click first on `Form1`, then on `Command1` on `Form1`, and finally on `Command1` on `Form2`. The value of `MyName` is known by all these procedures because it is a global variable.

11. Click `Command2` on `Form1` and notice that the global value of `MyName` is not printed on the Form. It is not available here because `MyName` is a local variable in that procedure, and is currently an empty, or null, string.

12. End the program. Open `Command2_Click` on `Form1` and change it to

```
Sub Command2_Click()
Dim MyName As String
MyName = "Shane"
Print MyName
EndSub
```

13. Run the program again, pressing all the buttons.

Notice that `MyName` has the value `Shane` only when the **Command2** button on `Form1` is pressed. The value reverts to `Bill` everywhere else. Thus the global definition persists everywhere but in the procedure `Command2_Click`, in which the local variable definition overrides the global definition.

Experiment with this code. Try defining `MyName` in different places to see what happens. Rather than defining it in the `Global` module, for example, define it in the declarations section of `Form1` (use a `Dim` statement rather than a `Global` one); or define it in the `Form_Load` procedure.

Strings and String Formulas

Now that you have a feel for variables and their scope, you can begin examining strings and string variables.

Defining Strings

The definition of a *string* is a sequence of text characters. Although most strings consist of printable characters, they also can contain any of the non-printing control characters such as the carriage return and line feed. A string also can be the null or empty string, which has a length of zero and doesn't contain any characters. All the Text boxes in the Vaccination Certificate program initially contain null strings.

A second type of string is a *substring*. A substring is an ordinary string that is contained in another string. In other words, it is a piece of another, longer string.

Characters actually are stored in the computer's memory and on disk as *ASCII* codes (ASCII stands for American Standard Code for Information Interchange). The standard set of ASCII codes ranges from 0 to 127 and includes all the standard typewriter symbols—see Appendix B, "ASCII\ANSI Code Chart." Codes from 128 through 255 are the extended character set. The extended character set contains many symbols, foreign characters, and Greek letters. The first 32 ASCII characters are *control characters.* Control characters are used to control data flow in communication programs, and line and page control on printers or the screen. The control codes you use regularly are backspace (8), tab (9), line feed (10), form feed (12), and carriage return (13).

There are two functions for converting between characters and ASCII codes, Asc() and Chr$(). You might wonder why you would want to use the codes at all when you can use the more readable characters. A simple example is inserting end-of-line characters (carriage return and line feed) within a string in a program. If you try to type a carriage return in a program, the program editor moves you down to the next line in the program rather than inserting that character in the string you were typing. (It probably will give you a syntax error, too.) To insert a carriage return in a string, you must create one with the function Chr$(13) and add it to your string. You will do this a little later in this chapter. The syntaxes of the Asc() and Chr$() functions are

```
Asc(string$)
Chr$(code)
```

Here, string$ is a string. Asc() returns the ASCII code of its first character, and code is an ASCII code. Chr$() returns the character that the code represents as a one-character string.

Declaring String Variables

There are several ways to declare a string variable. As I mentioned previously, all the string variables in the properties of objects are predefined, so they do not have to be defined explicitly before they are used. User variables can be used without being defined; however, it is a much better programming practice to declare everything first in the appropriate procedure or

(declarations) section. Doing so ensures that if you use the name of a global variable as a local variable, the two variables are kept separate. Another way to define a string variable is to append a $ to it. For example,

```
MyName$
```

also is a string variable. Notice that it is the same variable as the string variable MyName defined previously with the Dim statement. That is, the $ is not included as part of the variable name.

Using String Formulas

After you define a variable, you have to create a string and store it in the variable. Assigning a value to a string is done with an Assignment statement. The syntax of an Assignment statement is

```
Variable = Formula
```

In this case, Variable is a string variable, and Formula is a string formula or constant. The equal sign makes this an Assignment statement. When it is executed, the formula on the right is evaluated, and the string result is assigned to the variable on the left. You have used Assignment statements in this book to change the values of the properties of objects.

A string formula consists of a combination of quoted strings of text and string functions linked with the *concatenation* operator (+). Concatenation is the act of combining two short strings into a long string by placing the strings end to end. For example, the formula

```
Name = "Bill " + "Orvis"
```

combines the strings "Bill " and "Orvis" into the longer string "Bill Orvis" and assigns the result to the string variable MyName. As another example,

```
Dim MyName As String, YourName As String
MyName = "Bill"
YourName = "Julie"
OurName$ = MyName + " Loves " + YourName
```

combines the two string variables with the string " Loves " to create the string "Bill Loves Julie", which is assigned to the string variable OurName$. Here MyName and YourName are defined as string variables with a Dim statement. OurName$ is defined as a string variable because it has the $ suffix.

Strings Displayed in Labels and Text Boxes

After you have created a string, you have to display it. Printing it on a Form is an adequate way to display the string; however, in this age of dialog boxes and windows, inserting the string in a Label or Text box is more modern. Both Labels and Text boxes dynamically display text on the screen. The difference between them is that the user can edit the text in a Text box, but cannot edit the text in a Label.

Setting the Text with the Properties Bar

The simplest way to display text in a Label or Text box is to use the Properties bar at design time. For a Label, select the Caption property and type the text into the Settings box. For a Text box, find the Text property and again type the text into the Settings box. Although it is simple to do, setting the text in a box using the Properties bar is good only for static text (text that won't change) or to set an initial string for a Text or Caption property that is changed later by the program.

Setting the Text with a Formula

To dynamically change the text in a box, use Assignment statements in your program. The Assignment statement to change a property of an object has the following format:

```
object.property = formula
```

in which the formula must evaluate to a value consistent with the property being changed. The construct object.property is treated like any other variable that is defined at the Form level and refers to the contents of the property of the object. For text properties such as Text and Caption, formula must evaluate to a string of text.

The LOVES Program

Take the preceding example and turn it into the LOVES program.

1. Open a new project and draw two Text boxes.

2. Add one Label on the Form, as shown in Figure 4.2.

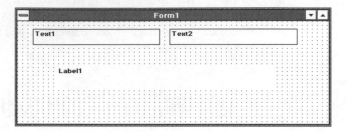

Figure 4.2. Layout for the LOVES application.

3. Select the `Text` properties of the two Text boxes and set them to the null string.

4. Select the `Caption` property of the Label and set it to the null string.

5. Open the Code window and select the (`general`) object and the (`declarations`) procedure. Then type

```
Dim MyName As String, YourName As String
```

This statement makes `MyName` and `YourName` global definitions in the Form. Thus, they are available to any procedure on the Form that wants to use them.

6. Select the `Text1_Change` procedure and type

```
Sub Text1_Change ()
MyName = Text1.Text
End Sub
```

This step stores the value of the `Text` property of the `Text1` box in the string variable `MyName`.

7. Select the Text2_Change procedure and type

```
Sub Text2_Change ()
YourName = Text2.Text
End Sub
```

This step does the same for the Text property of the Text2 box.

8. Select the Form_Click procedure and type

```
Sub Form_Click ()
Label1.Caption = MyName + " Loves " + YourName
End Sub
```

Here, the two string variables are combined with the string "Loves" and are stored in the Caption property of the Label1 box.

9. Now run the program. Type your name in the first Text box. Type the name of someone special in the second box, and click the Form.

Your program now should look like Figure 4.3 (your names replace mine and Julie's, of course).

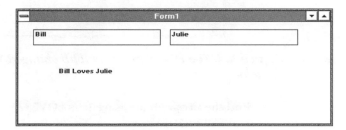

***Figure 4.3.** The running LOVES application.*

10. End the program by selecting **End** from the **Run** menu and save it as LOVES1 (LOVES1.MAK and LOVES1.FRM).

Try this program again, but without the declarations in the (declarations) procedure. The program won't work because the Form_Click procedure won't know the value of MyName or YourName. MyName and YourName now are local to the procedures that contain them.

Changing the Text Attributes

The text attributes in the Label and Text boxes are set in exactly the same manner as the text attributes of a Form. You change them either at design time with the Properties bar, or at run time with Assignment statements. To set the properties at run-time,

1. Select the Label and change the following properties:

```
Label1.Alignment = 2 - Centered
Label1.FontName = Script
Label1.FontSize = 24
```

2. Run the program again. It now looks like Figure 4.4.

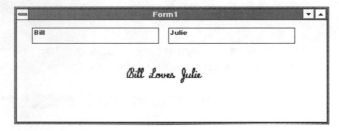

Figure 4.4. *The LOVES program with changed* Text *properties in the Label box.*

3. End the program and save it as LOVES2 (LOVES2.MAK and LOVES2.FRM).

The Manipulation of Strings

As you might expect, you can do more to strings than simply concatenate them. Visual Basic has a set of functions that deal exclusively with strings. The set includes functions to locate substrings, and others to extract a substring from a string. Table 4.1 contains a complete list of the string functions available in Visual Basic. See Chapter 15, "Command Reference," for descriptions of the individual functions.

Table 4.1. String functions.

Function	*Description*
Asc()	Converts a character to an ASCII code.
Chr$()	Converts an ASCII code to a character.
Format$()	Converts a number to a string with a specific format.
InStr()	Locates a substring in a string.
LCase$()	Converts a string to all lowercase.
Left$()	Extracts the left side of a string.
Len()	Determines the length of a string.
LSet()	Left-justifies a string.
LTrim$()	Removes leading spaces from a string.
Mid$()	Extracts a substring from a string.
Right$()	Extracts the right side of a string.
RSet()	Right-justifies a string.
RTrim$()	Removes trailing spaces from a string.
Space$()	Returns a string of spaces.
String$()	Returns a string of a specific character.
UCase$()	Converts a string to all uppercase.

4

If your program has to deal with a string typed by the user or sent by another program, the first thing you usually do is test it to see whether it is the one you expected to receive. You can calculate its length with the Len() function, or search for a specific substring with InStr(). If the Len() function returns a length of 0, the string is empty, a situation that your program must be able to deal with. The InStr() function searches for a specific substring within another string and returns the character location of the start of that substring. If it doesn't find the substring, it returns a zero. The syntaxes of the Len() and InStr() functions are

```
Len(string$)
InStr([start-position,]string$,substring$)
```

After you have found a substring, you might want to extract it, or some other substring. Do this with the Mid$(), Left$(), and Right$() functions. The Mid$() function extracts any substring within a string. The Left$() and Right$() functions are special cases of Mid$() that extract some number of characters from the left or right side of a string. The syntaxes of these functions are

```
Mid$(string$,start-character[,length])
Left$(string$,length)
Right$(string$,length)
```

Here, string$ is the string from which to extract a substring, start-character is the number of the first character to include in the substring, counting from the first character in string$, and length is the length of the substring to extract from string$. In Mid$(), if you omit the length argument, the entire right side of the string is extracted.

Mid$() also can be written as a statement (on the left side of a formula rather than on the right) that replaces a substring in a string with another string of equal length. That syntax is

```
Mid$(string$,start-character[,length]) = substring$
```

Here, the substring in string$ that starts at start-character and is length long is replaced with length characters from substring$. If length is omitted, all substring$ is used. In both cases, the resulting length of string$ is the same length as the original string$.

The Envelope Addresser Program (Version 1)

The LOVES application is cute, but you can make something more useful. Often when you write a letter, you have to type an envelope to go with it. Here is a program that prints addresses on envelopes. The program has a built-in return address. It accepts the address that is to be typed in a Text box. When your address is ready, click the Form to print the address.

1. Start with a new project and a single Form.

2. Draw a Text box on Form1 that is large enough to hold an address. Reduce the size of the Form by dragging its borders until it looks like Figure 4.5. Set the property Multiline = True so the Text box can contain more than one line of text. Set the Text property to null.

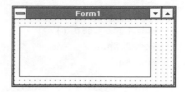

Figure 4.5. Form1 *setup for the Envelope Addresser.*

3. Create a second Form with the New Form command. Drag its borders until it looks like Figure 4.6.

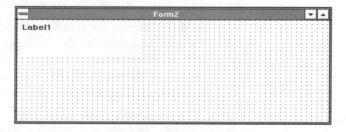

Figure 4.6. Form2 *setup for the Envelope Addresser.*

4. Draw a Label box in the upper-left corner for the return address. Set the property FontSize = 10.

5. Select Form2. Set FontSize = 10 and AutoRedraw = True.

The FontSize property increases the size of the text printed on the Form to 10 points. AutoRedraw must be turned on so the Form remembers text that is printed on it. Otherwise, when it is printed to the printer, only the text in the Labels and Text boxes is printed. AutoRedraw also makes it possible to cover a Form with another Form, uncover it, and still have the text appear.

 AutoRedraw is needed only for forms and picture boxes, because Text boxes and Labels already store the text printed on them in one of their properties.

6. Select Form1 and open its Code window. Select the Form_Load procedure and type

```
Sub Form_Load ()
Form2.Show
End Sub
```

This procedure is executed when Form1 loads. It loads Form2 and makes it visible.

7. Select the Text1_Change procedure and type

```
Sub Text1_Change ()
TheLine = Text1.Text
End Sub
```

This procedure extracts the text from the Text box as it is typed and stores it in the string variable TheLine. The Change event causes this procedure to be executed every time the user types a character into the Text box. To pass the value of TheLine from Form1 to Form2 where it is printed, define it in the Global module.

8. In the Project window, select the Global module. Open its Code window and type

```
Global TheLine As String
```

9. Select Form2 and open its Code window. Select the (declarations) procedure and type

```
Dim eol$
```

The string eol$ is a constant that is needed in two routines on Form2. By defining it in the (declarations) section of Form2, you have to define its value only once. You can't give it a value here with the Const declaration because you can't type a carriage return and a line feed into a string. Such functions as Chrs$(13) are not allowed in the (declarations) section.

10. Select the Form_Load procedure and type the following text. Substitute your own return address for the one I use here.

```
Sub Form_Load ()
  eol$ = Chr$(13) + Chr$(10)
Label1.Caption = "William J. Orvis" + eol$
Label1.Caption = Label1.Caption + "123 Some St." + eol$
Label1.Caption = Label1.Caption + "Anywhere, CA  91234"
End Sub
```

This routine inserts the return address into the Label. This must be done with code because you can't type a return in a Label. The routine first defines eol$, the end-of-line string, as a carriage return (Chr$(13)) and a line feed (Chr$(10)). Next, it combines the text of the return address into a single string with the end-of-line separating each line. This string is stored in the Caption property of the Label1 Label.

11. Select the Form_Click procedure and type

```
Sub Form_Click ()
start = 1
Form2.Cls
Print eol$ + eol$ + eol$ + eol$ + eol$ + eol$ + eol$ + eol$
Print Space$(80); Mid$(TheLine, start, InStr(start, TheLine,
    eol$) - start)
start = InStr(start, TheLine, eol$) + 2
Print Space$(80); Mid$(TheLine, start, InStr(start, TheLine,
    eol$) - start)
start = InStr(start, TheLine, eol$) + 2
Print Space$(80); Right$(TheLine, Len(TheLine) - start + 1
Form2.PrintForm
Form1.Show
End Sub
```

This procedure uses eol$, which was given a value in the Form_Load procedure and passed to this routine through the Form's (declarations) section. It then initializes the variable start, clears the Form, and prints eight new-line characters on the Form. The next Print statement uses the Space$() function to print 80 blank spaces. It then uses the Mid$() function to extract the name line of the address from TheLine. TheLine was passed to Form2 from Form1 through the Global module. You get the length of string to extract by using the InStr() function to look for the first end-of-line after character number start. Next, the procedure changes the value of start to point to the beginning of the next line (the first character after the two-character end-of-line). The address is extracted and printed in the same way. Then the city and state are extracted with the Right$() function. Finally, this procedure prints the Form to the printer (on your envelope) and then redisplays Form1 so you can address a second envelope.

One limitation of this procedure is that it must receive a three-line address. It does not make allowances for addresses with two lines, four lines, or any other number of lines but three. The book will discuss putting protections in programs later.

12. Save the program as ADDR1 (ADDR11.FRM, ADDR12.FRM, and ADDR1.MAK).

13. Run the program. Type the address for your letter in the Text box on Form1. When you are ready, insert an envelope in your printer (or leave the paper in it if you just want to experiment), and click Form2.

    Your address and return address now should be printed on the envelope.

The Use of an InputBox$

In the envelope-addressing program, you created a small Form to use when inputting the address to be printed on the envelope. In effect, you created what is called an *Input box*. The InputBox$ function performs a similar function, although you can input only one line of text at a time. The syntax of the function is

```
InputBox$(prompt$,[title$[,default$[,xpos%,ypos%]]])
```

Here, xpos% and ypos% are the location of the top-left corner of the Input box, default$ is a default string of text placed in the box, title$ is a string to be used as the title of the box, and prompt$ is a string of text describing what you are supposed to do with the box. When you execute this function, it presents the user with an Input box with the specified prompts and titles, and with **OK** and **Cancel** buttons. When you click **OK**, what you typed in the box is returned by the function.

The Envelope Addresser (Version 2)

Modify the envelope addresser to use an InputBox$ to get the address.

1. Open the ADDR1.MAK project file. Save it as ADDR2.MAK so you won't accidently overwrite the previous version of this program.

2. Select Form1 and delete it with the **R**emove File command on the File menu.

3. Select Form2 and open the Code window to the Form_Click procedure. Change the procedure to

```
Sub Form_Click ()
start = 1
```

```
Form2.Cls
Print eol$ + eol$ + eol$ + eol$ + eol$ + eol$ + eol$ + eol$
Print Space$(80); InputBox$("Name", "Mailing Address")
Print Space$(80); InputBox$("Address" , "Mailing Address")
Print Space$(80); InputBox$("City and State"  "Mailing Ad
    dress")
Form2.PrintForm
End Sub
```

Here, you first replace the Mid$() function with an InputBox$ with the string Name as the prompt and the string Mailing Address as the box title—see Figure 4.7. What the user types is printed immediately on Form2. The second and third lines of the address are done the same way. Then the Form is printed.

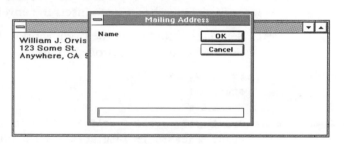

***Figure 4.7.** The first Input box requesting the name.*

4. Save the Form as ADDR2.FRM by selecting it and executing the Save File **As** command on the **File** menu. Save the project again as ADDR2.MAK.

5. Run the program. A dialog box appears and asks you to select the start-up routine. Select Form2 and click **OK**. Form1 is the default start-up Form, and because it was deleted, you have to tell Visual Basic which Form or procedure to use. This happens only the first time you run the program; the next time you run it, Visual Basic can recall the Form used for start up.

6. Click the Form. The Input box shown in Figure 4.7 appears. Type the name and press Enter.

7. After pressing Enter, another similar Input box appears. Type the address in the Input box.

8. After pressing Enter, a third similar Input box appears. Type the city and state and press Enter.

At this point, Form2 is filled out and printed to the printer.

The Use of a MsgBox

If you simply want to send a message to the user rather than requesting input from him, you can use the MsgBox function. The syntax of the MsgBox function is

```
MsgBox(msg$[,type[,title$]])
```

in which msg$ is the message to be shown, type is a number indicating the number and type of buttons on the box (see Chapter 15, "Command Reference," for a complete list), and title$ is a string title for the box. If you omit type, a simple message box with a single **OK** button is used. Add this to the envelope addresser program so the program pauses before printing. As a result, the user has time to insert the envelope in the printer.

1. Select Form2 and open the Code window to the Form_Click procedure. Change the the procedure to

   ```
   Sub Form_Click ()
   start = 1
   Form2.Cls
   Print eol$ + eol$ + eol$ + eol$ + eol$ + eol$ + eol$ + eol$
   Print Space$(80); InputBox$("Name", "Mailing Address")
   Print Space$(80); InputBox$("Address", "Mailing Address")
   Print Space$(80); InputBox$("City and State", "Mailing Address")
   Print
   MsgBox ("Insert an envelope in the printer and click OK")
   Form2.PrintForm
   End Sub
   ```

   The extra Print statement in line 8 is needed to overcome what seems to be a bug in Visual Basic. Without it, the third line of the address does not print.

2. Run the program again. After entering the city and state, the message box in Figure 4.8 appears.

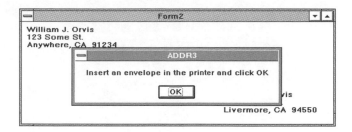

Figure 4.8. Using a message box for a pause in the Envelope Addresser.

3. End the program. Save the Form as ADDR3.FRM and the project as ADDR3.MAK.

What You Have Learned

Now you know all about strings and string functions. As you have seen, strings are important in Visual Basic, because all communication with the user is done with them. Keyboard input starts as a string, which is then turned into numbers and commands. Output to the screen or printer can start as numbers, but must be converted to strings to be printed. In this chapter you

*   Defined variables as storage locations for information.

*   Examined the scope of variables.

*   Defined strings and string variables.

*   Created string formulas.

*   Manipulated strings using the string functions.

*   Used Input and Message boxes.

*   Created an envelope addresser.

Using Numbers and Control Structures

In most computer language books, numeric variables are discussed first and strings are mentioned almost as an afterthought. In Visual Basic, however, they are discussed prior to the numeric types in a chapter of their own because they play such an important part in communicating with the user. Now that you know all about strings, it's time to look at numeric values and control structures.

In This Chapter

This chapter describes numeric variables and control structures. Numeric variables are variables that contain a number rather than a string of characters as a binary value. Although you can only display or store strings,

you can perform real numeric operations with numeric variables. In addition, control structures make it possible to examine the value of a variable and alter the order of execution of a program based on that value. In this chapter you learn to

- Compare the different numeric types.

- Examine integers.

- Examine floating-point numbers.

- Examine currency format.

- Define numeric variables.

- Create formulas using numeric variables.

- Examine array variables.

- Examine control arrays.

- Create logical formulas.

- Control program flow with loops and logical variables.

The Numeric Types of Visual Basic

There are six different data types in Visual Basic. The five numeric types are `Integer`, `Long`, `Single`, `Double`, `Currency`, and the `String` type. I discussed the `String` data type in the previous chapter. `Integer` and `Long` data types are used for storing whole numbers (numbers with no fractional parts). `Single` and `Double` data types are used for storing real numbers (numbers with fractional parts). `Currency` is a special data type designed to do calculations with decimal numbers rather than binary numbers. This data type is used to eliminate the round-off errors caused by converting binary numbers to decimal notation. Table 5.1 lists the numeric types available in Visual Basic and describes their properties.

Table 5.1. Data types in Visual Basic.

Type	Preface Character	Memory Usage	Range	Description
Integer	%	2 bytes	−32,768 to 32,767	Two-byte integer

Long	&	4 bytes	–2,147,483,648 to 2,147,483,647	Four-byte integer.
Single	!	4 bytes	–3.37E–38 to 3.37E+38	Single-precision floating-point number. This is the default for unspecified variables.
Double	#	8 bytes	–1.67D–308 to 1.67D+308	Double-precision floating-point number
Currency	@	8 bytes	–9.22E+14 to 9.22E14	Fixed-point number with two digits after the decimal. Math is done in decimal to eliminate round-off errors when converting from binary to decimal.
String	$	1 byte + 1 byte per character		String of characters.

Integers

The Integer and Long data types represent whole numbers only. They cannot be used to represent fractions. As a result, they take less storage space than floating-point numbers. Mathematical operations that involve Integers and Long types are much faster than those involving floating-point numbers. Use Integers when you know you do not have a fractional number. Use Long integers when you have to store values larger than those allowed by the Integer data type.

95

You might wonder why the limits in Table 5.1 are such odd numbers. Why should a type have a limit of 32,767 rather than a nice round number like 33,000? The fact is they *are* nice round numbers—in binary. The Integer data type is stored in two bytes (16 bits) of memory. The first bit is used as the sign bit (+ or -), and the rest represent the number in binary notation. The largest number that a sequence of n bits can represent is 2^n, which in this case is $2^{15} = 32,767$.

Floating-Point Numbers

Single- and Double-precision floating-point numbers are used to represent real numbers (numbers with fractional parts). The Single-precision floating-point number is the default numeric type for variables that are not defined with the prefix characters, or with Global, Dim, or Const statements. Single-precision numbers have about 7-digit precision, whereas Double-precision numbers have about 15-digit precision. The precision of a data type is its ability to store a certain number of digits. If you try to store a number with more digits than the precision allows, the extra digits are lost.

On input and output, large floating-point numbers are expressed in E or D format as

```
1.94E+04 = 19,400.
9.2279E-28 = 0.00000000000000000000000000092279
0.3141592653589793D+01 = 3.141592653589793
```

in which E represents the Single-precision floating-point, D is the Double-precision floating-point, and the numbers following the E or D are the powers of 10 used to multiply the number on the left.

Currency

The Currency numeric type is a fixed-point type used to calculate money values. In most cases, calculations are done in binary. The result is converted to decimal when it is printed or displayed on the screen. In the conversion process, round-off errors are caused often by the fact that there are decimal numbers that cannot be represented exactly in binary. As a result, you often get results like 0.99999 rather than 1.00. In many cases, this is no problem. However, if you are dealing with money, you usually want the results to be exact to the penny. A number like 0.99999 is not acceptable when 1.00 is expected. The Currency numeric type takes care of this by doing calculations in decimal rather than in binary, albeit decimal calculations are much slower than binary calculations. Currency type numbers have about 14-digit precision.

Defining Numeric Variables

Numeric variables are defined in exactly the same manner as the String data type. Moreover, all the arguments about the range of a variable apply equally to numeric types. In the Global module, you use the Global statement. Elsewhere you use Dim statements such as

```
Global Width As Single
Dim Account As Currency
Dim RoadLen As Double, Counter As Integer
```

In addition, you can use the variable prefix characters listed in Table 5.1 to define the type of any local variable or to override the type of a Global variable.

Onc defining statement you have not looked at so far is the Const statement. The Const statement is used anywhere you want to give a constant a name. This is different than defining a variable and assigning it a name, because once the variable is defined, the value of a constant cannot be changed. The syntax of the Const statement is

```
[Global] Const variable = value [,variable = value ...]
```

Here, the Global prefix is needed only in the Global Module; *variable* is the name of the constant, and *value* is its value. *Value* can consist of simple numbers, other constants, and all the operators except those for exponentiation and concatenation. *Value* cannot include any functions. The numeric type of *variable* is determined either by the value assigned to it, or by the placement of a variable prefix character on it. Strings also can

be constants. However, as mentioned previously, they cannot be concatenated, and you cannot use the Chr$() function to insert carriage returns or line feeds in your constant string. For example,

```
Global Const RED = &HFF&
```

defines the constant, RED, as the hexadecimal value for the red color. The constant then is used in the different procedures of the program rather than the hexadecimal value, making the procedures more readable.

Using Arrays

An array isn't actually a different numeric type. It is an indexed group of variables of the same type that can be referenced as a single object. An array variable must be defined with a Global or Dim statement, with the following syntax:

```
Dim ArrayName([lower To] upper[,[lower To] upper])[ As type]
```

Here, each set of *lower* and *upper* is a dimension of the array, with *lower* as the lower limit of the index and *upper* as the upper limit. If you leave out the lower limit, its default value is 0. The range of array limits is the same as the range of the integer data type (–32,768 to –32,767). The maximum number of dimensions for a single array is 60. For example,

```
Dim TaxRate(5)
Dim CostTable(2,5 To 8)
```

The first example defines TaxRate as a one-dimensional array variable with five elements. Each element is accessed by placing an index within the parentheses. The value of the index then identifies the array element to be used. For example, the elements of TaxRate are

```
TaxRate(0)
```

```
TaxRate(1)
```

```
TaxRate(2)
```

```
TaxRate(3)
```

```
TaxRate(4)
```

```
TaxRate(5)
```

The second example, `CostTable` (2,5 to 8), defines a two-dimensional, three-cell-by-three-cell array named `CostTable`. A two-dimensional array is like the two-dimensional grid of cells in a spreadsheet. The first number is the row index, and the second is the column. The array elements are accessed as

```
CostTable(0,5) CostTable(0,6)    CostTable(0,7)
CostTable(1,5) CostTable(1,6)    CostTable(1,7)
CostTable(2,5) CostTable(2,6)    CostTable(2,7)
```

You can imagine a three-dimensional array as a cube of cells with a row, column, and depth index. Higher-dimensional arrays such as this are a little difficult to imagine, but they are occasionally useful.

Arrays are used for storing large blocks of data. For example, imagine you are working on your super stock estimator, which needs the average daily value of a stock over several months. You don't want to create a program with several hundred variables to hold all these values (Day1, Day2, Day3, ...). Instead, create a single array variable to hold them, such as Day(Index1). Then the value of Index1 selects the value of the stock for any specific day.

You can use this process for three different stocks as well; just create a two-dimensional array with three elements on one direction and a few hundred in the other. For example, Day(1 To 300, 1 To 3), with the values retrieved with Day(Index1,Index2). (Index1 selects the day and Index2 selects the stock.) Assume you want to store the high and low values as well as the average. Add another dimension to the array when you define it, Day(1 To 300, 1 To 3, 1 To 3), then access the elements with Day(Index1,Index2,Index3), where Index1 selects the day, Index2 selects the stock and Index3 selects high, low, or average.

Inputting Numbers

In Chapter 4, "Using Strings and Text Boxes," you saw how to input strings of text from the user. But what about inputting numbers? You get numbers from the user in exactly the same way you get strings. In fact, you input the number as a string, using the methods of the previous chapter, and then convert it into a number. Conversion of strings into numbers is performed with the Val() function, which has the syntax

```
Val(string$)
```

Here, *string*$ is any string representation of a number. The string can have leading white space (spaces, tabs, and line feeds). However, it cannot have leading nonnumeric characters. The function converts the numeric characters into numbers. The function continues until it encounters a character it cannot convert, then it stops. For example,

```
Val("     456abs") = 456
Val("456 789") = 456
Val("a345") = 0
Val(" 0 ") = 0
```

As you can see by the previous two examples, you must be careful what strings you give to the Val() function. A string with a mistyped leading character—in this example, it's a—causes the result to be 0, even when the rest of the string contains a number. No error is generated if the function can't find a number in a string.

Displaying Numbers

Again, numbers are displayed in the same manner as strings. They are converted to a string first. Then the string is either printed or displayed in a Label or Text box. The simplest routine for converting numbers to text is the Str$() function. The Str$() function takes a number as an argument and converts it into a string. The format of the string is the simplest format that can display the full precision of the number. If you want the number formatted in a specific format, use the Format$() function. The syntaxes of these functions are

```
Str$(number)
Format$(number[,format-string$])
```

in which *number* is the value to be converted to a string, and *format-string*$ is a formatting string that controls how the string is converted. In the formatting string, place zeros or pound signs (0 or #) where you want the digits of the number to go. Insert commas and the decimal point where you want them. If you use the pound signs, the space in the output string of the Format$() function is reserved for a number. If you use zeros rather than pound signs, leading and trailing zeros are included at those positions, if needed. Specific formatting strings also exist for dates and times. See Chapter 15, "Command Reference," for a complete list. You can insert +, -, $, (,), and spaces in the string; those characters are included in the output, where they were placed in the formatting string. To insert any other characters in the output, they have to be surrounded by double quotation marks (use Chr$(34), not "). For example,

```
ANumber = 1234.567
Str$(ANumber) = " 1234.567"
Format$(ANumber,"#####.") = "1235."
Format$(ANumber,Chr$(34)+"Balance = "+Chr$(34)+"$00000.00"=
     "Balance = $01234.57"
Format$(ANumber,"##.##") = "1234.57"
ANumber2 = 0.123
Format$(ANumber2,"##.#####") = ".123"
Format$(ANumber2,"00.#####") = "00.123"
```

Users of other versions of BASIC should recognize the formatting capabilities of the PRINT USING statement contained in the Format$() function.

Calculating Mathematical Formulas

Mathematical formulas in Visual Basic look much like the equivalent algebraic formula for the same calculation. In other words, they are Assignment statements like those discussed for strings, with a numerical

variable on the left and a formula that evaluates to a numeric result on the right. Visual Basic has a complete set of operators and mathematical functions to use when constructing a mathematical formula.

Arithmetic Operators

The arithmetic operators available in Visual Basic are listed in Table 5.2. They include the standard set of addition, subtraction, multiplication, division, and powers (such as 10^4), as well as modulus arithmetic and integer division. The precedence of the operators tells you which operation is done first in an expression involving more than one operator.

Table 5.2. The Visual Basic arithmetic operators and precedences.

Operator	Operation	Precedence
^	Power	1
–	Negation (unary operation)	2
*	Multiplication	3
/	Division	3
\	Integer division	4
Mod	Modulus	5
+	Addition	6
–	Subtraction	6

Addition, subtraction, multiplication, and powers operate as you would expect, in the algebraic sense. The modulus operator is defined as the remainder of an integer division. First, the operands are rounded to integers. Then the modulus operation is performed. For example, if you had 6.9 Mod 2, 6.9 would be rounded to 7 and then divided by 2. The remainder (the Mod) would be 1. The integer division operator also rounds the operands to integers, performs a normal division operation, and then truncates the result to an integer. For example, if you had instead specified 6.9\2, 6.9 again would be rounded to 7, then divided by 2. The answer would be 2. Table 5.3 shows more examples.

Table 5.3. Modulus and integer division.

Modulus Division	Integer Division
5 Mod 3 = 2	5\3 = 1
-5 Mod 3 = -2	-5\3 = -1
5.8 Mod 3 = 0	5.8\3 = 2

As you can see, the modulus and integer division operators perform a complementary set of operations. The modulus operator is most often used to unwind cyclical events, such as the actual angle between two lines when it is specified as a number greater than 360 degrees. It also can be used to determine the day of the week (or the year) when the number of days between now and then is greater than a week (or a year). For example, to find the day of the week 138 days from now you could use

```
138 Mod 7 = 5
```

If today is a Monday, 138 days from now would be Monday plus five days, or Saturday.

Relational Operators

The relational operators shown in Table 5.4 compare two values and return a logical result. If the relationship between the two values is the same as the one expressed by the operator, the expression returns True (−1) otherwise, it returns False (0). All the relational operators have the same precedence, so use parentheses to ensure that the correct comparisons are done.

Table 5.4. The Visual Basic relational operators.

Operator	Operation
=	Equals
>	Greater than
<	Less than

5

continues

Table 5.4. continued.

Operator	Operation
<>	Not equal to
<=	Less than or equal to
>=	Greater than or equal to

Logical Operators

The logical operators shown in Table 5.5 apply a logical operation to one or two logical values, and return a logical value. In addition, if they are applied to numeric values rather than logical values, the operation is performed bit by bit to each bit in the numeric values. All the Logical operators have the same precedence, so use parentheses to ensure the operations are performed in the order you want. The logical operators are explained more, later in this chapter.

Table 5.5. The Visual Basic logical operators.

Operator	Operation
Not	Negation
And	Logical and
Or	Logical or
Xor	Logical exclusive or
Eqv	Logical equivalence
Imp	Logical implies

Precedence of the Operators

As stated before, the precedence of the operators tells you which operation is done first in an expression involving more than one operator. When the computer has a choice between two operations, the operation with the highest precedence is performed first. When two operations have the same precedence, they are evaluated left to right. Parentheses always override the precedence of operators, so use them to control the order of calculation. If you are unsure what the order is in a situation, use parentheses to make the formula calculate in the order in which you want it to be calculated. Inserting unnecessary parentheses won't hurt anything, and they assure you the calculations are being done in the order you want. Some examples are

```
A * B^C + D
A*B + C
A*(B + C)
```

In the first example, the power, B^C, is done first. Then this result is multiplied by A and added to D. In the second example, the multiplication, A*B, is done first. Then the result is added to C. The third example reverses the order of the second by using parentheses: The addition, (B + C), is done first. Then the result is multiplied by A.

Numeric Functions

The numeric functions consist of arithmetic functions, trigonometric functions, and logarithms. Table 5.6 lists the numeric functions available in Visual Basic.

Table 5.6. The numeric functions in Visual Basic.

Arithmetic Functions	
Function	*Result*
Abs( )	Absolute value
CCur( )	Convert to Currency

continues

Table 5.6. continued.

Arithmetic Functions

Function	Result
CInt()	Convert to Integer
CDbl()	Convert to Double
CLng()	Convert to Long
CSng()	Convert to Single
Fix()	Truncate to an integer
Int()	Round to an integer
Randomize()	Initialize the random number generator
Rnd()	Generate a random number
Sgn()	The sign of the argument
Sqr()	Square root

Trigonometric Functions

Function	Result
Sin()	Sine
Cos()	Cosine
Tan()	Tangent
Atn()	Arctangent

Logarithmic Functions

Function	Result
Exp()	Exponential
Log()	Natural logarithm

There are four functions for converting a floating-point number to an integer: `CInt()`, `CLng()`, `Fix()`, and `Int()`. The first two, `CInt()` and `CLng()`, force the result to be an `Integer` or `Long` type by rounding the floating-point number to an integer. For example, `CInt(6.8)` would equal the integer 7. `Fix()` forms an integer by truncating the fractional part of the floating-point number. `Int()` returns the largest integer that is less than or equal to the argument. For example,

```
CInt(4.7) = 5       CLng(4.7) = 5      Fix(4.7) = 4     Int(4.7) = 4
CInt(4.3) = 4       CLng(4.3) = 4      Fix(4.3) = 4     Int(4.3) = 4
CInt(-4.7) = -5     CLng(-4.7) = -5    Fix(-4.7) = -4   Int(-4.7) = -5
CInt(-4.3) = -4     CLng(-4.3) = -4    Fix(-4.3) = -4   Int(-4.3) = -5
```

The `Randomize()` and `Rnd()` functions initialize and return random numbers. The numbers are not truly random, but they are generated by a pseudo-random function. The `Randomize` function is normally executed inside a program to initialize the seed of the random number generator. By setting the *seed* (starting number) of that generator, you can either repeat a set of random numbers or give the generator a random starting place. If you execute `Randomize` with no argument, the random number generator gets a random starting point using the `Timer` function. If you use a numeric argument with `Randomize`, the generator uses it as the seed, and `Rnd(1)` returns the same set of numbers every time. A new random number is generated every time the `Rnd()` function is executed with a positive argument.

The available trigonometric functions are sine, cosine, tangent, and arctangent. The rest of the common trigonometric and hyperbolic functions can be calculated using the built-in functions and the well-known rules of trigonometry.

The logarithmic functions available in Visual Basic calculate the natural logarithm (base e = 2.71828) and the exponential (power of e). To calculate the common logarithm (base 10), use

```
Log10(x) = Log(x)/Log(10)
```

Type Conversion

Because five different numeric types are available in Visual Basic (`Integer`, `Long`, `Single`, `Double`, and `Currency`), some type of conversion has to take place when you create a formula that contains different types. Before a

calculation takes place, Visual Basic converts all the values on the right side of the formula into the most precise Form before performing the actual calculations. For example, if a formula combines Single-precision floating-point numbers and integer numbers, Visual Basic converts everything to Single-precision floating-point before performing the calculation. After the result is calculated, it is converted to the type of the variable on the left side of the formula.

The Self-Paced Learning Program (Version 1)

My son is learning mathematics and needs to practice for his weekly tests. The following program automatically creates a test for him to practice.

1. Start with a new project.

2. Draw five Labels (615 x 500 twips) on Form1, as shown in Figure 5.1.

3. Draw five Text boxes (615 x 260 twips).

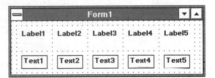

Figure 5.1. *The initial form layout of the Self-Paced Learning program.*

4. For each Text box set the following. Note that `""` stands for the empty or null string; therefore, delete the contents of the Text property.

```
BorderStyle = 0 - None
FontName = Courier
Text = ""
```

5. For each Label set

```
FontName = Courier
```

In these previous two steps, the font is Courier, a monospaced font (in which all characters are the same width). The numbers in the top row are then lined up with those in the bottom row.

6. Draw another five Label boxes, each with a width of 615 twips and a height of 20 twips. Use BorderStyle = 1 - Single to create the 10 horizontal lines between the Labels and the Text boxes, as shown in Figure 5.2.

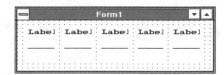

Figure 5.2. *Modified form layout for the Self-Paced Learning program.*

7. Open the Code window for the Form. Select the (declarations) section and type

```
Dim Probs(2, 5) As Single
```

This line defines the array Probs, which has three rows and six columns as a Single-precision array. The array is to hold the two numbers per addition problem. I define it here so the numbers are available for other routines to use. In the following step, don't forget you can use the **Copy** and **Paste** commands on the **Edit** menu to make multiple copies of a line, then go back and edit the difference.

8. Select the Load event and type

```
Sub Form_Load ()
Rem Initialize the random number generator
Randomize
Rem Define the end-of-line character
eol$ = Chr$(13) + Chr$(10)
Rem Fill the probs array with 2 sets of 5 values
Rem between 0 and 100
Probs(1, 1) = Int(Rnd(1) * 100)     'line 8
Probs(1, 2) = Int(Rnd(1) * 100)
Probs(1, 3) = Int(Rnd(1) * 100)
Probs(1, 4) = Int(Rnd(1) * 100)
Probs(1, 5) = Int(Rnd(1) * 100)
Probs(2, 1) = Int(Rnd(1) * 100)
Probs(2, 2) = Int(Rnd(1) * 100)
Probs(2, 3) = Int(Rnd(1) * 100)
Probs(2, 4) = Int(Rnd(1) * 100)
Probs(2, 5) = Int(Rnd(1) * 100)     'line 17
Rem Insert the random numbers into the labels
```

continues

109

```
Label1.Caption = Format$(Probs(1, 1), " 00") + eol$ +
    Format$(Probs(2, 1), "+00")
Label2.Caption = Format$(Probs(1, 2), " 00") + eol$ +
    Format$(Probs(2, 1), "+00")
Label3.Caption = Format$(Probs(1, 3), " 00") + eol$ +
    Format$(Probs(2, 1), "+00")
Label4.Caption = Format$(Probs(1, 4), " 00") + eol$ +
    Format$(Probs(2, 1), "+00")
Label5.Caption = Format$(Probs(1, 5), " 00") + eol$ +
    Format$(Probs(2, 1), "+00")
End Sub
```

The second line of code contains a `Rem` or `remark` statement used to store remarks about what your code is doing. Visual Basic ignores anything following the `Rem` keyword at the beginning of a line or a single quotation mark anywhere in a line. I use remarks of this type to mark lines of code as I describe them.

Be liberal with `remark` statements in your code. They won't slow anything down much, and they immensely improve the comprehension of your code. If you are one of those people who can remember every word you have ever written and why you wrote it, and your code is never going to be read by anyone else, you can forget about including `remark` statements. However, if you are like me, you should use many `remark` statements so you don't forget what you have done and why.

Line 3 initializes the random number generator. Line 5 creates an end-of-line string as you have done before. Lines 8 through 17 fill the array `Probs()` with random numbers between 0 and 100. The `Rnd(1)` function generates random numbers between 0 and 1. Multiplying by 100 extends the range of the numbers from 0 to 100. `Randomize` utilizes the random number generator and should be called at least once in a program that uses random numbers.

Lines 19 through 23 insert the numbers into the five Label boxes. First the numbers are converted to strings with the `Format$()` function. Then those strings are combined with an end-of-line character and stored in the `Caption` property of the Label boxes.

There is a bug in the first version of Visual Basic that should be fixed in later versions. The # placeholder does not hold a place as it is supposed to. Even if you use two #s in the format statement, numbers less than 10 won't line up correctly with numbers greater than 10. Using the "00" format instead is a simple way to work around the bug. This format prints 01 through 09 for the numbers 1 through 9. Another option is to right-justify the text in the Label using the Alignment property.

9. Run the program. A Form like Figure 5.3 appears on the screen (your numbers will be different). Type the first answer. Then press Tab to go to the next problem.

   My son now can take this math test by typing his answers in the Text boxes below the problems. Maybe he will think this is another computer game and will spend hours practicing his math problems.

10. Save the project as MATH1 (MATH1.FRM and MATH1.MAK).

Form1				
65	26	64	28	69
+41	+60	+42	+45	+85

Figure 5.3. Running the Self-Paced Learning program (Version 1).

This test was purposefully made into a five-problem test so it would be less confusing to explain. You can increase the number of problems to 10 or 20 easily by increasing the number of Labels and Text boxes, enlarging the Probs() array, and filling in the extra elements. Now you can exercise a young mind.

Using Loops and Control Arrays

If you look closely at the code in step 7, you notice two blocks of nearly identical statements. You shouldn't have to write the same statement repeatedly when the only difference is the value of an index. Loops are a good way to shorten the length of a program (and the amount of typing you have to do) by repeatedly executing a single block of statements rather than having multiple copies of that block.

There are three types of loops in Visual Basic: For/Next, While/Wend, and Do/Loop. The For/Next loop is a counted loop, which executes a block of statements a fixed number of times. I use this type of loop most often. The While/Wend loop executes a block of statements until some condition is no longer satisfied. The Do/Loop loop executes a block of statements as long as a condition is satisfied or until one condition becomes satisfied. The syntaxes of the loops are

```
For counter = start To end [Step stepsize]
    block of statements
[Exit For]
    block of statements
Next [counter[,counter]]

While condition
    block of statements
Wend

Do [{While|Until} condition]
    block of statements
[Exit Do]
    block of statements
Loop

Do
    block of statements
[Exit Do]
    block of statements
Loop [{While|Until} condition]
```

Here, *counter* is a variable used to count the number of times the For/Next loop is iterated, *start* is the beginning value of the counter, *end* is the stopping value of the counter, and stepsize is the increment given to the counter at each step. If the Step phase is omitted, step 1 is assumed. For the While/Wend and Do/Loop loops, *condition* is a numeric formula that results in the value True (–1) or False (0). The While and Until keywords determine how the condition is used. While continues executing the block until condition becomes False. Until continues executing the block as long as condition is False. With the Exit For and Exit Do statements, you can terminate a loop prematurely and go on to the next statement after the Next or Loop statement.

The Self-Paced Learning Program (Version 2)

A For/Next loop is made for the code in the Self-Paced Learning program, because you want things done exactly two times in five places. The data used in the program is stored in an array so individual elements are accessible with an index value. To use a loop here, you also have to be able to access the Text properties of five Text boxes using an index . Do this by combining the Text boxes into a control array. A control array is one or more controls with the same name. Individual controls in the control array are accessed with an index, like an array variable is.

To save a project with a new name:

1. Select a Form or module.

2. Use **File**, Save **As** with a new name.

3. Continue this process until you have saved all the Forms and modules.

4. Execute **File**, Sav**e** Project As to save the project with a new name.

A control array is created by giving all the controls (Text boxes in this case) the same CtlName and then setting the Index property to 1, 2, 3, and so on, to identify the individual control.

1. Select the Label1 box and set Index = 1.

2. Select the Label2 through Label5 Label boxes, and set CtlName = Label1. The Index property is incremented automatically when you add a control to a control array.

3. Open the Code window for the Form. Select the Load event and change the code to

```
Sub Form_Load ()
Rem Initialize the random number generator
Randomize
```

continues

113

```
Rem Define the end-of-line
eol$ = Chr$(13) + Chr$(10)
Rem Fill the probs array with 2 sets of 5 values
Rem between 0 and 100
For I = 1 To 2       'line 8
  For J = 1 To 5
    Probs(I, J) = Int(Rnd(1) * 100)
  Next J             'line 11
Next I
Rem Insert the random numbers into the labels
For J = 1 To 5       'line 14
  Label1(J).Caption = Format$(Probs(1, J), " 00") + eol$ +
    Format$(Probs(2, J), "+00")
Next J
End Sub
```

4. Save the code as MATH2 (MATH2.FRM and MATH2.MAK), then run
    it. The results should be similar to those in Figure 5.3, but with
    different numbers.

When saving a modified project with a new name, be sure to save the
Forms and modules first with the File Save As command on the File
menu, then save the Project with the Save Project As command. If you
save the project first, it is saved with the Form and module names of
the previous version.

As you can see, this is much simpler than the code in step 7, but it
performs exactly the same functions. In lines 8 and 9, I start two nested `For`/
`Next` loops that surround line 10. They are called *nested loops* because the
loop for the counter `J` is within the loop for counter `I`. When line 8 is
executed, `I` is set to 1. In line 9, `J` is set to 1. In line 10, `Probs(1,1)` is loaded.
When the execution reaches line 11, the bottom of the `J` loop, it jumps back
up to line 9, where `J` is set to 2, and lines 10 and 11 are executed again. This
continues until `J` equals 5, at which point the `J` loop is finished. Execution
moves to line 12. Line 12 is the bottom of the `I` loop, so execution jumps
back up to line 8, where `I` is set to 2. Line 9 is executed again, starting up
the `J` loop again to go through five more iterations. At this point, both the
`I` loop and the `J` loop are done, so execution moves to line 14, where
another `J` loop is started to load the `Caption` properties of the Label boxes.
The five Label boxes now are a control array named `Label1()`. Inserting an
integer between the parentheses selects the particular Label box to access.

Something else you should notice in this piece of code is the use of indentation. The indentation is purely for visual delineation of the blocks of code associated with the For/Next loops. It has no effect on the actual execution of the code, although it does make the code much more readable. Everything between the For I =... and the Next I statements is indented two spaces, which makes it easy to see the block iterated by that loop. The statements between the For J =... and the Next J statements are indented an additional two spaces. Again, the use of indentation has no effect on the operation of the code, but it greatly improves the readability.

Creating Logical Formulas

Logical formulas (or *conditionals*) are formulas that have a numerical result of –1 (True) or 0 (False). They are created by relating two formulas with one of the relational operators from Table 5.5. If the two formulas fit the relation specified by the operator, the value of the formula is True. Otherwise it is False. For example,

```
(3 > 5) = 0 (False)
(3 + 1 = 4) = -1 (True)
A = 4: B = 5: (A <= B) = -1 (True)
```

Logical formulas are the *conditions* used to determine when to terminate the Do/Loop and While/Wend loops discussed previously. They are the arguments also of the If Then Else branching statements I discuss in a few moments. Logical formulas are how you make a decision in a program to control what is done.

The logical operators (listed in Table 5.5) have two functions. They are most commonly used to connect two or more logical formulas into a more complicated logical formula. Second, they perform bitwise operations on one or two numbers. A bitwise operation on one number is applied to every bit in that number as if each bit were a separate entity. Bitwise operations are used only for specialized applications that must access the individual bits in a computer word. For example, if you want to know whether the fourth bit in an integer is null or 1, create a mask with only that bit set to 1, then And it with the integer. If the result is null, the bit is null; otherwise the bit is 1.

5

115

Table 5.7 is a *truth table* for the logical operators. A truth table shows the result for all combinations of `True` and `False` inputs. The `Not` operator switches `True` to `False` and `False` to `True`. The `And` operator returns `True` only when both operands are true. The `Or` operator returns `True` when either of the operands is true. `Xor` is the Exclusive `Or` operator, which returns `True` when either of the operands is true, but not both. `Eqv` is the equivalence operator, which returns `True` whenever both operands are the same. `Imp` is the implies operator, which always returns `True`, except when the first operand is true and the second is false. For example,

```
(3 > 2) And (5 <= 7) = True
(2 = 2) Xor (5 > 3) = False
```

The logical operators all have the same precedence, so you must use parentheses to control the order of evaluation. Otherwise, you might not get the results you expect. For example, the only difference in the following statements is the placement of parentheses; however, each statement gives a different result.

```
False And True Or True = True
(False And True) Or True = True
False And (True Or True) = False
```

Table 5.7. Truth table of the logical operators T = True (–1), F = False (0).

A	B	Not A	A And B	A Or B	A Xor B	A Eqv B	A Imp B
T	T	F	T	T	F	T	T
T	F	F	F	T	T	F	F
F	T	T	F	T	T	F	T
F	F	T	F	F	F	T	T

Branching—Controlling Program Flow

The programs created in this book so far are relatively linear in function. Every step in the program is executed in order from the first to the last.

Branching is the capability to change the order in which statements are executed. The simplest branch is the unconditional GoTo. The GoTo statement has the syntax

```
GoTo label
```

in which label is a line label or number. In older versions of BASIC, all lines in a program had to be numbered. Visual Basic supports this numbering but does not require it. More modern programming languages use line labels on only those lines that need special access. A label consists of an alphabetic name that follows the same rules as a variable name and ends with a colon. When a GoTo statement is executed, execution branches immediately to the statement following the label. Although the GoTo statement is extremely powerful, it is better programming practice to use structured branches such as the loops or If Then Else statements whenever possible. A program with many GoTo statements rapidly becomes unmanageable.

A conditional branch uses a logical formula to decide which block of code to execute. The most heavily used conditional branch statement is the If Then Else statement, which examines a condition and branches accordingly. The If Then Else statement has two forms: a simple, one-line Form, and the block If statement. The syntax of the simple If statement is

```
If condition Then iftrue [Else iffalse]
```

Here, condition is a logical formula that results in a True (–1) or False (0) value, and iftrue and iffalse are statements that are executed if condition is True or False. Iftrue and iffalse are Visual Basic statements, such as Assignment or GoTo statements.

The preferred form of the If Then Else statement is the block form. It is preferred because the statements comprising the Then and Else clauses are within the If Then Else block, making it simpler to see what is going on. The syntax of the block If statement is

```
If condition1 Then
block of statements
[ElseIf condition2 Then]
block of statements
[Else]
block of statements
End If
```

Here, if condition1 is True, the *block of statements* between the If and ElseIf statements is executed, and control passes to the statement after the End If statement. If condition1 is False, control passes to the first

ElseIf statement where *condition2* is tested. If it is True, the statements between the ElseIf statement and the Else statement are executed. There can be multiple ElseIf statements to test for different conditions. Visual Basic tests each one in turn until it finds one with a True condition. If none of the conditions is True, control passes to the Else statement, and the *block of statements* between the Else and End If statements is executed.

The Self-Paced Learning Program (Version 3)

Something that's missing from the Self-Paced Learning program is a test of the answers. The computer easily can calculate the correct answer for the math problems and compare them to the numbers my son types. In addition, it keeps track of the number of correct and incorrect answers and produces a percentage score at the end of the test.

1. Start with version 2 of the Self-Paced Learning program.

2. Select Text1 on Form1 and set Index = 1 to start a control array.

3. Select Text2 through Text5 and set CtlName = Text1 to create the rest of the control array.

4. Enlarge the Form as shown in Figure 5.4. Add a Label (2655 x 260 twips), and set

   Caption = " Wrong   Right   Score"

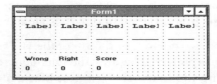

Figure 5.4. Layout for the Self-Paced Learning program (Version 3).

5. Below the word Wrong, place a Label (615 x 260 twips), and set

   ```
   CtlName = NumWrong
   Caption = ""
   ```

6. Below the word Right, place a Label (615 x 260 twips), and set

   ```
   CtlName = NumRight
   Caption = ""
   ```

7. Below the word Score, place a Label (615 x 260 twips), and set

   ```
   CtlName = Score
   Caption = ""
   ```

8. Open the (declarations) section and change it to

```
Const NumProbs = 5
Dim Probs(2, NumProbs) As Single, Answer(NumProbs) As Single
Dim GotIt(NumProbs) As Integer
Const True = -1
Const False = 0
Const Red = &HFF
```

I have added some arrays and defined five constants in the (declarations) section. NumProbs is the number of problems on the Form. I could use the number 5 in the program, but using the variable name makes the code more readable. Using the variable also makes it simpler to expand the program to more problems. True and False are given their default values here so I can use the words rather than the numbers. Red is defined as the hexadecimal string that produces the color red. To get it, I selected the ForeColor property of a box, opened the Color Palette window, selected red, and copied the value out of the Settings box. The &H at the beginning of the number specifies that the following characters are a hexadecimal (base 16) value.

9. Select the Form_Load event. Change it to read

```
Sub Form_Load ()
Rem Initialize the random number generator
Randomize
Rem Define the end-of-line character
eol$ = Chr$(13) + Chr$(10)
Rem Fill the probs array with 2 sets of 5 values
Rem between 0 and 100
For I = 1 To 2
  For J = 1 To NumProbs
    Probs(I, J) = Int(Rnd(1) * 100)
  Next J
Next I
Rem Insert the random numbers into the labels and
Rem calculate the answers
For J = 1 To NumProbs
      Label1(J).Caption = Format$(Probs(1, J), " 00") + eol$
          + Format$(Probs(2, J), "+00")
  Answer(J) = Probs(1, J) + Probs(2, J)        'added line
Next J
End Sub
```

Here I have added one line (marked **added line**) near the end of the procedure, to calculate the answers for each of the displayed problems.

10. Select the Text1_KeyPress event, and type

```
Sub Text1_KeyPress (Index As Integer, KeyAscii As Integer)
Rem Test for a return, if not, go on
If KeyAscii <> 13 Then GoTo SkipIt        'line 3


Rem Block one
Rem test for right or wrong answer when CR is pressed
If Text1(Index).text = "" Then            'line 7
  Rem No value typed, do nothing
  GoTo SkipIt
ElseIf Val(Text1(Index).text) = Answer(Index) Then
  Rem solution correct
  GotIt(Index) = True
Else                                      'line 13
  Rem solution wrong
  GotIt(Index) = False
End If


Rem Block 2
Rem When the last problem is done, score the test.
If Index = NumProbs Then                  'line 20
  Rem Calculate scores
  NRight = 0
  NWrong = 0
  For I = 1 To 5
    If GotIt(I) = True Then
      NRight = NRight + 1
      Text1(I).FontStrikethru = False
      Text1(I).Forecolor = Red
    Else
      NWrong = NWrong + 1
      Text1(I).FontStrikethru = True
    End If
  Next I
  NumRight.Caption = Str$(NRight)         'line 34
  NumWrong.Caption = Str$(NWrong)
  Score.Caption = Format$(NRight / (NumProbs), "##%")
```

```
Else
   Text1(Index + 1).SetFocus           'line 38
End If

SkipIt:
End Sub
```

The `Text1_Keypress` event automatically is passed two values, `Index` and `KeyAscii`. `Index` is the value of the `Index` property of the control in the control array that had the event. `KeyAscii` is the ASCII code of the key that was pressed. The user types the answer in a Text box and presses Enter. When Enter is pressed, the code checks the answer and moves the *focus* to the next problem. When the last problem is done, the program counts the right and wrong answers, calculates the score, and displays the results.

The *Focus*, in Visual Basic and in Windows programs in general, refers to the control or Form that is currently active. The control or Form currently with the focus receives any events generated by the keyboard or mouse. Thus, if a Command button is active, pressing Enter activates that Command button; if a Text box has the focus, anything you type appears in that Text box. To move the focus to a different object on a form, press the Tab key. To move the focus to the menu bar, press the Alt key, then use the arrow keys to move from menu item to menu item. Press Esc to move back to the form. To move the focus with code, use the `SetFocus` method. The syntax of `SetFocus` is

object.SetFocus

where *object* is the name of the Form or control you want to move the focus to.

In line 3, the value of `KeyAscii` is tested to see whether Enter (13) was pressed. If not, the code jumps to `SkipIt` and returns control to the Text box. If Enter was pressed, the procedure executes block 1.

Block 1 is a block `If` statement that checks for three different situations. First, in line 7, it checks for no value in the Text box, which occurs if the user presses Enter without typing anything. If that happened, the `GoTo` statement in line 10 jumps to `SkipIt`, ignoring the improper Return. Next, it compares what the user typed with the value in the array `Answers()` to see whether the user got it right. If he did, the array `GotIt()` is set to `True` for that problem. If the user has answered wrong, the code jumps to line 13, which changes `GotIt()` to `False`.

121

Block 2 of the code checks now to see whether this is the last problem. If not, the focus is moved to the next problem in line 38. The code starting in line 22 counts the number of correct answers and the number of incorrect answers. It does this by first zeroing the counters NRight and NWrong.

It then loops over each problem and, using another block If statement, adds one to either NRight or NWrong. Then it turns on the Strikethru property and changes the Forecolor to red for any incorrect answers. Starting in line 33, the code inserts the number of right and wrong answers in the Label boxes at the bottom of the Form and calculates the percent score. The fraction correct is calculated and converted to text using the Format$() function and the percent field specifier. The percent field specifier automatically multiplies the value it is converting by 100.

11. Save the program as MATH3 (MATH3.FRM and MATH3.MAK), run it, and try to answer a few problems. Your results should look like Figure 5.5 (with different numbers, of course). I purposely answered the second problem incorrectly to demonstrate what happens when the user misses a question.

		Form1		▼ ▲
53 +42	96 +84	56 +92	49 +36	22 +95
95	~~144~~	148	85	117
Wrong	Right	Score		
1	4	80%		

Figure 5.5. *Running version 3 of the Self-Paced Learning program.*

Although this is a simple, five-problem math test, you easily could make it include more problems by increasing the sizes of the arrays and adding more labels to the Form.

For a challenge, try changing the logic so the user gets more than one try per problem. Also, you could make the program tell the user whether the answer is correct as soon as it is typed. There are many variations, depending on what you want to do. A structure like this can be adapted to other forms of self-paced teaching, such as multiple-choice problems.

What You Have Learned

This chapter has been devoted to defining and using numeric data types. In addition, you have controlled program flow with loops and logical branches. You have learned

- About the different numeric types.

- About the capabilities of integers, floating-point numbers, and Currency type numbers.

- How to define numeric variables.

- How to create formulas using numeric variables.

- About array variables.

- About control arrays.

- About logical formulas.

- How to control program flow with loops and logical variables.

- How to create a Self-Paced Learning program.

Using Controls

In This Chapter

Everything placed on a Form is a control. Even the Label and Text boxes are controls, because they not only display text, they also initiate actions when they are changed or clicked. This chapter investigates the more traditional controls: buttons, check boxes, and scroll bars. More complex controls (such as menus) are discussed in later chapters; it's easier to learn the simplest control methods first. This chapter shows you the use of

- Command buttons.
- Option buttons.
- Check boxes.
- Scroll bars.

Using a Command Button to Initiate an Action

A Command button is a standard push button, which you push or click to make something happen. You can also double click it, or press a key while it has the focus to initiate an action. A Command button is created in exactly the same manner as any other control: select the Command button tool from the Toolbox window, and draw the button on a form.

The Advanced Annuity Calculator

Creating an annuity calculator, with buttons to select the calculation to perform, is a good exercise in using Command buttons. I realize that almost every book on programming calculates annuities as an example, and I'm going to do it, too. Although annuities are calculated using well-known but nasty little formulas, they are immensely useful in many home and business situations.

An annuity calculator enables you to deal with accounts that have periodic deposits or withdrawals, and that grow or deplete at a specific interest rate. You can calculate what you owe the bank every month when you finance a house or car. Annuities also tell you how fast an investment grows in an interest-bearing account, or how much money you must put into an account now, to have some specific amount later.

The Advanced Annuity Calculator has five Text boxes and five Command buttons to calculate the interest rate, payment, number of periods, present value, and future value. It uses cash flow conventions to determine the sign of the dollar values—that is, cash received is positive and cash paid out is negative. Whether a transaction is paid in or out depends on your point of view. If you are the bank, a car payment is positive; if you are the car buyer, the payment is negative. Be sure to pick your point of reference before using the calculator.

To calculate one of these five values, you must solve one of two equations for that value. The first (Equation 6.1) is used for all calculations in which IRate, the interest rate, is nonzero. The second (Equation 6.2) is used whenever IRate is zero.

$$PVal\,(1+IRate\,)^{NPer} + Pmt\left(\frac{(1+IRate\,)^{NPer}-1}{IRate}\right) + FVal\ = 0$$

Equation 6.1. *Used if* PVal *is not equal to zero.*

$$PVal + Pmt * NPer + FVal = 0$$

Equation 6.2. *Used if* Pval *is equal to zero.*

Here, IRate is the fractional interest rate per period (the fraction, not the percent), NPer is the number of payment periods, Pmt is the periodic payment, PVal is the present value—that is, the amount of money in the account now—and FVal is the future value, or the amount of money in the account at some future time. If you are dealing with a savings account in a bank, then the payment rate is probably zero, the present value is your initial deposit, and the future value is what you will have after several years. If you are calculating a car loan, then the present value is what you owe, and you want the future value to be zero, indicating you have paid off the loan.

To create this calculator, you need five sets of formulas: solutions of the two annuity equations (6.1 and 6.2) for each of the values. The results of solving these two equations are one pair of equations for each value but the rate, and a transcendental equation for the rate. A transcendental equation is one for which an analytical solution does not exist. To solve it, use the iterative numerical method known as successive approximations.

First, draw the user interface for the problem. The interface has five Text boxes for inputting or outputting numerical results, and five Command buttons to determine which value to calculate. Follow these initial steps:

1. Open a new project.

2. Select the form and adjust its size to 3885 by 2680 twips. Set its Caption property to Advanced Annuity Calculator.

3. Draw five Text boxes on the form as shown in Figure 6.1. The top three are 1095 by 380 twips; the bottom two are 1575 by 380 twips.

Figure 6.1. *Layout of the form in the Advanced Annuity Calculator.*

4. Selecting the Text boxes from left to right, top to bottom, set the Text properties to blank, and the CtrlName properties to: Rate, Per, Pay, PV, and FV.

5. Below the five Text boxes, draw five Command buttons the same size as the Text boxes.

6. For the five Command buttons, set the Caption properties to: Rate, Periods, Payment, Present Value, and Future Value. Set the CtrlName properties to: RateButton, PerButton, PayButton, PVButton, and FVButton.

Now that the interface is drawn, define some global variables in the Form so they can be passed between procedures on the Form. Here, five variables are defined to hold the numeric results. IRate is the interest rate, and is defined as a single precision floating point number. NPer is the number of periods, and is defined as an integer. Pmt, FVal, and PVal are the payment, present value, and future value, defined as double precision floating point numbers. Double precision is needed here so large numbers, like the mortgaged amount on a home, can be calculated accurately. The Currency type does not work here, it appears that the intermediate values calculated in some of the formulas cause numeric overflow errors.

7. Open the Code window for the form, select the declarations procedure, and type

```
Dim IRate As Single, NPer As Integer, Pmt As Double
Dim FVal As Double, PVal As Double
```

Whenever a number is typed into one of the Text boxes, extract it, convert it to a number, and store it in the appropriate variable.

8. Open the Code windows, one at a time, for the five Text boxes, and type the following Change procedures.

```
Sub Rate_Change ()
IRate = Val(Rate.text)
End Sub

Sub PV_Change ()
PVal = Val(PV.text)
End Sub

Sub Per_Change ()
NPer = Val(Per.text)
End Sub
```

```
Sub Pay_Change ()
Pmt = Val(Pay.text)
End Sub

Sub FV_Change ()
FVal = Val(FV.text)
End Sub
```

Now, if you solve the annuity equations for the number of periods, you get the following two equations. These equations are calculated whenever the PerButton Command button is pressed.

$$NPer = \frac{Log\left(\dfrac{Pmt - FVal * IRate}{Pmt + PVal * IRate}\right)}{Log(1 + IRate)}$$

Equation 6.3. *Used if* NPer *is not equal to zero.*

$$NPer = \frac{-(FVal + PVal)}{Pmt}$$

Equation 6.4. *Used if* NPer *is equal to zero.*

9. Open the Code window for the PerButton Command button and type

```
Sub PerButton_Click ()
If IRate <> 0 Then
  NPer = Log((Pmt - FVal * IRate) / (Pmt + PVal * IRate))
  / Log(1 + IRate)
Else
  NPer = -(FVal + PVal) / Pmt
End If
Per.text = Str$(NPer)
End Sub
```

This procedure uses a block If statement to select the equation to calculate, according to whether IRate is zero or not. If IRate isn't zero, the formula in line 3 is calculated; otherwise, the formula in line 5 is calculated. After the value of NPer is calculated, it is converted to text

129

in line 7 and stored in the Text property of the Per Text box. The Payment, Present Value, and Future Value buttons follow in the same way.

The formulas for the payment are

$$Pmt = \frac{IRate \; (PVal \; (1 + IRate)^{NPer} + FVal)}{1 - (1 + IRate)^{NPer}}$$

Equation 6.5. *Used if* Pmt *is not equal to zero.*

$$Pmt = \frac{-(FVal + PVal)}{NPer}$$

Equation 6.6. *Used if* Pmt *is equal to zero.*

10. Open the Code window for the PayButton procedure, and type

```
Sub PayButton_Click ()
If IRate <> 0 Then
  Pmt = IRate * (PVal * (1 + IRate) ^ NPer + FVal)
    / (1 - (1 + IRate) ^ NPer)
Else
  Pmt = -(FVal + PVal) / NPer
End If
Pay.text = Format$(Pmt, "####.00")
End Sub
```

This is largely the same as the PerButton_Click procedure, except the conversion of the number Pmt into a string of text is accomplished with a Format&() function. You could use dollar signs in the formatting strings, or commas to make the numbers more readable, but the Val() function won't be able to read them correctly if you do.

Don't use dollar signs or commas in the formatting strings. Although they do make the numbers more readable, the Val() function is not able to convert the text strings back into numbers correctly. This is because the Val() function stops converting characters into numbers when it reaches a non-numeric character such as a dollar sign or comma.

Replace the Val() function in these procedures with code that can convert a numeric text string containing dollar signs and commas into a numeric value, then use dollar signs and commas in the Format$() function. Hint: Use the string functions to remove the dollar signs and commas, then use the Val() function to convert the string into a number.

Do the same for the PVButton, and the FVButton. The equations for the present value and future value are

$$PVal = \frac{-FVal - Pmt\left(\frac{(1+IRate)^{NPer}-1}{IRate}\right)}{(1+IRate)^{NPer}}$$

Equation 6.7. *Used if* Pval *is not equal to zero.*

$$PVal = -FVal - * NPer$$

Equation 6.8. *Used if* Pval *is equal to zero.*

$$FVal = -PVal(1+IRate)^{NPer} - Pmt\left(\frac{(1+IRate)^{NPer}-1}{IRate}\right)$$

Equation 6.9. *Used if* Fval *is not equal to zero.*

$$FVal = -PVal - Pmt * NPer$$

Equation 6.10. *Used if* Fval *is equal to zero.*

11. Open the code window for the PVButton_Click procedure and type

```
Sub PVButton_Click ()
If IRate <> 0 Then
  PVal = -(FVal + Pmt * ((1 + IRate) ^ NPer - 1)
    / IRate) / ((1 + IRate) ^ NPer)
Else
  PVal = -FVal - Pmt * NPer
End If
PV.text = Format$(PVal, "######.00")
End Sub
```

12. Open the Code window for the FVButton_Click procedure and type

```
Sub FVButton_Click ()
If IRate <> 0 Then
  FVal = -PVal * ((1 + IRate) ^ NPer)
   - Pmt * ((1 + IRate) ^ NPer - 1) / IRate
Else
  FVal = -PVal - Pmt * NPer
End If
FV.text = Format$(FVal, "######.00")
End Sub
```

When you try to solve the annuity equations for the interest rate, you can't get an analytic solution. To solve this equation numerically, use a method known as successive approximations. "The Method of successive approximations" might sound exotic and complicated, but it is actually quite simple. You do a series of calculations (approximations) to bring the two sides of the equation as close in value as possible (convergence).

The equation is first solved so IRate is on the left side of the equal sign, and a function of IRate is on the right. Because there is more than one way to do this, the results may diverge (grow further apart) as you iterate, if you choose the wrong approach. The simplest way to determine whether you have solved the equation correctly is to try it and see if it converges to a solution. If it doesn't, try solving the equation a different way.

$$IRate = \frac{Pmt\,(1 - (1 + IRate)^{NPer})}{PVal\,(1 + IRate)^{NPer} + FVal}$$

Equation 6.11. *Used if* Pmt *is not equal to zero.*

$$IRate = -1 + \left(-\frac{FVal}{PVal}\right)^{\frac{1}{NPer}}$$

Equation 6.12. *Used if* Pmt *is not equal to zero.*

Next, guess a value of IRate, insert it in the right side of the equation, and calculate a new approximation. Insert this new approximation on the right to produce yet another approximation to IRate. Continue this iteration until the value of IRate inserted on the right converges with the value calculated by that insertion. Actually, you could iterate forever without getting identical values, so make them the same within some tolerance (0.001 in this case).

13. Open the `RateButton_Click()` procedure and type

```
Sub RateButton_Click ()
Dim Denom As Double
If Pmt <> 0 Then
  Rem Give IRate an initial guess
  IRate = .5
  IRateOld = 0
  counter = 0
  Rem Use the method of successive approximations
  Rem to solve for the value of IRate
  Rem Test for convergence and loop again if IRate isn't
  Rem converged.
  Do While Abs((IRate - IRateOld) / IRate) > .001    'line 12
   counter = counter + 1
   Rem Quit if it didn't converge after 20 iterations
   If counter > 200 Then
     MsgBox "Problem didn't converge after 20 iterations", 0
     Exit Do
   End If
   IRateOld = IRate      'line 19
   Denom = PVal * (1 + IRateOld) ^ NPer + FVal
   If Denom = 0 Then
     Rem Go here if Denom is zero.
     IRate = 0
     MsgBox "The interest rate is undefined (divide by zero)", 0
     Exit Do
   Else
     Rem Use this equation if Pmt and Denom are not 0
     IRate = Pmt * (1 - (1 + IRateOld) ^ NPer) / Denom
   End If
 Loop
Else
  Rem Use this equation if Pmt is 0.
  IRate = -1 + (-FVal / PVal) ^ (1 / NPer)       'line 32
End If
Rate.text = Format$(IRate, "0.0000 ")
End Sub
```

In this procedure, the first statement defines `Denom`, a double precision floating point variable. Next, a block `If` statement test `PMt` to see if it is zero. If it is, the alternate formula in line 33 is used to calculate

the rate. If `Pmt` is not zero, the next four lines select the initial guess for `IRate` and also initialize the variables `IRateOld` and `Counter`. `IRateOld` holds the value inserted in the formula, and `IRate` holds the new value calculated from the formula. `Counter` counts the number of times the loop is iterated so you can cancel the calculation if it isn't converging.

Line 12 starts a `Do` loop, which then ends with the `Loop` statement in line 30. The loop terminates when `IRateOld` and the calculated value `IRate` differ by only a tenth of a percent. The next six lines increment `Counter`, and test it to see whether it is greater than the 200 iteration limit. If the calculation reaches 200 iterations, it probably isn't going to converge, so the procedure displays a Message box informing you of that fact.

In line 19, `IRateOld` is set equal to the previously calculated value of `IRate`.

In line 20, the denominator of the function is calculated. In line 21, a block `If` statement tests the value of the denominator to see whether it is zero. If it were zero, and you used it anyway, the program would crash. Testing the denominator prevents this problem; the program puts up a Message box if the denominator is zero. If it's not zero, the new value of `IRate` is calculated in line 28.

14. Save the project as ANVT (ANVT.MAK and ANVT.FRM).

15. Run the program, and type **0.01** (1%) in the rate box, **36** in the Periods box, **10000** in the Present Value box, and **0** in the Future Value box. This represents a loan, typical of one for a new car ($10,000 for three years at 12% a year).

16. Press the **Payment** button to calculate the payment of $–322.14. Your Advanced Annuity Calculator should now look like Figure 6.2.

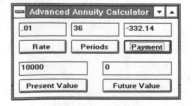

Figure 6.2. *Advanced Annuity Calculator after calculating the payment required on a $10,000 loan at 12% per year.*

Notice the $10,000 is positive, because you receive it from the bank, and the payment of $–322.14 is negative because you pay it to the bank. Note also, that because you have not tested for every possible invalid value, such as a negative interest rate, or both PVal and FVal as zero, this program can still crash. If that happens, just rerun the program with different values, or insert more protection (If statements) in the RateButton procedure to check for invalid data.

See if you can make this program uncrashable by testing the inputs for inconsistent or out-of-range data before calculating a value. Each Command button will have its own set of invalid values. Look at the denominators of the fractions in the formulas to see what combinations of values make them zero. These sets of values are invalid, and should not be allowed in the input. Check also for large values that cause overflow errors.

To calculate any other quantity, insert values in the boxes for all but the one you want to calculate, then press the button to calculate that value. For example, you can find out what interest rate you must have so $10,000 grows to $20,000 in five years. Type **60** in the Periods box (five years x 12 months/year), **0** in the Payment box, **10000** in the Present Value box (positive because the bank is receiving the money), **-20000** in the Future Value box (negative because the bank is giving you back the money in the future), and press the **Rate** button. The program would now look like Figure 6.3, with the value 0.0116 in the rate box, which represents 13.92% per year (0.0116 x 12 months x 100%).

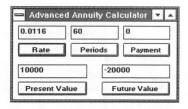

Figure 6.3. The Advanced Annuity Calculator after calculating the interest rate necessary for $10,000 to increase to $20,000 in five years.

Using Option Buttons to Select an Option

Option buttons are used in groups, which are defined by placing the Option buttons on a Form, Frame, or Picture window. All the Option buttons placed directly on a single Form, Frame, or Picture window constitute one group. Option buttons are often called "radio buttons" because they operate much like the station-changing buttons on a car radio. Only one Option button in a group can be pressed at any one time, and pressing one button releases the previously pressed button.

To add Option buttons to an application, first draw a frame with the Frame tool, then draw the Option buttons within the frame. Option buttons have the property `Value`, which is `True` (–1) if the button is pressed or `False` (0) if it is released.

The Self-Paced Learning Program (Version 4)

To demonstrate the use of Option buttons, add some to the Self-Paced Learning Program developed in Chapter 5, "Using Numbers." Version 3 of the program creates an addition test. This new version gives you the choice of addition, subtraction, multiplication, or division, selected with a group of four Option buttons.

1. Open the MATH3 program (MATH3.MAK), and save it as MATH4 (MATH4.MAK, and MATH4.FRM) so you don't accidentally overwrite the previous version.

 2. Using the Frame tool, draw a frame (1575 by 860 twips) to the right of the Score Text box as shown in Figure 6.4.

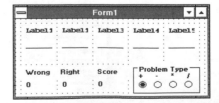

Figure 6.4. Layout for version 4 of the Self-Paced Learning program.

 3. Draw four Option buttons (255 by 260 twips), from left, along the bottom of the frame.

4. Draw four Labels (255 by 260 twips) above the four Option buttons.

5. Select each Labels and set the Caption properties to +, -, *, and /.

6. Select the first Option button on the left, and set the property, Value = True.

7. Select the frame and set the Caption property to Problem Type.

This completes the changes to the user interface. Now change the Form_Load procedure to check the Option buttons when it sets up the problems. You also have to add Click procedures to the Option buttons to run the Form_Load procedure whenever one of the buttons is pressed.

8. Open the Code window, select the declarations section, and add the definition for black color, as shown.

```
Const NumProbs = 5
Dim Probs(2, NumProbs) As Single, Answer(NumProbs) As Single
Dim GotIt(NumProbs) As Integer
Const True = -1
Const False = 0
Const Red = &HFF
Const Black = &H0
```

9. Select the Form_Load procedure, and change it to the following. The changes are in the last block.

```
Sub Form_Load ()
Rem Initialize the random number generator
Randomize
Rem Define the end-of-line character
eol$ = Chr$(13) + Chr$(10)
Rem Fill the probs array with 2 sets of 5 values
Rem between 0 and 100
For I = 1 To 2
  For J = 1 To NumProbs
    Probs(I, J) = Int(Rnd(1) * 100)
  Next J
Next I
Rem Insert the random numbers into the labels and
Rem calculate the answers
For J = 1 To NumProbs
  If Option1.Value = True Then      'line 16
```

continues

```
 Label1(J).Caption = Format$(Probs(1, J), " 00")
      + eol$ + Format$(Probs(2, J), "+00")
   Answer(J) = Probs(1, J) + Probs(2, J)
 ElseIf Option2.Value = True Then
 Label1(J).Caption = Format$(Probs(1, J), " 00")
      + eol$ + Format$(Probs(2, J), "-00")
   Answer(J) = Probs(1, J) - Probs(2, J)
 ElseIf Option3.Value = True Then
 Label1(J).Caption = Format$(Probs(1, J), " 00")
      + eol$ + Format$(Probs(2, J), "*00")
   Answer(J) = Probs(1, J) * Probs(2, J)
 ElseIf Option4.Value = True Then
 Label1(J).Caption = Format$(Probs(1, J), " 00")
      + eol$ + Format$(Probs(2, J), "\/00")
   Answer(J) = Probs(1, J) / Probs(2, J)
 End If
 Text1(J).text = ""        'line 29
 Text1(J).FontStrikethru = False
 Text1(J).ForeColor = Black
Next J
NumRight.Caption = ""
NumWrong.Caption = ""
Score.Caption = ""
End Sub
```

The changes start in line 16, with a block If statement. Each block of the block If statement checks the Value property of one of the Option buttons, to find the one that is pressed. The contents of each block are nearly the same; the first line (line 17, for example) inserts the numbers in the Label, along with the symbol for the type of operation (+, -, *, /). Each block inserts a different symbol. The second statement in each block (line 18, for example) calculates the correct answer for the problem using the operator selected with the **Option** button.

The second Format$() function in line 26 must have a division operator (/), but a slash used in a formatting string is a date separation operator. To insert a formatting operator as a literal symbol rather than the operator, precede it with a backslash (\). The pair of characters \/ produces a single / in the printed string.

Line 29 removes any old answers left from a previous test, and lines 30 and 31 reset the `FontStrikeThru` and `ForeColor` properties that were previously set for wrong answers. Lines 31, 32, and 33 remove any old scores. You also must move the focus back to the first Text box, but this is not the place to do it. The first time the `Form_Load` routine is called, the form has not been loaded yet, so there is no Text box to move the focus to. The routine would fail if you tried to move the focus to it. The next step takes care of that problem.

10. Select the `Option1_Click` procedure and type

```
Sub Option1_Click ()
Form_Load
Text1(1).SetFocus
End Sub
```

Here I introduce a new piece of the BASIC language, procedure calling. Up to now, all the procedures have been called by the system. When you click a control, the system calls the `Click` procedure; if a Text box is changed, the system runs the `Changed` procedure. Not only can the system call a procedure, but any procedure can call any other procedure in its scope. To call a procedure, simply type its name in your code. When the called procedure completes, execution returns to the procedure that called it and begins at the statement after the calling statement.

The rules of scope for procedures are the same as they are for variables. Any procedure on a form is accessible by any other procedure on the same form, and any procedure in a Module is available to any procedure in the application. Chapter 8, "Writing Custom Procedures," discusses procedures in more detail.

In the `Option1_Click` procedure, the second line calls the `Form_Load` procedure and runs it. When it is complete, control returns to the third line, which moves the focus to the first Text box. The other three `Option` procedures work the same way.

11. Select the `Option2_Click` procedure and type

```
Sub Option2_Click ()
Form_Load
Text1(1).SetFocus
End Sub
```

12. Select the `Option3_Click` procedure and type

```
Sub Option3_Click ()
Form_Load
Text1(1).SetFocus
End Sub
```

13. Select the `Option4_Click` procedure and type

```
Sub Option4_Click ()
Form_Load
Text1(1).SetFocus
End Sub
```

14. Save the project, then run it.

You now can change the test type by pressing one of the Option buttons. Notice how pressing one button releases whichever one was previously pressed.

The subtraction test can have large numbers subtracted from small ones with a negative result. Add code to reverse the top and bottom numbers in the subtraction test when that is the case. Negative numbers are too advanced for most children.

Using a Check Box to Set an Option

Unlike Option buttons, Check boxes are independent of each other, and more than one can be checked at the same time. Otherwise, they behave much like Option buttons. When a Check box is checked, its `Value` property is 1; if it's unchecked, the value is zero. The `Value` property also can be 2 if the Check box is grayed (disabled). You draw Check boxes in almost the same way you draw Option buttons, except they do not have to be on a Frame because they are independent of each other. However, you can put them on a Frame if you want to visually group them.

The Envelope Addresser (Version 3)

As an example, add the following options to the envelope addresser.

- Optional return address.

- Bold or plain text.

- Large or small type.

Follow these steps to add the options to version 1 of the envelope addresser to include the options.

1. Open the ADDR1.MAK project file and then save it as ADDR3.MAK so you won't accidently overwrite the previous version of this program. Save the two forms as ADDR31.FRM and ADDR32.FRM, and the global module as ADDR3.BAS.

2. Select Form1 and enlarge it to 3900 by 3540 twips.

3. Using the Check box tool, draw three Check boxes on the form as shown in Figure 6.5.

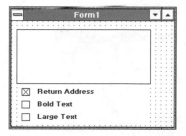

Figure 6.5. *Setup of* Form1 *for version 3 of the Envelope Addresser.*

4. Change the Caption properties of the three Check boxes to

```
Check1.Caption = Return Address
Check2.Caption = Bold Text
Check3.Caption = Large Text
```

5. Select the first Check box and change its Value property to 1 - Checked.

6. Because most people want a return address, make it the default. Select Form2 and add the Label box Label2 (3375 by 1220 twips) as shown in Figure 6.6.

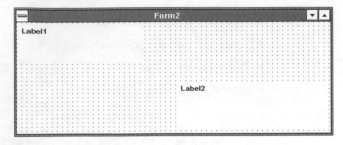

Figure 6.6. *Setup of* Form2 *for version 3 of the Envelope Addresser.*

This completes the changes to the interface. Now make some adjustments to the code so it reacts to changes in the Check boxes.

7. Select Form1, open the Code window for the Check1_Click procedure, and type

```
Sub Check1_Click ()
RetAddr = Check1.Value
End Sub
```

8. Select the Check2_Click procedure and type

```
Sub Check2_Click ()
BoldFace = Check2.Value
End Sub
```

9. Select the Check3_Click procedure and type

```
Sub Check3_Click ()
LargeType = Check3.Value
End Sub
```

10. Open the Global module, and insert references to these three options so they are passed to the procedures on Form2. Also, define the values True, False, Checked, and Unchecked.

```
Global TheLine As String
Global RetAddr As Integer, BoldFace As Integer
Global LargeType As Integer
Global Const True = -1, False = 0
Global Const Checked = 1, Unchecked = 0
```

In the original version of the envelope addresser, the return address is printed on the form by the Form_Load procedure. This has to be moved to the Form_Click procedure so you can use logical statements to decide to print it or not.

11. Cut the three lines, which define the return address, from the Form_Load procedure (saving them for the Form_Click procedure) using the Cut command on the Edit menu. Add the default values of the Check boxes to the Form_Load procedure, which should now read

```
Sub Form_Load ()
eol$ = Chr&(13) + Chr$(10)
RetAddr = Checked
BoldFace = Unchecked
LargeType = Unchecked
End Sub
```

12. Change the Form_Click procedure to read as follows. First, paste text from the Form_Load procedure into the Form_Click procedure using the Paste command on the Edit menu.

```
Sub Form_Click ()
If BoldFace = Unchecked Then
  Label1.FontBold = True
  Label2.FontBold = True
Else
  Label1.FontBold = False
  Label2.FontBold = False
End If
If LargeType = Unchecked Then
  Label1.FontSize = 12
  Label2.FontSize = 12
Else
  Label1.FontSize = 10
  Label2.FontSize = 10
End If
If RetAddr = Unchecked Then
  Label1.Caption = "William J. Orvis" + eol$
  Label1.Caption = Label1.Caption + "123 Some St." + eol$
  Label1.Caption = Label1.Caption + "Anywhere, CA  91234"
Else
  Label1.Caption = ""
End If
Label2.Caption = TheLine            'line 23
Form2.PrintForm
Form1.Show
End Sub
```

Notice there are three independent block If statements. They are independent because each Check box is independent of the others. The first block If statement in lines 2 through 8 checks whether the Bold Text check box is checked, and changes the FontBold property of both labels to True or False. The second block in lines 9 through 15 does the same for the FontSize property of the two Label boxes. The third If block in lines 16 through 22 checks the value of the Return Address Check box, and if it is true, inserts the return address into the Caption property of the Label1 box. If it isn't True, it blanks the Caption property. In line 23, the value of the address is placed in the Caption property of the second label box, and in line 24, the form is printed. Line 25 redisplays Form1 so you can print a second envelope.

13. Save the project and run the program. Type the address for the envelope in the Text box on Form1; select the options you want and then click Form2 to print the envelope.

Using Scroll Bars to Set a Value

The last control discussed in this chapter is Scroll bars, which are used to select a numeric value in some range. Because of their more familiar use to control windows, you might not have thought of Scroll bars as a way to set a value. However, a Scroll bar returns a number that indicates the relative location of the thumb (the white square that slides along the Scroll bar). When you move the thumb up and down (or left and right) the number stored in the Value property of the Scroll bar changes accordingly.

It is up to the attached program to convert changes in that number to movement of a window. Also, there is no reason that a Scroll bar can only control windows. In any program where an integer has to be selected from a range, a Scroll bar can be used. It also can be used like a gauge with the program changing the Value property, which makes the thumb move along some scale. There are two properties that control the range of the number returned in the Value property, as listed.

Min - The minimum value of the Scroll bar when the thumb is at the left of a horizontal Scroll bar or at the top of a vertical one.

Max - The maximum value of the Scroll bar when the thumb is at the bottom or right.

Changing the `Value` property by a program causes the thumb to move, and moving the thumb with the mouse changes `Value`. Thus, a Scroll bar can be used either as an indicator, or as an input device.

The Self-Paced Learning program currently uses numbers between 0 and 100 to create the math problems. My son has been complaining that the numbers in the multiplication test are too big for him, so I added a pair of horizontal scroll bars to the program to enter the maximum range for the first (top) and second (bottom) numbers. This way, he can start with small numbers and, as he grows more proficient, he can increase the size of the numbers.

The Self-Paced Learning Program (Version 4)

Make the upper limits of the numbers used in the math test adjustable with two horizontal Scroll bars.

1. Open version 3 of the Self-Paced Learning Program (MATH3.MAK) and save it as version 4 (MATH4.MAK and MATH4.FRM).

2. Select `Form1` and increase its size to 4635 by 3520 twips.

3. Add two horizontal Scroll bars (3135 by 260 twips).

4. Add two Labels (735 by 260 twips) as shown in Figure 6.7. Change the `CtlName` property of the upper label to `TopRange` and change the lower label to `BottomRange`.

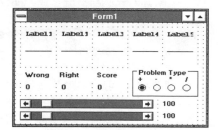

Figure 6.7. *Setup for version 4 of the Self-Paced Learning program.*

5. Select the Scroll bars and set their properties.

```
Max = 1000
Min = 0
Value = 100
LargeChange = 10
```

The LargeChange property controls how large a change you get when you click the gray area of a Scroll bar above or below the thumb. Setting the Value property sets the initial, or default, position of the thumb.

6. Select the two new label boxes and set the Caption properties to 100.

7. Open the HScroll1_Change Code window and type

```
Sub HScroll1_Change ()
TopRange.Caption = Str$(HScroll1.Value)
End Sub
```

8. Select the HScroll2_Change Code window and type

```
Sub HScroll2_Change ()
BottomRange.Caption = Str$(HScroll2.Value)
End Sub
```

These two routines set the values in the two Labels whenever you move the thumb on the Scroll bar.

9. Select the Form_Load procedure and change it as follows. The changes are in lines 7 through 10.

```
Sub Form_Load ()
Rem Initialize the random number generator
Randomize
Rem Define the end-of-line character
eol$ = Chr$(13) + Chr$(10)
Rem Fill the probs array with 2 sets of 5 values
For J = 1 To NumProbs        'line 7
    Probs(1, J) = Int(Rnd(1) * HScroll1.Value)
    Probs(2, J) = Int(Rnd(1) * HScroll2.Value)
Next J                'line 10
Rem Insert the random numbers into the labels and
Rem calculate the answers
For J = 1 To NumProbs
  If Option1.Value = True Then
   ⤷Label1(J).Caption = Format$(Probs(1, J), " 00")
     + eol$ + Format$(Probs(2, J), "+00")
   Answer(J) = Probs(1, J) + Probs(2, J)
  ElseIf Option2.Value = True Then
   ⤷Label1(J).Caption = Format$(Probs(1, J), " 00")
     + eol$ + Format$(Probs(2, J), "-00")
   Answer(J) = Probs(1, J) - Probs(2, J)
```

```
  ElseIf Option3.Value = True Then
↳   Label1(J).Caption = Format$(Probs(1, J), " 00")
      + eol$ + Format$(Probs(2, J), "*00")
    Answer(J) = Probs(1, J) * Probs(2, J)
  ElseIf Option4.Value = True Then
↳   Label1(J).Caption = Format$(Probs(1, J), " 00")
      + eol$ + Format$(Probs(2, J), "\/00")
    Answer(J) = Probs(1, J) / Probs(2, J)
  End If
  Text1(J).Text = ""
  Text1(J).FontStrikethru = False
  Text1(J).ForeColor = Black
Next J
NumRight.Caption = ""
NumWrong.Caption = ""
Score.Caption = ""
End Sub
```

The only changes in this routine are in lines 7 through 10, where the multipliers of the RND() functions are changed to the values from the two Scroll bars. This version differs from version 4 of this program in that the outer Loop is replaced with two equations, one for the upper values and one for the lower values.

10. Save the project, then run it. Change the lower Scroll bar until the value reads 10, then press the multiplication Option button. A test similar to Figure 6.8 appears. See also Plate IV, inside back cover.

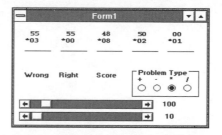

Figure 6.8. *A multiplication test with numbers between 0 and 100 for the upper values and numbers between 0 and 10 for the lower values.*

What You Have Learned

This chapter has examined the more traditional controls: Command buttons, Option Buttons, Check boxes, and Scroll bars. In this chapter you

- Learned that Command buttons initiate actions; Option buttons select one of a set of options; Check boxes enable individual options, and Scroll bars input integer values.

- Created an Advanced Annuity Calculator, two versions of a Self-Paced Learning Program, and a version of the Envelope Addresser.

- Studied more complicated logical statements, remote procedures, and the method of successive approximations for solving transcendental equations.

Using Custom Menus

Rather than pressing buttons and checking boxes, you can control programs conveniently with pull-down menus. When you select a menu command it executes a procedure, and that procedure can set options or carry out complex calculations.

In This Chapter

Menus are attached to Forms using the Menu Design window, then procedures are written and attached to the commands on the menu. This chapter shows you how to

- Construct menus with the Menu Design window.

- Attach procedures to menus.

- Create the standard File and Edit menus.

● Access the Clipboard with the Edit menu.

● Implement the Undo command.

Using the Menu Design Window

In contrast to controls you draw on a Form, menus are created in a Menu Design window, as shown in Figure 7.1. The top half of the window is used to set the properties of the currently selected menu item, and the bottom half lists all the menus and menu items on a Form. A menu item is any of the menu names or commands that show on a menu. The buttons along the center of the window insert and move menu items.

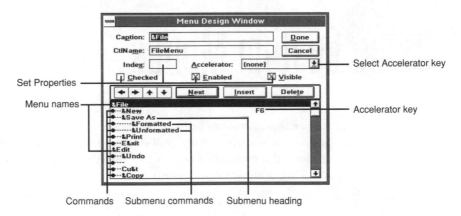

Figure 7.1. The Menu Design window.

The left-hand items in the list at the bottom of the window in Figure 7.1 are the menu names that appear in a Form's menu bar. In this figure, File and Edit are the two menus defined for this Form. Menu commands and submenu headings are indented below the menu names. Here, New, Print, and Exit are menu commands under the File menu, and Undo, Cut, Copy, and Paste (Paste is scrolled off the bottom of the window) are menu commands under the Edit menu. Submenu headings have additional menu items indented below them. When a submenu heading is selected, the submenu drops to the left or right of the submenu heading. Save As is a submenu heading under the File menu with Formatted and Unformatted as the submenu commands. Figure 7.2 shows the menus defined in the Menu Design window in Figure 7.1, including the Save **As** submenu.

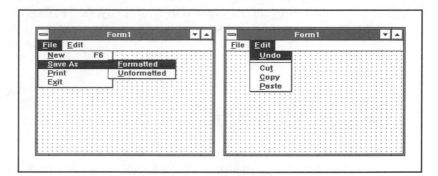

***Figure* 7.2.** *The File menu with the Save As submenu open and the Edit menu.*

Although there can be five levels of submenus in a Visual Basic program, try not to go beyond one or two. Too many levels causes your program to become confusing and the menus become difficult to select— see Figure 7.3, for example.

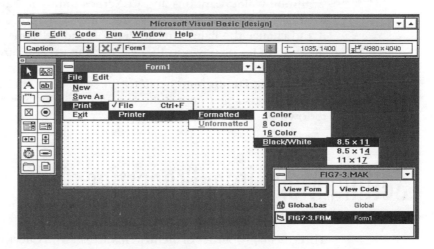

***Figure* 7.3.** *Multiple levels of submenus can be confusing.*

151

A separator bar also can appear on a menu. For example, in Figure 7.2 there is a separator bar on the **E**dit menu between the **U**ndo and **C**ut commands. Separator bars are for purely visual separation of commands on a menu, and are created by typing a hyphen as the `Caption` of a menu item. Separator bars also must have control names, even though they are never selected or executed.

Editing Menu Items

To create a menu, open the Form you want to attach a menu to, and open the Menu Design window above it. Type a menu name in the Caption box, and it appears in the bottom window. Type a control name, which must be a legal variable name, in the CtlName box. You must supply a control name for each menu item (including separator bars, as mentioned earlier), even if you do not intend to attach code to the menu item.

Click the **N**ext button and type another Caption and CtlName. If this is a menu command or submenu name, click the right arrow to indent it. Continue typing Captions and CtlNames until you have inserted all the menu items for all your menus in the window. To edit a menu item, select it and change the names in the Caption and CtlName boxes. To move a menu item up or down in the list, use the up and down arrows on the window. Change the indent level with the left and right arrows on the window. The **Delete** button deletes the selected menu item, and the **Insert** button inserts a new item at the selection point by moving all those below it down one line.

Setting Menu Item Properties

Three main properties of menu items are set with Check boxes in the Menu Design window: **Checked**, **Enabled**, and **Visible**. These properties not only are set at design time, but are adjustable at run time.

The Checked Check box places a check mark to the left of the item's name—see the **F**ile **P**rint File command in Figure 7.3—and sets the `Checked` property to `True`. The `Checked` property is used most often to show whether the option accessed by the menu item is enabled. You can write code so selecting a menu item sets the check mark and enables the option, and selecting it again disables the option and removes the check mark. This is done by changing the value of the Checked property. Note that you cannot check a menu name or submenu head.

The Enabled property determines whether a menu item is executable. Disabled menu items are grayed on the menu, and cannot be selected—see the File Print Printer Unformatted command in Figure 7.3. You should disable menu items for commands and options that are currently unavailable. If you disable a menu name, the whole menu is disabled.

The Visible property is another way to control access to menu items. When the visible box is not checked or the Visible property is False, the menu item and all its submenus disappear from the menu bar. By having several menus, with some visible and others not, you can make different menus, or different versions of the same menu, available at different times during the execution of your program. Making a menu name invisible makes the whole menu invisible.

Two more properties of menu items can be set only at design time: Shortcut keys, and Access keys. *Shortcut keys* are command or function keys that access a menu command directly from the keyboard, without pulling down the menu. Shortcut keys are created by selecting them from the Accelerator box on the Menu Design window. As a reminder, the selected key or key combination appears on the menu to the right of the command name. For example, in Figure 7.2, if you pressed F6, the File New command would be executed, or, in Figure 7.3, if you pressed Ctrl-F, the File Print File command would be executed.

Access keys allow you to select menus and menu items without using the mouse. The Access key for any menu item is underlined in the item's name. (In this book, access keys are in bold.) When a program is running, the Menu bar is activated by pressing the Alt key, then a menu is pulled down by pressing its Access key. When a menu is open, menu items are selected with the up and down arrow keys, or by pressing the Access key for the item you want.

The Access key for a menu item is selected when you type the Caption property. Place an ampersand (&) before the letter you want to use (as shown for the File menu in Figure 7.1); it appears underlined in the menu—see the File menu in Figure 7.2. You don't have to use the first letter in a file item's name as the Access key, though it is a good idea for frequently used items. You can place the ampersand anywhere in the file item's name,

and the letter following the ampersand becomes the Access key. Be careful what letters you select for access keys, because if two menus or two items on the same menu have the same key, only the first item is selectable.

Attaching Code to a Menu

Code is attached to a menu command in the same way you attach it to the other controls. To open a Code window attached to a menu item, you can either open the Code window for a Form, then select the CtlName of the menu item, or select the menu command directly on the Form. Menu items respond to only one event, the Click event, which corresponds to selection of the command from its menu. The menu names also respond to the Click event, and any code placed in that procedure is executed before the menu drops down.

Creating the Standard Menus

Most Windows applications contain a minimum of two menus, the **File** menu and the **Edit** menu. The **File** menu starts and stops the application, and opens, closes, and prints documents. The **Edit** menu contains the standard editing commands, **U**ndo, **Cu**t, **C**opy, and **P**aste.

If you plan to open and close files, or you want to edit your application, it's important to make the commands operate in the standard way so other users do not have to learn new methods. For example, you might have invented the best method for editing text, but if your application does not have a working **Edit** menu with the standard **Cu**t, **C**opy and **P**aste commands, your frustrated users will be thinking unkind things about you. If, however, they can use your code without having to learn anything new, they might not notice—but they will not be calling you to complain, either.

If you plan to have your application share data through the Clipboard with other Windows applications, you must have the **Edit** menu, and the appropriate code to access the Clipboard. The Clipboard is a special area in Windows available to all running applications. When you cut or copy data in an application, a copy of the current selection is placed on the Clipboard. When you paste data, the contents of the Clipboard is inserted at the insertion point, or replaces the current selection.

Creating the File Menu

A standard **File** menu contains the **New**, **Open**, **Close**, **Save**, Save **As**, **Print**, and **Exit** commands, or some similar set with the same functions. In a particular program, one or more of these commands might be missing, or there might be additional commands. The **File** menu in Visual Basic is a good example; it contains commands for opening, saving and deleting Forms and projects, creating new Forms and projects, printing, and ending the program.

The Envelope Addresser Program (Version 4)

The Envelope Addresser Program is currently designed to print an envelope when you click the Form. The only ways to end the program are to end it in Visual Basic or to close the window. Both of these commands could be placed on a menu. This example also shows you how to add a **Print** Options submenu, move the options originally set on Form1 to that menu, delete Form1, and type the address directly on Form2.

1. Open version 3 of the Envelope Addresser ADDR4.MAK, and save it as ADDR5.MAK.

2. Select Form1 and delete it with the **File** **Remove** File command.

3. Select Form2 and save it as ADDR52.FRM. Select the Global module and save it as ADDR5.BAS.

   Because the start-up Form has been deleted, redefine it with the Set Startup Form command on the **Run** menu.

4. Under the **Run** menu, execute the Set Startup Form command and select Form2.

   To type the address directly on Form2, you need a Text box on Form2 because you cannot type on a Label. Also, it would be nice to have an outline around the Text box so you can see where you are typing, but that goes away when the Form is printed. However, the Outline property cannot be changed at run time, only at design time. To solve this difficulty, draw two Text boxes, one with an outline and one

155

without, and one visible and the other invisible. When you type the visible, outlined box, the text is sent to the invisible, unoutlined box. At print time, switch the visible box for the invisible box to get the address without an outline.

5. Select `Label2` on `Form2` and delete it.

6. Draw a Text box 3375 by 1220 twips where `Label2` used to be. Change its properties as

```
CtlName = PrintBox
Text = ""
BorderStyle = 0 - None
Multiline = True
```

7. On top of the first Text box, draw a second Text box exactly the same size. Change the Text box properties to:

```
CtlName = EditBox
Caption = ""
BorderStyle = 1 - Fixed Single
Multiline = True
```

Now, attach the menu to `Form2`. It has a **N**ew command to clear the Form, a **P**rint command to print it, a Print **O**ptions menu to allow changes in any of the options, and an **E**xit command to end the program.

8. Open the Menu Design window, and type the following table of values, listed in Table 7.1, and shown in Figure 7.4. Use the arrow button to indent the menus and press Done when you are finished.

Table 7.1. Menu definitions for the Address program 4.

Caption	CtlName	# of indents
&File	FileMenu	0
&New	NewCmd	1
-	SepBar1	1
&Print	PrintCmd	1
Print &Options	OptionMenu	1
&Return Address	RetAddrCmd	2
&Bold Text	BoldTextCmd	2

Caption	CtlName	# of indents
&Large Text	LargeTextCmd	2
-	SepBar2	1
E&xit	ExitCmd	1

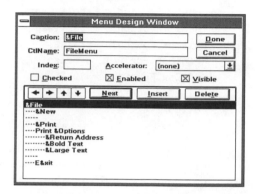

Figure 7.4. Menu Design window for version 5 of the Envelope Addresser.

This completes the interface. Now change the code. Much of the code can be copied from the old version of the program into the new one, or retyped as you please. First, change the global definitions. Actually, TheLine does not have to be defined here, because you are no longer passing it from one Form to another. It also could be defined in the declarations section of Form2. However, because it is already here, leave it alone.

9. Open the Global module and change it to read:

```
Global TheLine As String
Global Const True = -1, False = 0
```

10. The declarations section of Form2 is not changed, and should still read:

```
Dim eol$
```

11. Open the Form_Load procedure and change it to the following. Pieces of this were copied from the old Form_Click procedure.

```
Sub Form_Load ()
eol$ = Chr$(13) + Chr$(10)
Rem set initial values
```

continues

157

```
RetAddrCmd.Checked = True
BoldTextCmd.Checked = False
LargeTextCmd.Checked = False
Rem Insert return address
Label1.FontBold = False
Label1.FontSize = 10
Label1.Caption = "William J. Orvis" + eol$
Label1.Caption = Label1.Caption + "123 Some St." + eol$
Label1.Caption = Label1.Caption + "Anywhere, CA  91234"
EditBox.FontBold = False
PrintBox.FontBold = False
EditBox.FontSize = 10
PrintBox.FontSize = 10
EditBox.Text = ""
End Sub
```

Line 2 of this procedure defines the eol$ (end-of-line) character, then lines 3 through 6 set the initial values of the options. Lines 7 to the end carry out the initial options, such as inserting the return address, turning off bold, and setting the size of the text.

The next procedure is executed whenever the Return Address menu command is executed. The procedure toggles the return address option on or off each time the menu command is executed. Much of this also can be copied from the Form_Load procedure.

12. Open the RetAddrCmd_Click procedure and type

```
Sub RetAddrCmd_Click ()
Rem Reverse the check mark
RetAddrCmd.Checked = Not RetAddrCmd.Checked
If RetAddrCmd.Checked = True Then
  Label1.Caption = "William J. Orvis" + eol$
  Label1.Caption = Label1.Caption + "123 Some St." + eol$
  Label1.Caption = Label1.Caption + "Anywhere, CA  91234"
Else
  Label1.Caption = ""
End If
End Sub
```

Line 3 uses the NOT operator to change the Checked property of the Return Address command. The NOT operator changes True to False or False to True. Lines 4 through the end of this procedure are a block If statement that checks the state of the check mark, and if it is True, inserts the return address in the Label1 Label. If it's False, it blanks the contents of the Label. The next procedure performs a similar function for the **B**old Text command.

13. Open the BoldTextCmd_Click procedure and type

```
Sub BoldTextCmd_Click ()
Rem Reverse the check mark
BoldTextCmd.Checked = Not BoldTextCmd.Checked
If BoldTextCmd.Checked = True Then
 Label1.FontBold = True
 EditBox.FontBold = True
 PrintBox.FontBold = True
Else
 Label1.FontBold = False
 EditBox.FontBold = False
 PrintBox.FontBold = False
End If
End Sub
```

Again, line 3 switches the state of the check on the Bold Text menu command, and the block If statement changes the FontBold property in the Label1 Label box and the EditBox and PrintBox Text boxes.

The next procedure does exactly the same thing for the **L**arge Text menu command. First, it switches the state of the check mark, then it changes the property in the three boxes.

14. Open the LargeTextCmd_Click procedure and type

```
Sub LargeTextCmd_Click ()
Rem Reverse the check mark
LargeTextCmd.Checked = Not LargeTextCmd.Checked
If LargeTextCmd.Checked = True Then
 Label1.FontSize = 12
 EditBox.FontSize = 12
 PrintBox.FontSize = 12
Else
 Label1.FontSize = 10
 EditBox.FontSize = 10
 PrintBox.FontSize = 10
End If
End Sub
```

The `EditBox_Change` procedure makes sure that whenever the `EditBox` is changed, the invisible `PrintBox` also is changed. This way, when the Form is printed, the `PrintBox` contains the correct text.

15. Open the `EditBox_Change` procedure and type

```
Sub EditBox_Change ()
PrintBox.Text = EditBox.Text
End Sub
```

16. Open the `PrintCmd_Click` procedure and type

```
Sub PrintCmd_Click ()
Rem switch between the edit box with the border and
Rem the edit box without the border for printing
EditBox.Visible = False
PrintBox.Visible = True
Form2.PrintForm
Rem Switch back to the edit box
PrintBox.Visible = False
EditBox.Visible = True
End Sub
```

The **Print** menu command executes the `PrintCmd` procedure, as shown previously. It first makes `EditBox` invisible and `PrintBox` visible to eliminate the bounding box surrounding the address. The bounding box makes it easier to type the address, but you don't want it to be printed on the envelope. Next, the procedure prints the Form using the `PrintForm` method, and then turns the bounding box back on.

The next two procedures are relatively simple. The **New** menu command calls the `Form_Load` procedure again to reset everything as it was at the beginning, and the Exit menu command executes the `End` statement to end the program.

17. Open the `NewCmd_Click` procedure and type

```
Sub NewCmd_Click ()
Form_Load
End Sub
```

18. Open the `ExitCmd_Click` procedure and type

```
Sub ExitCmd_Click ()
End
End Sub
```

19. Select the Form_Click procedure and delete it by selecting its contents and pressing Delete. We no longer need this procedure because all its functions have been moved to other procedures.

20. Save the project and run it. The Form looks like Figure 7.5.

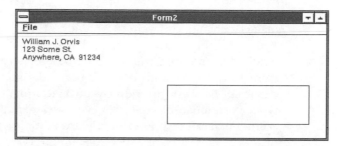

Figure 7.5. *Startup of version 4 of the Envelope Addresser.*

21. Type an address in the Editbox, and select any options from the Print Options submenu as shown in Figure 7.6.

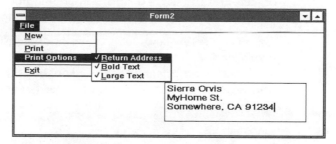

Figure 7.6. *Changing options in version 4 of the Envelope Addresser.*

22. Print an envelope by selecting **P**rint from the **F**ile menu. To print another envelope, either edit the old address or clear the Form with the New command and type a new address. Then print again.

Creating the Edit Menu

The next standard menu is the **E**dit menu, which is used to transfer text and graphics between the Clipboard and a running application. The standard

Edit menu commands are Undo, Cut, Copy, and Paste. Like the File menu, the Edit menu can have more or fewer commands, depending on the application.

Of all the commands, the Undo command is the most difficult to program. Undo returns the program to the state it had just before the last command was executed, or editing was done. Thus, any procedure that makes a change you want to be able to Undo must save the original state, and signal the Undo command that something can be undone. Unfortunately, I cannot give you much help here, because what you do or don't want to undo depends on your particular application. Take editing, for example. Because you don't want Undo just to undo the last character typed, you must select certain events to mark the beginning of a piece of editing that can be undone. Standard editing actions include deleting one or more characters, or executing a menu command.

The Cut, Copy and Paste commands transfer data between the application and the Clipboard. Because the Clipboard is a part of the system, all Windows applications have access to material placed on it. Text is transferred between a program and the Clipboard using the `Clipboard` object, and the `GetText` and `SetText` methods. Other methods exist for transferring pictures and other data to the Clipboard.

The `GetText` and `SetText` methods transfer text between the Clipboard and a Visual Basic program. The `GetText` method works like a function and returns any text stored on the Clipboard. `SetText` does just the opposite and places text on the Clipboard, replacing any text already there. The syntax of these methods are

```
Clipboard.GetText([type])
Clipboard.SetText String$, type
```

Where *type* is a constant that indicates the type of data to get or put on the Clipboard. If *type* is omitted, the default type is text. *String$* is a string containing the text to be placed on the Clipboard.

Three Text box properties are needed to correctly perform the Cut, Copy and Paste functions: `SelLength`, `SelStart`, and `SelText`. The `SelLength` property is a `Long` integer that contains the number of characters selected in the Text box. The `SelStart` Property is also a `Long` integer that contains the location of the first selected character, or the insertion point if no characters are selected. The `SelText` property is a string that contains the selected text. The `SelText` property has a unique characteristic: if you change it, the selected text in the Text box is replaced with the changed text. Thus, the Cut, Copy, and Paste commands can be implemented by simply copying or changing the `SelText` property.

This characteristic makes it very easy to implement the Cut, Copy, and Paste commands. To Copy the selected text, simply copy the contents of `SelText` to the Clipboard. To Cut the selected text, copy it first with the Copy command then set `SelText` equal to the null string, deleting the selected text. To implement the Paste command, equate `SelText` to the `GetText` method, which replaces the currently selected text with the contents of the Clipboard.

The Envelope Addresser Program (Version 5)

When you write a letter using a word processor program, you usually have typed the address already. Rather than typing it again in the Envelope Addresser program, add an Edit menu to that program so you can paste the address into it after copying the address onto the Clipboard in the word processor. Additionally, implement the Undo command on the Edit menu. To implement the Undo command, you have to decide what is "undoable." In this case, any Cut or Paste is "undoable," and any sequence of Backspaces or Deletes is "undoable."

1. Open version 4 of the envelope addresser ADDR4.MAK, and save it as version 5, ADDR5.MAK, ADDR52.FRM, and ADDR5.BAS.

   First, add the Edit menu to `Form2`.

2. Open `Form2`, open the Menu Design window, and add the following menu, using the values shown in Table 7.2. Don't remove the File menu in the process, but add this to the end, as shown in Figure 7.7.

Table 7.2. Menu definitions for version 5 of the Envelope Addresser program.

Caption	CtlName	# of indents
&Edit	EditMenu	0
&Undo	UndoCmd	1
-	SepBar3	1
Cu&t	CutCmd	1
&Copy	CopyCmd	1
&Paste	PasteCmd	1

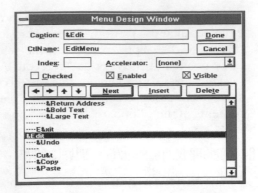

Figure 7.7. Menu Design window showing the added Edit menu.

The Undo procedure has to watch for the Backspace and Delete keys to determine when to start saving editing changes, so put constant definitions of the key codes for those two keys in the Global module.

Key codes are numeric codes for the different keys on the keyboard (see Appendix C). You can either type them into your program, or copy them from the file CONSTANT.TXT where they are stored as Global constants. To copy them into a program, open the CONSTANT.TXT file as if it were a Form with the **Add** File command on the File menu. Next, scroll through the Code window until you find the definitions you want, then use the **Copy** command on the Edit menu to copy them onto the Clipboard. Select the Global module, open its Code window and paste the definitions using the **Paste** command on the **Edit** menu. After you have pasted all the definitions you need, remove the CONSTANT.TXT file from the project by selecting it and executing the **Remove** File command on the File menu.

3. Open the code window of the Global module, and add the two key definitions at the end so it reads:

```
Global TheLine As String
Global Const True = -1, False = 0
Global Const KEY_BACK = &H8, KEY_DELETE = &H2E
```

4. In the declarations section of Form2, define the three variables to store the state of the system for the Undo command.

```
Dim eol$
Dim UndoText As String, UndoLength As Long, UndoStart As Long
```

5. Open the Code window for the `Form_Load` procedure and add the three statements at the end to initialize the Undo variables.

```
Sub Form_Load ()
eol$ = Chr$(13) + Chr$(10)
Rem set initial values
RetAddrCmd.Checked = True
BoldTextCmd.Checked = False
LargeTextCmd.Checked = False
Rem Insert return address
Label1.FontBold = False
Label1.FontSize = 10
Label1.Caption = "William J. Orvis" + eol$
Label1.Caption = Label1.Caption + "123 Some St." + eol$
Label1.Caption = Label1.Caption + "Anywhere, CA   91234"
EditBox.FontBold = False
PrintBox.FontBold = False
EditBox.FontSize = 10
PrintBox.FontSize = 10
EditBox.Text = ""
UndoText = ""
UndoStart = 0
UndoLength = 0
End Sub
```

6. The `CopyCmd_Click` procedure implements the Copy command. The selected data in `EditBox` is copied to the Clipboard. The selected text is accessed with the `SelText` property and passed to the Clipboard using the `SetText` method.

7. Select the `CopyCmd_Click` procedure and type

```
Sub CopyCmd_Click ()
Clipboard.SetText EditBox.SelText
End Sub
```

The next three procedures save the state of the system for the Undo command. In the `CutCmd_Click` and the `PasteCmd_Click` procedures, the contents of `EditBox` are saved before the command is carried out. Also saved are the `SelStart` and `SelLength` properties; this way, the cursor position and the selection size also can be restored. The third procedure, `EditBox_KeyDown`, intercepts keypresses being sent to `EditBox`, and saves the contents of `EditBox` whenever one or more Backspaces or Deletes are pressed.

165

The CutCmd_Click procedure implements the Cut command. After the data is saved for the Undo command, the selected data in EditBox is copied to the Clipboard as in the CopyCmd_Click procedure. The selected text is then deleted in line 9 by equating SelText to a null string.

8. Open the CutCmd_Click procedure and type

```
Sub CutCmd_Click ()
Rem Save state for undo
UndoText = EditBox.Text
UndoStart = EditBox.SelStart
UndoLength = EditBox.SelLength
Rem Cut the selected text out of the Text box
Rem and put it on the Clipboard
Clipboard.SetText EditBox.SelText
EditBox.SelText = ""
End Sub
```

The PasteCmd_Click procedure implements the **Paste** command. Lines 2 through 5 save the data for the Undo command. Line 8 then replaces the selected text with the contents of the Clipboard.

9. Select the PasteCmd_Click procedure and type

```
Sub PasteCmd_Click ()
Rem Save state for undo                    line 2
UndoText = EditBox.Text
UndoStart = EditBox.SelStart
UndoLength = EditBox.SelLength
Rem Replace the selected text with the contents
Rem of the Clipboard
EditBox.SelText = Clipboard.GetText()      line 8
End Sub
```

10. Open the EditBox_KeyDown procedure and type

```
Sub EditBox_KeyDown (KeyCode As Integer, Shift As Integer)
Static Flag As Integer
If KeyCode = KEY_BACK Or KeyCode = KEY_DELETE Then
  If Flag = False Then
    Flag = True
    UndoText = EditBox.Text
    UndoStart = EditBox.SelStart
    UndoLength = EditBox.SelLength
```

```
   End If
Else
   Flag = False
End If
End Sub
```

The EditBox_KeyDown procedure watches for KeyDown events directed at EditBox. This procedure captures those events before they are sent to EditBox. The key pressed is stored in the variable KeyCode, and Shift contains the state of the Ctrl, Shift, and Alt keys. The value of KeyCode and Shift must not be changed if you want the typed characters to eventually reach EditBox. The second statement defines the variable Flag as a Static variable. Normally, all the local variables in the EditBox_KeyDown procedure disappear as soon as the procedure ends. In this case, you want the variable Flag to stay around. Flag is initially False, but is set to True the first time Backspace or Delete is pressed. Note that the initial value of all numeric values is null, and all strings are the null string.

The next statement tests the key pressed to see whether it is the Backspace or the Delete key. If it isn't either of these, the block If statement sets Flag to False and ends. If a Backspace or Delete key is pressed, the If statement starting in line 4 is executed, testing the value of Flag. If Flag is False, this is the first Backspace or Delete pressed, and it is time to save the contents of EditBox and to set Flag to True. If Flag is True, this is one of several Backspaces or Deletes pressed in a row, and you don't have to do anything.

11. Open the UndoCmd_Click code window and type

```
Sub UndoCmd_Click ()
Rem Restore the state
EditBox.Text = UndoText
EditBox.SelStart = UndoStart
EditBox.SelLength = UndoLength
End Sub
```

This procedure actually performs the Undo command, and restores the contents of EditBox, the location of the cursor and the characters selected.

12. Save the project, and run it. Try typing some text in EditBox, then select, Cut and Paste it to a different place. Try the Undo command. Try copying an address in your favorite word processing program, switch to the Envelope Addresser, then paste the address into EditBox.

167

Add a menu command to select one of two or three return addresses. Add another menu command to open a dialog box so you can input the return address. Add a menu to select one of several, frequently used, built-in addresses, and place the menu in the Text box.

When you execute the Cut command, the selected text should disappear, and the cursor should be located at the point where the text was removed. When the Paste command is executed, the selected text is replaced by the contents of the Clipboard. If no text is selected, the Clipboard contents are inserted at the insertion point. The cursor should be located at the end of the pasted text. The Copy command should make no apparent change to the text or the location of the insertion point. After a Cut or Paste command, the Undo command should return EditBox to the same state as before the Cut or Paste command, including the location of the cursor and the text selected. After typing some changes, Undo returns the EditBox to its state when the last Cut or Paste command was executed, or to the state when the last Backspace or Delete was pressed.

What You Have Learned

A common way of controlling Windows programs is with menus, and this chapter has investigated how you create and use them. Rather than pressing buttons and checking boxes, menus are used to set options, and execute commands. Menus are created using the Menu Design window, which attaches them to the top Form. Procedures are attached to menu commands in exactly the same way as other controls, by inserting code in the Code window for that command. Specifically, you learned to

● Construct menus with the Menu Design window.

● Set the Checked, Enabled, and Visible properties.

● Attach Shortcut and Access keys to menu items.

● Attach procedures to menu commands.

- Create the standard **File** and **Edit** menus.

- Access the Clipboard with **Cut**, **Copy** and **Paste**.

- Implement the Undo command in the Envelope Addresser Program.

Writing Custom Procedures

The code in this book, until now, has been written in procedures that are attached to controls and forms. These procedures are actually event-procedures, because they are executed when some specific event (such as a control being clicked) occurs to the control or Form it is attached to. In a couple of instances, you also executed an event-procedure directly by placing its name in another procedure. Now it's time to look at the creation and use of procedures.

In This Chapter

This chapter investigates Function and Sub procedures, two types of procedures that differ only slightly from the event-procedures used so far in this book. Specifically, you learn how to

- Use Sub procedures.
- Use user-defined functions.

● Pass arguments to procedures.

● Use List boxes.

You also will create the Automatic Check Register program, a program that records checks and deposits and automatically maintains the account balance.

What are Procedures?

A *procedure* is a self-contained block of code that performs a specific task. The more specific the task, the easier the procedure is to write and maintain. Procedures enable you to group a block of statements together, give them a name, and use the name to execute the specified code. Procedures are the building blocks of a computer program.

When writing a program in Visual Basic, you naturally break it into procedures as you attach code to the different controls and Forms. These event-procedures break a program into tasks that are performed when each event occurs. Although these procedures are automatically created by Visual Basic, any other procedures must be created by the programmer.

You might wonder, "Why bother with procedures?" You know what you want your code to do, so why separate it with artificial barriers? In the early days of computing, that's exactly the philosophy people followed. Memory was expensive, so programmers spent much of their time writing the most compact code possible. This compact code became known as "spaghetti code," because, unfortunately, the point of execution would jump all over the place with apparently random intent. Maintaining this code was only barely possible if you were the original programmer, and modifying it was usually impossible. It was generally faster to write a new program than to try to decipher someone else's program. Procedures were available, but were used only to reuse common blocks of code.

As restrictions on memory usage have rapidly diminished, program design has focused more on maintainability than on size. Modern programming practice encourages the use of procedures to not only reuse blocks of code, but to functionally organize a program. Procedure use has increasingly modularized codes, making codes more readable, and much easier to maintain or modify.

Procedures isolate not only the code associated with a task, but the data. All variables used in a single procedure, and not defined at a higher level (in the declarations section of a Form, or in the Global module), are available only in that procedure. A variable of the same name in another procedure is unaffected by changes in the first variable. As discussed before, these are local variables.

Communication with a procedure is by way of global variables defined at a higher level, and through variables passed to a procedure via its arguments.

Creating Sub Procedures

All the event-procedures attached to controls are Sub procedures. A Sub procedure or subroutine begins with the keyword Sub and the procedure name, followed by an optional argument list in parentheses. Procedures that deal only with global variables do not have an argument list, but must still have the parentheses.

The argument list consists of the names of the local variables that receive the values sent to the Sub procedure by the calling routine, plus any needed type declarations (As Integer, for example). All Sub procedures end with an End Sub statement. The syntax of the Sub statement, which is the heading of the Sub procedure, is

```
[Static] Sub subname [(arguments)]
End Sub
```

where *subname* is the name of the Sub procedure, and *arguments* is the argument list. The Static option makes all the variables defined in the Sub procedure persist from one call of the Sub procedure to the next. For example, a subroutine to calculate the sum of two numbers and return the value in a third could be written as follows:

```
Sub AddEmUp (NumOne As Single, NumTwo As Single, TheSum As Single)
TheSum = NumOne + NumTwo
End Sub
```

Now, this procedure is so simple you would probably never write it yourself, but it does illustrate all the parts of a Sub procedure. The first line declares the procedure name and arguments, with each argument getting

an explicit type declaration. The second line adds the first two arguments together and stores that value in the third, which is passed back to the calling routine in the argument list. You also could pass the value back in one of the first two arguments.

To execute or call a procedure from some other procedure, type its name followed by the arguments you want sent to the procedure. In contrast to the argument list in the heading of the Sub procedure, the argument list in the calling statement is not surrounded by parentheses. However, each argument in the calling statement corresponds, one for one, with the arguments in the procedure heading. If an argument is passing a value back to the calling procedure, a variable must be used to receive it; otherwise you could use constant values. For example, to call the AddEmUp procedure from the Form_Click procedure, type

```
Sub Form_Click ()
A = 185
B = 723
AddEmUp A, B, C
Form1.Print A, B, C
AddEmUp 5, 7, ANumber
Form1.Print ANumber
End Sub
```

The first line defines the Form_Click event-procedure. The second and third lines load the variables A and B with the values 185 and 723. The fourth line calls the procedure AddEmUp with A, B, and C as the arguments. Note that there are no parentheses around the arguments as there are in the definition of AddEmUp. The fifth line prints the values of the three arguments after control returns from AddEmUp. The sixth line calls the procedure again, this time with constant values, rather than variables, as two of the arguments. The third argument still must be a variable, because it receives the result of the Sub procedure's calculation. When this procedure is run, it produces this text on the Form:

```
185             723                908
12
```

To write a procedure on a Form in Visual Basic, move to the general object of a Form, and execute the New Procedure command on the Code menu. Alternately, type the first line of the procedure. As soon as you press Enter, Visual Basic creates a template for the new procedure under the general object, including the End Sub statement. To find the procedure, select the general object, and locate the procedure in the Proc. List box. Do the same to create a Sub procedure in any module but the Global module, which is only for declarations.

User-Defined Functions

In addition to Sub procedures, you also can create Function procedures. A Function procedure is similar to such built-in functions as Sin() or Mid$(). A Function procedure, like a Sub procedure, can modify its arguments and execute BASIC statements. In addition, it returns a value stored in the function's name. The syntax of a function statement is

```
[Static] Function funcname [(arguments)] [As type]
End Function
```

Here, *funcname* is the name of the function, and *arguments* are the names of the local variables that receive the arguments from the calling procedure. Because a Function procedure returns a value in the function name, that name must have a type like any other variable. To set the type of the function name, either declare it globally with a Global or Dim statement, use a type declaration suffix on the name, or include the As *type* clause in the function statement. The Static option makes the variables persist from one calling of the function to the next.

Before the end of the Function procedure, an assignment statement must assign a value to a variable with the same name as the function, to be returned by it when the End Function statement is reached. For example, the following function returns the sum of its two arguments.

```
Function AddEmUpFunc (VarOne As Single, VarTwo As Single) As Single
AddEmUpFunc = VarOne + VarTwo
End Function
```

Again, this function is overly simple, but it demonstrates the syntax of the Function statement. A function need not be this simple; it can contain many statements, including calls to other Function and Sub procedures. The first line defines the function name, its data type, and the types of the arguments it expects. The second line calculates the sum of the two arguments and assigns that value to the function name. The third line ends the procedure.

The calling syntax of a function is somewhat different than that of a Sub procedure, due to the value returned. A Function procedure is called in exactly the same way as any of the built-in functions. For example, this function might be called, in lines 4 and 6 of the Form_Click procedure, as

```
Sub Form_Click ()
```

```
A = 185
B = 723
C = AddEmUpFunc(A, B)
Form1.Print A, B, C
Form1.Print AddEmUpFunc(5, 7)
End Sub
```

This procedure gives exactly the same results as the one that used the AddEmUp Sub procedure. Note that only two arguments are passed to the function, and the third is returned as the function name. The value assigned to C could just as easily have been returned as an argument in the Sub procedure. Note in the sixth line that the value returned by the function isn't assigned to a variable, but is passed directly to the Print method as one of its arguments.

Passing Arguments to Procedures

There are two ways to pass an argument to a Sub or Function procedure: as an address, or as a value. The default is to pass arguments to a procedure by address. An address is the location of the variable in memory. By passing the address as an argument, the procedure that was called operates on the same variable as the one that called it, even though it might have a different name in the called procedure.

If you don't want the procedure you are calling to have access to the original variable, pass it as a value, using the ByVal keyword in front of the variable name when it is declared in the first line of the procedure. An alternate approach is to surround the argument with parentheses in the calling statement. When a variable is passed as a value, a copy of the original variable is made, and that copy is passed to the procedure. Because the procedure is no longer operating on the original variable, any changes it makes to the copy are not reflected in the original.

Formulas used as arguments of procedures are always passed as values, even though the default is by address. The values of properties cannot be passed by address. They must either be passed by value, or assigned to another variable first, then passed to the procedure. Be careful of passing array variables by value, because the whole array must be duplicated to do so.

This example demonstrates calling by value and by address:

```
Sub Form_Click ()
A = 1
B = 2
C = 3
D = 4
PassTest A, B
Form1.Print A, B
PassTest (C), D
Form1.Print C, D
End Sub

Sub PassTest (One As Single, ByVal Two As Single)
Form1.Print One, Two
One = 10
Two = 20
End Sub
```

When this program is run, and the Form clicked, the following values are printcd.

```
1          2
10         2
3          4
3          4
```

Lines 2 through 5 of the Form_Click procedure initialize the four variables A, B, C, and D, as 1, 2, 3, and 4. In line 6, the PassTest Sub procedure is called, and is passed A and B as arguments. In the PassTest procedure, the first line specifies that the second argument is passed by value and the first is by address. The second line then prints the two variables One and Two, which have been passed the values 1 and 2. In lines 3 and 4, the PassTest procedure changes the values of the arguments to 10 and 20, and then ends in line 5.

In line 7 of the Form_Click procedure, the current values of A and B are printed. Because the first argument is passed by address, the new value of 10 is passed back from the variable One in the PassTest procedure to the variable A in the Form_Click procedure. The second argument was passed by value, so the new value of 20 for variable Two is not passed back to the variable B.

In line 8, the variables C and D are passed to the PassTest procedure. As before, the value of the second variable, D, is passed by value, and is

unchanged by the procedure. This time, however, the parentheses around C pass the first argument by value as well, so neither variable is changed outside the PassTest procedure.

Displaying and Selecting With Lists

Two new controls are List boxes and Combo boxes. A List box holds a list of strings the user can choose from. A Combo box combines a List box with a Text box, so users also can type a value not on the list.

There are three types of Combo boxes, selected with the Style property. Figure 8.1 shows a List box and the three types of Combo boxes.

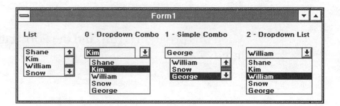

Figure 8.1. *A List box and three types of Combo boxes.*

> The drop-down Combo box in Visual Basic looks different from those in other Windows applications. The drop-down Combo box has a space between it and the down arrow button that causes the list to drop down. Everywhere else, there is no space.

A List box contains a list of values, and the user can select only one value from the list. A Combo Box combines a List and a Text box, and offers more options. A Style 0 Combo box is a *Drop-down Combo* box, with a Text box at the top and a List box that drops down when the small down arrow on the right is pressed. If a list item is selected in the list part of the Combo box, it is placed in the text part of the Combo box where it can be edited. Style 1 is a *Simple Combo* box, which also has a Text box at the top and a List box below it. The only difference between a Style 0 and Style 1 Combo box is that the list does not drop down in the Style 1 Combo box, but is permanently displayed. A Style 2 Combo box is a *Drop-down List* box, which is actually a List box rather than a Combo box because the box at the top only displays the currently selected item, and cannot be edited.

Use List and Drop-down List boxes when you have a specific list of values for users to choose from, and don't want users to be able to type their own values. Use the Simple and Drop-down Combo boxes when you have a list of possible values for users to select, but users also can type their own values. The drop-down versions of these boxes also save space on a Form.

Although all these boxes respond to the `Click` event when an item is selected, it is better to let the user select an item, then use a button to signify acceptance of that item. This is especially true if the action performed is irreversible, such as the deletion of a file. You could then add a `DoubleClick` event on the list or Combo box that also executes the button's event-procedure. That way, a user can click an item in the list and press the button to accept it, or double click it to get the same effect.

Combo and List boxes have some special properties and methods for dealing with them. The important methods are

`AddItem`—Adds an item to a list.

`RemoveItem`—Removes an item from a list.

The properties are

`List`—An array of strings, containing all the items in the list.

`ListCount`—The number of items in a list.

`ListIndex`—The index of the currently selected item.

`Sorted`—An indicator of whether the list is sorted or displayed as input.

All of the Text box properties, such as `SelLength`, `SelStart`, `SelText`, and `Text`, also apply to the Text box part of the Combo boxes. You cannot insert values in the list part of these boxes at design time, but must insert them at run time using the `AddItem` method. The syntax of the `AddItem` method is

`[`*form.*`]` *control*`.AddItem` *item$* `[`*,index%*`]`

where *form* is the name of the Form the control is attached to, *control* is the `CtlName` of the List or Combo box, and *item$* is a string to insert into the list. (The *form* variable defaults to the Form containing the statement if the variable is omitted.) The optional *index%* argument controls where the item

is inserted in the list. If *index%* is omitted, the new item is inserted at the bottom of the list, unless the Sorted property is True, in which case the item is inserted into its alphabetical location.

As you might expect, the RemoveItem method performs the opposite function of the AddItem method. The syntax is

[*form.*]*control*.RemoveItem *index%*

Items in a list are indexed from the top, starting with index number 0. The second item is index number 1, the third is 2, and so on. The ListCount property contains the number of items currently in the list, and the ListIndex property contains the index number of the currently selected item. To see the contents of the currently selected item, use the List property with ListIndex as the argument in the following manner:

Item$ = [*form.*] *control*.List*(*[*form.*]*control*.ListIndex*)*

As you can see, the List property is an array of strings, and you are selecting the current one using the ListIndex property. The Text property also contains the currently selected item when the item is selected, but can be changed afterwards by the user.

The Automated Check Register Program

The Automated Check Register program is an automated check register stored in the computer. It automatically inserts the next check number and date, has a Combo box containing several common entries for the description field, and automatically maintains the account balance. The register is stored in a List box, and selecting an item in that list brings it into the Text boxes for editing.

First, draw the user interface:

1. Open a new project, and save it as CKREG (CKREG.MAK and CKREG1.FRM).

2. Open Form1, adjust its size to 8625 by 3320 twips, and set the following properties

   ```
   Caption = Check Register
   ControlBox = False
   MaxButton = False
   BorderStyle = 3 - Fixed Double
   ```

3. Draw five Labels on the Form, as shown in Figure 8.2, and type the properties, as shown in the following table.

	Label1	Label2	Label3	Label4	Label5
Caption =	Number	Date	Description of Transaction	Amount	Balance
Height =	260	260	260	260	260
Width =	900	1215	2775	1455	1455
Top =	120	120	120	120	120
Left =	120	960	2160	5280	6840

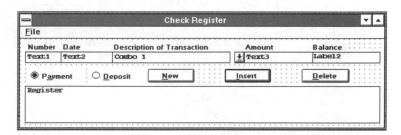

Figure 8.2. *Layout of the Form for the Check Register program.*

Draw a row of Text, Label, and Combo boxes to use as input boxes for an entry into the check register, as shown in Figure 8.2. The three Text boxes are for the check number, the date, and the amount of the check or deposit, all which are editable quantities. The Combo box is for the description of the transaction, and has a list of standard transactions, plus an editable box to insert a transaction not on the list. The Label box is for the balance, which cannot be edited because it depends on the previous balance and the current entry.

4. Draw a Text box on the Form to hold the check number, and set its properties.

```
CtlName = CkNumBox
Height = 380
Width = 855
Top = 360
Left = 120
FontName = Courier
FontSize = 10
```

181

5. Draw another Text box on the Form to hold the date, and set its properties.

```
CtlName = DateBox
Height = 380
Width = 1215
Top = 360
Left = 960
FontName = Courier
FontSize = 10
```

6. Draw a third Text box on the Form to hold the amount, and set its properties.

```
CtlName = AmountBox
Height = 380
Width = 1575
Top = 360
Left = 5280
FontName = Courier
FontSize = 10
```

7. Draw a Label on the Form to hold the balance, and set its properties.

```
CtlName = BalanceBox
Height = 380
Width = 1575
Top = 360
Left = 6840
FontName = Courier
FontSize = 10
```

8. Draw a Combo box on the Form to hold the description of the transaction, and set its properties.

```
CtlName = DescBox
Height = 380
Width = 3135
Top = 360
Left = 2160
Style = 0 - Dropdown Combo
FontName = Courier
FontSize = 10
```

The font name and size is changed to 10 point Courier in all these boxes, because the data is going to be stored in strings in the following List box, and you want the strings to line up. Use Courier because it's a monospace font; if you used a proportionally spaced font, the data wouldn't line up.

9. Draw a List box on the Form and type its properties.

```
CtlName = Register
Height = 1100
Width = 8295
Top = 1320
Left = 120
FontName = Courier
FontSize = 10
```

Next, attach two Option buttons to select whether the current entry is a payment or deposit, then three Command buttons to control insertion and deletion of new records. (Your screen will look like Figure 8.2.) The **New** button sets up the entry boxes for a new entry, setting the current date, check number and balance. The **Insert** button inserts the data currently in the Text boxes into the check record, either at the end for a new entry, or to replace an entry selected for corrections. The **Delete** button deletes the selected entry from the check record.

Note the ampersand (&) in the Caption properties of the controls for these buttons. That marks the following letter in their names as an Access key for the controls, just as it did for the menu commands in Chapter 7, "Using Custom Menus." A control with an Access key can be selected by pressing Alt and the Access key. Note also that the **Insert** button has the Default property set to True. Only one control on a Form can have its Default property set, and that control is clicked if the Enter key is pressed, assuming the focus is not on another Command button.

10. Draw an Option button on the Form and set its properties.

```
CtlName = Debit
Caption = P&ayment
Height = 380
Width = 1215
Top = 840
Left = 240
Value = True
```

11. Draw a second Option button on the Form and set its properties.

```
CtlName = Credit
Caption = &Deposit
Height = 380
Width = 1215
Top = 840
Left = 1680
Value = False
```

12. Draw a Command button on the Form and set its properties.

```
CtlName = NewCmd
Caption = &New
Height = 380
Width = 1095
Top = 840
Left = 3000
```

13. Draw a second Command button on the Form and set its properties.

```
CtlName = InsertCmd
Caption = &Insert
Height = 380
Width = 1575
Top = 840
Left = 4440
Default = True
```

14. Draw a third Command button on the Form and set its properties.

```
CtlName = DeleteCmd
Caption = &Delete
Height = 380
Width = 1095
Top = 840
Left = 6600
```

Change the tab order of the controls so pressing the Tab key moves the focus to the object that you most likely will want to access next.

15. Select the NewCmd Command button, and change its TabIndex property to 0. Select the rest of the controls on the Form, in order, and set the TabIndex property according to Table 8.1.

Table 8.1. `TabIndex` values for the Check Register program.

CtlName	*TabIndex*
NewCmd	0
Register	1
DescBox	2
AmountBox	3
Debit	4
Credit	5
InsertCmd	6
CkNumBox	7
DateBox	8
DeleteCmd	9

16. Open the menu design window and create a File menu according to Table 8.2.

Table 8.2. File menu setup for the Check Register program.

Caption	*CtlName*	*# of indents*
&File	FileMenu	0
&Print	PrintCmd	1
-	SepBar1	1
E&it	ExitCmd	1

This completes the visual interface, which should now look like Figure 8.2. The next step is to add code to these controls. First, define the constants `True` and `False`, then declare some variables at the Form level to hold the check number (`CkNum`), and current balance (`Balance`). `NewFlag` is a flag that indicates whether this is a new record being inserted into the check record, or an old record being edited. `InitialBalance` is the starting balance for the program.

17. Open the `declarations` section of `Form1`, and type

```
Const True = -1, False = 0
Dim CkNum As Integer, Balance As Double, NewFlag As Integer
Dim InitialBalance As Double
```

The `Form_Load` procedure initializes the variables and sets up the program. The procedure inserts the initial balance into the register, as if it were a deposit. I chose a starting number of 1000 for the checks in line 3 and an initial balance of $980 in line 4. Lines 6 through 14 load values in the `DescBox` List box. Because a List box cannot be loaded at design time, it must be loaded by the running code. Lines 16 through 21 load the initial values in the Text boxes, then the routine `Box2List` is called in line 22. The `Box2List` routine takes the data from all the Text boxes, stores it in a string, and returns that string to the argument `Entry$`. In line 23, the `AddItem` method inserts `Entry$` into the `Register` List box.

You don't want users to be inserting data or changing the entry type until they have either initialized a new record with the **New** button, or selected a list item from the `Register` for editing, so the rest of this procedure disables the **Insert** and **Delete** buttons and the **Debit** and **Credit** Option buttons. Once you have pressed `New` or have selected a record, the buttons are enabled again.

18. Open the `Form_Load` procedure and type

```
Sub Form_Load ()
InitialBalance = 980      'Set the initial values
CkNum = 1000
Balance = InitialBalance
'Insert some items in the Description list
DescBox.AddItem "Shane's Grocery"
DescBox.AddItem "Sierra Bank and Trust"
DescBox.AddItem "Skye's Sewing Shop"
DescBox.AddItem "Today Computers"
DescBox.AddItem "Julie's Day-care"
DescBox.AddItem "B.J.'s Consulting"
DescBox.AddItem "Orvis Cattle Co."
DescBox.AddItem "Pay"
DescBox.AddItem "Royalty Payment"
'Insert the initial balance in the register as a deposit
line 15
CkNumBox.Text = ""
DateBox.Text = "01-01-1992"
```

```
DescBox.Text = "Starting Balance"
Credit.Value = True
AmountBox.Text = "          980.00"
BalanceBox.Caption = "          980.00"
Box2List Entry$      'Store the data in the string Entry
Register.AddItem Entry$      'Store the new item in the Regis-
ter
'Disable the Insert and Delete Buttons
InsertCmd.Enabled = False
DeleteCmd.Enabled = False
'Disable the Payment/Deposit options
Debit.Enabled = False
Credit.Enabled = False
End Sub
```

The **New** Command button sets up the Text boxes for a new entry. First, in lines 2 and 3, the **Debit** and **Credit** Option buttons are enabled. In lines 5 through 11, the default values for a check are entered into the Text boxes. In line 13, the NewFlag is set to indicate that this is a new entry. A new record has now been initialized, so enable the **Insert** Command button in line 14 so the record can be stored, then disable the **Delete** button. The most logical thing for the user to do next is to select the description, so move the focus to the Description box in line 16.

19. Open the NewCmd_Click procedure and type

```
Sub NewCmd_Click ()
Debit.Enabled = True
Credit.Enabled = True
'Set default values for a new check
Debit.Value = True
CkNumBox.Text = Str$(CkNum)
DateBox.Text = Date$
DescBox.Text = ""
AmountBox.Text = ""
Balance = GetBalance(Register.ListCount - 1)
BalanceBox.Caption = Format$(Balance, "0.00")
'Set the new flag and enable the Insert command
NewFlag = True
InsertCmd.Enabled = True
DeleteCmd.Enabled = False
DescBox.SetFocus
End Sub
```

187

After pressing the **New** button, you might want to insert a deposit rather than a check. Clicking the **Deposit** button executes the `Credit_Click` procedure, which changes the entry to a deposit, and deletes the check number. Clicking the **Payment** button executes the `Debit_click` procedure, changes the entry back to a check record, and inserts the check number back into the check number Text box. Both procedures end by calling the `AmountBox_Change` procedure to update the balance.

20. Open the `Credit_Click` and `Debit_Click` procedures and type

```
Sub Credit_Click ()
CkNumBox.Text = ""
AmountBox_Change
End Sub

Sub Debit_Click ()
CkNumBox.Text = Str$(CkNum)
AmountBox_Change
End Sub
```

After you have completed filling the Text boxes for a record, press the **Insert** button. The procedure attached to this button first calls the `Box2List` procedure to copy the data from the Text boxes and return it in the string `Entry$`. In line 3, a block `If` statement breaks the routine into two different parts, one for a new record, and one for a changed record. If the record is a new one, it is added to the `Register` List box with the `AddItem` method in line 4. Then, if the entry was for a check (`Debit.Value = True`), it adds one to the variable `CkNum` to advance the check number, and updates the current balance. It then disables the **Insert** and **Delete** buttons so you can't insert or delete a record until you either press `New` or select a record in the `Register` List box.

If the entry was for a changed record rather than for a new one, the block of code starting in line 14 is executed. Instead of using the `AddItem` method to add a new entry, this statement uses the `List` property of the `Register` List box to replace the existing entry with the edited one in the string `Entry$`.

The `List` property is an array of strings containing the items in the list, and the `ListIndex` property contains the currently selected one. Because an entry has been changed, the current balance in the replaced entry and all those following it might not be correct, so the `FixBalance` procedure is called in line 15 to recalculate the balance for all the entries in the `Register`. Then the `Register_Click` procedure is called to read the corrected data back into the Text boxes. The last few lines of the routine disable the Option buttons and move the focus to the **New** command button.

21. Open the `InsertCmd_Click` procedure and type

```
Sub InsertCmd_Click ()
Box2List  Entry$    'copy the data into the string Entry
If NewFlag = True Then
  Register.AddItem Entry$
  If Debit.Value = True Then
    CkNum = CkNum + 1
  End If
  Balance = GetBalance(Register.ListCount - 1)
  Rem If you wanted to print checks from this program
  Rem you would call a check printing routine here.
  InsertCmd.Enabled = False
  DeleteCmd.Enabled = False
Else
  Register.List(Register.ListIndex) = Entry$
  FixBalance       'Recalculate the Balance field
  Register_Click
End If
Debit.Fnabled = False
Credit.Enabled = False
NewCmd.SetFocus
End Sub
```

The `Register_Click` procedure is executed whenever an item in the `Register` List box is clicked. It first sets the flag `NewFlag` to `False`, indicating this is an old record rather than a new one. Then, in lines 4 and 5, it extracts the selected record into the string variable `Entry$`, and calls the `List2Box` Sub procedure to put the values in the Text boxes. In line 6, it uses the `GetBalance` Function procedure to get the current balance from the record just before the selected one (`Register.ListIndex - 1`). It finally enables the **Insert** and **Delete** buttons.

22. Open the `Register_Click` procedure and type

```
Sub Register_Click ()
NewFlag = False
'Get the entry from the Register and put it in the Text boxes
Entry$ = Register.Text
List2Box Entry$
Balance = GetBalance(Register.ListIndex - 1)
'Turn on the Insert and Delete commands
InsertCmd.Enabled = True
DeleteCmd.Enabled = True
End Sub
```

The DeleteCmd_Click procedure is executed when the **Delete** button is pressed. It first checks to ensure that the selected list item is not the first list item that contains the starting balance. If it isn't, the procedure deletes the selected item with the RemoveItem method. Because removing an item will probably make the current balance incorrect, the procedure calls the FixBalance Sub procedure to recalculate it. Finally, the procedure disables the **Delete** and **Insert** buttons.

23. Open the DeleteCmd_Click procedure and type

```
Sub DeleteCmd_Click ()
If Register.ListIndex > 0 Then
Register.RemoveItem Register.ListIndex
FixBalance
End If
DeleteCmd.Enabled = False
InsertCmd.Enabled = False
End Sub
```

The PrintCmd_Click procedure is executed whenever the **Print** command is selected from the **File** menu. The procedure starts a For/Next loop counting over the number of items in the List box (0 to ListCount-1.). The integer variable I% is the loop counter for the For/Next loop, and is used to select the list item in line 30. It then uses the Print method to print the list item. At the end, it executes the EndDoc method to tell the printer it is done, and to begin printing.

24. Open the PrintCmd_Click procedure and type

```
Sub PrintCmd_Click ()
For i% = 0 To Register.ListCount - 1
  Printer.Print Register.List(i%)
Next i%
Printer.EndDoc
End Sub
```

25. Open the ExitCmd_Click procedure and type

```
Sub ExitCmd_Click ()
End
End Sub
```

The ExitCmd_Click procedure is executed when the **Exit** command is selected from the **File** menu. It simply executes an End statement to end the program. The AmountBox_Change procedure is executed whenever you type a number into the Amount Text box. It checks to see whether this is a deposit or a payment, and recalculates the value in the `BalanceBox` Label accordingly. As a result, the value in the `Balance` box changes dynamically as you type a deposit or withdrawal.

26. Open the `AmountBox_Change` procedure and type

```
Sub AmountBox_Change ()
If Debit.Value = True Then
    BalanceBox.Caption = Format$(Balance
        - Val(AmountBox.Text), "0.00")
Else
    BalanceBox.Caption = Format$(Balance
        + Val(AmountBox.Text), "0.00")
End If
End Sub
```

This completes the event-procedures; now the user-defined procedures are discussed. As you type these procedures, be sure to select the correct type—`Function` or `Sub`—otherwise the program does not work. The first user-defined procedure is `Box2List`, which copies the data from the Text boxes and returns it in a string variable so it can be stored in the List box. The data is stored in the string variable, according to Table 8.3.

Table 8.3. Breakdown of the `TheString$` variable.

Contents	Starting Character	Length
Check number	1	6
Date	8	10
Description	19	25
Debit or Credit	45	1
Amount	47	14
Balance	62	14

The procedure first initializes the value of TheString$ as a string of 81 spaces. In line 3, the Mid$ statement is used to insert the check number in the first six character positions. Line 4 puts the date in 10 character positions starting at position number 8. Line 5 inserts the description in 25 characters, starting at position number 19. Lines 6 through 10 insert a D or C at character position 45, depending on whether this is a payment or deposit. Next are two dollar amounts. Although all the items so far have been left justified into the string locations, dollar amounts look better if they are right justified. To right justify the variables, create a temporary variable, Temp$, containing 14 blanks. Use the RSet method to right justify the dollar amounts into the temporary variable, then insert the temporary variable into TheString$. Lines 11 through 13 insert the amount of the debit or credit starting at position 47, and lines 14 through 16 insert the balance starting in position 62.

27. Select the general section of the Form and create a template for the Box2List Sub procedure. Either use the **New Procedure** command on the **Code** menu, or type Sub Box2List at the bottom of the declarations section, open the procedure and type

```
Sub Box2List (TheString$)
TheString$= Space$(81)
Mid$(TheString$ , 1, 6) = CkNumBox.Text
Mid$(TheString$, 8, 10) = DateBox.Text
Mid$(TheString$, 19, 25) = DescBox.Text
If Debit.Value = True Then
   Mid$(TheString$, 45) = "D"
Else
   Mid$(TheString$, 45) = "C"
End If
Temp$ = Space$(14)
RSet Temp$ = Format$(Val(AmountBox.Text), "0.00")
Mid$(TheString$, 47, 14) = Temp$
Temp$ = Space$(14)
RSet Temp$ = BalanceBox.Caption
Mid$(TheString$, 62, 14) = Temp$
End Sub
```

The List2Box Sub procedure reverses the process of the Box2List procedure. Substrings are extracted from TheString$ using the Mid$() function and stored in the Text boxes.

28. Create a template for the List2Box Sub procedure, and type

```
Sub List2Box (TheString$)
CkNumBox.Text = Mid$(TheString$, 1, 6)
DateBox.Text = Mid$(TheString$, 8, 10)
DescBox.Text = Mid$(TheString$, 19, 25)
If Mid$(TheString$, 45, 1) = "D" Then
  Debit.Value = True
Else
  Credit.Value = True
End If
Debit.Enabled = False
Credit.Enabled = False
AmountBox.Text = LTrim$ (Mid$(TheString$, 47, 14))
BalanceBox.Caption = LTrim$ (Mid$(TheString$, 62, 14))
End Sub
```

The FixBalance Sub procedure loops over all the list items in Register, and calculates and updates the running balance. The balance is calculated in line 5 using the GetBalance() Function procedure to get the previous balance, and the GetChange() Function procedure to get the current debit or credit. It updates the balance with the PutBalance Sub procedure.

29. Create a template for the FixBalance Sub procedure, and type

```
Sub FixBalance ()
Rem Fix the balance column after an adjustment
If Register.ListCount > 0 Then
  For i% = 0 To Register.ListCount - 1
    Balance = GetBalance(i% - 1) + GetChange(i%)
    PutBalance i%, Balance
  Next i%
End If
End Sub
```

The GetChange() procedure returns the debit or credit amount from the record indicated by its argument. Because this procedure returns a single value, make it a Function procedure. This procedure first checks to be sure the argument index is valid, then uses it to select a list item in Register and store it in Entry$. It extracts the amount from Entry$ in line 6, and stores it in a temporary double precision variable, temp#. It then tests to see whether this is a debit or credit, and accordingly returns a positive or negative value in GetChange.

193

30. Create a template for the `GetChange()` Function procedure, and type

```
Function GetChange (index As Integer) As Double
If index < 0 Then
  GetChange = 0
Else
  Entry$ = Register.List(index)
  Temp# = Val(Mid$(Entry$, 47, 14))
  If Mid$(Entry$, 45, 1) = "D" Then
    GetChange = -Temp#
  Else
    GetChange = Temp#
  End If
End If
End Function
```

The `GetBalance()` and `PutBalance()` procedures either get or change the balance in the list item selected with the index. GetBalance is a `Function` procedure because it returns a single value, and you want to use it like a function. `GetBalance()` first checks for an out-of-range index. It then extracts the list item into the string `Entry$`, then extracts the numeric value of the balance and returns it in `GetBalance`. `PutBalance()` does just the opposite; it also checks the index, then it extracts the list item into `Entry$` in line 3. It then replaces the value in the list item with the new value in lines 4 through 6, then stores the list item back into the list in line 7.

31. Create a template for the `GetBalance()` Function procedure, and type

```
Function GetBalance (index As Integer) As Double
If index < 0 Then
  GetBalance = InitialBalance
Else
  Entry$ = Register.List(index)
  GetBalance = Val(Mid$(Entry$, 62, 14))
End If
End Function
```

32. Create a template for the `PutBalance()` Sub procedure, and type

```
Sub PutBalance (index As Integer, bal As Double)
If index > 0 Then
  Entry$ = Register.List(index)
```

```
      Temp$ = Space$(14)
      RSet Temp$ = Format$(bal, "0.00")
      Mid$(Entry$, 62) = Temp$
      Register.List(index) = Entry$
   End If
End Sub
```

33. Save the procedure and run it. Click the **New** button, then click
    the down arrow on the right side of the Drop-down Combo box.
    Your screen should look like Figure 8.3.

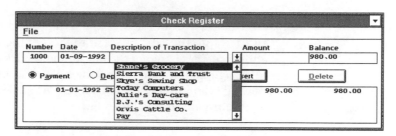

Figure 8.3. *The Automated Check Register program with the description list pulled down.*

Select Shane's Grocery as the description, type **50** as the amount, and
press Enter, or click the **Insert** button. The check register should now
look like Figure 8.4.

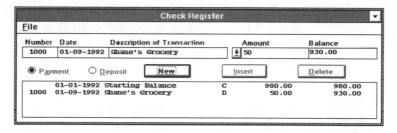

Figure 8.4. *The Automated Check Register program with the first entry
inserted.*

34. Type several more entries, both payments and deposits. The check
    register should look something like Figure 8.5.

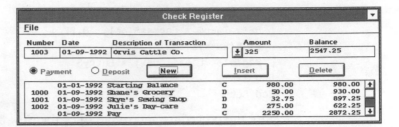

Figure 8.5. *The Automated Check Register program with several entries.*

35. Select an entry from the Register List box, and note how it is extracted into the Text boxes at the top of the Form, as shown in Figure 8.6. Try changing the amount and click **Insert** to carry out the change and update the balance. Try deleting an entry by selecting it and pressing the **Delete** button. Try printing with the **P**rint command on the **F**ile menu.

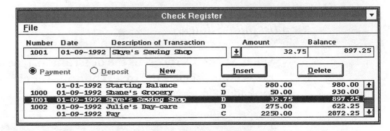

Figure 8.6. *The Automated Check Register program with a list item selected.*

This check register program lacks a command to insert new records within the record rather than at the end. However, that would be a relatively easy command to add. Just follow the logic of the Insert command, but insert the record using an index with the AddItem method.

Because you have already typed all the names and numbers, you could add a command to read the Register and to print your checks for you. You would have to tell the routine which check to start with and to skip any deposits. In addition, you could create a similar command that reads deposits and prints deposit slips.

Right now, the program also lacks a way to save all the entries after they have been entered, so don't spend a week typing all your checks into this program—you will be upset when you exit the program and everything disappears. Saving the lists is covered in Chapter 9, "Using Sequential Files."

With some modification, this program could be used as a general purpose journal, which forms the beginning of an accounting system.

What You Have Learned

This chapter examined how to create procedures to modularize a program and reuse code. There are two types of procedures: Sub procedures and Function procedures. They are quite similar, except the Function procedures return a value stored in the functions name. The chapter also looked at List and Combo boxes for inputting and storing lists of data. You have explored the details of

- Sub procedures.
- Function procedures.
- Arguments passed to procedures as values or addresses.
- List boxes.
- An Automated Check Register program.

Using Sequential Files

Until now, you have saved programs in disk files with the save commands on Visual Basic's File menu, but you haven't saved the data within your programs. Saving data is essential; in the last chapter, for example, the Check Register program you developed is useless if you can't save the data in the register. So now it's time to look at the different ways to use disk files to save and retrieve data.

In This Chapter

There are three types of disk files in Visual Basic: sequential, random access, and binary. Binary disk files are used for advanced applications that require access to the raw bytes of a data file, and are beyond the scope of this book.

Random access files are discussed in Chapter 10, "Using Random Access Files." This chapter discusses:

- Creating and opening sequential files.

- Reading and writing data to sequential files.

- Creating file access dialog boxes.

Storing Data In Disk Files

The three types of data files used in Visual Basic are sequential, random access, and binary. Sequential files are text files, read or written sequentially (from the beginning to the end) as a linear sequence of variable-length lines of text, with a line-feed carriage return at the end of each line. They are text files that can be listed on the screen or printer with the DOS TYPE or PRINT commands, or can be opened with any word processor. Numbers are stored as a sequence of digits, much as you would type them on the screen. Because they are linear, they can either be read or written, but not both simultaneously. That is, you cannot be reading part of a file at the same time you are writing another part, although you can be reading two different parts at the same time.

Random access files, as the name implies, are not accessed in linear fashion. They are accessed in fixed-length blocks, known as records, in any order.

The third file type, binary, is actually similar to random access, except that it is read and written byte by byte rather than record by record, and no special significance is placed on the value of any byte (such as the carriage return line-feed pair). I won't discuss any more details of binary files here.

Opening and Closing Sequential Files

Sequential files and, in fact, all files, are created or opened with the Open statement. The syntax of the Open statement is

```
Open name$ [For mode] [Access access] [lock] As [#]filenumber%
[Len = rlen%]
```

Here, name$ is a string variable, or quoted string containing the name of the file to open, and the path, if it isn't in the default directory. The path, in Windows as in DOS, is the list of disk name and directories you must traverse to reach a file. For example, let's say that the absolute path to the file FILE.TXT is

```
D:\DIR1\DIR2\DIR3\FILE.TXT
```

where D is the disk letter, DIR1, DIR2, and DIR3 are the directories you must traverse, and FILE.TXT is the file name and extension of the file. In this case, the file FILE.TXT is in directory DIR3, which is in directory DIR2, which is in directory DIR1, which is in the root directory of disk D. A path can also be relative to the current default directory. For example, if DIR2 is the current default directory, then the path

```
DIR3\FILE.TXT
```

points to the same file. The default directory is changed by several commands and programs, so you can't always depend on it to be a specific directory. In any program, it's much safer to use absolute paths because they always point to a specific file.

The *mode* of the file is either Append, Binary, Input, Output, or Random. The access argument controls the file access type, and is either Read, Write, or Read Write. The lock argument has the value Lock Read, or Lock Write, and controls access to a file by other processes. The filenumber% is a unique number that identifies the open file to all the other file access commands. The rlen% argument is the record length, in bytes, to use with random access files.

For sequential files, the acceptable modes are Input, Output, or Append. When a file is opened For Input, the file already must exist, and you can only read data from it. When a file is opened For Output, it is opened if it exists, or created if it does not, and you can only write data to it. When an existing file is opened For Output, writing starts at the first record, overwriting any old data in the file. The Append mode is a variation of Output. When the file is opened, writing starts at the end, preserving the old data.

The *access* and *lock* arguments apply to networked environments, where multiple users may have access to the same file. The access argument controls what access you want for the file, in case someone else already has it open, and the lock argument controls what access to the file you are willing to allow others if you are the first to open the file. These are unneeded in a single-user situation.

201

The *filenumber* argument must be included with every `Open` statement, and used with every command that accesses the file. Because you might have more than one file open at any one time, this number uniquely identifies each file. Usually, the first file you open is file number 1, the second is 2, and so forth. If you close a file, you can reuse its file number. If you know how many files you have open, you can assign a constant for the file number. However, if you don't know how many files your program has open, such as when you are using a word processor that has multiple files open simultaneously, use the `FreeFile` function to give you the next available file number. For example,

```
InputFileNum% = FreeFile
Open "MYFILE.TXT" For Input As # InputFileNum%
```

This opens the file named MYFILE.TXT as a sequential file for reading only. The file number is selected with the `FreeFile` function, so use the variable `InputFileNum%` whenever the file is accessed. If this is the only file that is accessed by a program, you could simply use the file number 1 to open the file and, as the following example shows, use the file number 1 with every file access command.

```
Open "MYFILE.TXT" For Input As #1
```

When you are done with a file, close it with the `Close` statement. The `Close` statement empties all Visual Basic's file buffers and gives the information to the system for writing to the disk. The `Close` statement also releases the file numbers for reuse with other files. The syntax is

```
Close [[#]filenumber%] [,[#]filenumber%]...
```

where `filenumber%` is the file number used when the file was opened. To close all open files, use the `Close` statement without the file numbers.

File systems don't write bytes to open disk files as you send them, but collect the bytes in file buffers. A file buffer is simply a place in memory where the information is stored until it is written to disk. When a buffer is full, it is written to disk all at once. This is why you must close files before removing a disk. If you don't do so, the file might not be there in its entirety.

Writing Sequential Files

Data is written to sequential files using the `Print #` and `Write #` statements in the same way that data is printed on the screen or on the printer. The `Print #` statement writes data to disk files in exactly the same way that the `Print` method writes data on the screen. The printed data is converted to text, and the text is sent to the disk file. All the formatting conventions discussed previously apply here as well. The format of the `Print #` statement is

```
Print # filenumber%, expressionlist [{;¦,}]
```

where `filenumber%` is the file number used when the file was opened, and `expressionlist%` is a comma- or semicolon-separated list of expressions to be printed. Expressions that evaluate to strings are printed as is; expressions that evaluate to numbers are converted to strings before being sent to the file. If expressions are separated by commas, the point of printing moves to the next tab stop (one every 14 spaces) before printing the next item. If the expressions are separated by semicolons, the next item is printed immediately following the last. Normally, a carriage-return line feed pair is inserted at the end of every `Print #` statement, unless it ends in a semicolon or comma. For example, the fragment

```
A = 5.3
Print #1, "The length = ";A
```

would print (write)

```
The length = 5.3
```

in file number 1.

The second way to send data to a disk file is with the `Write #` statement. The `Write #` statement works much the same as the `Print #` statement, except that commas are inserted between printed expressions, and strings are surrounded by quotations. Data written with a `Write #` statement is easier to read back into a program than that written with `Print #`. Thus, the `Print #` statement is used mostly for creating files that are eventually read or printed on a printer, and `Write #` is used for data that is going to be read back into a BASIC program. For example, the fragment

```
A1 = 5.355
B1 = 4.788
Print #1, "The values, are: ", A1, B1, " units"
Write #1, "The values, are: ", A1, B1, " units"
```

would produce the following code in a disk file.

```
The values, are:            5.355      4.788            units
"The values, are: ",5.355,4.788," units"
```

Reading Sequential Files

After you have written data to a sequential file, you might want to read it back into a program. Actually, any text file can be read by Visual Basic as a sequential file. To read a sequential file, use the Input # and Line Input # statements, and the Input$() function.

The Input # statement

The Input # statement reads data from a disk file into its arguments. The syntax is

Input # filenumber% , expressionlist

where filenumber is the number that opened the file, and expressionlist is a list of Visual Basic variables that receive data that is read from the file.

When reading a file, leading spaces are always ignored. For a number, the first nonblank character is assumed to be the start of the number, and the first blank, comma, or the end of the line terminates it. For a string, the first nonblank character starts the string, and a comma or the end of the line terminates it. If the string is quoted, everything between the quotations is included in the string, including commas. Thus, data written with the Write # statement is more accurately read than data written with Print #. For example, reading the disk file you previously created with the Print # and Write # statements, with the code fragment

```
Input #1, A$, B, C, D$
Input #1, E$, F, G, H$
```

would store the following data in the variables:

```
A$ = "The values"
B = 0
C = 5.355
D$ = "4.788          units"
E$ = "The values, are: "
F = 5.355
G = 4.788
H$ = " units"
```

Note how the first Input # statement stopped reading the string into A$ at the first comma, so that the first numeric input, B, sees text rather than a number and gets a value of zero. Then the second numeric input, C, reads the first number, and the remaining number and string end up in D$.

The Line Input # Statement

The Line Input # statement inputs one line of text into a single string variable. It reads everything in a line up to a carriage return, including leading spaces, trailing spaces, commas, and quotation marks. The syntax is

```
Line Input # filenumber%,string$
```

where filenumber% is the file number used in the Open statement, and string$ is a string variable. For example, if you redo the previous example with Line Input # statements, as such,

```
Line Input #1, A$
Line Input #1, B$
```

the variables contain exactly what is in the file.

```
A$ = The values, are:        5.355      4.788          units
B$ = "The values, are: ",5.355,4.788," units"
```

The Line Input # statement is typically used to input text files for a word processor or similar program, or in a program where you are going to use the string functions, such as Mid$(), to extract portions of a line.

The Input$() Function

The last input method for sequential files is the `Input$()` function. The `Input$()` function is used to input every byte in a file, including line terminators. The `Input #` and `Line Input #` statements skip carriage returns and line feeds, but the `Input$()` function reads every byte in a file and returns a string. The syntax is

```
Input$(numbytes%[#]filenumber%)
```

where `numbytes%` is the number of bytes to return and `filenumber%` is the file number used in the `Open` statement. For example, again using the same input file as the preceding one,

```
A$ = Input$(5,#1)
```

The string variable, `A$`, contains

```
A$ = The v
```

The EOF() Function

An auxilary function used with sequential files is the `EOF()` function. It returns `True` if you have reached the end-of-file. If you attempt to read past the end-of-file, your program generates an error, so use the `EOF()` function to test a file before reading from it, if you don't know where the end-of-file is. The syntax of the function is

```
Flag% = EOF(filenumber%)
```

where `filenumber%` is the file number used in the `Open` statement. In the following example, `EOF(1)` is tested, and if it is `False` (0), another record is needed.

```
False = 0
If Not EOF(1) = False Then Input#1, A$
```

Creating File Access Dialog Boxes

Most Windows programs that access files selected by the user do so with a file access dialog box. A file access dialog box is a Form that lets you select the drive, directory (folder) and file from a list, rather than typing a file name. A file access dialog box is created using three special list controls: the Drive, Directory, and File List boxes. A Drive List box contains a drop-down list of all the drives on your machine. Selecting a drive from the list puts the drive letter in the list's Path property.

A Directory List box contains a list of the directories on the current drive. Selecting a directory from the list places the path to that directory in the box's Path attribute. A File List box displays a list of the files in the directory in its Path property. Clicking a file places the file's name in the box's FileName property.

An Open Dialog Box

Combining these three lists and some code on a Form creates a file access dialog box. The three lists aren't connected in any way, so changing the drive in the Drive List box doesn't change the Directory List box. You need some simple pieces of code to connect the three box types.

Changing the drive in the Drive List box creates a Click event on that box and changes the Path property. In the Click event Code window, change the Path property of the Directory List box to equal the new Path in the Drive List box. Clicking a directory in the Directory List box also creates a Click event and changes the Path variable, so insert a formula to change the Path property of the File List box to that in the Directory List box. Add a button to combine the FileName and Path properties, and you have an Open dialog box. Add a Text box to insert a new file name, and you have a Save dialog box.

The Check Register Program (Version 2)

This new version of the Check Register program is actually a continuation of the example started in Chapter 8, "Writing Custom Procedures," because without a save capability, the Check Register program isn't much use. In this chapter, you will add Open, Save, and Save As commands to the File menu,

and attach two new Forms containing an Open Dialog box and a Save As Dialog box. The rest of the program remains largely unchanged.

1. Open the Check Register program, and display Form1.

2. Open the Menu Design window and add **O**pen, **S**ave, and Save **A**s commands to the File menu according to Table 9.1.

Table 9.1. Menu design for the check register program, version 2.

Caption	CtlName	# of indents
&File	FileMenu	0
&Open	OpenCmd	1
&Save	SaveCmd	1
Save &As	SaveAsCmd	1
-	SepBar2	1
&Print	PrintCmd	1
-	SepBar1	1
&Quit	QuitCmd	1

The following three procedures are attached to the three new commands on the File menu. Their only function is to pass control to the file access dialog boxes. Note the constant AsModal following the Show method in each procedure. It's defined as the number 1 in the Global module and it makes the Dialog boxes *modal*. When a Form is modal, you can't select any other Forms until you have edited or viewed the modal Form and closed it. Also, any code following the Code method for a modal Form isn't executed until the Form is hidden or unloaded. If a Form isn't modal, you can move to other Forms by clicking them. The SaveCmd_Click procedure tests the global variable FileName to see whether it is blank. If it's not blank, a file already is attached to this program, so the procedure calls the SaveIt Sub procedure to save the contents of the Register List box. If FileName is blank, the data hasn't been saved yet, and the procedure calls the SaveDialog Form to attach a file.

3. Open the `OpenCmd_Click` procedure and type

```
Sub OpenCmd_Click ()
OpenDialog.Show AsModal
End Sub
```

4. Open the `SaveCmd_Click` procedure and type

```
Sub SaveCmd_Click ()
If FileName <> "" Then
  SaveIt
Else
  SaveDialog.Show AsModal
End If
End Sub
```

5. Open the `SaveAsCmd_Click` procedure and type

```
Sub SaveAsCmd_Click ()
SaveDialog.Show AsModal
End Sub
```

Move all the declarations and definitions to the Global module, so they are available to these Forms.

6. Open the declarations section of `Form1` and cut everything there. Open the Global module and paste it all. Change `Dim` to `Global` and add `Global` before each constant declaration. Add the definition for the `FileName` variable and `modal` constant. It should now read

```
Global Const True = -1, False = 0, AsModal = 1
Global CkNum As Integer, Balance As Double, NewFlag As Integer
Global InitialBalance As Double
Global FileName As String
```

7. Add two new Forms to this project with the New Form command on the File menu. Save them as CKREG2.FRM and CKREG3.FRM. Select the first one and change its properties as follows:

```
Caption = Open
Height = 2640
Width = 4845
ControlBox = False
FormName = OpenDialog
MaxButton = False
MinButton = False
```

8. Draw a File List box on the Form with these properties

```
Top = 120
Left = 120
Height = 1820
Width = 1575
Pattern = *.*
```

The `Pattern` property controls what files are listed in the box. Using `*.*` (wild card) lists all the files in the directory.

Because the `Pattern` property controls which files are visible in the File List box, you might want to allow the user to change that property. The simplest way to do this is to add a Text box and have its `Change` procedure set the `Pattern` property of the File List box. You also can select a standard pattern with a set of option buttons, or select from a menu. A third option is to have a Text box display the currently selected file in the File List box, and if you type something that isn't a file name, use it to set the pattern property.

9. Draw a Directory List box on the Form with these properties

```
Top = 600
Left = 1800
Height = 1340
Width = 1335
```

10. Draw a Drive List box on the Form with these properties

```
Top = 120
Left = 1800
Width = 1335
```

11. Draw a Command button on the Form with these properties

```
Caption = OK
CtlName = OKCmd
Top = 120
Left = 3360
Height = 380
Width = 1215
Default = True
```

12. Draw another Command button on the Form with these proper-
    ties. (The Form should now look like Figure 9.1.)

```
Caption = Cancel
CtlName = CancelCmd
Top = 600
Left = 3360
Height = 380
Width = 1215
```

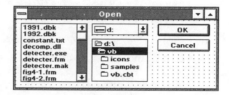

Figure 9.1. *Layout of the Open Dialog box.*

13. Open the Drive1_Change procedure and type the following. This
    links the directory shown in the Directory list to changes in the
    drive from the Drive list.

```
Sub Drive1_Change ()
Dir1.Path = Drive1.Drive
End Sub
```

14. Open the Dir1_Change procedure and type the following. This links
    the File list to the directory selected in the Directory list.

```
Sub Dir1_Change ()
File1.Path = Dir1.Path
End Sub
```

15. Open the OKCmd_Click procedure and type

```
Sub OKCmd_Click ()
If File1.FileName = "" Then
  MsgBox "Please select a file first."
  Exit Sub
End If
FileName = File1.Path + "\" + File1.FileName    'line 6
ClearIt
ReadIt
OpenDialog.Hide
End Sub
```

When the **OK** button is clicked, this procedure first checks the FileName property of the File List box to see whether a file has been selected. If not, it displays a Message box asking you to select a file name first, then executes the Exit Sub statement to exit this Sub procedure. If a file name has been selected, line 6 combines the Path property with a backslash and the file name to produce a complete path to the selected file. Next, the ClearIt procedure is called to clear the contents of the Register List box on Form1. Then the ReadIt procedure is called to read the contents of the selected file into the Register List box. Line 9 then hides the Open Dialog box, passing control back to Form1.

16. Open the CancelCmd_Click procedure and type the following. This command changes nothing, and returns control to Form1.

```
Sub CancelCmd_Click ()
OpenDialog.Hide
End Sub
```

17. Open the File1_DblClick procedure and type the following. This procedure makes double clicking a file name in the File List box the same as clicking the file and pressing the **OK** button.

```
Sub File1_DblClick ()
OKCmd_Click
End Sub
```

A Save As Dialog Box

This completes the Open Dialog box. Next, create the Save As Dialog box, which is nearly identical to the Open Dialog box, but adds a Text box for the new file name.

1. Select the third Form saved as REG3.FRM. Change its properties to

```
Caption = Save As
Height = 2640
Width = 4845
ControlBox = False
FormName = SaveDialog
MaxButton = False
MinButton = False
```

2. Draw a File List box on the Form with these properties

```
Top = 600
Left = 120
Height = 1460
Width = 1575
Pattern = *.*
```

3. Draw a Directory List box on the Form with these properties

```
Top = 600
Left = 1800
Height = 1460
Width = 1335
```

4. Draw a Drive List box on the Form with these properties

```
Top = 120
Left = 1800
Width = 1335
```

5. Draw a Command button on the Form with these properties

```
Caption = OK
CtlName = OKCmd
Top = 120
Left = 3360
Height = 380
Width = 1215
Default = True
```

6. Draw another Command button on the Form with these properties

```
Caption = Cancel
CtlName = CancelCmd
Top = 600
Left = 3360
Height = 380
Width = 1215
```

7. Draw a Text box with these properties (the Form should now look like Figure 9.2.)

```
CtlName = FName
Top = 120
Left =120
Height = 380
Width = 1575
Text = 1111
```

213

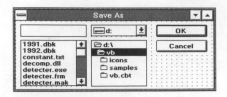

Figure 9.2. *Layout of the Save As Dialog box.*

As with the Open dialog, much of the code in the Save As dialog is the same. Keep in mind that the names of the controls on both of these dialog boxes are the same, but because they are on two different Forms, the names are local to those Forms.

8. Open the `Drive1_Change` procedure and type the following. This action links the directory shown in the Directory list to changes in the drive from the Drive list.

```
Sub Drive1_Change ()
Dir1.Path = Drive1.Drive
End Sub
```

9. Open the `Dir1_Change` procedure and type the following. This links the File list to the directory selected in the Directory list.

```
Sub Dir1_Change ()
File1.Path = Dir1.Path
End Sub
```

10. Open the `CancelCmd_Click` procedure and type the following. This command changes nothing, and returns control to `Form1`.

```
Sub CancelCmd_Click ()
SaveDialog.Hide
End Sub
```

11. Open the `OKCmd_Click` procedure and type

```
Sub OKCmd_Click ()
Dim thePath  As String
'Test for no file name    line 3
If FName.Text = "" Then
```

```
    MsgBox "Type a file name first"
    Exit Sub
End If
'Test for path      line 8
If InStr(FName.Text, "\") <> 0 Or InStr(FName.Text, ":") <> 0
Then
    MsgBox "File name only, no path"
    Exit Sub
End If
'Test for missing extension add .CKR if missing      line 13
FName.Text = LTrim$(RTrim$(FName.Text))
If InStr(FName.Text, ".") = 0 Then
    FName.Text = Left$(FName.Text,8) + ".CKR"
End If
thePath = Dir1.Path + "\" + FName.Text
'Check for existing file      line 19
If Dir$(thePath) <> "" Then
    Action = MsgBox("File exists, overwrite?", 257)
    If Action = 2 Then Exit Sub
End If
'Open the file and save the check register data      line 24
FileName = thePath
File1.Refresh
SaveIt
SaveDialog.Hide
End Sub
```

This OKCmd_Click procedure is a little more complex than that in the Open command, but only because it has to verify the file name before using it. The block of code from line 3 to line 7 checks to see whether you have typed a file name in the Text box. If you haven't, it displays a Message box asking you to do so first, then exits the procedure with an Exit Sub statement. Lines 8 through 12 check to see whether you have typed a path in the Text box as well as the file name by checking for the \ or : characters. Because you are going to create the path, you don't want users to type their own. A more complex Save As dialog could let users type their own paths.

Change the OKCmd procedure so users can type a complete path rather than a file name. If the user types a path without a file name, make the procedure change the Path properties of the File List box, the Directory List box, and the Drive property of the Drive List box, then exit. If the path includes a file name, change the Path properties and open the file. If a pattern is typed rather than a file name, change the Pattern property of the File List box to that pattern.

Lines 13 through 18 check to see whether the user has typed an extension on the file name by looking for the period. If not, the code block adds the .CKR extension in line 16. The LTrim$() and RTrim$() functions remove any blanks from the left or right sides of the file name. The Left$() function in line 16 extracts up to 8 characters from the left side of the file name, ensuring that the name part of the file name is no more than 8 characters long. In line 18, the complete path to the file is created by combining the directory path from the Path property of the Directory box with a backslash and the file name from the Text box.

Lines 19 through 23 check for an existing file using the Dir$() function. The Dir$() function returns the name of the file if it exists; otherwise it returns an empty string. If the file already exists, a Message box is displayed with an **OK** and a **Cancel** button (the 257 argument of the MsgBox statement; see Chapter 15, "Command Reference," for a list of codes). If the user presses **Cancel**, the Message box returns a value of 2, and the Exit Sub statement is called to exit the procedure without overwriting the file. If the point of execution reaches Line 24, the file can be created or opened, so pass the path to the Global variable FileName, and call the SaveIt Sub procedure to save the file.

12. Open the File1_Click procedure and type the following. This step puts a selected file name in the Text box if the user clicks it in the File List box.

```
Sub File1_Click ()
FName.Text = File1.FileName
End Sub
```

13. Open the File1_DblClick procedure and type the following. This procedure makes double clicking a file name in the File List box the same as clicking the file and pressing the **OK** button.

```
Sub File1_DblClick ()
OKCmd_Click
End Sub
```

This completes the Save As Dialog box. Now create a module for the SaveIt, ClearIt and ReadIt Sub procedures.

14. Execute the **New Module** command on the **File** menu, and save the module as CKREGM.BAS.

15. Open the SaveIt Sub procedure and type

```
Sub SaveIt ()
Dim I As Integer
'Open the file and save the contents of Register
Open FileName For Output As #1          'line 4
Write #1, Form1.Register.ListCount, CkNum, Balance,
InitialBalance
For I = 0 To Form1.Register.ListCount - 1          'line 6
  Print #1, Form1.Register.List(I)
Next I
Close #1
End Sub
```

This procedure saves the contents of the Register List box in the file specified by the Global variable FileName. Line 4 opens the file for sequential output. Line 5 writes the number of items in the list, and the value of CkNum, Balance, and InitialBalance. These three values also are needed to restart the program from a datafile. Note how the Register object on Form1 is accessed from this module by prefacing the object name with the Form name. Unfortunately, you can't do this for user-defined variables, only Visual Basic objects. User-defined variables have to be passed through the Global module.

Note also that I have used the Write # statement to ensure that I can extract the values correctly later. Lines 6 through 8 loop through all the items in the List box, and print each item to the disk file. I use the Print statement here because I am writing complete lines to the file, not individual values. Line 9 closes the file.

16. Open the ClearIt Sub procedure and type

```
Sub ClearIt ()
'Clear the contents of Register
While Form1.Register.ListCount > 0
Form1.Register.RemoveItem 0
Wend
End Sub
```

9

This procedure simply clears the contents of the Register List box on Form1. Note again how I have added the Form name to the List box name, so I can access the object in Form1 from this module. The procedure works with a While/Wend loop that checks the number of items in the Register List box using the ListCount property. As long as there is still at least one item in the list, it executes the RemoveItem method on the first item (item number 0). It continues until there are no more items in the List box.

17. Open the ReadIt Sub procedure and type

```
Sub ReadIt ()
Dim NumEntries As Integer, aLine As String
'Open the file and read into Register
Open FileName For Input As #1
Input #1, NumEntries, CkNum, Balance, InitialBalance
For i = 1 To NumEntries
Line Input #1, aLine
Form1.Register.AddItem aLine
Next i
Close #1
End Sub
```

This procedure complements the SaveIt Sub procedure. It first opens the file that has its name in the Global variable FileName for sequential input. You can use the same file number here (1) as you used in the SaveIt procedure because you close the file when you end that procedure. If that file were still open, you would have to use a different file number. After opening the file, the procedure reads the number of entries into NumEntries, then reads the three values saved with the Write # statement back into the same variables using the Input # statement. Using the NumEntries number, you will know exactly how many lines of data to read, so you won't need to use the EOF() function each time to check for the end of the file. In this case, loop over the number of entries that you previously wrote to the file. Because you wrote complete lines of text to the file, you can read them back with the Line Input # statement into the variable aLine, and then insert that line into the Register List box on Form1 using the AddItem method. Finally, close the file.

18. Save the project; it's done. Run the program and insert a few values, then execute the **S**ave command on the **F**ile menu. Note that it brings up the Save **A**s Dialog box, as shown in Figure 9.3,

because you have not saved this data yet. Select a disk and directory by clicking the List boxes, type a file name (REG1), and press **OK**. The data is saved.

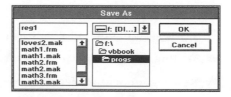

Figure 9.3. *The Save As Dialog box.*

19. Change the data by adding a few more items, then execute **Save** again. This time the program doesn't bring up the Save **As** dialog because it already knows where to store the data.

20. Change the data again, then execute the **O**pen command. The Open dialog, as shown in Figure 9.4, appears. Select the old file and click **OK**. The old data is read, replacing the data currently in the Register List box.

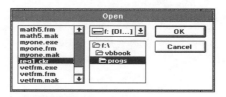

Figure 9.4. *The Open Dialog box.*

You now have an operating check register program to keep track of your bank account. This program demonstrates linear record keeping or journaling, which attaches each new entry to the end of the file of data. This is just one possible type. A ledger, for example, requires randomly accessed files, which are discussed in Chapter 10, "Using Random Access Files."

What You Have Learned

Three types of disk files are available in Visual Basic, and this chapter investigated the most common, sequential access files. Random Access files

are discussed in Chapter 10, "Using Random Access Files." The third type, binary files, is used primarily with advanced applications. To access files within an application, you created Open and Save As Dialog boxes and attached them to the Check Register program. In this chapter, you learned about

- Using `Open` to open or create sequential files.

- Writing sequential files with `Write #` and `Print #`.

- Reading sequential files with `Input #`, `Line Input #`, and `Input$()`.

- Creating file access dialog boxes using Drive, Folder, and File lists.

Using Random Access Files

The second most useful file type in Visual Basic is the random access file. A random access file is different from a sequential access file in that the individual records are read and written in any order, rather than only from the beginning to the end. The primary use of random access files is for database-type programs such as a general ledger or inventory manager.

In This Chapter

Random access files are opened and closed in much the same manner as sequential files, but the record length is fixed rather than variable like sequential files. This fixed record length is necessary so individual records can be located and accessed asynchronously. To implement the storing of

values in fixed length records, use a record type variable composed of one or more standard type values, such as integers and strings. In this chapter, you will learn to

- Create user-defined record type variables.

- Create and open random access files.

- Read and write records in random access files.

- Create a Datebook database program.

Storing Data in Random Access Disk Files

Your computer actually reads data from a disk in fixed-length pieces called sectors, and a sector holds 512 bytes. If a record is 512 bytes long, or some number that is evenly divisible into 512 (a power of 2 = 1, 2, 4, 8, 16, 32, 64, 128...), then no record crosses a sector boundary. If a record crosses a sector boundary, the computer must read two sectors rather than one to get the whole record.

For example, if your record length is 500 bytes (a nice, round number), the first record is contained in the first 500 bytes of the first sector. The second record is in the last 12 bytes of the first sector and the first 488 bytes of the second. The third record uses the last 24 bytes of the second sector and the first 476 bytes of the third. On the other hand, if the record is just 12 bytes longer, every record is completely contained within a single sector. If you can't use the extra bytes, you are still only wasting about 2.5% of your disk space in exchange for cutting the access time in half. The trade-off is file space versus file access time. What you do depends on your application. If you have huge data files that don't get accessed often, you might want to sacrifice speed for reduced size. On the other hand, if your application spends too much time accessing the files, you might want to sacrifice some file space for increased speed.

Random access files, as the name implies, are not accessed in a linear fashion. They are accessed in fixed length blocks, known as records, in any order. Random access files are also text files, but you may not be able to read any of the numbers stored in them. Numbers are stored as binary data rather than character data. This procedure saves a considerable amount of memory, because a 5-digit integer takes at least 5 bytes to be stored as text, and only 2 bytes to be stored as a binary integer.

Record lengths in random access files are fixed, and the default length is 128 bytes. Although record lengths of any size (up to 32,767 bytes) are allowed, sizes that are powers of two are more efficient. The record length is specified when you open the file.

Defining Record Type Variables

In addition to the built-in variable types such as `Integer` and `String`, you can define your own variable types by combining other types. Then, a single variable name passes the whole contents of a record rather than a single value. To create a record type variable, you must first define the variable type with a `Type` statement. The `Type` statement defines which of the built-in or user-defined variable types make up the record, and in what order. The syntax of the `Type` statement is

```
Type newtypename
  elementname As typename
  elementname As typename
  .
  .
  .
End Type
```

Here, `newtypename` is the name you are giving to the `type` definition, `elementname` is the name you are giving to the element that is going to be a part of this type, and `typename` is the type of variable that `elementname` is. `Typename` can be any of the built-in types (`Integer`, `Long`, `Single`, `Double`, `Currency`, or `String`), or some other user-defined type.

For example, the following `Type` definition defines the variable type `DayType`, which consists of three elements. The first is `theDate`, which is a `Double` precision floating point number for storing a date. The second is an `Integer` named `Flags`, and the third is a fixed length `String` named `Msg`. Strings are normally variable length and might be so in a general, user-defined type; but because the record length in a random access file is fixed, the length of any strings that make up the record variable also must be fixed.

10

Fixed length String variables are created by adding an asterisk (*) and the string length following the String type name.

```
Type DayType
   theDate As Double
   Flags As Integer
   Msg As String * 118
End Type
```

If you add up the number of bytes needed to store this new variable, you will notice that it adds up to 128 bytes exactly (8 bytes for the Double, 2 for the Integer, and 118 for the String), one of the efficient lengths for random access file records. The length of a record type variable must be less than or equal to the length of a record defined with the Open statement. After you have defined a new type, you must then define a variable with that type so you can use it. Defining a variable as a new type is done in exactly the same way as the built-in type definitions, by using Dim and Global statements. For example,

```
Dim aLine As String, Today as DayType
Global theMonth(1 To 31) As DayType
```

The first line defines aLine as a string variable and Today as the new variable type DayType. The second line defines an array named Month of 31 DayType variables. To access the parts of a user-defined variable type, combine the variable name with the element name, separated with a dot. For example,

```
Today.Flags = 2
Month(5).Msg = "Some interesting message"
Today.theDay = Now
```

The first line stores the number 2 in the Flags element of Today (the Integer), the second inserts a string in the Msg element of the fifth element of Month, and the third line uses the function Now to insert today's date and time into the theDay element of Today.

Opening A Random Access File

To open a random access file, use the Open statement, defined in Chapter 9, "Using Sequential Files," or use a mode of Random, and include the record length. For example,

```
Open "MYFILE.DBK" For Random As #1 Len = 128
```

opens the file MYFLE.DBK in the default directory as a random access file, with file number 1 and with a record length of 128 bytes. The default record length for random access files is 128 bytes, so the length argument could have been omitted. It is better to specify the length, however, so when you are reading the program, you immediately know what the record length is.

When you are done with this file, close it in exactly the same way as a sequential file, using a `Close` # statement:

```
Close #1
```

Reading and Writing Random Records

Now that you have the file open, you have to be able to read and write records. Records from a random access file are read with the `Get` # statement. The `Get` # statement syntax is

```
Get [#] filenumber%,[recordnumber&],recordvariable
```

Here, the `filenumber%` is the file number used in the Open statement, `recordnumber&` is the number of the record you want to read, and `recordvariable` is the name of the record type variable that receives the data. If you omit the record number, you will get the next record in the file after the last one you read. For example,

```
Get #1,225,Today
```

reads record number 225 from file number 1 and stores it in the `DayType` record variable `Today`. After you have read a record into a record variable, you can access the contents of that record by accessing the elements of the record variable.

Records are written in exactly the same manner as they are read, using the `Put` # statement. The syntax and arguments are identical to those for the `Get` # statement,

```
Put [#] filenumber%,[recordnumber&],recordvariable
```

An example is

```
Put #1, 12, Month(3)
```

which stores the third element of the array of record variables, Month( ), in record 12 of file number 1. If that record doesn't exist yet, the file is automatically extended to include it.

The Datebook Program

The Datebook program is a year-long electronic calendar of important dates and notes. When it starts, it automatically checks a week ahead and beeps if any of the dates are marked important. It then displays the current month with important dates marked in shades of gray. Clicking a date brings up a second window that shows the note attached to that date. In that window, you can create or edit the note and save it in the database file. The program consists of two Forms: one contains a monthly calendar showing the important dates with attached notes, and the other shows the note attached to the selected date.

The monthly calendar Form is made with 37 Labels arranged in five rows of seven, plus one row of two. This structure holds any month. Also on the Form are two arrows, used to move forward or backward one month. The **F**ile menu contains commands to create a new yearly database, or to open a database other than the current year. A **M**onth menu contains all the month names to rapidly move to a different month in the current year.

1. Open a new project, select the Form, and change its properties to the following. This holds a calendar for one month, as shown in Figure 10.1.

```
Caption = Date Book
BorderStyle = 3 - Fixed Double
MaxButton = False
Height = 5500
Width = 5460
```

Setting the BorderStyle to 3 and MaxButton to False makes it impossible for other users to change the size of the Form, which would spoil your user-interface.

2. Draw a Label at the top to hold the name of the current month, and set its properties to

```
Caption = Month
CtlName = MonthBox
Top = 0
Left = 1440
Height = 380
Width = 2415
```

```
Alignment = 2 - Center
BorderStype = 1 - Fixed Single
FontSize = 12
```

Figure 10.1. Layout for Form1 *of the Datebook program.*

The next step is to create the two arrow buttons to move the calendar forward or backward one month. Because there is no control that looks like an arrow, create one using a Picture box, an icon of the arrow, and the Picture box's Click procedure.

A Picture box has a Picture property into which you can load a drawing or icon, which is then displayed in the box. The types of picture files that can be loaded into a Picture box include bitmap files (.BMP), icon files (.ICO), and Windows Metafile files (.WMF). One of the most common graphics file types is the bitmap file. Many programs create bitmap files, including most of the popular paint programs such as Paintbrush, included with Windows. An icon is simply a specialized bitmap file with a maximum size of 32 by 32 pixels. You can create your own icons, using the Iconwrks sample program included with Visual Basic (see Plate II).

Visual Basic includes a small library of icons, including a whole list of arrows. To attach an icon to a picture box (or a Form), select the box, then select the Picture property. The type of attached picture, if there is one, shows in the Settings box. To the right of the Settings box is an ellipsis (...). When you click the ellipsis, an Open dialog box appears. Use that dialog box to select the file containing the picture or icon you want to use. To load a picture at run-time, use the LoadPicture function.

3. Draw a Picture box on the upper left, with the following attributes. To set the Picture property, select it, and click the ellipsis on the right side of the Settings box to open a File Open dialog box.

227

Locate the ARW07LT.ICO file containing the left arrow icon. It's located in the \VB\ICONS\ARROWS directory (the \VB directory is the Visual Basic directory). Click the file name and click **OK**.

```
CtlName = LeftArrow
Picture = ARW07LT.ICO
Top = -120
Left = 240
Height = 500
Width = 615
```

4. Draw a second Picture box on the upper right, with the following attributes. Attach the right pointing arrow to it.

```
CtlName = RightArrow
Picture = ARW07RT.ICO
Top = -120
Left = 4440
Height = 500
Width = 615
```

5. Draw seven Labels across the Form containing the first letter of the days of the week, according to Table 10.1.

Table 10.1. Properties for Datebook Labels.

Caption	Left	Top	Height	Width
S	360	600	260	255
M	1080	600	260	255
T	1800	600	260	255
W	2520	600	260	255
T	3240	600	260	255
F	3960	600	260	255
S	4680	600	260	255

Now, create a control array of Labels to form the calendar. Each Label is a date square on the calendar, and also is a button to get access to the note attached to that date. Create the array by drawing the first box, then use the **C**opy and **P**aste commands on the **E**dit menu to create the rest.

6. Draw a Label with the following properties.

```
Caption = Day
CtlName = DayButton
Top = 960
Left = 120
Height = 620
Width = 735
BorderStype = 1 - Fixed Single
```

7. Select the Label and execute the Copy command, then execute the Paste command. A dialog box appears asking you whether you want to create a control array. Click **Yes**.

8. Select the newly pasted Label and drag it to the right of the first one. Continue pasting and dragging until you have five rows of seven boxes and one row of two boxes, as shown in Figure 10.1.

   There are two menus on this application. One is the standard file menu with **New**, **Open** and **Exit** commands, the second is a **Month** menu with all the months of the year on it. The Month menu will quickly move you to any month in the current year.

9. Open the Menu Design window and create a **File** and a **Month** menu according to Table 10.2. The Month menu is a control array containing all the months of the year.

Table 10.2. Menu design for the Datebook program.

Caption	CtlName	# of indents	Index
&File	FileMenu	0	
&New	NewCmd	1	
&Open	OpenCmd	1	
-	SepBar1	1	
&Exit	ExitCmd	1	
&Month	MonthMenu	0	
&Jan	MonthCmd	1	1
&Feb	MonthCmd	1	2
Ma&r	MonthCmd	1	3

continues

Table 10.2. continued.

Caption	CtlName	# of indents	Index
&Apr	MonthCmd	1	4
Ma&y	MonthCmd	1	5
J&un	MonthCmd	1	6
Ju&l	MonthCmd	1	7
Au&g	MonthCmd	1	8
&Sep	MonthCmd	1	9
&Oct	MonthCmd	1	10
&Nov	MonthCmd	1	11
&Dec	MonthCmd	1	12

10. Save the Form as DBOOK1.FRM.

    This completes the design for the first Form, which contains the calendar. Now, create a second Form to use for reading and writing the notes being attached to the dates on the calendar.

11. Add a second Form to the project with the New Form command on the **F**ile menu, and set its properties as follows.

    ```
    Caption = Reminder
    BorderStyle = 3 - Fixed double
    MaxButton = False
    MinButton = False
    Height = 2740
    Width = 5145
    ```

12. Draw a Text box on the Form as shown in Figure 10.2, and set its properties. This is where you type the notes.

    ```
    CtlName = Message
    Top = 720
    Left = 120
    Height = 1340
    Width = 3495
    Text = " "
    ```

Figure 10.2. *Layout for* Form2 *of the Datebook program.*

Next, create a control array of three option buttons for setting the importance of a note. The array has three option buttons marked **None**, **Routine**, and **Important**. The **None** button clears the current note. The **Routine** button colors the date light blue (cyan) on the calendar, and the **Important** button colors the date red.

13. Create a control array of the following three Option buttons. You can either create the first button, then **C**opy and **P**aste it to create the others, or draw three Option buttons and give them all the same CtlName. Use Table 10.3 for the appropriate values for each button. These three buttons are used to indicate whether the attached note is routine or important.

Table 10.3. Values for the Option buttons.

Caption	Left	Index	Value	Height	Width	Top
&None	120	0	True	500	1095	120
&Routine	1200	1	False	500	1095	120
&Important	2400	2	False	500	1095	120

There are two command buttons on this Form. The first is the **OK** button, which attaches the note to the calendar and saves it in the disk file. The **Cancel** button discards any changes and returns you to the calendar.

14. Draw an **OK** Command button with these properties:

```
Caption = OK
CtlName = OKCmd
Top = 120
Left = 3840
Height = 500
Width = 1095
Default = True
```

231

15. Draw a **Cancel** Command button with these properties:

```
Caption = Cancel
CtlName = CancelCmd
Top = 720
Left = 3840
Height = 500
Width = 1095
Default = False
```

16. Draw a Label below the **Cancel** button with these properties:

```
Caption = Reminder for
Top = 1320
Left = 3840
Height =260
Width = 1215
```

17. Draw a Label to hold the date with these properties:

```
CtlName = DateBox
BorderStype = 1 - Fixed Single
Top = 1680
Left = 3840
Height = 380
Width = 1095
```

18. Save the Form as DBOOK2.FRM.

This completes the second Form. Now attach code to the project. First is the Global module; it contains the definitions for `True`, `False` and `asModal`, a list of color definitions copied from the file CONSTANT.TXT included with Visual Basic and the definition for the `DayType` type. The type definition must come before any attempt to use it.

Next are some Global variable definitions: `FileName` is a string variable that contains the name of the currently open file, `theYear` is an integer containing the current year as a number, `theMonth` contains the current month as a number, `EOL` holds the end-of-line characters—carriage return, and line feed. The variable `ChangeDate` is a record variable of type `DayType`, `Months( )` is an array of 12 strings, each string containing the name of a month; `thisMonth( )` is an array that holds the serial date numbers for each day in the current month, and `OldBackColor` and `OldForeColor` are double precision variables to hold the values of the background and text colors.

Serial date numbers are used in Visual Basic to store dates and times. The date is stored in the integer part of the number as the integer number of days since 12/30/1899. Negative values describe dates back to 1/1/1753. The time is stored in the fractional part of the number as a fraction of a whole day; for example, 0.5 is noon. The functions Day( ), Weekday( ), Month( ), and Year( ) convert serial date numbers into integers representing the day of the month, day of the week, month of the year, and year. The function DateValue( ) converts a text representation of a date into a serial date number, and DateSerial(year,month,day) converts the three integers year, month, and day into a serial date number.

19. Open the Global module and type

```
Global Const True = -1, False = 0, asModal = 1
Global Const BLACK = &H0&          'Colors from the file
Global Const RED = &HFF&           'CONSTANT.TXT
Global Const GREEN = &HFF00&
Global Const YELLOW = &HFFFF&
Global Const BLUE = &HFF0000
Global Const MAGENTA = &HFF00FF
Global Const CYAN = &HFFFF00
Global Const WHITE = &HFFFFFF
Global Const LT_GRAY = &H808080
Global Const DK_GRAY = &H404040
Type DayType                       'Type declaration for the
  TheDate As Double                'record DayType, 128 bytes
  Flags As Integer                 'long
  Msg As String * 118
End Type
Global FileName As String          'The disk file name and path
Global theYear As Integer          'The current year
Global theMonth As Integer         'The current month
Global EOL As String               'End-Of-Line character
Global ChangeDate As DayType       'Serial date being changed
Global Months(1 To 12) As String   'Text names of the months
Global thisMonth(36) As Double     'Array to hold datenumbers
Global OldBackColor As Double      'Store old background color
Global OldForeColor As Double      'Store old text color
```

20. Save the Global module as DBOOKG.BAS.

The `Form_Load` procedure sets up the problem. The first 15 lines define the `EOL` variable and fill the `Months( )` array with the text of the 12 month names. Line 16 is a call to the `ClearMonth` procedure which initializes the 36 Labels on the calendar. Line 18 creates a file name from the current year by using the `Now` function to get the current serial date number, and the `Year( )` function to extract the current year. The year (4 digits) is then combined with the .DBK file extension to form the file name. In line 19, the `Dir$( )` function is used to see whether the file exists. If it doesn't, the procedure exits; otherwise, the file is opened as a random access file with file number 1 in line 20. In line 21, the `Get #` statement is used to extract the first record. The actual year stored in the file is extracted from the `TheDate` item of the `aDay` record variable in line 22 and the file is closed in line 23. This ensures that there actually is a file for the desired year.

In line 24, the `Now` function is used again with the `Month( )` function to get the current month and store it in `theMonth`. In line 25, the `FillMonth` procedure is executed to insert the days and notes in the currently open year and month. In line 27, the `LookAhead` procedure is called with an argument of seven days. This procedure scans ahead the number of days specified, then beeps and prints a message if any day has the **Important** button set. The last two lines before the `End Sub` statement load `Form2`, then hide it. This gets `Form2` into memory so it can be displayed when it is needed, and so its controls can be accessed before `Form2` is displayed.

21. Select the first Form, open the `Form_Load` procedure, and type

```
Sub Form_Load ()
Dim aDay As DayType
EOL = Chr$(13) + Chr$(10)      'End-of-line character
Months(1) = "January"        'Fill Months array
Months(2) = "February"
Months(3) = "March"
Months(4) = "April"
Months(5) = "May"
Months(6) = "June"
Months(7) = "July"
Months(8) = "August"
Months(9) = "September"
Months(10) = "October"
Months(11) = "November"
Months(12) = "December"
```

```
ClearMonth
'If a file for the current year exists, get it    line 17
FileName = Format$(Year(Now), "0000") + ".DBK"
If Dir$(FileName) = "" Then Exit Sub
Open FileName For Random As #1 Len = 128
Get #1, 1, aDay
theYear = Year(aDay.TheDate)
Close #1
theMonth = Month(Now)
FillMonth
'Look ahead one week for important days'
LookAhead (7)
Load Form2
Form2.Hide
End Sub
```

The New command creates a new year's data file. Lines 4 through 11 use an Input box so you can enter a year, and then test the value returned. If the value is a blank, the procedure exits. Otherwise, it stores the value in the variable theYear. Lines 11 through 18 convert the date into a file name, as before, and test to see whether a file already exists. If it does, the pro-cedure sends a message to you, asking whether it is OK to overwrite the old file. If you do not want to overwrite it, press the **Cancel** button, and the procedure exits. Otherwise, it opens or creates the file. In lines 19 through 22, the record variable is filled with blank data, except for the first field, which contains the date of the record.

In lines 23 through 29, the file is opened, and the blank data is written out to it. This initializes the file by deleting any existing data in the file that could be mistaken for a message. The only thing that changes is the date, which is updated each pass through the loop. Finally, the procedure checks to see whether this is the current year. If it is, it switches to the current month. If not, it starts with January. FillMonth is called at the end to draw the current month.

22. Open the NewCmd_Click procedure, and type

```
Sub NewCmd_Click ()
Dim aDay As DayType, i  As Integer, aYear As String
Dim aMsg As String, Action As Integer
'Get a year from the user. Exit if blank.
theYear = 0
If theYear < 1753 Or theYear > 2078 Then
```

```
      aYear = InputBox$("Type the year")
      If aYear = "" Then Exit Sub
      theYear = Val(aYear)
   End If
   'Make a file name with the year and check for an existing   line 11
   'file. Ask if it is OK to overwrite it.
   FileName = Format$(theYear, "0000") + ".DBK"
   If Dir$(FileName) <> "" Then
      aMsg = "File already exists" + EOL + "Overwrite it?"
      Action = MsgBox(aMsg, 257)
      If Action = 2 Then Exit Sub   'If Cancel is pressed, exit
   End If
   'load the record variable    line 19
   aDay.TheDate = DateSerial(theYear, 1, 1) - 1
   aDay.Flags = 0
   aDay.Msg = Space$(118)
   'Open the file and fill with data.   line 23
   Open FileName For Random As #1 Len = 128
   For i = 1 To 366
      aDay.TheDate = aDay.TheDate + 1
      Put #1, i, aDay
   Next i
   Close #1
   'If the new file is this year, display the current month
   If theYear = Year(Now) Then
      theMonth = Month(Now)
   Else
      theMonth = 1

   End If
   FillMonth
   End Sub
```

The **Open** command works much the same way as the **New** command, but can be used only when the file already exists. The procedure first asks you for the year in line 10, using an Input box. When the year is validated, it uses the `Dir$( )` function in line 17 to see whether the file exists. If it doesn't, a message box is displayed in line 18, asking you to use the **New** command instead.

If the file exists, it's opened as a random access file in line 24, and the first record is read in line 25. The current year is then extracted from the first record. In lines 28 through 34, the program determines if it is the current year, and displays the current month if it is.

23. Open the OpenCmd_Click procedure, and type

```
Sub OpenCmd_Click ()
Dim aDay As DayType, i  As Integer, aYear As String
Dim OldFileName As String, OldYear As Integer
'Save the old year in case the user changes his mind
OldYear = theYear
OldFileName = FileName
'Get a year from the user. Exit if it is a blank
theYear = 0
If theYear < 1753 Or theYear > 2078 Then
  aYear = InputBox$("Type the year")
  If aYear = "" Then Exit Sub
  theYear = Val(aYear)
End If
'Make and validate a file name. Restore the old one and
line 14
'exit if it doesn't exist.
FileName = Format$(theYear, "0000") + ".DBK"
If Dir$(FileName) = "" Then  'Check for existing file
  MsgBox "File doesn't exist, use New"
  FileName = OldFileName
  theYear = OldYear
  Exit Sub
End If
'Open the file and get the correct year    line 23
Open FileName For Random As #1 Len = 128
Get #1, 1, aDay
theYear = Year(aDay.TheDate)
Close #1
'If it's this year, display the current month    line 28
If theYear = Year(Now) Then
  theMonth = Month(Now)
Else
  theMonth = 1
End If
FillMonth
End Sub
```

Set the right and left arrow picture boxes so they seem like real buttons; the buttons turn black when pressed with the mouse and white when released. To do this, use the MouseDown and MouseUp events rather than the Click event to activate the code. The MouseDown event

is passed information about the state of the mouse, but changing the background color to black requires only the information that the mouse was pressed. In the MouseUp procedure, turn the background color back to white (or whatever it was). For the left arrow, subtract 1 from theMonth and for the right arrow, add 1. In both cases, make the value in theMonth wrap at 0 and 12 months so that pressing the left arrow in January causes a move to December, and pressing the right arrow in December moves to January. Finally, call the FillMonth procedure to draw the new month.

24. Open the LeftArrow_MouseDown procedure, and type

```
Sub LeftArrow_MouseDown (Button As Integer, Shift As Integer,
        X As Single, Y As Single)
LeftArrow.BackColor = BLACK
End Sub
```

25. Open the LeftArrow_MouseUp procedure, and type

```
Sub LeftArrow_MouseUp (Button As Integer, Shift As Integer,
        X As Single, Y As Single)
LeftArrow.BackColor = WHITE
theMonth = theMonth - 1
If theMonth = 0 Then theMonth = 12
FillMonth
End Sub
```

26. Open the RightArrow_MouseDown procedure, and type

```
Sub RightArrow_MouseDown (Button As Integer,
        Shift As Integer, X As Single, Y As Single)
RightArrow.BackColor = BLACK
End Sub
```

27. Open the RightArrow_MouseUp procedure, and type

```
Sub RightArrow_MouseUp (Button As Integer,
        Shift As Integer, X As Single, Y As Single)
RightArrow.BackColor = WHITE
theMonth = theMonth + 1
If theMonth = 13 Then theMonth = 1
FillMonth
End Sub
```

The MonthCmd_Click procedure is executed whenever one of the months is selected on the Month menu. The value of Index is equal to 1 for January, 2 for February, and so forth, so insert the value of Index into the variable theMonth and call FillMonth to draw the new month.

28. Open the `MonthCmd_Click` procedure, and type

```
Sub MonthCmd_Click (Index As Integer)
theMonth = Index
FillMonth
End Sub
```

29. Open the `ExitCmd_Click` procedure, and type

```
Sub ExitCmd_Click ()
End
End Sub
```

The Labels that form the calendar are also buttons that open the appropriate note. They are handled in much the same way as the left-arrow and right-arrow buttons. The `DayButton_MouseDown` procedure changes the background color to black and the text color to white. The `DayButton_MouseUp` procedure reverses that step to make the button seem like it was pressed. In line 5, the record number containing the data for this date is calculated by subtracting the serial date number for January 1 of the current year from the selected date stored in the array `thisMonth( )`, plus 1. This gives the correct record number, because the records are stored in the file as sequential days starting with January 1. The program then reads the record, and inserts the data into the controls on `Form2`. Then the Form is made visible as a modal Form.

30. Open the `DayButton_MouseDown` procedure, and type

```
Sub DayButton_MouseDown (Index As Integer,
        Button As Integer, Shift As Integer, X As Single, Y As
                Single)
OldBackColor = DayButton(Index).BackColor
OldForeColor = DayButton(Index).ForeColor
DayButton(Index).BackColor = BLACK
DayButton(Index).ForeColor = WHITE
End Sub
```

31. Open the `DayButton_MouseUp` procedure, and type

```
Sub DayButton_MouseUp (Index As Integer, Button As Integer,
        Shift As Integer, X As Single, Y As Single)
DayButton(Index).BackColor = OldBackColor
DayButton(Index).ForeColor = OldForeColor
Open FileName For Random As #1 Len = 128
RecNo = thisMonth(Index) - DateSerial(theYear, 1, 1) + 1
Get #1, RecNo, ChangeDate
Close #1
```

```
Form2.DateBox.Caption = Format$(ChangeDate.TheDate, "mm-dd-yyyy")
Form2.Message.Text = ChangeDate.Msg
Form2.FlagOpt(ChangeDate.Flags).Value = True
Form2.Show 1
End Sub
```

32. Save the Form.

When Form2 appears, any existing data for the selected date is displayed on the Form for you to edit or delete. Whenever any changes are made to the large Text box on Form2, the Message_Change procedure is executed. It simply stores the changed message in the Msg item of the ChangeDate record variable. It then checks the option buttons, and automatically clicks the **Routine** button, (FlagOpt(1)), if the message was previously empty.

33. Select the Message_Change procedure and type

```
Sub Message_Change ()
ChangeDate.Msg = Message.Text
If FlagOpt(0).Value = True And Message.Text <> ""
        Then FlagOpt(1).Value = True
End Sub
```

The FlagOpt_Click procedure is called whenever one of the option buttons is pressed. When it is executed, it first stores the current state of the option buttons in the Flags item of the ChangeDate record variable. Next, it checks to see whether the **None** Option button (Index = 0) was pressed, and if so, clears the contents of the Message Text box. Finally, it moves the focus to the Message Text box. The If statement is needed here to prevent this code from trying to move the focus while the Form is hidden. Because the DayButton procedure makes changes to the values on this Form before it makes the Form visible, an error would be generated if this code attempted to set the focus while the Form was hidden.

34. Select the FlagOpt_Click procedure and type

```
Sub FlagOpt_Click (Index As Integer)
ChangeDate.Flags = Index
If Index = 0 Then Message.Text = ""
If Message.visible Then Message.SetFocus
End Sub
```

After making any changes, you press the **OK** button. The **OK** button opens the data file, calculates the record number, and stores the edited record in the file. It then hides Form2 and calls the FillMonth procedure to redraw the month on Form1.

35. Select the second Form, open the OKCmd_Click procedure, and type

```
Sub OKCmd_Click ()
Open FileName For Random As #1 Len = 128
RecNo = ChangeDate.TheDate - DateSerial(theYear, 1, 1) + 1
Put #1, RecNo, ChangeDate
Close #1
Form2.Hide
FillMonth
End Sub
```

The **Cancel** button simply hides Form2 without making any changes to the data file.

36. Select the CancelCmd_Click procedure and type

```
Sub CancelCmd_Click ()
Form2.Hide
End Sub
```

37. Save the Form.

Several procedures stored on the module do the real work of this program. The ClearMonth procedure loops over all the Labels on Form1, deletes their captions, disables them, and resets the default background and foreground colors.

38. Add a new module using the New Module command on the File menu. Select the general procedure and type the ClearMonth procedure.

```
Sub ClearMonth ()
Dim I As Integer
For I = 0 To 36
Form1.DayButton(I).Caption = ""
Form1.DayButton(I).Enabled = False
Form1.DayButton(I).BackColor = WHITE
Form1.DayButton(I).ForeColor = BLACK
Next I
End Sub
```

The FillMonth procedure inserts the data for the current month into the calendar. It first clears the calendar using the ClearMonth procedure in line 5. In line 6, it inserts the name of the current month and the year into the MonthBox at the top of the Form. In lines 7, 8, and 9, it loops over all the months in the **Month** menu and unchecks them.

It's easier here just to uncheck every item on the menu rather than trying to figure out which item is checked. In line 10, the procedure checks the current month on the **Month** menu.

The next block of code inserts the data into the calendar. In line 11, the serial date number of the first day of the month is placed in the variable StartDate. Next, the data file is opened, and the record number containing the data for the first of the month is calculated. The record is read, the day is extracted from the serial date number (should be 1) in line 15, and the day of the week is extracted in line 16. The day of the week is used to determine which of the DayButton procedures on Form1 holds the dates for this month.

In line 18, a loop starts that continues until the serial date number advances to the next month; thus it cycles over all the days in the current month. In line 19, the current date is combined with an end-of-line (carriage return-line feed) and the current day's messages, and is inserted in the Caption property of the DayButton procedure. In line 20, the Label is enabled, and in line 21, the current serial date number is stored in the array, theMonth( ). In lines 22 through 24, the day is checked to see whether it is today; if it is, it's marked with an asterisk (*) inserted before the date and colored yellow.

Lines 26 through 31 check the state of the Option buttons to see whether this date has a note attached, and whether it's important. If a note is attached, the background color is changed to light blue (cyan). If the note is important, the background color is changed to dark gray and the text is changed to white. I used shades of gray here because they print better in a book, but you can use any of the colors defined in the Global module. Finally, this procedure increments the index for the next day, reads the next record, and extracts the day. This loop continues until the day is in the next month.

39. Type the FillMonth procedure.

```
Sub FillMonth ()
Dim StartDate As Double, aDay As DayType
Dim theDay As Integer, RecNo As Integer
Dim Index As Integer, I  As Integer, FirstIndex As Integer
ClearMonth
Form1.MonthBox.Caption = Months(theMonth) + Str$(theYear)
For I = 1 To 12
  Form1.MonthCmd(I).Checked = False
```

```
Next I
Form1.MonthCmd(theMonth).Checked = true
StartDate = DateSerial(theYear, theMonth, 1)      'line 11
Open FileName For Random As #1 Len = 128
RecNo = StartDate - DateSerial(theYear, 1, 1) + 1
Get #1, RecNo, aDay
theDay = Day(aDay.TheDate)
FirstIndex = Weekday(StartDate) - 1      'line 16
Index = FirstIndex
While theMonth = Month(StartDate + Index - FirstIndex)
  Form1.DayButton(Index).Caption = Str$(theDay) + EOL + aDay.Msg
  Form1.DayButton(Index).Enabled = true
  thisMonth(Index) = aDay.TheDate
  If aDay.TheDate = Fix(Now) Then
    Form1.DayButton(Index).Caption = "*" +
    Form1.DayButton(Index).Caption
    Form1.DayButton(Index).BackColor = YELLOW
  End If
  If aDay.Flags = 1 Then      'line 26
    Form1.DayButton(Index).BackColor = CYAN
  ElseIf aDay.Flags = 2 Then
    Form1.DayButton(Index).BackColor = RED
    Form1.DayButton(Index).ForeColor = WHITE
  End If
  Index = Index + 1
  RecNo = RecNo + 1
  Get #1, RecNo, aDay
  theDay = Day(aDay.TheDate)
Wend
Close #1
end sub
```

The LookAhead procedure is executed by the Form_Load procedure of
Form1. It checks Days days ahead of the current day and beeps and
displays a Message box if it finds one with the Important option set.
In line 6, the variable StartDate is set to the serial date number for
today. The Fix( ) function removes any fraction of a day returned by
the Now function. Lines 10 through 14 loop over the number of days
ahead to look, extract the records for each of those days, and check
the state of the Option buttons. In line 12, if a date is found that has
the Important option set (aDay.Flags = 2), then FoundIt is set to True,
and the program beeps. In line 19, if FoundIt was set to True, it will
display a Message box that tells you there are important messages.

40. Type the LookAhead procedure.

```
Sub LookAhead (Days As Integer)
'Look ahead Days for messages and beep if important
Dim StartDate As Double, aDay As DayType
Dim RecNo As Integer, Foundit As Integer
Dim I  As Integer
StartDate = Fix(Now)
Open FileName For Random As #1 Len = 128
RecNo = StartDate - DateSerial(theYear, 1, 1) + 1
Foundit = False
For I = 1 To Days      'line 10
  Get #1, RecNo, aDay
  If aDay.Flags = 2 Then
    Foundit = true
    Beep
  End If
  RecNo = RecNo + 1
Next I
Close #1
If Foundit Then MsgBox "You have important dates this week"
End Sub
```

41. Save the module as DBOOKM1.BAS, then save the project.

42. Run the program. The first time there is no data file, so execute the New command and give it the current year. When the program finishes creating the new data file, the calendar window looks something like Figure 10.3, with the current month visible, and the current day marked with an asterisk and a yellow background.

43. Click a date and the Reminder window opens, as shown in Figure 10.4. In the Reminder window, click the **Important** Option button and type a note. Only the first couple of words show on the calendar window, so make sure they indicate what the note is about—see also Plate IV.

Click **OK** to add the note and return to the calendar window. After adding a few routine or important dates, the calendar window should look something like Figure 10.5.

This completes the Datebook program; use it for all your important dates.

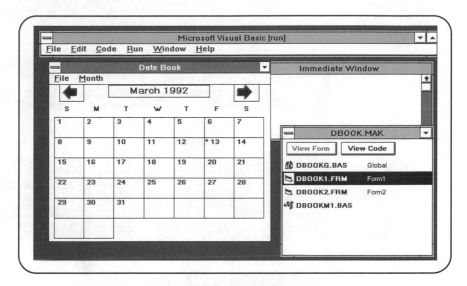

Figure 10.3. *The Datebook program—startup at the current month.*

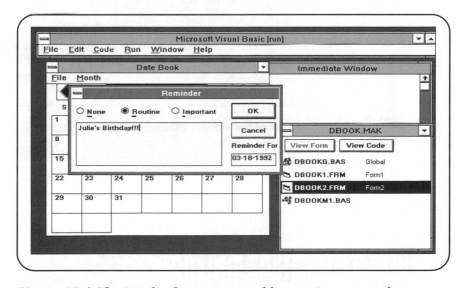

Figure 10.4. *The Datebook program—adding an important date.*

Current date (Yellow) ——   —— Routine note (Cyan)

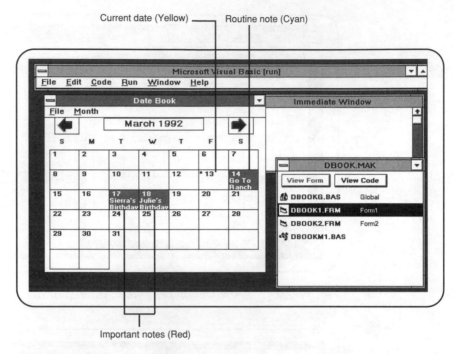

Important notes (Red)

Figure 10.5. *The Datebook program with notes added to some important dates.*

Try some of the other options, such as clicking the arrow buttons or using the Month menu to change the month. You could compile the program and make it a Windows startup document so every time you start up windows, you see your current calendar.

What You Have Learned

This chapter discussed the use of random access files. A random access disk file is one in which the individual records are read or written independently of all the other records in the file. All records are defined the same length when the file is opened. The contents of a record is determined by a record type variable defined with the Type statement. Specifically, this chapter investigated

- Using Type to create user-defined variables.

- Using Open to open or create a random access disk file.

- Reading and writing records with Get # and Put #.

- Creating a Datebook database program to store important events.

11

The Use of Color

Before you can draw graphics with Visual Basic, you have to set up the drawing environment. In addition to the obvious drawing properties such as the colors, the drawing environment includes setting the drawing mode, controlling the redrawing of windows when they have been uncovered, and setting the coordinate system. Redrawing of graphic windows is especially important in a window's environment where windows can be covered or uncovered at any time. The colors and drawing mode control how the drawing methods discussed in Chapter 12, "Drawing with Visual Basic," paint color on the screen, and the coordinate system determines what units you have to use when drawing on the screen.

In This Chapter

This chapter shows you how to manipulate color and the drawing properties, so you can control the drawing environment of Visual Basic. Properties exist to control the style of drawing, the colors used, and the scale of the drawing. Properties also exist to control redrawing of graphic images when a Form is uncovered. In this chapter, you will learn to

● Control redrawing of a graphic.

● Set the scale used when drawing.

● Set the colors.

● Set the drawing mode.

● Set the scale of a graphic.

Setting Drawing Properties

Drawing on the screen only occurs on a Form or Picture box; you cannot draw on any of the other controls. In addition to the screen, you can draw on the `Printer` object to obtain printed images. Forms and Picture boxes have special properties, shown in Table 11.1, for controlling how and where drawing occurs on them. These properties set the default colors used for foreground and background objects, the initial drawing location, and the coordinate system used on a Form.

Table 11.1. Graphics properties of Forms and Picture boxes.

Property	Description
AutoRedraw	Sets the object to remember what was drawn on it
BackColor	Sets the background color
CurrentX	The current horizontal location
CurrentY	The current vertical location
DrawMode	Controls how new drawing is combined with old

Property	Description
DrawStyle	Controls line dashing
DrawWidth	Controls the width of lines
FillColor	Controls the color used to fill circles and rectangles
FillStyle	Controls the pattern used to fill circles and rectangles
ForeColor	Sets the foreground color
Image	Provides access to the persistent bitmap
Picture	Provides access to the displayed graphic image
ScaleHeight	The height of the drawing area in the scale units
ScaleLeft	The x coordinate of the left side of the drawing area
ScaleMode	The coordinate system to use in the drawing area
ScaleTop	The y coordinate of the top of the drawing area
ScaleWidth	The width of the drawing area in scale units

Controlling Redrawing of a Graphic

Whenever a Form is covered and then uncovered by another window, its contents are erased by the covering window and have to be redrawn if you want to see them. Text boxes, Labels, Lists, and Combo boxes all contain the text drawn on them, so they automatically redraw themselves. File List boxes, Directory List boxes and Drive List boxes also contain the text they display, and also redraw themselves. Forms and Picture boxes with graphic images loaded into them at design time contain those images, and automatically redraw themselves. However, Forms and Picture boxes with graphic images drawn on them at run time or with text printed on them do not contain those images, and thus do not redraw themselves. Redrawing these objects must be handled by the Windows operating system or your program.

Although the File, Directory, and Drive List boxes automatically redraw themselves, their contents are not updated unless you change a directory. If you have added a file to a directory, or added a new subdirectory with your program, execute the Refresh method for that box to make it update its contents.

There are two ways to redraw a window, let the system do it, or do it yourself. The AutoRedraw property controls who does the redrawing when a window is uncovered. If AutoRedraw is set to True, then the Windows operating system stores a copy of everything drawn on the Form or Picture box in what is known as the persistent bitmap. It's persistent, because it isn't erased by an overlaying window. Whenever a Form or Picture box needs redrawing, the system paints a copy of the persistent bitmap on the screen, recreating the image.

If AutoRedraw is set to False, then uncovering a Form or Picture box causes a Paint event for that object, and, if you want the object redrawn, you must place code in the Paint event procedure to redraw it.

Accessing The Graphic Images

The Picture and Image properties provide a link to the graphic images displayed on a Form or Picture box. The Picture property is a link to the image displayed on the screen. It can be used to either load or store a graphic image. The Image property is a link to the persistent bitmap for a Form or Picture box, and is used to extract that image.

To store an image in a Form or Picture box at design time, select the Picture property from the Properties list, then click the ellipses to the right of the Settings box. A File open dialog box appears for you to select the picture file. Only bitmaps (.PCX), icons (.ICO), Windows metafiles (.WMF), and device-independent bitmaps (.DIB) files can be stored in a Form or Picture box. To load these properties at run time, use the GetData method to copy a picture from the Clipboard, or the LoadPicture function to load one from a disk file. To save an image, use the SetData method to put it on the Clipboard, or the SavePicture statement to put it in a disk file. See Chapter 15, "Command Reference," for the details.

Although it is certainly more convenient to let the system redraw uncovered objects, especially if the image is difficult to reconstruct, there are some caveats to using the AutoRedraw property.

1. Persistent bitmaps can use up to 30K of memory. If you have only one graphic in an application, then it probably isn't a problem. If you have many Forms and Picture boxes that contain graphics, then it could become a problem, because each of those has its own persistent bitmap.

2. When AutoRedraw is True, drawing and printing is done on the persistent bitmap. When your drawing procedure finishes, and your program is in the *idle-loop*, the persistent bitmap is copied to the screen. (A program is in the idle-loop when it is waiting for you to do something, such as press a button.) If you have a graphic procedure that takes a long time to run, you won't see anything on the screen until it finishes.

3. You can override the problem in number 2 by executing the Refresh method for the object whenever you want the persistent bitmap copied to the screen. However, this slows down your program significantly by causing your whole drawing to be drawn multiple times; once on the persistent bitmap, and again on the screen every time you execute Refresh.

4. If you change AutoRedraw from True to False at run time, then everything in the persistent bitmap becomes the background of the Form or Picture box, and is not erased with the Cls method. If you later change AutoRedraw back to True, the image in the persistent bitmap replaces everything drawn since you changed AutoRedraw to False when the image is refreshed. The image isn't immediately refreshed, but waits until you make a change and enter the idle-loop, or until you execute the Refresh method.

5. You must set AutoRedraw to True if you want to print graphics drawn on a Form or Picture box using the PrintForm method.

Setting The Scale

The default scale used in a Form or Picture box is twips, measured from the upper-left corner of the drawing area (just below the title bar of a Form). The horizontal or *x* coordinate is measured to the right from the left edge of the drawing area, and the vertical or *y* coordinate is measured down from the top edge of the drawing area. The location of the drawing point is stored in the CurrentX and CurrentY properties of the object that is being drawn. The drawing point is where the next drawing method will begin drawing, or where the next printed character will appear. Because this coordinate system is inverted, and uses units that most people are not used to, Visual Basic has the capability to redefine the coordinate system used on the drawing area of a Form, Picture box, or printer.

First is the ScaleMode property, which sets one of seven standard coordinate systems in a window (see Table 11.2). The origin is not changed by setting this property, but the unit system is. Setting this property does not change the size or physical location of any object drawn on a Form or Picture box, just the system used to measure it.

Table 11.2. Settings of the ScaleMode property.

Setting	Description
0	User-defined scale, automatically set when the scale is manually changed
1	Twips (default)
2	Points
3	Pixels
4	Characters
5	Inches
6	Millimeters
7	Centimeters

In addition to these seven built-in scales, you can define your own scale with the ScaleLeft, ScaleTop, ScaleWidth, and ScaleHeight properties. ScaleLeft and ScaleTop define the coordinates of the upper-left corner of the drawing area. ScaleWidth and ScaleHeight then define the width and height of the drawing area. Setting the ScaleHeight property to a negative number, and setting the ScaleTop property to a positive number of the same magnitude, flips the coordinate system. This moves the origin to the lower-left corner, and also makes the vertical coordinate increase as you go upwards. The Scale method is a convenient way to set the ScaleHeight, ScaleWidth, ScaleLeft, and ScaleTop properties all at once. The syntax of the Scale method is

```
[object.]Scale [(x1!,y1!) - (x2!,y2!)]
```

where *object* is the object that has its four properties changed; *x1!*, *y1!* is the *x, y* location in the new scale of the upper-left corner of the window, and *x2!*, *y2!* are the *x, y* coordinates of the lower-left corner window. These values are then combined to create the four Scale properties. When you set any of the four Scale properties, or use the Scale method, the ScaleMode property of the object is automatically changed to 0 - User Defined.

Setting Screen Colors

The ForeColor and BackColor properties control the default colors used for foreground and background objects. Foreground objects consist of lines, text, and the borders of rectangles and circles. The background is the blank area of a Form or Picture box. Two other properties, FillColor and FillStyle, control the default color and pattern used in the two fillable drawing objects, rectangles and circles—see Chapter 15, "Command Reference," for a list of values.

Colors are set at design time using the Color Palette window, or at run time using either the defined colors from the CONSTANT.TXT file included with Visual Basic, or with the RGB() and QBColor() functions. You have already set some of the colors using both the Color Palette window and color constants. Now, let's look at the numbers themselves. A color is stored as a single Long integer, but it actually contains four separate numbers stored in the four bytes of the Long integer.

The right-most three bytes contain the color in RGB format. The right-most byte contains the intensity of red, next is the intensity of green, and the third is blue. Each of the three intensities has a range of 0 to 255, where 0 is no color or black, and 255 is the brightest.

The simplest representations of these values are as hexadecimal numbers. Hexadecimal numbers are base 16, rather than base 10 like decimal numbers. The digits in a hexadecimal number range from 0 through 9, and then A through F to represent the numbers 10 through 16. In a hexadecimal number, each byte is represented by a pair of these digits. For example, &H02 is equal to 2 in decimal; the &H designator tells you that the following digits are hexadecimal and not decimal: &H09 = 9, &H0A = 10, &H0B = 11, &H0F = 15, &H10 = 16, &H11 = 17, and so on through &HFF = 255. Table 11.3 contains the hexadecimal values for the standard colors available in the file CONSTANT.TXT, included with Visual Basic. As you did in Chapter 10, "Using Random Access Files," the definitions can be loaded into the Global module and then used throughout a program.

Table 11.3. Hexadecimal color numbers for some standard colors.

Color	Hexadecimal Value
BLACK	&H000000
RED	&H0000FF
GREEN	&H00FF00
YELLOW	&H00FFFF
BLUE	&HFF0000
MAGENTA	&HFF00FF
CYAN	&HFFFF00
WHITE	&HFFFFFF

The right-most byte controls the meaning of the Long integer. If it is 0, the Long integer represents an RGB color as described above. If it has a hexadecimal value of &H80, the Long integer becomes a selector of one of the default system colors shown in Table 11.4. The default system colors are those set in the Windows control panel. Use these colors when you want parts of your application to appear the same as similar parts of the system.

Table 11.4. The hexadecimal color numbers for the system default colors.

System Color	Hexadecimal value
Gray area on Scroll bars	&H80000000
Desktop background	&H80000001
Caption of an active window	&H80000002
Caption of an inactive window	&H80000003
Menu background	&H80000004
Window background	&H80000005
Window frame	&H80000006
Menu text	&H80000007
Window text	&H80000008
Caption text	&H80000009
Border of an active window	&H8000000A
Border of an inactive window	&H8000000B
Background of MDI applications	&H8000000C
Selected items	&H8000000D
Selected text	&H8000000E
Command button	&H8000000F
Command button edge	&H80000010
Disabled text	&H80000011
Push buttons	&H80000012

The RGB() function is an alternate way of creating colors without using the constant values from CONSTANT.TXT. The RGB() function takes three integer arguments, one each for the red, green, and blue intensities, and returns the number for that color. The syntax is

```
RGB(red%,green%,blue%)
```

where `red%`, `green%`, and `blue%` are integer values in the range 0 to 255. For example,

```
Color = RGB(255,0,0)
```

would give the variable `Color` the value `&H0000FF`, which, according to Table 11.3, is bright red.

A second function, `QBColor()`, sets the color value for the 16 standard Quick Basic colors. The color is set with a simple integer argument in the range 0 to 15 according to Table 11.5.

The numbers and colors in Table 11.5 correspond to the QuickBasic, GW-BASIC, and BASICA color attributes.

Table 11.5. The color codes for use with the `QBColor` function.

Code	Color
0	Black
1	Blue
2	Green
3	Cyan
4	Red
5	Magenta
6	Yellow or Brown
7	White
8	Gray
9	Light Blue
10	Light Green
11	Light Cyan
12	Light Red
13	Light Magenta
14	Light Yellow
15	Bright White

Color Test Program

To look at some of these colors, create the Color Test program. This program allows you to set the colors and display the color values used in Labels. Use Scroll bars to set the values.

1. Open a new project, select Form1 and set its properties to

   ```
   Height = 3700
   Width = 4950
   Caption = Color Test
   ```

2. Draw a Picture box on the Form, as shown in Figure 11.1 and set its properties to

   ```
   Height = 1100
   Width = 1095
   Top = 360
   Left = 120
   ```

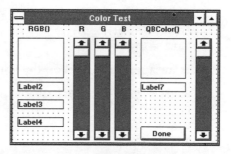

Figure 11.1. Layout of the Color Test program.

3. Draw a second Picture box on the Form and set its properties to

   ```
   Height = 1100
   Width = 1095
   Top = 360
   Left = 3000
   ```

4. Draw a Label on the Form and set its properties to

   ```
   Caption = R     G     B
   Height = 260
   Width = 1215
   Top = 0
   Left = 1440
   ```

259

5. Draw three Labels on the Form and set their properties to

```
BorderStyle = 1 - Single
Height = 260
Width = 1095
Left = 120
Top = 1560, 2040, 2520
```

6. Draw a Label above the `Picture1` box and set its properties to

```
Caption = RGB()
Height = 260
Width = 735
Top = 0
Left = 360
```

7. Draw a Label above the `Picture2` box and set its properties to

```
Caption = QBColor()
Height = 260
Width = 855
Top = 0
Left = 3120
```

8. Draw a seventh Label on the Form and set its properties to

```
BorderStyle = 1 - Single
Height = 260
Width = 1095
Top = 1560
Left = 3000
```

9. Create a control array of three Vertical Scroll bars with the properties

```
CtlName = VScroll()
Height = 2780
Width = 375
Max = 255
Min = 0
Top = 360
Left(3 values) = 1440, 1920, 2400
```

10. Draw a Vertical Scroll bar with the properties

```
CtlName = VScroll1
Height = 2780
```

```
Width = 375
Max = 15
Min = 0
Top = 360
Left = 4320
```

11. Draw a Command button with the properties

```
Caption = Done
Height = 380
Width = 1095
Top = 2760
Left = 3000
```

12. Open the Command1_Click procedure and type

```
Sub Command1_Click ()
End
End Sub
```

The following procedure is for the control array of three Vertical Scroll bars. The procedure is executed whenever the thumb of one of the Scroll bars is moved. In line 2, the Value properties of the three bars, and the RGB() function are used to set the intensity of Red, Green, and Blue in the background of the Picture1 Picture box. In line 3, the text R = is combined with the intensity of Red and stored in the Caption property of Label2. Lines 4 and 5 do the same for Green and Blue.

13. Open the VScroll_Change procedure and type

```
Sub VScroll_Change (Index As Integer)
Picture1.BackColor = RGB(VScroll(0).Value, VScroll(1).Value,
  VScroll(2).Value)
Label2.Caption = "R = " + Str$(VScroll(0).Value)
Label3.Caption = "G = " + Str$(VScroll(1).Value)
Label4.Caption = "B = " + Str$(VScroll(2).Value)
End Sub
```

The following procedure uses the Value property of the VScroll1 Scroll Bar to set the color code in the QBColor() function. That color is then used for the background of the Picture2 Picture box. The contents of the Value property are displayed in Label7.

14. Open the VScroll1_Change procedure and type

```
Sub VScroll1_Change ()
Picture2.BackColor = QBColor(Int(VScroll1.Value))
```

continues

```
Label7.Caption = Str$(VScroll1.Value)
End Sub
```

When the Form first loads, the following procedure executes both of the Change procedures to insert the initial values and colors into the Labels and Picture boxes.

15. Open the Form_Load procedure and type

```
Sub Form_Load ()
VScroll_Change 0
VScroll1_Change
End Sub
```

16. Save the project as COLOR.MAK, and COLOR.FRM.

17. Run the program, and move the three Scroll bars on the RGB() side to see how the different combinations of red, green, and blue change the color of the first picture window. Move the Scroll bar on the QBColor() side and see what colors the 16 values of the argument give. The Form should look something like Figure 11.2.

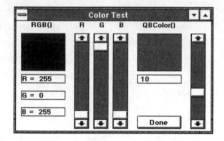

Figure 11.2. *The Color Test program.*

Controlling the Drawing Mode

Three picture properties control the drawing mode of the graphic pen; DrawMode, DrawStyle, and DrawWidth. The graphic pen is a convenient abstraction to understand drawing on a Form or Picture box. When foreground graphics are being created on a Form or Picture box, you can imagine a pen drawing those graphics. The three Draw properties described here control how the ink flows out of that fictitious pen. DrawMode is an Integer code that controls how the color being drawn on the graphic (the

Pen) combines with what is already there (the Screen). The color numbers for the pen's color and the existing screen colors are combined using the logical formulas given in Table 11.6.

Table 11.6. Codes for the `DrawMode` property.

Code	Definition	Description
1	Black	Black
2	Not Merge Pen	NOT (Pen AND Screen)
3	Mask Not Pen	NOT Pen OR Screen
4	Not Copy Pen	NOT Pen
5	Mask Pen Not	Pen OR NOT Screen
6	Invert	NOT Screen
7	Xor Pen	Pen XOR Screen
8	Not Mask Pen	NOT (Pen OR Screen)
9	Mask Pen	Pen OR Screen
10	Not Xor Pen	NOT (Pen XOR Screen)
11	Transparent	Screen
12	Merge Not Pen	NOT Pen AND Screen
13	Copy Pen (Default)	Pen
14	Merge Pen Not	Pen AND NOT Screen
15	Merge Pen	Pen AND Screen
16	White	White

Of the 16 possible modes shown, only the following six give results that are easily predictable.

1 - Black, draw with a black pen.

6 - Invert, draw with the inverse of whatever is already there.

7 -XOR Pen, draw with the colors that are not common to both the pen and screen.

11 - Transparent, don't draw anything.

13 - Copy Pen, draw with the current ForeColor (default).

16 - White, draw with a white pen.

Drawing twice with mode 7 restores the screen to what it was before it was drawn on. The other 10 values are not easily predictable, so experimenting with them is the best way to see what they do.

> A useful project would be to create a program like the Color Test program, that changes the DrawMode and DrawStyle for different foreground and background colors. You would need to draw a foreground object across the Picture boxes to have something to combine with the background colors.

The DrawStyle property sets the style for lines drawn on a Form or Picture box. Table 11.7 lists the different line styles you can set with this property. Styles 1 through 4 work only if the DrawWidth property is set to 1; otherwise the setting defaults to 0 - Solid. That is, you cannot draw wide dotted or dashed lines.

Table 11.7. Values of the DrawStyle property.

Value	Definition
0	Solid (Default)
1	Dashed line
2	Dotted line
3	Dash-dot
4	Dash-dot-dot
5	Invisible
6	Inside solid

The DrawWidth property controls the width of lines drawn on a Form or Picture box. Its value specifies the width of a line in pixels.

What You Have Learned

This chapter has dealt with the Visual Basic methods that draw on a Form, and the properties and methods that set the colors to draw with and the modes in which colors are combined. Forms and Picture boxes are the only screen objects that can be drawn on. The Printer object also can be drawn on to produce printed graphics. In detail, you have learned about

- Controlling the redrawing of a graphic.

- Loading and saving a graphic image.

- Setting the scale with the Scale method, and the ScaleHeight, ScaleWidth, ScaleLeft, and ScaleTop properties.

- Setting the foreground and background colors with constants, and the RGB( ) and QBColor( ) functions.

- Controlling how new drawing combines with what is already on a graphic.

- Drawing dotted and dashed lines.

Drawing with Visual Basic

Although Visual Basic does not have an extensive set of drawing tools, it does have a line and rectangle tool, a circle tool, and a point plotting tool. Using these simple tools, and the capability to set the screen colors, you can draw many useful figures. Or, using the graphic file importing capability, you can load a figure that has been created elsewhere directly into a Visual Basic window.

In This Chapter

This chapter shows you how to create graphics images with Visual Basic. Visual Basic has three methods for drawing on the screen, Line, Circle, and PSet. The Line method draws lines and rectangles, the Circle method draws circles and the PSet method sets the color of a single point. In addition, Visual Basic can import several of the standard picture format files and display them on a Form or picture window.

267

In this chapter, you learn to

- Draw circles and pie sections.

- Draw lines and rectangles.

- Set the color of a point on the screen.

- Import and export pictures.

Making Circles and Pie Slices

The `Circle` method is used to draw circles, filled circles, arcs, pie slices, and filled pie slices on Forms, Picture boxes, and the `Printer` object. The syntax of the `Circle` method is

```
[object.]Circle[Step](xc!,yc!),radius![,[color&],
    [startang!][,[endang!][,aspect!]]]]
```

where *object* is the object to be drawn on, (*xc!*,*yc!*) is the location of the center of the circle, *radius!* is the radius of the circle, *color&* is the color to use to draw the outline of the circle or arc, *startang!* and *endang!* are the starting and ending angles (in radians) of the pie slice, and *aspect!* is the aspect ratio of the object. If you use the *Step* argument, the coordinates of the center of the circle are treated as relative to the current drawing location. If the *startang!* and *endang!* arguments are positive, they mark the end points of an arc. If they are negative, they still mark the end points of an arc, but a line also is drawn from the center of the circle to the end of the arc, creating a pie slice.

The Drawing Test Program

The drawing test program is a simple program used to experiment with the drawing tools. First add a Picture window and some buttons to a Form. Then attach code to the buttons to experiment with circles.

1. Open a new project and select `Form1`. Set its properties as follows.

   ```
   Caption = Drawing
   Height = 4100
   Width = 6240
   ```

2. Draw a Picture box on the Form with these properties.

   ```
   CtlName = BlackBoard
   Height = 2300
   ```

```
Width = 4575
Top = 240
Left = 1440
```

3. Draw the **Q**uit Command button on the Form as shown in Figure 12.1, with these properties.

```
CtlName = QuitCmd
Caption = Quit
Height = 380
Width = 615
Top = 2640
Left = 3400
```

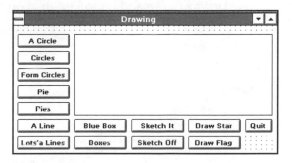

Figure 12.1. *Layout of the Drawing program.*

4. Open the `QuitCmd_Click` procedure and type

```
Sub QuitCmd_Click ()
End
End Sub
```

5. Open the Global module and type the following. The first block of color definitions comes from the CONSTANT.TXT file included with Visual Basic. The rest of the definitions are used later in this example.

```
' BackColor, ForeColor, FillColor (standard RGB colors:
  form, controls)
Global Const BLACK = &H0&
Global Const RED = &HFF&
Global Const GREEN = &HFF00&
Global Const YELLOW = &HFFFF&
Global Const BLUE = &HFF0000
Global Const MAGENTA = &HFF00FF
```

continues

```
Global Const CYAN = &HFFFF00
Global Const WHITE = &HFFFFFF
Global SketchMode As Integer
Global Const True = -1, False = 0
Type FlagType
  Xmin As Single
  Xmax As Single
  Ymin As Single
  Ymax As Single
  Stripe As Single
  Rbox As Single
End Type
```

6. Draw a Command button on the Form with the following properties.

```
CtlName = CircleCmd
Caption = A Circle
Height = 380
Width = 1215
Top = 240
Left = 120
```

7. Open the CircleCmd_Click code window and type

```
Sub CircleCmd_Click ()
'Draw a Blue circle
BlackBoard.ScaleMode = 1          '  Twips
BlackBoard.DrawStyle = 0          '  Solid
BlackBoard.FillStyle = 0          '  Solid
BlackBoard.FillColor = BLUE
BlackBoard.Cls
BlackBoard.Circle (2000, 1000), 800, RED
End Sub
```

This procedure first resets ScaleMode to twips, in case it had been changed by another command. It then turns off-line and fill patterns by setting both DrawStyle and FillStyle to 0 - Solid. It sets the FillColor to blue, then executes the Cls method on the Picture box. The Cls, or Clear Screen, method clears any drawing in the box and sets the whole box to the background color. Finally, the Circle method is applied to the Picture window. It draws a circle in the window centered on the point 2000 twips from the left side of the box and 1000 twips from the top. The radius of the circle is 800 twips, the outline color is red, and the fill color is blue.

8. Save the project as FLAG.MAK, FLAG1.FRM, and FLAGG.BAS (the reason for saving it with this name will be apparent soon). Run the program and click the **A Circle** button; the Form should look like Figure 12.2.

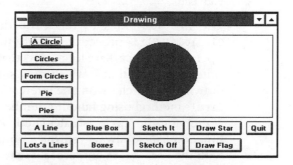

Figure 12.2. *Result of pressing the* **A Circle** *button.*

Now this isn't terribly exciting, even though it is a pretty blue circle with a bright red rim. Draw a few more circles to make things more interesting.

9. Add another Command button below the first and set its properties to

```
Height = 380
Width = 1215
Top = 720
Left = 120
Caption = Circles
CtlName = CirclesCmd
```

10. Open the CirclesCmd_Click procedure and type

```
Sub CirclesCmd_Click ()
'Draw 100 random circles
Dim Color As Long, I As Integer
BlackBoard.ScaleMode = 1          ' - Twips
BlackBoard.DrawStyle = 0          ' - Solid
BlackBoard.FillStyle = 0          ' - Solid
BlackBoard.Cls
For I = 1 To 100
 XC = Rnd(1) * BlackBoard.ScaleWidth        'line 9
 YC = Rnd(1) * BlackBoard.ScaleHeight
 Radius = Rnd(1) * BlackBoard.ScaleHeight / 2
```

continues

271

```
    Color = QBColor(Rnd(1) * 15)
    BlackBoard.FillColor = Color
    BlackBoard.Circle (XC, YC), Radius, Color
Next I
End Sub
```

The first few lines of this procedure are the same as in the `CircleCmd_Click` procedure, where the drawing environment is set up. In line 8, a For/Next loop starts that iterates the enclosed block of statements 100 times, which draws 100 circles on the Form. Just drawing 100 circles won't be interesting, so set the arguments of the `Circle` method using random numbers. In lines 9 and 10, a random center for the circle is calculated. Because the random number function `RND(1)` always returns a number between 0 and 1, scale it with the `ScaleWidth` and `ScaleHeight` properties of the Picture box. This ensures that the center is always within the Picture box.

In line 11, calculate the radius of the circle and scale it to be a maximum of one half the height of the Picture box. In line 12, use the `QBColor()` function and the `Rnd()` function to randomly select one of the 16 standard colors. Finally, in line 13, the `Circle` method is called to draw the circle.

> You can be more creative and use the `RGB()` function rather than `QBColor()`, because it's capable of creating over 16 million colors.

11. Save the program and run it. Press the **Circles** button and see what happens. You should see something like Figure 12.3 (kind of pretty, don't you think?).

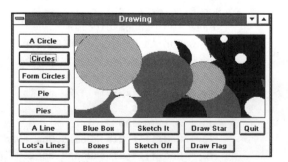

Figure 12.3. Execution of the Circles *program.*

You can draw on a Form as well as on a Picture box, as you will see.

12. Draw a command button and set its properties to

```
Height = 380
Width = 1215
Top = 1200
Left = 120
Caption = Form Circles
CtlName = FCirclesCmd
```

13. Open the `CirclesCmd_Click` procedure and copy everything but the first and last lines. Open the `FCirclesCmd_Click` procedure and paste into the template, then edit it until it reads as follows. All you have to do is to remove the name of the Picture box so that the drawing defaults to the Form.

```
Sub FCirclesCmd_Click ()
'Draw 100 random circles on the form
Dim Color As Long, I As Integer
ScaleMode = 1 ' - Twips
DrawStyle = 0 ' - Solid
FillStyle = 0 ' - Solid
Cls
For I = 1 To 100
  XC = Rnd(1) * ScaleWidth
  YC = Rnd(1) * ScaleHeight
  Radius = Rnd(1) * ScaleHeight / 2
  Color = QBColor(Rnd(1) * 15)
  FillColor = Color
  Circle (XC, YC), Radius, Color
Next I
End Sub
```

14. Save the project and run it. Click the **Form Circles** button and circles appear on the Form as shown in Figure 12.4. Note how they don't overwrite the buttons or the Picture box, but are drawn behind them.

The `Circles` method is capable of more than simply creating circles. It creates ellipses if you make the *aspect!* argument different from 1. It also creates arcs and filled pie slices if you use the *startang!* and *endang!* arguments. If *startang!* and *endang!* are positive, the method draws an arc. If they are negative, the method draws a filled pie slice.

273

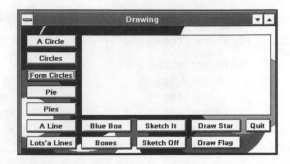

Figure 12.4. Execution of the Form Circles *program.*

15. Draw a Command button and set its properties to

```
Height = 380
Width = 1215
Top = 1680
Left = 120
Caption = Pie
CtlName = PieCmd
```

16. Open the PieCmd_Click procedure and type the following. You can copy most of it from the previous procedure to save yourself some typing.

```
Sub PieCmd_Click ()
'Draw a Red pie slice
BlackBoard.ScaleMode = 1 ' - Twips
BlackBoard.DrawStyle = 0 ' - Solid
BlackBoard.FillStyle = 0 ' - Solid
BlackBoard.FillColor = RED
BlackBoard.Cls
BlackBoard.Circle (2000, 1000), 800, BLACK, -1, -2, 1
End Sub
```

This procedure works like the Circle program, with the addition of -1 and -2 for the starting and ending angles. The angles are measured in radians, starting from the positive *x* axis (that is, 3 o'clock is 0 and noon is $\pi/2$ radians). Thus, the arc is drawn from 1 radian (1 x 180/π = 57.3 degrees) to 2 radians (114.6 degrees). The two values are negative, so lines also are drawn from the center of the circle to each end of the arc. The arc is filled with the FillColor, red, and outlined in black, as specified in the color argument of the method.

17. Save the project and run it. It should look like Figure 12.5.

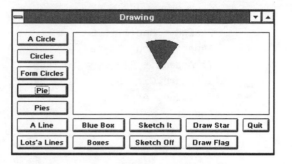

Figure 12.5. *Execution of the* Pie *program.*

Yawn, not terribly exciting, is it? But, if random circles were interesting, how about random pies?

18. Draw a Command button and set its properties to

```
Height = 380
Width = 1215
Top = 2160
Left = 120
Caption = Pies
CtlName = PiesCmd
```

19. Open the CirclesCmd_Click procedure and copy everything but the first and last lines. Open the PiesCmd_Click procedure and paste it into the template, then edit it until it reads as follows.

```
Sub PiesCmd_Click ()
'Draw 100 random pie slices
Dim Color As Long, I As Integer
Dim XC As Single, YC As Single
Dim Radius As Single
Dim PieStart As Single, PieEnd As Single
BlackBoard.ScaleMode = 1                    ' - Twips
BlackBoard.DrawStyle = 0                     ' - Solid
BlackBoard.FillStyle = 0                     ' - Solid
BlackBoard.Cls
For I = 1 To 100
  XC = Rnd(1) * BlackBoard.ScaleWidth
  YC = Rnd(1) * BlackBoard.ScaleHeight
  Radius = Rnd(1) * BlackBoard.ScaleHeight / 2 + 20
  Color = QBColor(Rnd(1) * 15)
  BlackBoard.FillColor = Color
```

continues

275

```
    PieStart = Rnd(1) * 6
    PieEnd = Rnd(1) * 6
    Aspect = Rnd(1) * 2
    If Aspect * Radius > 10 Then
BlackBoard.Circle (XC, YC), Radius, BLACK, -PieStart,
    -PieEnd, Aspect
    End If
Next I
End Sub
```

This is identical to the Circles program, with the addition of the PieStart, PieEnd, and Aspect variables. PieStart and PieEnd are given random values between 0 and 6 radians (6 is slightly less than 2π, the number of radians in a circle.) Aspect is given a value between 0 and 2. Note that an aspect of 1 is a circle, values less than 1 are ellipses with the long axis horizontal, and values greater than one produce ellipses whose long axis is vertical. Another difference is the addition of an If statement around the Circle method. There is a bug in the first version of Visual Basic that makes this method generate an overflow error for some cases where the aspect ratio and radius are small. This statement skips the Circle method if the product of the values is less than 10, which seems to prevent the method from crashing.

20. Save the project, run it, and press the **Pies** button. Yieoww! It looks like a Pac-Man attack—see Figure 12.6.

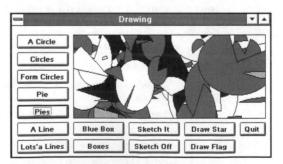

Figure 12.6. *Execution of the* Pies *program. (Look out, it's a Pac-Man attack!)*

276

Making Lines and Boxes

The Line method works much like the Circle method, except that it produces lines and filled rectangles rather than circles. The syntax of the Line method is

[*object.*]**Line**[[**Step**](*xst!*,*yst!*)]-[**Step**](*xen!*,*yen!*)[,[*color&*],**B**[**F**]]]

Here, *object* is the Form, Picture box, or Printer to be drawn on; *xst!* and *yst!* are either the *x,y* coordinates to the start of a line or the upper-left corner of a box; *xen!* and *yen!* are the *x,y* coordinates of the end of the line, or the lower-right corner of a box. If the starting point is omitted, drawing is from the current position specified by the CurrentX and CurrentY properties of the object. If Step is used, the coordinates are considered to be relative to the previous point plotted. The B parameter specifies that this is a box rather than a line, and the F parameter specifies that if it is a box, it is to be filled with the same color as the bounding line specified with *color&*, rather than using the FillColor property of the object. You can now draw a line on the Form.

1. Draw a Command button and set its properties to

```
Height = 380
Width = 1215
Top = 2640
Left = 120
Caption = A Line
CtlName = LineCmd
```

2. Open the LineCmd_Click procedure and type the following. You can copy most of it from the previous procedure and save yourself some typing.

```
Sub LineCmd_Click ()
'Draw a line
BlackBoard.ScaleMode = 1  ' - Twips
BlackBoard.DrawStyle = 0  ' - Solid
BlackBoard.FillStyle = 0  ' - Solid
BlackBoard.Cls
BlackBoard.Line (200, 500)-(4000, 2000), BLUE
End Sub
```

12

Here, the first few lines are the same as in the previous procedures. The Line method in the next-to-last line draws a blue line from a point 200 twips from the left and 500 twips from the top of the drawing area to the point 4000 twips from the left and 2000 twips from the top.

3. Save the project, run it, and press the **A Line** button. It should look like Figure 12.7.

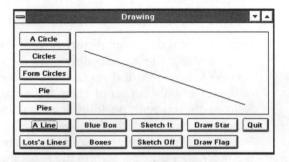

Figure 12.7. Execution of the A Line *program.*

4. Draw a Command button and set its properties to

```
Height = 380
Width = 1215
Top = 3120
Left = 120
Caption = Lots'a Lines
CtlName = LinesCmd
```

5. Open the LinesCmd_Click procedure and type the following. You can copy most of it from the Circles procedure and save yourself some typing.

```
Sub LinesCmd_Click ()
'Draw 100 random Lines
Dim Color As Long, I As Integer
Dim XL As Single, XR As Single
Dim YL As Single, YR As Single
BlackBoard.ScaleMode = 1 ' - Twips
BlackBoard.DrawStyle = 0 ' - Solid
BlackBoard.FillStyle = 0 ' - Solid
BlackBoard.Cls
```

```
For I = 1 To 100
  XL = Rnd(1) * BlackBoard.ScaleWidth
  YL = Rnd(1) * BlackBoard.ScaleHeight
  XR = Rnd(1) * BlackBoard.ScaleWidth
  YR = Rnd(1) * BlackBoard.ScaleHeight
  Color = QBColor(Rnd(1) * 15)
  BlackBoard.Line (XL, YL)-(XR, YR), Color
Next I
End Sub
```

Here, you generate four random numbers to specify the *x, y* coordinates of the start and end of a line and another random number for the color. These values are then used as arguments to the Line method, which draws a line.

6. Save the project, run it, and press the **Lots'a Lines** button. It should look like Figure 12.8.

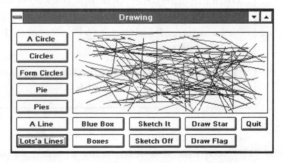

Figure 12.8. *Execution of the* Lots'a Lines *program.*

Now, try a box. Use the same procedure as the LineCmd_Click, but add the B parameter.

7. Draw a Command button and set its properties to

```
Height = 380
Width = 1215
Top = 2640
Left = 1440
Caption = Blue Box
CtlName = BoxCmd
```

An interesting variation on the Lines program is one I call Spinners, shown in Plate III. As with all the examples, it uses the Drawing Test Program as a base. First, two pairs of points are selected randomly. Next, the program moves 1/20 of the distance from one point to the next in a pair, and a line is drawn from there to the equivalent point between the other pair of points. The program then steps another 1/20 of the distance and draws another line. This continues until it reaches the second point in each pair. Then, two new pairs of points are created with the second point from each of the original two pairs, plus two new random points added to them. The program continues drawing lines and adding new points until it completes 20 pairs of points.

Another variation is to draw multisided geometric figures. Set the program up to calculate points on a circle, input the angle through which to move each step, and draw a line. Continue rotating and drawing lines until you come back to your starting point. If you set the angle to 120 degrees, you get a triangle. If you set it to 90 degrees, you get a square. If you set it to 88 degrees, the program draws around in a circle 44 times.

There are many other variations; have fun with this program and see what you can come up with.

8. Open the BoxCmd_Click procedure and type the following. You can copy most of it from the LineCmd_Click procedure and save yourself some typing.

```
Sub BoxCmd_Click ()
'Draw a blue box
BlackBoard.ScaleMode = 1  ' - Twips
BlackBoard.DrawStyle = 0   ' - Solid
BlackBoard.FillStyle = 0   ' - Solid
BlackBoard.FillColor = BLUE
BlackBoard.Cls
BlackBoard.Line (200, 500)-(4000, 2000), BLACK, B
End Sub
```

9. Save the project, run it, and click the **Blue Box** button. The window should now look like Figure 12.9.

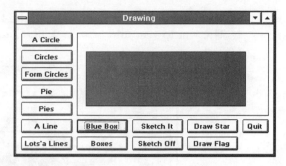

Figure 12.9. *Execution of the* Blue Box *program.*

Now, how about a bunch of boxes.

10. Draw a Command button and set its properties to

```
Height = 380
Width = 1215
Top = 3120
Left = 1440
Caption = Boxes
CtlName = BoxesCmd
```

11. Open the BoxesCmd_Click procedure and type the following code. Copy most of it from the LinesCmd_Click procedure to save yourself some typing.

```
Sub BoxesCmd_Click ()
'Draw 100 random boxes
Dim Color As Long, I As Integer
Dim XL As Single, XR As Single
Dim YL As Single, YR As Single
BlackBoard.ScaleMode = 1 ' - Twips
BlackBoard.DrawStyle = 0 ' - Solid
BlackBoard.FillStyle = 0 ' - Solid
BlackBoard.Cls
For I = 1 To 100
  XL = Rnd(1) * BlackBoard.ScaleWidth
  YL = Rnd(1) * BlackBoard.ScaleHeight
  XR = Rnd(1) * BlackBoard.ScaleWidth
  YR = Rnd(1) * BlackBoard.ScaleHeight
  Color = QBColor(Rnd(1) * 15)
  BlackBoard.FillColor = Color
  BlackBoard.Line (XL, YL)-(XR, YR), Color, B
Next I
End Sub
```

12. Save the project, run it, and click the **Boxes** button. Psychedelic! The window should now look like Figure 12.10.

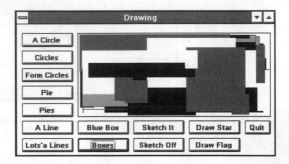

Figure 12.10. Execution of the Boxes *program.*

Drawing Points

Points on the screen are individually set with the PSet method, and read with the Point method. The syntax of the PSet method is

`[object.]PSet [Step](x!,y!)[,color&]`

Here, *object* is the Form, Picture box, or Printer to draw on, *x!* and *y!* give the *x,y* location of the point, and *color&* indicates the color you've chosen for the point. If Step is used, the point is relative to the previous point. If *color&* is omitted, the current foreground color is used. The syntax of the Point method is

`[object.]Point (x!,y!)`

The definitions of the arguments are the same as for the PSet method, except that this method returns the color rather than setting it.

To draw points on the screen, you need a way to select the point to color, and the mouse and the MouseMove event do the job. The MouseMove event is generated whenever the location of the mouse has changed after some short length of time. The MouseMove event procedure is passed the state of the mouse's buttons and its *x,y* location; use that information to make a black dot at the mouse location if the mouse button is down.

1. Draw a Command button and set its properties to

```
Height = 380
Width = 1215
Top = 2640
Left = 2760
Caption = Sketch It
CtlName = SketchCmd
```

2. Draw a second Command button below it and set its properties to

```
Height = 380
Width = 1215
Top = 3120
Left = 2760
Caption = Sketch Off
CtlName = UnSketchCmd
```

3. Open the SketchCmd_Click procedure and type the following code. This command initializes the Picture box and sets the flag SketchMode to True.

```
Sub SketchCmd_Click ()
'Turn on sketch mode
SketchMode = True
BlackBoard.ScaleMode = 1   ' - Twips
BlackBoard.DrawStyle = 0   ' - Solid
BlackBoard.FillStyle = 0   ' - Solid
BlackBoard.ForeColor = BLACK
BlackBoard.Cls
End Sub
```

4. Open the UnSketchCmd_Click procedure and type the following code. This command sets the flag SketchMode to False.

```
Sub UnSketchCmd_Click ()
'Sketch Mode off
SketchMode = False
End Sub
```

5. Open the BlackBoard_MouseMove procedure and type

```
Sub BlackBoard_MouseMove (Button As Integer,
   Shift As Integer, x As Single, y As Single)
If SketchMode = True And Button <> 0 Then
BlackBoard.PSet (x, y)
End If
End Sub
```

Whenever the mouse moves, this command is executed. It checks to see that SketchMode is True, and that a mouse button is down. If this is True, it sets the point at the mouse location to the current foreground color (black).

6. Save the project, run it, and click the **Sketch It** button. Move the mouse into the Picture box, press the button, and move the mouse.

   A trail of dots follows the mouse's motion. The spacing of the dots and the speed at which you move the mouse indicates how often Visual Basic checks to see whether the mouse has moved. The screen should look like Figure 12.11.

7. Click the **Sketch Off** button when you are done.

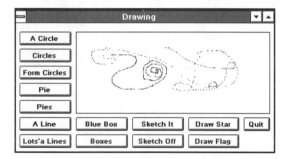

Figure 12.11. Execution of the Sketch It *program.*

Now that you know how to use the drawing programs, try something more interesting—drawing an American flag on the screen. The red and white stripes, a blue rectangle, and fifty white stars all can be drawn with the line method, the first two with the B option and the stars without this option.

The stars present a special problem, because they have to be filled with white, but there is no filled star method available, nor is there a Paint method. The Paint method is available in other BASICs, and it fills any enclosed area with a specific color. It isn't available in Visual Basic. Writing a Paint method would be an interesting evening's project, but you can live without it here, because the stars are going to be small, so you can fill them with lines. First create the star-drawing procedure. There is a Paint event, but it has nothing to do with filling in a graphic. The Paint event tells you when a window needs to be redrawn—see Chapter 11, "The Use of Color."

8. Draw a Command button and set its properties to

```
Height = 380
Width = 1215
Top = 2640
Left = 4080
Caption = Draw Star
CtlName = StarCmd
```

9. Open the StarCmd_Click method and type

```
Sub StarCmd_Click ()
'Draw a star
Dim theFlag As FlagType
theFlag.Xmin = 0      'Bounding box
theFlag.Xmax = 44
theFlag.Ymin = 0
theFlag.Ymax = 26
theFlag.Stripe = 0    'Stripe height
theFlag.Rbox = 44     'Right side of the star box
ScaleIt theFlag, BlackBoard
BlackBoard.Cls
BlueRec theFlag, BlackBoard
Star 44 / 2, 26 / 2, 26 / 2, BlackBoard
End Sub
```

This procedure uses the FlagType record type, defined in the Global module, to save space passing information to the Sub procedures. The FlagType type contains the *bounding box* of the rectangle to hold the flag, the width of a stripe, and the width of the blue rectangle. A bounding box is a rectangle that completely contains the flag. In this procedure, you want to draw a single star on a blue background, so set the stripe height to 0 and the width of the blue box to the width of the flag. After theFlag is loaded, the procedure calls the ScaleIt Sub procedure to scale the Picture box. Note that the procedure is passed only the name of the record type variable theFlag, rather than each of its components. The components are still passed, but in the record type variable.

Next, the procedure clears the Picture box, calls the BlueRec Sub procedure to draw the blue rectangle, and then calls the Star Sub procedure to draw a star. The arguments to the Star Sub procedure are the *x, y* location of the center of the star, the length of a side, and the object to draw them on. Now, create those three Sub procedures.

10. Open the general method and type

```
Sub ScaleIt (C As FlagType, Pic As Control)
If TypeOf Pic Is PictureBox Then
  Pic.ScaleMode = 0                ' - User defined scale
  Pic.Scale (C.Xmin, C.Ymax)-(C.Xmax, C.Ymin)
End If
End Sub
```

Note, in the heading of this procedure, the `Pic As Control` clause. The `Control` type allows you to pass a control name as an argument to a `Sub` procedure. Line 2 tests the control passed to the procedure to make sure it is a `PictureBox`. The procedure then sets the `ScaleMode` to `0 - User Defined`, and uses the `Scale` method to set the scales of the Picture box. The `Scale` method sets all the `Scale` properties at once.

11. Select the general procedure and type

```
Sub BlueRec (C As FlagType, Pic As Control)
'Draw blue rectangle
Pic.Line (C.Xmin, 6 * C.Stripe)-(C.Rbox, C.Ymax), BLUE, BF
End Sub
```

This routine draws the blue rectangle in the upper-left corner of the flag. To do so, it uses the `Line` method with the `B` and `F` options to draw a filled, blue rectangle.

12. Select the general procedure and type

```
Sub Star (XC, YC, Slen As Single, Pic As Control)
'Draw a 5 pointed star, one point at a time.
Dim Lmin As Single, Lmax As Single
Lmin = Slen * .25
Lmax = Slen * .75
PointAng = 1.26    'radians, 2*Pi/5, the angle between points
HPointAng = PointAng / 2  'the half angle of a point
RotAng = 1.57    'radians, rotate star
For K = 1 To 5
  'x,y location of the point
  Xpt = Lmax * Cos(RotAng + (K - 1) * PointAng) + XC
  Ypt = Lmax * Sin(RotAng + (K - 1) * PointAng) + YC
  'x,y location of the right valley
  XptR = Lmin * Cos(RotAng - HPointAng + (K - 1) * PointAng) + XC
  YptR = Lmin * Sin(RotAng - HPointAng + (K - 1) * PointAng) + YC
  'x,y location of the left valley
```

```
            XptL = Lmin * Cos(RotAng + HPointAng + (K - 1) * PointAng) + XC
            YptL = Lmin * Sin(RotAng + HPointAng + (K - 1) * PointAng) + YC
            'x,y location of the opposite valley
            XptB = Lmin * Cos((K - 1) * PointAng - RotAng) + XC
            YptB = Lmin * Sin((K - 1) * PointAng - RotAng) + YC
            'Draw the three lines
            Pic.Line (XptR, YptR)-(Xpt, Ypt), WHITE
            Pic.Line (Xpt, Ypt)-(XptL, YptL), WHITE
            Pic.Line (Xpt, Ypt)-(XptB, YptB), WHITE
        Next K
    End Sub
```

This procedure first defines Lmin and Lmax as one quarter and three quarters of the point length SLen. It then defines PointAng as 1.26 radians, which is the angle between two points on a 5-pointed star; HPointAng, which is half PointAng; and RotAng, the angle through which you want to rotate the star before drawing it.

Using this data, the procedure starts a For/Next loop over the five points on a star. The block of code within the loop calculates the following four x,y locations on a star's point.

- Xpt,Ypt: The location of the tip of the point.

- XptR,YptR: The valley between two points to the right of the first point.

- XptL,YptL: The location of the valley to the left of the first point.

- XptB, YptB: The location of the valley between two points, on the opposite side of the star from the point being drawn.

Finally, three lines are drawn on the object, one on each side of a point and one down the center. The line down the center fills the object when it is small. The loop causes five points to be drawn on the Picture window, rotating each to line up the valley points.

13. Save the procedure, run it, and press the **Draw Star** button. A star like the one in Figure 12.12 is drawn. Note how each point is made up of three lines. When they are drawn small, the points appear to be filled.

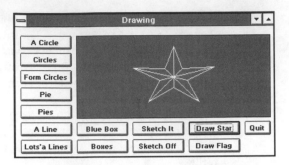

Figure 12.12. *Execution of the* Draw Star *program.*

Now, draw the flag.

14. Draw a Command button and set its properties to

```
Height = 380
Width = 1215
Top = 3120
Left = 4080
Caption = Draw Flag
CtlName = FlagCmd
```

15. Open the FlagCmd_Click procedure and type

```
Sub FlagCmd_Click ()
'Draw an American Flag
Dim theFlag As FlagType
theFlag.Xmin = 0       'Bounding box
theFlag.Xmax = 44
theFlag.Ymin = 0
theFlag.Ymax = 26
theFlag.Stripe = 2     'Stripe height
theFlag.Rbox = 26      'Right side of the star box
ScaleIt theFlag, BlackBoard
BlackBoard.Cls
DrawStripes theFlag, BlackBoard
BlueRec theFlag, BlackBoard
DrawStars theFlag, BlackBoard
End Sub
```

This time the theFlag record type variable is loaded with values that create a flag. The width of the bounding box is 44 user-defined units, and the height is 26; each stripe is 2 units tall, and the blue box is 26 units wide. After the record type variable is loaded, the ScaleIt

288

procedure is called to scale the Picture box, Cls is called to clear it, and the DrawStripes Sub procedure is called to draw stripes on it. Next, the BlueRec Sub procedure is called to draw the blue rectangle, and finally, the DrawStars Sub procedure is called to draw the stars.

16. Open the general procedure and type

```
Sub DrawStripes (C As FlagType, Pic As Control)
'Draw stripes
Dim I As Integer, Color As Double
'Calculate the position of the stripes, and
'alternate the colors between RED and WHITE.
Color = WHITE
For I = 1 To 13
If Color = WHITE Then Color = RED Else Color = WHITE
Pic.Line (C.Xmin, (I - 1) * C.Stripe)-(C.Xmax, I *
  C.Stripe), Color, BF
Next I
End Sub
```

This procedure draws the 13 alternating red and white stripes. There are actually 6 long stripes and 7 short stripes, but draw 13 long stripes, and then draw the blue rectangle over them. The procedure first defines the variable Color as white, and creates a loop over the 13 stripes, starting at the bottom. The first statement in the For/Next loop causes the value of Color to alternate between red and white. The second uses the Line command with the B and F options to draw a stripe.

17. Open the general procedure and type

```
Sub DrawStars (C As FlagType, Pic As Control)
Dim I As Integer, J As Integer
'Calculate the position of each star, then draw it.
DX = C.Rbox / 12
DY = 7 * C.Stripe / 10
'First the 5 rows of 6 stars
For I = 1 To 5
  For J = 1 To 6
    XC = -DX + J * 2 * DX
    YC = 6 * C.Stripe - DY + I * 2 * DY
    Star XC, YC, C.Stripe / 2, Pic
  Next J
Next I
'Next the 4 rows of 5 stars
For I = 1 To 4
```

continues

```
    For J = 1 To 5
      XC = J * 2 * DX
      YC = 6 * C.Stripe + I * 2 * DY
      Star XC, YC, C.Stripe / 2, Pic
    Next J
  Next I
End Sub
```

This last procedure calculates the position of each star on the blue rectangle, and calls the Star Sub procedure to draw them. It does this by first calculating the positions of five rows of six stars, and then calculating the positions of the remaining four rows of five stars. In both cases nested For/Next loops are used. The first loop selects the five rows, and the second selects the six stars along each row. DX and DY are the star-to-star spacings in the horizontal and vertical directions.

18. Save the project, run it, and click the **Draw Flag** button. The flag appears, as shown in Figure 12.13 (see also Plate I), and makes you want to stand up and cheer.

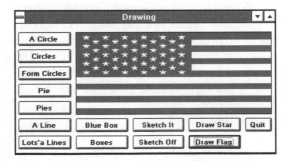

Figure 12.13. *Execution of the* Draw Flag *program.*

If you look at Plates I and III, you will notice that they are similar to those developed in the text, but enlarged to full screen. They are actually the same program as the Drawing Test program. I expanded the Form to full screen with the **Maximize** button, moved the buttons around and stretched the Picture box to fill most of the screen. Since the Picture box was used to scale the problem, no changes need to be made to the code. Try this variation, it's simple to do.

The Plot It Program

If you can tear yourself away from the circles and pies, you can put all this together and make something useful. The Plot It program is a simple data plotter that demonstrates the principles of creating a grid and plotting data. The program itself consists of two Forms, one for the plot and the second for inputting the data. It's not a sophisticated plotting program, but could easily be expanded, or incorporated into another program.

1. Open a new project, select Form1, and set its properties to

   ```
   Caption = Plot It
   Height = 3700
   Width = 7650
   BorderStyle = 3 - Fixed Double
   MaxButton = False
   ```

2. Draw a Picture box on the Form as shown in Figure 12.14 and set its properties to

   ```
   CtlName = PlotPic
   Height = 2540
   Width = 5055
   Top = 240
   Left = 2160
   ```

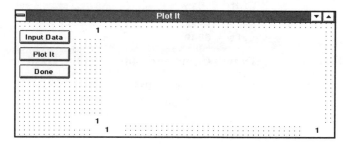

Figure 12.14. Layout of the Plot It *program.*

3. Draw a Label on the Form and set its properties to

   ```
   Caption = 1
   CtlName = YmaxLabel
   Alignment = 1 - Right Justify
   Height = 260
   Width = 615
   Top = 120
   Left = 1440
   ```

291

4. Draw a Label on the Form and set its properties to

```
Caption = 1
CtlName = YminLabel
Alignment = 1 - Right Justify
Height = 260
Width = 615
Top = 2640
Left = 1440
```

5. Draw a Label on the Form and set its properties to

```
Caption = 1
CtlName = XminLabel
Alignment = 2 - Center
Height = 260
Width = 615
Top = 2880
Left = 1920
```

6. Draw a Label on the Form and set its properties to

```
Caption = 1
CtlName = XmaxLabel
Alignment = 2 - Center
Height = 260
Width = 615
Top = 2880
Left = 6840
```

7. Draw a Command button on the Form and set its properties to

```
Caption = Input Data
CtlName = InputCmd
Height = 380
Width = 1215
Top = 240
Left = 120
```

8. Draw a Command button on the Form and set its properties to the following. Disable this button at the start, because you don't want to plot anything until some data has been inserted.

```
Caption = Plot It
CtlName = PlotItCmd
Enabled = False
```

```
Height = 380
Width = 1215
Top = 720
Left = 120
```

9. Draw a Command button on the Form and set its properties to

```
Caption = Done
CtlName = DoneCmd
Height = 380
Width = 1215
Top = 1200
Left = 120
```

10. Open the Global module and type

```
Global xyData(500, 2) As Single        'x,y data
Global DataLen As Single               'length of filled array
Global Xmin As Single, Xmax As Single  'x axis limits
Global Ymin As Single, Ymax As Single  'y axis limits
Global Const True = -1, False = 0
Global Const Modal = 1
```

The first line defines a large, two-dimensional array to hold the *x,y* data to be plotted. Next is DataLen, which contains the number of elements of xyData that have been filled with data. Xmin, Xmax, Ymin, and Ymax contain the upper and lower x and y limits for the plot. The last two lines define the constants True, False and Modal.

11. Open the InputCmd_Click procedure and type

```
Sub InputCmd_Click ()
InputDialog.Show Modal
PlotItCmd.Enabled = True
End Sub
```

This procedure displays the second Form as a Modal Form for inputting the data. When that procedure completes, this procedure enables the **Plot It** button.

12. Open the PlotItCmd_Click procedure and type

```
Sub PlotItCmd_Click ()
DrawAxes
PlotData
End Sub
```

This procedure simply calls two other procedures to create the plot, `DrawAxes` to draw the axes, and `PlotData` to plot the data.

13. Open the `DoneCmd_Click` procedure and type

```
Sub DoneCmd_Click ()
End
End Sub
```

14. Open the `general` procedure and type

```
Sub DrawAxes ()
Dim VTic As Single, HTic As Single
Dim ShapeFac As Single
PlotPic.ScaleMode = 1
ShapeFac = PlotPic.Width / PlotPic.Height
VTic = .02 * (Ymax - Ymin)
HTic = .02 * (Xmax - Xmin) / ShapeFac
PlotPic.Scale (Xmin - HTic, Ymax + VTic)-(Xmax + HTic, Ymin -VTic)
PlotPic.Line (Xmin - HTic, Ymin)-(Xmax + HTic, Ymin)  'line 9
PlotPic.Line (Xmin, Ymin - VTic)-(Xmin, Ymax + VTic)
PlotPic.Line (Xmax, Ymin - VTic)-(Xmax, Ymin + VTic)
PlotPic.Line (Xmax / 2, Ymin - VTic)-(Xmax / 2, Ymin + VTic)
PlotPic.Line (Xmin - HTic, Ymax)-(Xmin + HTic, Ymax)
PlotPic.Line (Xmin - HTic, Ymax / 2)-(Xmin + HTic, Ymax / 2)
XminLabel.Caption = Str$(Xmin)                       'line 15
XmaxLabel.Caption = Str$(Xmax)
YminLabel.Caption = Str$(Ymin)
YmaxLabel.Caption = Str$(Ymax)
End Sub
```

This procedure draws the axes on the `PlotPic` Picture box. In line 4, it resets the scale to twips, and then, in line 5, it calculates `ShapeFac`, a shape factor, from the width and height of the Picture box. `ShapeFac` is used to adjust the length of horizontal lines so that they appear the same length as similar vertical lines even though the box isn't square. Next, the routine defines `VTic` and `HTic`, the vertical and horizontal Tic mark lengths, as two percent of the height or width of the box, with `HTic` adjusted with `ShapeFac`.

Next, the routine uses the `Scale` method to set the scale of the Picture box to that stored in `Xmin`, `Xmax`, `Ymin`, and `Ymax`. The minimum and maximum values are moved in from the edge of the Picture box by the Tic amount so there is room to draw the Tic marks. In lines 9 through 14, the procedure uses the `Line` method to draw the *x* and *y* axes, and Tic marks at the ends and centers of each axis. In lines 15 through 18, the values of the upper and lower limits are inserted into the Label boxes that mark those limits.

15. Open the general procedure and type

```
Sub PlotData ()
Dim I As Integer
PlotPic.CurrentX = xyData(1, 1)
PlotPic.CurrentY = xyData(1, 2)
For I = 2 To DataLen
  PlotPic.Line -(xyData(I, 1), xyData(I, 2))
Next I
End Sub
```

The PlotData procedure plots the data on the existing grid. It first moves the drawing point to the first x,y data point by setting the values of the CurrentX and CurrentY properties. It then loops over all the data in the xyData array, using the Line method with only one data point to draw lines from the current position to that given in the argument to the method.

This completes the plotting portion of the program. Now it's time to plot some data. In this demonstration, I create a simple dialog box for inputting the data. Depending on your application, you might have the data produced by a calculation, or read from a data file. To make the plotting portion work, you have to fill the data array xyData(), put the number of data points in the DataLen variable, and set the plot limits in the Xmin, Xmax, Ymin, and Ymax variables.

16. Attach a new Form to the project and set its properties to

```
Caption = Input Dialog
Height = 3700
Width = 5250
BorderStyle = 3 - Fixed Double
MinButton = False
MaxButton = False
```

17. Draw a Text box on the Form, as shown in Figure 12.15, and set its properties to

```
CtlName = DataBox
Height = 2540
Width = 2295
Top = 480
Left = 120
ScrollBars = 2 - Vertical
MultiLine = True
Text = ""
```

295

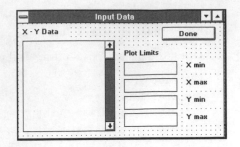

Figure 12.15. *Layout of the Input dialog box.*

 18. Draw four Text boxes to hold the plot limits, and set their properties according to Table 12.1.

Table 12.1. Properties for the four Text boxes.

CtlName	Height	Width	Left	Top	Text
XminBox	380	1335	2640	1080	""
XmaxBox	380	1335	2640	1560	""
YminBox	380	1335	2640	2040	""
YmaxBox	380	1335	2640	2520	""

 19. Draw a Label box on the Form and set its properties to

```
Caption = X-Y Data
Height = 260
Width = 1095
Top = 120
Left = 120
```

 20. Draw another Label on the Form and set its properties to

```
Caption = Plot Limits
Height = 260
Width = 1455
Top = 720
Left = 2640
```

 21. Draw four Labels on the Form and set their properties according to Table 12.2.

Table 12.2. Properties for the four Labels.

Caption	Height	Width	Left	Top
X min	260	855	4200	1080
X max	260	855	4200	1560
Y min	260	855	4200	2040
Y max	260	855	4200	2520

22. Draw a **Done** Command button and set its properties to

```
CtlName = DoneCmd
Caption = Done
Height = 380
Width = 1335
Top = 120
Left = 3600
```

The following four procedures copy the values of Xmin, Xmax, Ymin, and Ymax from the Text boxes into the variables whenever the user types in one of the boxes.

23. Open the XminBox_Change procedure and type

```
Sub XminBox_Change ()
Xmin = Val(XminBox.Text)
End Sub
```

24. Open the XmaxBox_Change procedure and type

```
Sub XmaxBox_Change ()
Xmax = Val(XmaxBox.Text)
End Sub
```

25. Open the YminBox_Change procedure and type

```
Sub YminBox_Change ()
Ymin = Val(YminBox.Text)
End Sub
```

26. Open the YmaxBox_Change procedure and type

```
Sub YmaxBox_Change ()
Ymax = Val(YmaxBox.Text)
End Sub
```

297

27. Open the `DoneCmd_Click` procedure and type

```
Sub DoneCmd_Click ()
Dim Start As Integer, End1 As Integer, End2 As Integer
'Check limit boxes
If (XmaxBox.Text = "" Or XminBox.Text = ""
    Or YmaxBox.Text = "" Or YminBox.Text = "") Then
  MsgBox "Type plot limits first."
  Exit Sub
End If
'Load the data array
DataLen = 0
Start = 1
End1 = InStr(Start, DataBox.Text, ",")                    'line 11
End2 = InStr(End1 + 1, DataBox.Text, Chr$(13))
While End1 <> 0 And End2 <> 0                             'line 13
  DataLen = DataLen + 1
  xyData(DataLen, 1) = Val(Mid$(DataBox.Text, Start, End1 - Start))
  xyData(DataLen, 2) = Val(Mid$(DataBox.Text, End1 + 1,
      End2 - End1 - 1))
  Start = End2 + 1
  End1 = InStr(Start, DataBox.Text, ",")
  End2 = InStr(End1 + 1, DataBox.Text, Chr$(13))
Wend
InputDialog.Hide
End Sub
```

This procedure must take the data out of the Text box, convert it to numbers, and store those numbers in the data array. You have to type *x, y* data into the Text box, separating the *x, y* values with commas and pressing Enter after each *y* data value. In line 4, the procedure first checks the four plot limit boxes to see that the user has typed data in each one. If not, the procedure puts up an error message and exits. If data is in all the boxes, the procedure begins looking for data in the `DataBox` Text box.

Using the `InStr()` function in line 11, it locates the first comma in the `Text` property of `DataBox` and assigns the character number to `End1`. In line 12 it looks for the first carriage return (ASCII code 13) and assigns its location to `End2`. The *x* data should be between the beginning of the string and the comma, and the *y* data should be between the comma and the carriage return. In line 13, the procedure starts a `While/Wend` loop that continues until the `InStr()` functions don't find any more values. If a pair of values is found, the values are added to the data array.

In line 14, the value of DataLen is incremented. In line 15 the Mid$() function is used to extract the substring containing the *x* value from the Text property of DataBox. The value lies between character positions Start and End1. The extracted substring is immediately converted to a value with the Val() function and stored in xyData. Line 16 does the same for the *y* value. In line 17, the starting position stored in Start is moved to one character beyond the carriage return. The procedure then looks for another comma and carriage return. This loop continues until it can't find any more numbers. The procedure then hides itself, and returns to Form1 so you can plot the data.

28. Save the project as PLOT.MAK, PLOT1.FRM, PLOT2.FRM, and PLOTG.BAS.

29. Run the program, press the **Input Data** button and type some data, including the plot limits. The Input dialog box should look like Figure 12.16.

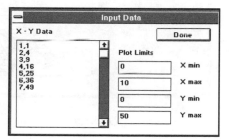

Figure 12.16. *The Input dialog box for the* Plot It *program.*

30. Click **Done** on the Input dialog box, then press the **Plot It** button on Form1. The data is plotted in the Picture box, which should now look like Figure 12.17.

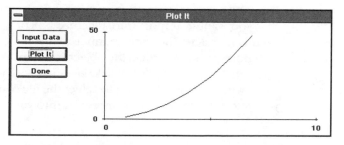

Figure 12.17. *Plotting data with the* Plot It *program.*

Many variations of this program can be created, because it is still in a primitive form. It lacks Labels for the axes and a title, which could be loaded in the Input dialog box. It also automatically could calculate the plot limits by examining the maximum and minimum values in the data. How you change it depends on what you want it to do. Don't let the fact that this is a simple plot program make you think that it has limited scope. As Figure 12.18 shows, you can use this program to create a 3D wireframe plot. In fact, the plot form is identical to that developed here in this text. The wireframe plot is created completely by manipulating the data. The plotted data is $\mathrm{Cos}(x\,\pi\,2)\mathrm{Cos}(y\,\pi/2)\,\mathrm{Exp}(xy/10)$.

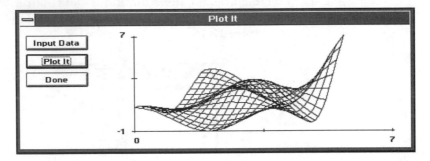

Figure 12.18. *A 3D wireframe plot created with the* `Plot It` *program.*

Importing a Picture

Drawing pictures is fun, but you might have a more complicated illustration that you want to import into a Picture box or a Form. At design-time, you do this in exactly the same manner that you created the arrow keys in the Datebook program. Select the object you want to attach the drawing to, and select its `Picture` property. Click the ellipsis (...) in the Settings window and a File window opens for you to select the file containing the picture. When you select it, the picture is imported into your object and displayed.

You can do similar things at run-time, using the `LoadPicture()` function. The function has the syntax

`LoadPicture[(`*path$*`)]`

Here, *path$* is the path and name of the picture file to load. Equate the `Picture` Property of a Form or Picture box to this function to load it. Visual Basic currently recognizes bit map (.BMP), icon (.ICO), and Windows metafile (.WMF) files.

If you have a picture in a window and want to save it in a file, use the `SavePicture` statement. The `SavePicture` statement has the syntax

`SavePicture` *picturevariable*, *path$*

Here, the *picturevariable* argument is the `Picture` or `Image` property of a Form or Picture box, and *path$* is a string containing the path and file name of the file in which to store the picture. Pictures are saved as bit maps (.BMP) files.

What You Have Learned

In this chapter, you read about with the Visual Basic methods that draw on a Form. Forms and Picture boxes are the only screen objects that can be drawn on. The Printer object also may be drawn on to produce printed graphics. In detail, you have read about

- Using the `Circle` method to draw circles and pie sections.

- Using the `Line` method to draw lines and rectangles.

- Using the `PSet` method to set the color of a point on the screen.

- Using the `Point` method to get the color of a point on the screen.

- Importing pictures with `LoadPicture` and saving pictures with `SavePicture`.

Debugging and Error Trapping

You've just completed your latest and greatest application that will surely bring the world rushing to your door, but when you run it, it does something entirely unexpected. Say hello to a programming bug. There is no way to completely avoid these little monsters, so now you must look at what you can do about them. (Kicking the computer might make you feel better, but won't make the bugs go away.)

In This Chapter

This chapter covers two related topics, debugging and error trapping. Although they sound similar, they are inherently different. Debugging is the process of eliminating known errors from a program. These errors include misspelled keywords, misplaced commas, and incorrect program logic. Error trapping is the process of handling errors that you cannot eliminate by changing the code. Errors which can be trapped include numeric

overflow and divide-by-zero. These types of errors are caused, for the most part, by unexpected values appearing in a formula. In this chapter, you learn how to

- Debug applications.

- Locate and fix syntax errors.

- Locate and fix logical errors.

- Use tools that find errors.

- Use error trapping.

- Handle trapped errors.

The Art of Debugging

Debugging computer programs is more art than engineering, which is often disconcerting to new programmers who are becoming used to the rigid structure of a computer language. But there is no rigorous method for locating programming bugs. Successfully locating logical errors in complex programs calls on all of a programmer's knowledge and experience. The more the programmer knows about the operation of the language, the problem being solved, and even the basic electronic operation of a computer, the more quickly he or she can locate the problem. Fixing a problem is usually trivial compared to finding it.

However, now that I have worried you somewhat, I must add that being able to locate and fix a problem in a huge mass of code is an extremely rewarding experience, with nearly immediate gratification. When a bug is fixed, the program works, (well, most of the time) right now. In no other branch of engineering can you so quickly fix a problem and see the results.

Luckily, the complexity of your programs increases gradually with your experience and ability, so the increase in bugs you generate is gradual, too. Don't be overly worried about the bugs in your programs; finding them is part of the fun.

The first step in debugging is having well documented, modularized code. Keep code blocks and procedures reasonably small and as single-minded as possible. That is, make sure the function of each block or procedure is well defined and well known. Use remarks liberally, especially whenever you do something that isn't obvious. This adds to the work of creating a code, but it dramatically reduces the time needed to correct or change one.

The second step in debugging is to realize that a computer is completely logical, and does exactly what you tell it to do. A program bug can make a computer seem to have a peculiar mind of its own, but realize it is actually doing what you told it to do, literally. With that in mind, read on and discover bugs.

Syntax Errors

The most common bug is the syntax error, and it is also the easiest to find. Most syntax errors are found by the Visual Basic interpreter as soon as you type a line of code. Others show up as soon as you try to run your code. Thus, syntax errors come in two flavors, design-time and run-time.

Syntax errors are generated when you stray from the strict guidelines, or grammar, of the computer language. They involve misspelling key words, inserting the wrong number or type of arguments to a function, and inserting the wrong punctuation in a programming statement.

Design-Time Syntax Errors

Design-time errors are revealed to you when you are typing your code. They are errors that involve the syntax of a single line of code, such as missed punctuation or misspelled key words. The design-time interpreter looks at each line you type as soon as you move the cursor out of that line. It then compares what you have typed with the syntax of the language. It cannot check the value or type of variables in a statement, only the number and punctuation. If it can't make sense of what you have done, it tells you so.

You probably already have seen several of these errors as you have typed the example programs in this book. Either that, or you are a splendid typist, and never make a mistake. I wish I had that capability, but my fingers don't always seem to do what my head is telling them to do, so I generate syntax errors frequently. Luckily, I know right away when I have made an error, and can fix it.

Run-Time Syntax Errors

The second type of syntax error is the run-time error (although not all run-time errors are syntax errors). Run-time errors occur when you use the wrong type of argument in a function, or have incorrect block structures. Most Visual Basic functions and methods require specific variable types as arguments. If you give a function the wrong variable type, the run-time syntax checker stops the program, displays the offending program line, and displays a message about possible corrections to the line. This can be done only at run time because the code that defines the variable types, in this case, the Dim and Global statements, is physically separated from the place the variable is actually used. For example,

```
Dim B as Integer
A = Val(B)
```

The Val() function expects B to be a String variable. As the point of execution reaches the first statement, B is defined as an Integer. When it reaches the second statement, Val() generates an error.

Another common run-time error is misused block structures, such as a block If statement missing its End If statement, or a For/Next loop missing its Next statement. Again, these errors cannot be determined at design time, but are revealed when you attempt to run the code and check whether blocks are incorrectly set up. For example,

```
A = 3 * 5
Printer.Print A
Next I
```

The Next I statement has to have a matching For statement, so this code generates a run-time error.

Arithmetic errors, such as overflow and divide-by-zero, are also common. Most of these errors are determined by the hardware, and passed back to Visual Basic, which stops the code and sends you a message. Arithmetic errors often result from a logical error in the program design, when the wrong values are inserted into a calculation. For example,

```
A = 3 * 0
B = 1/A
```

generates a divide-by-zero error because A is incorrectly set to zero.

File system errors occur when a requested file-related action cannot be completed. For example, when you open a file for input that does not exist, or print to a file that has not yet been opened. Again, these types of errors usually result from logical errors in a program's design. Table 13.1 contains a list of the Visual Basic run-time errors, and error numbers.

The first two columns of this table were generated with the following simple piece of code, which printed the table into the Immediate window. The Error$() function produces Visual Basic's error message for the given error number used as an argument. If there is no error defined for a number, it returns "User-defined error." The If statement skips all the undefined error numbers.

```
Sub Form_Click ()
For I = 1 To 1000
  If Error$(I) <> "User-defined error" Then
    Debug.Print I, Error$(I)
  End If
Next I
End Sub
```

Table 13.1. Visual Basic run-time errors.

Code	Error	Description
3	Return without GoSub	A Return statement was encountered without a corresponding GoSub.
5	Illegal function call	This is usually caused by calling a function with invalid or out of range arguments (for example, Sqr(-1)).
6	Overflow	The result of some calculation was greater than the largest number that can be stored in the variable to receive that result.

continues

Table 13.1. continued.

Code	Error	Description
7	Out of memory	Code and data storage have filled all available memory.
9	Subscript out of range	The value of an array subscript is not within the range defined in the `Dim` or `Global` statement.
10	Duplicate definition	A variable was defined with the same name as a variable that already exists.
11	Division by zero	A numeric calculation has a zero in the denominator.
13	Type mismatch	A string variable has been equated to a numeric variable, or a function argument is the wrong type.
14	Out of string space	All the strings in the modules or Forms use more than 64K bytes of memory.
16	String formula too complex	A string expression is too complicated to evaluate, break it into smaller segments.
17	Can't continue	A change was made in break mode that prevents a code from being restarted.
19	No Resume	An `On Error` statement is active and missing its `Resume` statement.
20	Resume without error	A `Resume` statement was encountered without an active `On Error` statement.
28	Out of stack space	The memory reserved for storage of local variables and procedure calls is full.
35	`Sub` or `Function` not defined	An undefined procedure was called.

Code	Error	Description
48	Error in loading DLL	Something is wrong with a DLL library file that was accessed.
49	Bad DLL calling convention	Something is wrong with the interface to a DLL routine.
51	Internal error	An internal Visual Basic error, probably a bug in Visual Basic.
52	Bad file name or number	A file name or number are being used for a file that hasn't been opened yet.
53	File not found	An attempt has been made to access a file that doesn't exist.
54	Bad file mode	Get # or Put # was used with a sequential file, or Input # or Print # were used on files opened for Output only or Input only.
55	File already open	An attempt has been made to Open a sequential file that is already open, or to Kill an open file.
57	Device I/O error	A device driver has issued an error.
58	File already exists	A Name statement was used to change a file name to one that already exists.
59	Bad record length	A record variable is larger than the record length specified in the Open statement.
61	Disk full	A disk filled up while writing a file.
62	Input past end of file	An attempt has been made to read beyond the end-of-file marker on a file.

continues

Table 13.1. continued.

Code	Error	Description
63	Bad record number	A negative record number was specified in a Get # or Put # statement.
64	Bad file name	A file name was specified that does not follow DOS conventions.
67	Too many files	The number of files open at any one time has been exceeded.
68	Device unavailable	A device, such as a printer, is currently off-line.
70	Permission denied	An attempt has been made to write to a locked or protected file.
71	Disk not ready	A floppy disk isn't inserted or the door on a drive isn't closed.
74	Can't rename with different drive	A Name statement attempted to move a file to a different drive.
75	Path/File access error	A path-file combination does not exist, or an attempt to write a write protected file occurred.
76	Path not found	A path does not exist.
260	No Timer available	An attempt has been made to allocate more than 16 Timers.
280	DDE channel not closed	Awaiting response from foreign application An attempt was made to start a new DDE connection before an old one was fully closed.
281	No More DDE channels	Too many DDE channels are open.

Code	Error	Description
282	No foreign application responded to a DDE initiate	A DDE initiate request was sent to an external application and it didn't reply. The foreign application may be closed, slow or may not recognize the request.
283	Multiple applications responded to a DDE initiate	More than one application responded to a DDE initiate request.
284	DDE channel locked	An attempt was made to use a DDE link that is already in use.
285	Foreign application won't perform DDE method or operation	An operation was requested that a foreign application doesn't recognize.
286	Timeout while waiting for DDE response	A foreign application is not responding.
287	User pressed Alt key during DDE operation	The Alt key was pressed while a DDE conversation was in progress.
288	Destination is busy	The foreign application is busy and won't respond to a DDE request.
289	Data not provided in DDE operation	An unexpected error occurred during a DDE conversation.
290	Data in wrong format	Data returned by a foreign application is the wrong type.
291	Foreign application quit	The foreign application quit without ending the DDE link.
292	DDE conversation closed or changed	The foreign application unexpectedly closed the link.
293	DDE Method invoked with no channel open	A DDE method was executed on a nonexistent link.
294	Invalid DDE Link format	The foreign application sent data that is not in DDE link format.

continues

13

311

Table 13.1. continued.

Code	Error	Description
295	Message queue filled; DDE message lost	When the DDE message queue is filled, new messages are lost.
296	`PasteLink` already performed on this control	An attempt to establish a link using the `PasteLink` command occurred to a control that is already involved in a link.
297	Can't set `LinkMode`; invalid `LinkTopic`	The `LinkTopic` is invalid in an attempt to change the `LinkMode`.
320	Can't use character device names in file names:	A device name, like `LPT1` was used as a file name.
321	Invalid file format	A Form file is damaged.
340	Control array element ' ' does not exist	A control array index is out of range.
341	Invalid object array index	A control array index is larger than 32,767 or less than 0.
342	Not enough room to allocate control array ' '	Not enough memory to create a control array.
343	Object not an array	An index was applied to an object that is not a control array.
344	Must specify index for object array	A control array was accessed without an index.
345	Reached limit: cannot create any more controls for this Form	Created more than 255 controls on a Form.
360	Object already loaded	A control specified in a control array is already loaded.
361	Can't load or unload this object	An attempt was made to load or unload a system object, such as a Printer, or to unload a nonarray control.

Code	Error	Description
362	Can't unload controls created at design time	An attempt was made to unload a control loaded at design time.
363	Custom control ' ' not found	A custom control on a Form is not yet attached to a project.
364	Object was unloaded	A Form was unloaded by its own `Form_Load` procedure.
365	Unable to unload within this context	A Form could not be unloaded.
380	Invalid property value	An invalid value was applied to a property.
381	Invalid property array index	An index applied to a property that accepts an index is less than 0 or greater than 32,767.
382	' ' property cannot be set at run time	An attempt was made to change a property that only can be changed at design time.
383	' ' property is read-only	An attempt was made to change a read-only property.
384	' ' property can't be modified when Form is minimized or maximized	An attempt was made to change `Top`, `Left`, `Height`, or `Width` with the Form maximized or minimized.
385	Must specify index when using property array	An attempt was made to access the `Fonts` or `List` property, without using an array index.
386	' ' property not available at run-time	An attempt was made to access `CtlName` or `FormName` at run-time.
387	' ' property can't be set on this control	An attempt was made to check a top level menu, or make all submenus invisible.
388	Can't set `Visible` property from a parent menu	A submenu head cannot set the visible property of a submenu item.

continues

313

Table 13.1. continued.

Code	Error	Description
400	Form already displayed; can't show modally	An attempt was made to make a Form modal that was already visible.
401	Can't show nonmodal Form when modal Form is displayed	An attempt was made to show a nonmodal Form while a modal Form is visible.
402	Must close or hide topmost modal Form first	An attempt was made to hide or unload a modal Form that has other modal Forms above it. Modal Forms must be unloaded from the top down.
420	Invalid object reference	An object was referenced on an unloaded Form.
421	Method not applicable for this object	An inappropriate method was applied to an object.
422	Property ' ' not found	A property was referenced that does not apply to the object in the reference.
423	Property or control ' ' not found	A property or control was referenced that is not part of the referenced Form.
424	Object required	A property was used in a refer-ence where an object should be.
425	Invalid object use	An attempt was made to assign a value to a control or Form rather than to a property.
430	No currently active control	`ActiveControl` was used and no control had the focus.
431	No currently active Form	`ActiveForm` was used and no Form was active.
460	Invalid Clipboard format	The specified Clipboard format is incompatible with the method being used.

Code	Error	Description
461	Specified format does not match format of data	The specified Clipboard format does not match the data being transferred.
480	Can't create `AutoRedraw` image	Not enough memory to create the persistent bit map.
481	Invalid picture	Data assigned to the `Picture` property isn't a recognizable picture.
482	Printer error	There is some problem with the printer.
520	Can't empty Clipboard	Another application is using the Clipboard and won't release it.
521	Can't open Clipboard	Another application is using the Clipboard and won't release it.

Logical Errors

Logical errors occur when the computer is doing what you told it to do, but not what you wanted it to do. When you are lucky, the cause is obvious and you fix it. More often, they are hard to find, because the cause of the error can be far from the statement that produced the outward appearance of the error. For example, if you get a divide-by-zero error, the statement that made the divisor zero can be far from the statement where the division operation occurred; or a logical error might not even generate an error message, but result in an incorrect value calculated and printed by a program. Here's where your experience and intuition come into play.

The Timer Program

This simple little program illustrates a logical bug—see whether you can find it. The program uses the last control on the Toolbox window, the Timer. The Timer is basically an alarm clock that runs in the background

and generates a Timer event whenever its time runs out. The Timer's Interval property stores the amount of time to wait, in milliseconds, before generating a Timer event. Using the Timer to generate one-second events, this program counts those events, and displays the value of the counter in a Label.

1. Open a new project, select Form1, and set its properties to

```
Caption = The Timer
Height = 1340
Width = 5130
BorderStyle = 3 - fixed double
ControlBox = False
MaxButton = False
MinButton = False
```

2. Draw a Label on the Form, as shown in Figure 13.1, with these properties:

```
Height = 620
Width = 3015
Top = 120
Left = 720
Caption = ""
FontSize = 24
```

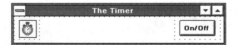

Figure 13.1. Layout for the Timer program.

3. Draw a Command button on the Form with these properties:

```
CtlName = OnCmd
Height = 500
Width = 855
Top = 120
Left = 3960
Caption = On/Off
```

4. Draw a Timer to the left of the Label. The location isn't important because the Timer is invisible in the running application. Set its properties to

```
Interval = 1000
Enabled = False
```

5. Open the `Timer1_Timer` procedure and type

```
Sub Timer1_Timer ()
Dim I As Integer
I = I + 1
Label1.Caption = Str$(I)
End Sub
```

This procedure is executed whenever the `Timer` event occurs, which is once per second. When executed, it increments the value of `I` by 1 and inserts that number in the `Caption` property of the Label; thus the Label counts seconds whenever the Timer is running.

6. Open the `OnCmd_Click` procedure and type

```
Sub OnCmd_Click ()
Timer1.Enabled = Not Timer1.Enabled
End Sub
```

This procedure turns the Timer on and off by applying the `Not` logical operator on the Timer's `Enabled` property. The `Not` operator changes `True` to `False` or `False` to `True`.

7. Save the project as TIMER.MAK and TIMER.FRM.

8. Run the program and click the **On/Off** button.

What happens? The Timer doesn't count, but displays a 1 all the time. This isn't what you told the computer to do—or is it? In the next few sections, you will learn how to track down the problem.

To locate a logical error, gather all the information you have about it—where it occurred, what the program was doing, what was the error, whatever you have. Use this information to estimate the most probable cause of the error and then check that piece of code. If that doesn't work, try using some of the debugging tools (discussed in the next section) to get more information about the bug and what it's doing. Keep gathering information and looking at the code until you find out what is happening.

Debugging Tools

Not all of debugging is done through intuition and magic. There are some excellent tools built into Visual Basic that greatly reduce the amount of work involved in locating and fixing programming bugs. In fact, it's much easier to debug Visual Basic programs than those in most other high-level languages, primarily because Visual Basic is an interpreted language, so you can make changes and adjustments in the code and immediately run it to see the results. In fact, you can make adjustments while the code is running by issuing the Break command, making the change, then issuing the Continue command.

The difference between a compiler and an interpreter is found in the way they convert and execute code. An interpreter directly executes the text file containing the code you have written, while a compiler converts it into a file of machine language codes first, then executes those machine language codes. Machine language codes are the numeric codes that the microprocessor in your computer executes. Interpreters have to still convert the text version of a code into machine language, but they do it one line at a time. An interpreter reads a single line of code, converts it to machine language, executes it, then continues with the next line of code. A compiler converts the whole code into machine language first, then it executes the machine language.

Breaking a Running Code

There are four ways to break a running code:

- Pressing Ctrl-Break.

- Selecting Break on the Run menu.

- Encountering a Stop statement in a program.

- Encountering a breakpoint inserted with the Toggle Breakpoint command on the Run menu.

A fifth way is encountering a run-time error, which automatically breaks the code at the line where the error occurs.

When a program is in Break mode you can examine code in the code windows, print values in the Immediate window, change the values of variables, and even change code. When you are done, issue the Continue command on the **Run** menu, and your code starts up where it left off.

To break a code using Ctrl-Break, or the **Break** command on the **Run** menu, the code must first be running. These two commands are somewhat imprecise about their stopping points in code, because as soon as you issue one of these commands, it immediately stops execution, opens a code window, and displays the next line it is going to execute surrounded by a black box. You see something similar when a code encounters a run-time error, but then you know the boxed statement is the one causing the error.

The Stop statement and Toggle **B**reakpoint command cause a code to stop in a specific place. You use these when you think you know where a problem is, and want to stop the execution at that spot. The Stop statement is like any other Visual Basic statement. You type it into your code, and when it is executed the code stops. It is different from the End statement for interpreted code. When an End statement is encountered, the code is stopped and unloaded, and all the variables are erased. You must restart the code from scratch if you use End. Stop, however, simply halts the code. Everything is still in memory and can be restarted from the stopping point. If you compile the code, though, the Stop statement behaves exactly the same way as an End statement.

To use the Toggle **B**reakpoint command, select the statement where you want the code to stop, and click the Toggle **B**reakpoint command. Your code behaves exactly as if you had inserted a Stop statement there. To remove a breakpoint, select the statement and press Toggle **B**reakpoint again, or click the Clear **A**ll Breakpoints command to remove them all.

Examining and Changing Things

When your code is in Break mode, you can examine code and variables, and even change things. To change code while in Break mode, simply type the changes in the appropriate code window. You can change most statements without affecting the running code. A few things that you can't change are

- Variable definitions, such as those in Dim and Global statements.

- Loop control statements, such as For/Next.

- Sub and Function procedure calls.

If you change these things, your code becomes inconsistent and must be restarted rather than continued. Visual Basic warns you when a change will force a restart.

To examine the values of variables, open the Immediate window and type `Print`, `?`, or the variable name; then press Enter, and the value of the variable is printed. For example, to see the value of a variable called `count`, type `Print count` or `?#count` in the Immediate window.

To change the value of a variable, type an Assignment statement in the Immediate window equating the variable to its new value. For example, to reset the value of `count`, you could type `count=0` in the Immediate window. You can examine or change only those variables in the active call chain. The active call chain includes procedures currently being executed, and those which call procedures that are being executed. Examining and changing any other procedures makes no sense anyway. For example, why would you want to examine a variable that hasn't even been defined yet? Its value has no meaning until it is in the active call chain.

You also can use the Immediate window to experiment with functions and formulas. The program executes just about any statement you type, and you can print the results using `Print`. The only restriction is that it can execute only a single line at a time, although you can stack several statements, separated by colons, on one line to execute a short piece of code in the Immediate window.

Use the Break mode to figure out what is wrong with the Timer program (bear with me if you have already figured it out).

1. The problem is probably in the `Timer1_Timer` procedure, so open it, insert the cursor in the first executable statement (`I = I + 1`), and execute the Toggle **B**reakpoint command. The statement is bolded, as shown in Figure 13.2, to indicate it has a breakpoint set.

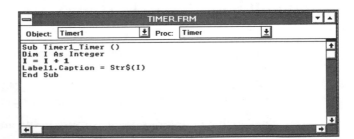

Figure 13.2. Setting a breakpoint.

2. Run the program and click the **On/Off** button. The program stops at the breakpoint and displays the Code window—see Figure 13.3.

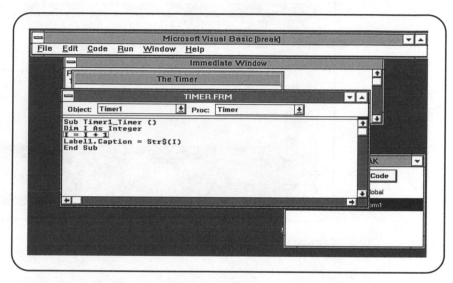

Figure 13.3. Stopped at a breakpoint.

3. Select the Immediate window, either by clicking it, or selecting it from the Windows menu. Type **Print I** and press Enter. The value 0 is printed in the Immediate window, as you would expect, the first time this procedure is executed.

4. As I mentioned, you can try almost anything in this window. Type **Print Sin(5)**, and the value of the sine of 5 radians appears, as shown in Figure 13.4.

5. Select the Continue command from the Run menu. The code runs for a moment, and then hits the breakpoint again. Select the Immediate window and type **Print I** again. It still returns 0. Do this step several times; the value of I is zero every time.

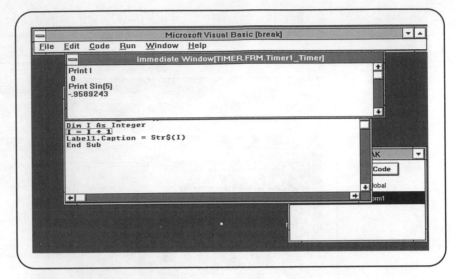

Figure 13.4. *Using the Immediate window.*

Step Mode

Rather than pressing **C**ontinue to continue running a program after it has been in Break mode, you can click the **S**ingle Step command on the **R**un menu (or press the F8 key) to execute one statement of the program and return to Break mode. You use this command to step through a program, one step at a time, so you can watch the execution and examine the value of the variables at each step.

The **P**rocedure Step command works the same way as the **S**ingle Step command, except when it reaches a call to another procedure. The **S**ingle Step command moves to the called procedure and begins executing code there, one step at a time. The **P**rocedure Step command runs all the code in the procedure and returns to Break mode only when the called procedure returns to the procedure that called it. Thus, the **S**ingle Step command moves you throughout your program, but the **P**rocedure Step command takes you step by step through a single procedure.

Also useful here are the Show Next Statement and Set Next Statement commands on the **Run** menu. In Break mode, the Show Next Statement command draws a black box around the next statement to be executed. Use it to see where you are in a program. The Set Next Statement command changes the execution point to a different statement. Use it to reexecute a statement or block of statements after making a change, and to see the effect of that change.

1. Press F8 (**S**ingle Step) and the execution point moves to the next statement, as shown in Figure 13.5. Select the Immediate window and type **Print I**, and the value 1 is returned as you would expect.

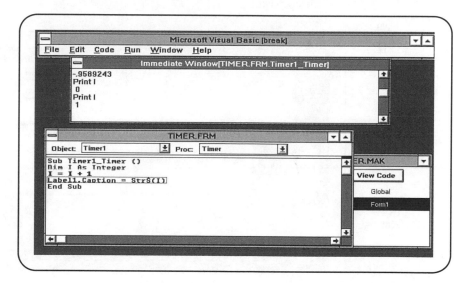

Figure 13.5. *Single stepping to the next statement and checking* I *again.*

2. Press F8 again, and the execution point moves to the End Sub statement. Press F8 a third time and it exits the procedure, waits for the next Timer event, reenters the Timer1_Timer procedure, and stops at the first executable statement (the I = I + 1 statement.) Select the Immediate window and type **Print I**, and the value 0 is returned again. I is being incremented as it is supposed to, but it is reset to 0 each time the procedure is called.

    The problem should be obvious by now: Each time a procedure ends, all its local variables are lost and reset to 0 when the procedure is called again. The variable I is local to this procedure because it was defined in the Dim statement at the beginning of the

procedure. To make this program work, you must make the value of I persist from one call of the procedure to the next. One way to do that is to move the definition of I to the declarations area of the Form, or to the Global module. A simpler way that keeps I local is to change the Dim statement to a Static statement.

3. Select the Timer1_Timer procedure, select the Dim statement, and change the word Dim to Static. Click elsewhere in the procedure and Visual Basic puts up a message that informs you to restart the program—see Figure 13.6. You must restart because you have changed a variable definition, making the running application inconsistent.

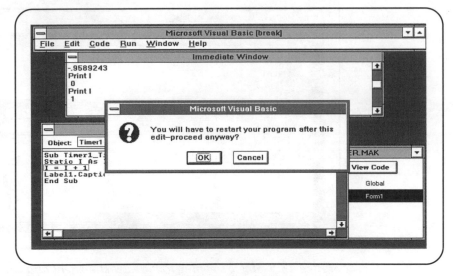

Figure 13.6. *Changing a* Dim *statement in break mode causes a restart.*

4. Click **OK**, select the I = I + 1 statement, execute the Toggle Breakpoint command to turn off the breakpoint, run the program again and click the **On/Off** button. It works!!! See Figure 13.7. Execute the **End** command to quit the program.

5. Execute the **Make Exe File** command on the **File** menu to compile the program as TIMER.EXE. Switch to the Windows Program Manager and open the File Manager. Find the TIMER.EXE file as shown in Figure 13.8, click it, hold the left mouse button down and drag it to the Visual Basic program group window on the Program Manager. This process installs the executable file in the Visual Basic group.

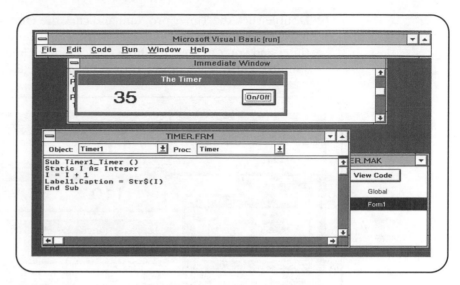

Figure 13.7. *The Timer program, working at last.*

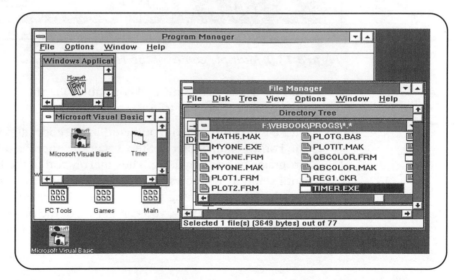

Figure 13.8. *Installing the executable program in the Visual Basic group window.*

6. Double-click the Timer program and click the **On/Off** button. You have a working Timer. Double-click the Timer program a few more times and you can have multiple copies of the Timer running simultaneously, each doing its own timing—see Figure 13.9.

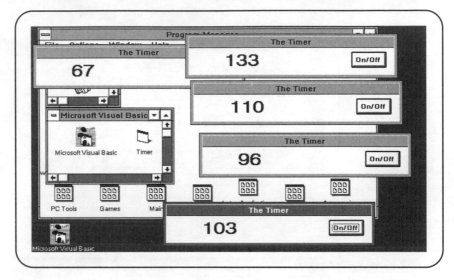

***Figure 13.9.** Multiple copies of the Timer program.*

7. End the Timer programs and continue. Oh, oh! Another logical error. There is no way to turn them off.

   There is no **Quit** or **Exit** command in the code, and you disabled the Form's control box in Step 1. Luckily, there is no way for these programs to hurt anything. They merrily run in the background until you quit Windows, at which time they are deleted. In fact, they have been running the whole time I have been typing these last few pages. Actually, you can get rid of the programs by pressing Ctrl-Esc to open the Windows task list, selecting the Timer, and pressing End Task.

Sounds

When debugging a program, often you don't want many details about a program's execution, but just want to know when it reaches a particular location in the code. In this situation, the Beep statement is very useful.

Simply insert it in an interesting area and your code beeps at you when it reaches that point. You can get more elaborate by inserting different beep codes at different points in your program to signal where you are.

Unfortunately, you can't string several Beeps in a row. The sounds all run together and you get a buzz rather than a beep, so you can't tell how many beeps you have. To create multiple beeps in a code, you can insert a simple procedure like this one:

```
Sub Beeper (NumBeeps As Integer)
Dim I As Integer, J As Integer
For I = 1 To NumBeeps
  Beep
  For J = 1 To 10000
  Next J
Next I
End Sub
```

Call this procedure in every location where you want to hear a marker. Follow the procedure name by the number of beeps you want to hear. That number is passed to the variable NumBeeps, which is used as the upper limit on a For/Next loop. The procedure executes a Beep, then executes a second For/Next loop. Note that the Next statement in the second loop immediately follows the For statement, so this loop does nothing but waste some time to create a pause between beeps. You might have to adjust the upper limit of the second loop so you can discern the number of beeps. The value 10,000 seems to work well for my machine, but the number you use is machine-dependent. Pick a number just large enough so you can hear the number of beeps.

An alternate for the second loop is a While/Wend loop that watches the value of the Timer() function. The Timer() function returns the number of seconds since midnight, so if you wait until its integer value changes, you get a one-second pause, though I find this too long.

```
Sub Beeper (NumBeeps As Integer)
Dim I As Integer, J As Integer
For I = 1 To NumBeeps
Beep
J = Timer
While J = Int(Timer)
Wend
Next I
End Sub
```

For example, in the nonworking version of the Timer program, you could insert the first Beeper procedure with I as the argument. Then the program would beep the value of I to you each time it executes. Try it and see.

Debugging Code

A final method of tracing bugs is the insertion of debugging code. Debugging code usually consists of Print statements strategically placed in a code to print their location and the values of important variables. Visual Basic makes this easy by including the Debug object. Anything printed to the Debug object appears on the Immediate window, so as your code runs, you can monitor the printed values to watch for suspicious changes.

If you have more than one Debug statement, be sure to include a short piece of text to identify the location of the statement doing the printing. In a large code, with many Debug statements, put a Debug flag in the Global module and use it in an If statement to control the execution of the Debug statements. For example,

```
If DebugFlag Then Debug.Print "I am here",J
```

Here, this statement does nothing if the value of DebugFlag is False. If it is True, it prints I am here, then the value of the variable J. This way you can leave the Debug statements in your code and they won't do much but slow it down a little. When you want to print the Debug values, either insert a statement at the beginning of your code that sets DebugFlag to True, or break the code, and type DebugFlag = -1 in the Immediate window. When you click Continue, the Debug statements are activated.

The Role of Error Trapping

Debugging involves searching for the causes of an error. When you figure it out, you fix your code and (you hope) never have that error again. Some errors you can't control—for example, trying to open a file for input that doesn't exist. If the user of your code does this, an error message appears and the code stops in break mode. If you are running a compiled version of your code, it quits and is removed from memory. Generally, you would prefer that did not happen—just as you would be thoroughly upset if, right after you had typed your Magnum Opus, your word processor quit without letting you save anything, just because you mistyped a file name. To handle problems like this, use error trapping.

Error trapping allows your program to take control when an error occurs. All of the run-time errors listed in Table 13.1 are "trappable" by your program. (Meaning that they can be captured by your code and handled internally.) When an error occurs, your error trap code takes control, checks to see what the error is, fixes it if possible, and then returns you to the place where the problem occurred. Each procedure has its own specific error-handling procedure. The error handler is enabled with the On Error statement. When enabled, if a run-time error occurs, the block of code pointed to by the On Error statement is executed.

How Visual Basic Traps Errors

When Visual Basic encounters a run-time error, it puts the error number from Table 13.1 in the variable Err, and checks whether any error handler is available. If so, it executes the handler, and lets it take care of the error. If the handler also generates an error, Visual Basic checks the procedure that called the procedure with the error, to see whether the calling procedure has an error handler. If no error handler is available, or if none can handle the error, the code quits and displays an error message concerning the original error.

If you are running the program in interpreted mode, it displays the error message, then displays the offending statement. If you are running a compiled version of the code, it quits after displaying the error message from Table 13.1.

Setting a Trap for Errors

To set up an error trap, insert an On Error Goto statement near the beginning of a procedure with the errors you want to trap. This statement must be placed before any statement that might cause a "trappable" error. The syntax of the statement is

```
On Error {GoTo label ¦ Resume Next ¦ GoTo 0}
```

If you use the GoTo *label* clause, where *label* is a valid Label within the same procedure, the block of code following that Label is set as the current error handling procedure. Control isn't passed to the error handler with this statement, the statement is only marked as where to go if an error occurs. While an error handler must be in the same procedure as the On Error statement, it might immediately call some other procedure to handle the error. This way you can combine all similar error handling in a Sub or Function procedure, then pass control to it from the different error handlers in a program.

If you use the Resume Next clause, your code skips the statement that caused the error and continues running with the next one. This statement does not define an error handler. Be careful of this, because skipping statements can make your code inconsistent. The main use for the Resume Next clause is to save an error to handle later. If you are doing something that should not be stopped to handle an error, such as receiving data in a telecommunications program, use the Resume Next statement. Note that only the last error encountered is stored in Err, so if you encounter a second error before handling the first, the error number of the first error is lost.

The last clause, GoTo 0, disables error trapping in this routine. Use this clause to turn off error checking after the vulnerable statements have been executed.

To test an error trap, use the Error statement. The Error statement takes a single number as its argument, and that number is the code for the error you want to simulate. Whenever Visual Basic executes an Error statement it simulates getting the error specified by that argument and either displays an error dialog or executes your error trapping code. The Error statement also is used to create your own errors. For example, in a File Open dialog box, if you already have an error handler for file-not-found errors that warns the user and requests a new file name, you can use the existing mechanism to handle files with an incorrect file type by creating a user-defined error. Otherwise, you will have to write practically the same block of code to handle the file type errors as you do for file-not-found errors.

You can use any of the missing numbers from Table 13.1 as user-defined errors, but make sure that if you have a user-defined error, you also have an error trap enabled to handle it. Also note that future versions of Visual Basic might use some of these unused error numbers.

Getting Information About an Error

After you have trapped an error, you must get information about it, such as what error occurred, and where it occurred. When error checking is not enabled, Visual Basic displays a dialog box that informs you what error occurred, and then, if you are running in interpreted mode, it displays the error message.

After an error has occurred, the variable Err contains the error number—see Table 13.1. To get the text of an error message, call the Error$() function with the error number as its argument. The function returns the text description of the error. This is the same description you get when Visual Basic displays an error message. Getting the location of the error is more difficult. In older versions of BASIC, each line in a program was consecutively numbered. If you number your lines, the number of the closest line to the line containing the error will be in Erl. Because Visual Basic programs rarely use line numbers, this might not be very useful unless you specifically number the statements with which you expect to have problems.

The Err and Erl functions are valid only in the procedure where the error occurs, and are reset to 0 whenever you execute a Resume or On Error statement. They also might be reset if you call some other procedure, so save the values they return at the beginning of your error handler if you plan to use them.

Creating an Error Handler

As mentioned previously, an error handler must reside in the same procedure as the On Error statement that activated it. However, you usually don't want it in a position where it can be executed during the normal operation of your procedure. A good place to put it is at the end of your procedure, separated from the rest of the procedure with an Exit Sub or Exit Function statement.

An error handler can contain whatever you choose; the only requirement is that it end with a Resume statement. Commonly, error handlers first use the Err function to see what the error is, and then use a block If statement to decide what to do in each case. Rarely would you code an error handler for all of the possible errors listed in Table 13.1. Usually, you

write code for the errors you expect and then write an Else clause for the rest that prints an error message and ends the program, or at least exits that procedure.

Every error handler must end with a Resume, Resume Next, or Resume *label* statement. The Resume statement returns the execution point to the statement that caused the problem, and tries to execute it again. This is the most common case: the handler corrects the problem and lets the program try again. The Resume Next statement returns execution to the next statement after the one that caused the problem. In this case, the error handler must handle the work of the statement that caused the problem, then skip it. The Resume *label* statement resumes execution at the statement following the Label.

For example, a formula that contains a division operation runs the risk of having zero as the divisor. An important case is the integrand of the Sine Integral Si(x). The integrand is equal to the sine of x divided by x. At x equals zero, the integrand is zero divided by zero, which is one; however, Visual Basic gives a divide-by-zero error. To make this work correctly, trap the divide-by-zero error and replace the result with one.

```
Function Si(x As Single) As Single
'function to calculate the sine integral
'statements to integrate sin(x)/x from x to infinity
 .
 .
 .

Integrand = Sin(xint)/xint
 .
 .
 .

End Function
```

Because the integral can pass through 0, xint equals 0 and the routine crashes. To fix this, create an error handler this way:

```
Function Si(x As Single) As Single
'function to calculate the sine integral
'statements to integrate sin(x)/x from x to infinity
On Error GoTo FixSin      'turn the error handler on
 .
 .
 .
Integrand = Sin(xint)/xint
```

```
.
.
.Exit Function
FixSin:
If Err = 11 Then
  Integrand = 1
Else
  MsgBox Error$(Err)
  Stop
End If
Resume Next
End Function
```

The error handler is enabled by line 4. If line 8 is executed and no error is encountered, the procedure continues normally. If an error is encountered, control passes to the block of code following the `FixSin:` Label. The error handler first checks whether the error is the expected divide-by-zero (error number 11.) If it is a divide-by-zero error, the procedure sets the value of `Integrand` to 1 and resumes with the statement after the one with the divide by 0 error. If it isn't a divide-by-zero error, this procedure sends the error message to the user and ends. You might want to move the `On Error` statement down to a position just before the `Integrand` statement and put an `On Error GoTo 0` statement after it. This assures you that the `Integrand` statement is the one with the problem and not some other statement with a division error.

The `Pies` procedure on the Drawing Test Program in Chapter 12, "Drawing with Visual Basic," found a small bug in Version 1 of Visual Basic. To work around that bug, I had to put the `Circle` method within a block `If` statement so I could check the input values and skip drawing the pie slice if the numbers looked bad. If you remove that protection and press the **Pies** button a few times, it eventually crashes with an overflow error. An overflow error occurs when numbers get too large to be represented by a variable.

1. Open the Drawing Test program (FLAG.FRM), open the `PiesCmd_Click` procedure, and remove the `If` and `End If` statements that surround the `Circle` method. One way to remove a line without actually deleting it from a program is to insert a `Rem` at the beginning of the line, turning it into a comment (the changed lines are bold).

   ```
   Sub PiesCmd_Click ()
   'Draw 100 random pie slices
   Dim Color As Long, I As Integer
   ```

continues

333

```
Dim XC As Single, YC As Single
Dim Radius As Single
Dim PieStart As Single, PieEnd As Single
BlackBoard.ScaleMode = 1              ' - Twips
BlackBoard.DrawStyle = 0              ' - Solid
BlackBoard.FillStyle = 0             ' - Solid
BlackBoard.Cls
For I = 1 To 100
  XC = Rnd(1) * BlackBoard.ScaleWidth
  YC = Rnd(1) * BlackBoard.ScaleHeight
  Radius = Rnd(1) * BlackBoard.ScaleHeight / 2 + 20
  Color = QBColor(Rnd(1) * 15)
  BlackBoard.FillColor = Color
  PieStart = Rnd(1) * 6
  PieEnd = Rnd(1) * 6
  Aspect = Rnd(1) * 2
Rem  If Aspect * Radius > 10 Then
    BlackBoard.Circle (XC, YC), Radius, BLACK, -PieStart, -
PieEnd, Aspect
Rem  End If
Next I
End Sub
```

2. Run the program. Press the **Pies** button a few times and it eventually crashes, as shown in Figure 13.10. (Oops, Copies of the Timer
   are still running in the background.)

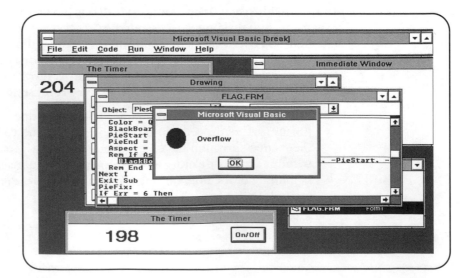

Figure 13.10. Crashing the Pies *procedure.*

3. Insert an error trap into the procedure so it reads as follows (the changed and added lines are bold).

```
Sub PiesCmd_Click ()
'Draw 100 random pie slices
Dim Color As Long, I As Integer
Dim XC As Single, YC As Single
Dim Radius As Single
Dim PieStart As Single, PieEnd As Single
BlackBoard.ScaleMode = 1              ' - Twips
BlackBoard.DrawStyle = 0             ' - Solid
BlackBoard.FillStyle = 0             ' - Solid
BlackBoard.Cls
On Error GoTo PieFix     'Enable error trapping
For I = 1 To 100
  XC = Rnd(1) * BlackBoard.ScaleWidth
  YC = Rnd(1) * BlackBoard.ScaleHeight
  Radius = Rnd(1) * BlackBoard.ScaleHeight / 2 + 20
  Color = QBColor(Rnd(1) * 15)
  BlackBoard.FillColor = Color
  PieStart = Rnd(1) * 6
  PieEnd = Rnd(1) * 6
  Aspect = Rnd(1) * 2
  Rem If Aspect * Radius > 10 Then
    BlackBoard.Circle (XC, YC), Radius, BLACK, -PieStart,
        -PieEnd, Aspect
    Rem End If
  Next I
Exit Sub
PieFix:        'this is the error handler
If Err = 6 Then
  Debug.Print "Got one"
  Resume Next
Else
  MsgBox Error$(Err)
  Stop
End If
End Sub
```

The Debug statement in the error handler prints Got one on the Immediate window whenever it traps an error. If it does trap an overflow error, it executes the Resume Next statement to skip drawing the pie slice with the Circle method.

4. Save the program, run it, and press **Pies** several times. The error trapping procedure now captures any errors and skips the Circle method, as shown in Figure 13.11. Note the Got ones printed on the Immediate window.

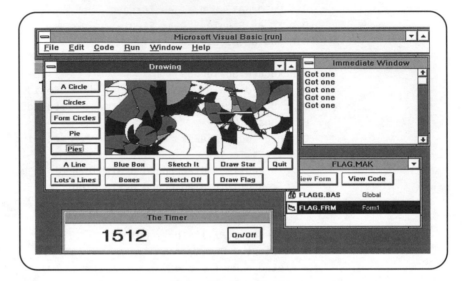

Figure 13.11. *Trapping run-time errors in the* Pies *procedure.*

5. Remove the Debug statement from the error handler and save the project.

What You Have Learned

This chapter discussed debugging programs and trapping errors. Debugging is finding and removing errors from a program, while error trapping is writing code to correct situations when the error can't be avoided. The types of errors involved in debugging are syntax errors and logical errors. Syntax errors occur because you have incorrectly applied the grammar of the Visual Basic language. Logical errors occur when your code does what you told it to do, but not what you wanted it to do. Error trapping can trap only run-time errors, and is used to capture errors that would normally crash an application. After it is captured, an error-handling routine determines what is to be done to correct the error. Specifically, this chapter discussed

- Syntax errors.

- Run-time errors.

- Logical errors.

- Examining a program in Break mode.

- Using sounds to mark sections of code.

- Using debugging code and the Immediate window.

- Error trapping with the `On Error` statement.

- Getting information about an error with `Err` and `Erl`.

- Exiting an error handler with `Resume`.

Advanced Language Features

The advanced features of Visual Basic are somewhat beyond the scope of an introductory book. However, they represent important capabilities that you might eventually want to include in your programs. These features include control of the DOS file system, Dynamic Data Exchange (DDE), and Dynamic Link Libraries (DLL). As your understanding of Visual Basic and Windows programming increases, you probably will want to use these capabilities, so I briefly discuss them here. You can work out the details as you need them.

In This Chapter

Visual Basic has several advanced features, including Dynamic Data Exchange (DDE), Dynamic Link Libraries (DLL), and the use of Binary files. This chapter discusses

- Dynamic Data Exchange.

- Dynamic Link Libraries.

- Binary files.

- Dragging and dropping.

- File system management.

Using Dynamic Data Exchange

Dynamic Data Exchange (DDE) is a windows capability that allows two running programs to exchange data. The programs must be especially equipped to handle DDE and set up a link with another program. Visual Basic has this capability built in, so you only have to enable it.

Servers and Clients

Every DDE link has two ends, the *server* and *client*. The server provides data for the client and the client receives the data. The linking is generally between two similar objects in the two programs, or at least between two objects that understand the same type of data. For example, a cell in a Microsoft Excel worksheet and a Text box in Visual Basic can be linked in a DDE link. If Excel is the server and Visual Basic is the client, then whenever the contents of the worksheet cell changes, that change is passed to the Text box. If Visual Basic is the server and Excel is the client, then changing the contents of the Text box changes the contents of the worksheet cell.

In any DDE exchange, a program can be both a server and a client, depending on the needs of the communication. For example, a worksheet cell could be a server for a Label, and a Text box could be a server for a worksheet cell. Thus the two programs can pass data between them. Be careful with this; don't make the same item both a server and a client. If you do, an unending loop is set up with one program changing the other, and the change in the other initiating a change in the first. If you have to send data to a server, and if the server is capable of accepting data as well as sending it, a LinkPoke method is available. See Chapter 15, "Command Reference," for more details.

Hot and Cold Links

DDE links come in two temperatures, hot and cold. A hot DDE link updates the client's data whenever the data changes in the server. Because this is not ideal in some cases, the DDE link also can be cold: the client's data is updated only when the client asks for it with the LinkRequest method. For example, pictures contain a large amount of data that must be transferred over the link. If the link between two pictures is hot, the whole picture is sent every time you change a single bit on the picture on the server. With a cold link, you can wait until you have finished changing the picture before sending it over the link.

Initiating a Link

A client-server relationship is initiated by the client asking the server for service. To establish the link, a LinkOpen request must first be passed to the Windows operating system. Windows then passes the request to the selected program. A LinkOpen request contains the following data:

```
application|topic!item
```

The *application* is the name of the server application. This name can be different from the name of the running application, for example, the application name for Microsoft Excel is Excel. The application name for a Visual Basic program running in the Visual Basic environment is the name of the Project window minus the .MAK extension. If the Visual Basic program is compiled, the application name is the name of the executable file minus the .EXE extension.

The *topic* is usually the name of the document that contains the needed data. For Excel, it is the name of the worksheet window. In Visual Basic, it's the name of the Form (see the FormName property).

The *item* is a reference to the object containing the data. In Excel, it is a reference to the cell containing the data in RC format; that is, R3C5 stands for the cell at the intersection of row 3 and column 5. For Visual Basic, the item is the name of the Label, Text box or Picture box that contains the data.

To initiate a DDE link with Visual Basic as the client, change the LinkTopic property of a Form, Label, Picture box, or Text box to *application¦topic*, the LinkItem property to *item*, and the LinkMode property to 1 (Hot), or 2 (Cold). Your Visual Basic program then attempts to establish a link with the external application. You don't have to do anything else. To close the link, change the LinkMode property of the Form or control back to 0 (none).

For example, the following procedure establishes a link between an Excel worksheet and Visual Basic (Microsoft Excel is needed for this example). Whenever the **Command1** button is pressed, the following short procedure establishes a link between the Text1 Text box and cell B2 (R2C2) on Sheet1.XLS of an Excel worksheet. Figure 14.1 shows both the cell in the worksheet and the Text box in Visual Basic. Changing the contents of the cell causes the Text box to change, as well.

> Because Microsoft Excel is needed for this example and you might not have it, check the documentation of some of your other Windows programs to see how they handle DDE and use them instead. Another option is to create a second Visual Basic application to respond to your DDE requests, as is done later in this chapter.

1. Open a new project and draw a Command button and Text box on the Form.

2. Open the Command1_Click procedure and type

```
Sub Command1_Click ()
Text1.LinkTopic = "Excel¦Sheet1.XLS"
Text1.LinkItem = "R2C2"
Text1.LinkMode = 1
End Sub
```

3. Run Microsoft Excel, type some text in cell B2, and save the worksheet as Sheet1.XLS.

4. Run the Visual Basic program and click the **Command1** button. The contents of the Excel worksheet should appear in the Text1 Text box. You will note two little bar-like symbols next to the text. They are markers for the carriage return-line feed that Excel appended to the text. Because the box is a single line box (Multiline = False) the carriage return-line feed appears as symbols. If Multiline were True, the symbols would make the cursor move down a line.

5. Switch to Excel and change the contents of cell B2. See what happens in the Text1 Text box.

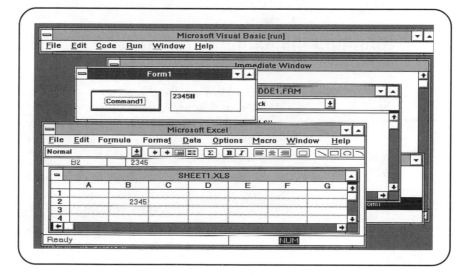

Figure 14.1. *A Dynamic Data Link between cell* B2 *on an Excel worksheet and a Text box.*

Sending Data to the Server

Excel can accept a Poke event, so add the following command button to the program. When you press the button, the data in the Text1 Text box is sent to the worksheet, changing the value of the linked cell in the worksheet.

343

6. Add another Command button to the Form, open the
Command2_Click procedure and type

```
Sub Command2_Click ()
Text1.LinkPoke
End Sub
```

7. Excel should still be running, so run the Visual Basic program and
click the **Command1** button to initiate the link. The Text1 Text
box and cell B2 should contain the same thing.

8. Change the contents of the Text1 Text box. Nothing happens in
the worksheet, because the Text box is the client, not the server.
Click the **Command2** button and the contents of the Text box is
sent to cell B2 on the worksheet.

Sending Commands to the Server

In addition to linking data, some DDE servers can accept commands from the client. For example, Excel accepts any valid macro
commands, surrounded by square brackets, from a linked client.
Using macro commands, Excel can be asked to open files, change
settings, change data and so forth.

For example, the following procedure informs Excel to select cell
B2 and change its value to Good Morning. Note that double quotation marks are needed in the command strings, so they have to be
created with Chr$(34) and concatenated into the command string.
The comments show what the command string looks like. The first
command informs Excel to activate Sheet1.XLS, the second command selects cell B2 (R2C2), and the third command changes its
value to Good Morning. The result is shown in Figure 14.2.

9. Add another button to the Form, open the Command3_Click
procedure and type

```
Sub Command3_Click ()
    'Send the command: [ACTIVATE("SHEET1.XLS")]
⮌ Text1.LinkExecute "[ACTIVATE(" + Chr$(34) + "SHEET1.XLS" +
    Chr$(34) + ")]"
    'Send the command: [SELECT( "R2C2" )]
```

```
   Text1.LinkExecute "[SELECT(" + Chr$(34) + "R2C2" +
      Chr$(34) + ")]"
      'Send the command: [FORMULA("Good Morning")]
   Text1.LinkExecute "[FORMULA(" + Chr$(34) +
      "Good Morning" + Chr$(34) + ")]"
End Sub
```

10. Run the program, press **Command1** to establish the link, then press **Command3** to send the macro commands to Excel.

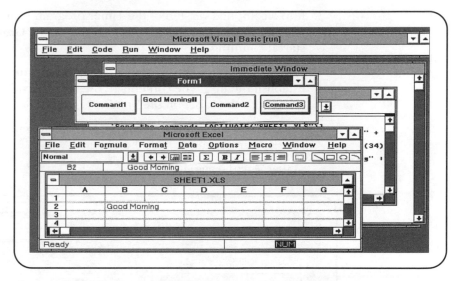

Figure 14.2. *Sending commands to a DDE server (Excel).*

Making Visual Basic the Server

To make a Visual Basic program the server in a DDE link, the LinkMode property of the Form you want to be the server must be set to 1 - Server. Note that this is the default setting, so you don't have to do anything to make a Visual Basic program a server. Any program that attempts to link to it sends Visual Basic a link request with the proper application, topic, and item. In Excel, the cell formula is =application¦Topic!Item.

For example, run a copy of the Timer program, then link to the Label using another Visual Basic program, and a cell in an Excel worksheet. All three cells count together, as shown in Figure 14.3.

1. Open a new project and draw a Command button and Text box on the Form.

2. Open the `Command1_Click` procedure and type

```
Sub Command1_Click ()
Text1.LinkTopic = "Timer¦Form1"
Text1.LinkItem = "Label1"
Text1.LinkMode = 1
End Sub
```

3. Run a compiled version of the Timer program from Chapter 13, "Debugging and Error Trapping," and click the **On/Off** button to start it counting.

4. Run the Visual Basic program and click the **Command1** button to establish the link. The contents of the `Text1` Text box now counts along with the Label on the Timer.

5. Select Excel, and set cell `B3` to the following command. Now it, too, is counting along with the Timer.

```
=Timer¦Form1!Label1
```

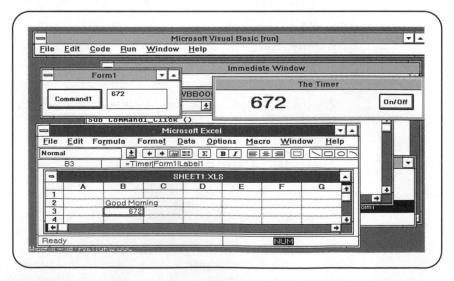

Figure 14.3. *A Dynamic Data Link between two Visual Basic programs and an Excel worksheet.*

Linking to Dynamic Link Libraries

A Dynamic Link Library is a special library of functions external to Visual Basic. Dynamic Link Libraries all have the .DLL extension. To use the functions in a DLL, you first must have the library documentation. There are several libraries that come with Windows, and the documentation is in the "Microsoft Windows Programmers Reference" by Microsoft Press. The Visual Basic DLLs are in the VBRUN100.DLL run-time library and include the Visual Basic procedures. Many of the Windows and Visual Basic procedures are defined in the examples included with Visual Basic.

Armed with this description of the library interface, add a `Declare` statement to the Global module to tell Visual Basic the names and argument types. After it is declared, you can use the function like any other internal `Sub` or `Function` procedure. Call the function with any numeric types, and Visual Basic converts the numbers to the correct types and passes them to the library routine.

For example, the following declares the interface to the DLL function `InvertRect`, in the library User.DLL. It has two arguments, `hdc` which is passed by value, and a user-defined type `lpRect`, passed by address.

```
Declare Function InvertRect Lib "User" (ByVal hdc, lpRect
As RECT)
```

The `InvertRect` function could now be used in a program, such as

```
Rval = InvertRect(Ctrl.hdc, rect)
```

Here, `Rval` is a dummy variable that receives any value returned by `InvertRect`.

Binary Files

Binary data files are actually any data file type opened with the Binary file type in the `Open` statement. When a file is opened `As Binary`, every byte of the file is accessible and changeable as if it were a random access file with

one-byte-long records. Use this file type when you have to look at the raw bytes of a file. A virus checker would be one such program, because it needs to search the contents of an executable file for a particular sequence of bytes. Any file can be opened as Binary, including executable (.EXE and .COM) files.

Use the Get and Input$ statements to read data from the Binary file and the Put statement to store data. When using Get and Put, the number of bytes read or written is equal to the number of bytes in the variables used as arguments to the statements.

Dragging and Dropping

If you want movable controls rather than fixed ones on a Form, you have two options, change the DragMode property of the control to 1 - Automatic, or use the Drag method in the controls MouseDown event procedure. Whichever of these methods you use, when you place the mouse pointer on the control and press the mouse button, you can drag an outline of the control around the Form. To actually move the control, use the Move method in the Form's DragDrop event procedure. For example, drag a Picture box around on a Form.

1. Draw a small Picture box on a Form, and set its DragMode property to 1 - Automatic.

2. Run the program, place the mouse pointer on the Picture box, press the left mouse button, and drag an outline of the Picture box around the screen.

   When you release the mouse button to drop Picture box, the Picture box jumps back to its original location, because you have not moved the Picture box; you have only dragged its outline around. To actually move it, add a Move method to the Form's DragDrop procedure.

3. End the program, open the Form_DragDrop procedure and type the following.

```
Sub Form_DragDrop (Source As Control, X As Single,
   Y As Single)
Source.Move X, Y
End Sub
```

The DragDrop event occurs whenever a control is dragged over a Form (or other control) and dropped. The Source argument contains the name of the control (the Picture box) that was dragged over and dropped on the Form. The X and Y arguments contain the location of the mouse pointer when the control was dropped. The Move method is used here to actually move the control to the new coordinates. A difficulty here is that the upper-left corner of the control is moved to the x, y location supplied by the DragDrop procedure. The x, y location is not the upper-left corner of the outline being dragged around the Form, but the location of the mouse pointer on that outline. When you Run this program you will see what I mean.

4. Run the program and drag and drop the Picture box around on the Form. Note where the outline is, and where the Picture box moves when you release the mouse button. End the program when you are done.

   If you want the dragged control to align with the outline when it is moved, you must capture the x, y coordinates of the MouseDown event on the control and subtract that location from the x, y coordinates in the DragDrop procedure.

5. Open the general procedure on the Form and define the variables for the x and y offsets. Also, define two constants to be used later.

```
Dim XOffset As Single
Dim YOffset As Single
Const StartDrag = 1
Const Drop = 2
```

6. Select the Picture1_MouseDown procedure and type the following.

```
Sub Picture1_MouseDown (Button As Integer,
   Shift As Integer, X As Single, Y As Single)
XOffset = X
YOffset = Y
Picture1.Drag StartDrag
End Sub
```

   This procedure stores the location of the MouseDown event on Picture1, and manually initiates dragging with the Drag method.

7. Select the Form_DragDrop procedure and change it to the following.

```
Sub Form_DragDrop (Source As Control, X As Single, Y As
   Single)
Source.Drag Drop
Source.Move X - XOffset, Y - YOffset
End Sub
```

349

This procedure ends manual dragging and moves the Picture box. The procedure offsets that move by the location of the initial MouseDown on the Picture box.

8. Click the **View Form** button on the Project window, select the Picture1 Picture box and change its DragMode property to **0 - Manual**.

9. Run the program and drag and drop the Picture box. Again, note where the outline is, and where the Picture box moves when the mouse button is released. Now they should align. End the program when you are done and save it if you like.

This method works for all controls that have a MouseDown event, which includes List boxes, Labels, File List boxes and Picture boxes. For all other controls, such as Command buttons, you can either manually insert the values of XOffset and YOffset that offset the move to the center of the control (the most obvious place to click a control before dragging it), or use a custom icon stored in the controls DragIcon property. The custom icon is always centered on the mouse pointer so you can manually insert the size of the offset. See Chapter 15, "Command Reference," for more information on using these properties.

File System Management

File system control is not truly an advanced feature, but it is covered here because it is not widely used in BASIC anymore. The original BASICs were the operating systems for several early machines, and as such, had to be able to control the file system. Current BASICs are programming environments within the current operating system, so they rarely have to move and copy files, but the capability from the earlier versions still exists. The DOS file system is controlled from within a Visual Basic program with commands similar to the DOS system commands. The following statements and functions can be used in any Visual Basic program to control the file system. See the descriptions of the individual commands in Chapter 15, "Command Reference," for more information.

ChDir	Change to a different default directory
ChDrive	Change the current drive

`CurDir$`	Get the current directory path
`Dir$`	Return a list of files
`Kill`	Delete a file
`MkDir`	Create a subdirectory
`Name As`	Change the name of a file or move it to a different directory
`RmDir`	Delete a subdirectory

What You Have Learned

14

This chapter points you to some of the advanced capabilities of Visual Basic. These features are somewhat beyond the scope of an introductory book, but I expect that you will eventually want to use them, if only to experiment with the capabilities of Visual Basic. To try them out, create some simple applications like those in this chapter and experiment with the functions and methods. This chapter examined

- Linking Applications with DDE.
- Using DLL Libraries.
- Using Binary files.
- Dragging and dropping.
- Managing the file system.

Congratulations to all of you who have made it to the end of Part II. By now, you should be able to use the essential capabilities of Visual Basic. Parts III and IV are reference sections, so—unless you read technical manuals for fun—you probably will find it most useful for explanations of the specific aspects of Visual Basic you are using.

Part III

Visual Basic
Reference

Command Reference

This chapter of the reference section contains an alphabetical list of Visual Basic functions, operators, statements, data types, and methods. Chapter 16, "Properties," lists Visual Basic properties. Chapter 17, "Events," lists Visual Basic events, and Chapter 18, "Objects," lists the Visual Basic objects.

Each section in this chapter addresses a single language element, giving its **Purpose** followed by the **Syntax**, the **Arguments**, a more complete **Description**, any values it **Returns**, usage under **For Example**, and a list of similar or complementary functions under **See also**.

Purpose

The **Purpose** section is a brief statement of the function of the language element.

Arguments

The **Arguments** section describes each of the arguments listed in the Syntax section.

Syntax Statements

As in Part II of this book, syntax statements have a structured form to list all the options and arguments:

- The parts of the command that must be literally typed are shown in monospace bold type, such as `End`.

- Placeholders for variables are in `monospace italic` and, where appropriate, are prefaced with a variable type prefix character such as `$` or `%`.

- Optional arguments are surrounded by [square brackets].

- Mutually exclusive items are separated by vertical ¦ lines and surrounded by {curly braces}. You may use only one item from a list of mutually exclusive items.

- Repeated clauses are followed by an ellipsis (...).

Example 1:

`End [{Function¦Select¦Sub¦Type}]`

In this example, the key word `End` must be typed verbatim, so it is in bold. `End` is followed by a list of optional arguments; remember that options are shown in [brackets]. Only one of the four key words shown—`Function`, `Select`, `Sub`, or `Type`—may be used as an argument with `End`. We know that we must choose one because they are surrounded by {curly braces} and separated by vertical ¦ bars.

Example 2:

MsgBox(*msg$*[,*type%*[,*title$*]]**)**

In this example, the key word **MsgBox** and the parentheses must be typed verbatim so they are shown in bold. The string argument *msg$* is a placeholder for a string constant or a string variable, as shown by its italics. The two other arguments are optional and so are shown in [brackets].

But is there an extra bracket around *title$*? When you see brackets within brackets, treat the arguments as a pair. In this case the second argument, *type%*, is optional and can be used alone; if the third argument, *title$*, is used, the second, *type%*, must be included.

Arguments

The **Arguments** section describes each of the arguments listed in the Syntax section. For variables such as *type%* you are not required to use the prefix characters when using the functions; they merely indicate the type of variable the function or statement expects. For numeric values, any variable type can be used and automatically converted to the type shown in the descriptions. In most cases, you can use either of the following for the argument.

- A variable containing the required value

- A literal value for the argument. A literal is simply a number typed at the correct location in the argument list, or, if a string argument is required, a string of text between double quotation marks.

The prefix characters are

Type	*Prefix*
Integer	%
Long	&
Single	!
Double	#
Currency	@
String	$

In cases having many options, such as the Open statement, I have simplified the syntax statements by using placeholders for the options and including the option list in the **Arguments** section.

For functions and operators, the value returned by the function or the result of the operation is described in the **Returns** section.

 Abs

Purpose   The Abs() function calculates and returns the absolute value of *number*

Syntax   `Abs(number)`

Arguments   *number*—a number of any type, or a formula that evaluates to a number.

Description The absolute value of a number is the value of the positive magnitude of the number.

Returns   The result is the absolute (positive) value of a number. The numeric type of the result is the same type as the argument.

For example The following two assignment statements both assign the value 1 to the variables on the left.

```
A = Abs(-1)     'Assigns the value 1 to A
aVal = Abs(1)   'Assigns the value 1 to aVal
```

See also   Sgn() function

 AddItem

Purpose   The AddItem method adds a new entry to a List or Combo box.

Syntax   `[form.]control.AddItem item$[,index%]`

Arguments   *control*—the name of a List or Combo box. If the name of the Form isn't included, this argument defaults to the Form containing this method.

item$—the string item to add to the control's list.

index%—the location in the list of items in the List or Combo box at which to insert the item. The first item is number 0, the second is 1, and so forth. If this argument is omitted and the Sorted property is False, the item is added at the end of the list. If this argument is omitted and Sorted is True, the item is inserted in its alphabetical location.

Description   The AddItem method adds new items to the List property in a List or Combo box. List and Combo boxes can be loaded with items only at run time; they cannot be loaded at design time.

For example   The example code fragment adds the text A new item to the List3 List box on Form1. This code adds the new text to the end of the list unless the Sorted property is True, in which case it adds it at its alphabetical position in the list.

```
Form1.List3.AddItem "A new item"
```

See also   RemoveItem method
List property
ListCount property
ListIndex property

And

Purpose   The And operator combines two logical expressions or all the bits in two numeric values using the logical AND operation.

Syntax   *express1* **And** *express2*

Arguments   *express1, express2*—a logical expression, numeric expression, or numeric value.

Description   The And operator combines two logical values according to the following truth table. If two numeric values are combined, the operator is applied bit by bit to the corresponding bits in the two values; that is, each bit in the result is equal to the logical AND of the corresponding bits in the two values.

A	B	A And B
True	True	True
True	False	False
False	True	False
False	False	False

Returns   The logical AND of the two expressions equals (True (−1) or False (0)) if *express1* and *express2* are logical expressions. If *express1* and *express2* are numeric expressions, the result is the bitwise logical AND of the same bits in each of the two expressions.

For example   The following If statement causes a beep only if both A and B are True.

```
If A And B Then  Beep
```

See also   Eqv operator
Imp operator
Not operator
Or operator
Xor operator

 Any

Purpose   The data type Any suppresses data type checking and matches any data type in a Declare statement.

Syntax   *variable* **As Any**

Arguments   *variable*—a variable name.

Description   The data type Any is used in Declare statements to disable data type error checking for values passed to a Dynamic Link Library (DLL) procedure.

For example   The following statement declares the name and arguments to a Sub procedure (DoItAgain) in an external DLL library (MYLIB.DLL). The argument ArgA is not checked for type when a value is passed to the external procedure. The argument ArgB must be an Integer and is checked for type before being passed to the external procedure.

```
Declare Sub DoItAgain Lib "MYLIB.DLL" (ArgA As Any,
    ArgB As Integer)
```

See also   Declare statement
Type statement
Control data type
Currency data type
Double data type
Form data type

Integer data type
Long data type
Single data type
String data type

 # AppActivate

Purpose The AppActivate statement activates the **Program** window of another running application. The **Program** window is the first, or main, window that an application opens.

Syntax `AppActivate progtitle$`

Arguments *progtitle$*—a string containing the text in the title bar of the **Program** window to activate. It must match character for character, but is not case sensitive.

Description The AppActivate statement activates another running program under the control of Visual Basic. Once activated, use the SendKeys statement to send keystrokes to the activated application.

For example The following Sub procedure activates the Timer program created in Chapter 13, "Debugging," and presses the **On/Off** button.

```
Sub ActivateTimer
AppActivate "The Timer"
SendKeys "{Enter}", -1
End Sub
```

See also SendKeys statement

Asc

Purpose The Asc() function returns the ASCII code of the first character of the string argument.

Syntax `Asc(astring$)`

Arguments *astring$*—a string of any length; only the first character is examined.

Description   The ASCII character set consists of 128 standard characters, plus a second set of 128 characters defined in the ANSI standard. Each character has a code between 0 and 255. The Asc() function returns the code for the first character in the argument. Use the Chr$() function to convert codes back to characters.

> The second 128 characters are different in DOS and Windows applications.

Returns   The result is the ASCII code for the first character in the string argument.

For example   The following two assignment statements assign the variables A and B to the ASCII codes for R and 7.

```
A = Asc("R")      'assigns A the code 82
B = Asc("7")      'assigns B the code 55
```

See also   Chr$() function

 **Atn**

Purpose   The Atn() function calculates and returns the first quadrant arctangent of number.

Syntax   Atn(*number*)

Arguments   *number*—a number of any numeric type, or a formula that evaluates to a number.

Description   The arctangent of a number is the angle whose tangent is the number. The arctangent function is the inverse of the tangent function. This function returns an angle in the positive half space between $-\pi/2$ and $\pi/2$. The actual angle also could be in the negative half space, because

$$\mathrm{Tan}(\theta) = \mathrm{Tan}(\theta + \pi)$$

for any angle θ. To convert from degrees to radians, multiply by $\pi/180$. To calculate the arcsine and arccosine using the arctangent function, use:

```
arcsine(T) = Atn(T/Sqrt(1 - T^2))
π = 3.141593
arccosine(T) = π/2 - Atn(T/Sqrt(1 - T^2))
```

Returns   The result is the arctangent of *number* expressed in radians. It is in the range $-\pi/2$ to $\pi/2$, where π is 3.141593.

For example   The following two assignment statements assign the arctangent of 3.25 to the variable on the left, one in radians and one in degrees.

```
A = Atn(3.25)                'Assigns the arctangent in radians
                             'of 3.25 to A.
B = Atn(3.25)*180/3.141593   'Assigns the arctangent
                             'in degrees of 3.25 to B.
```

See also   Sin() function
Cos() function
Tan() function

S | Beep

Purpose   The Beep statement causes a system beep.

Syntax   **Beep**

Arguments   None

Description   The Beep statement causes a system beep out of the computer's speaker.

For example   The following Sub procedure emits NumBeeps beeps, each separated by a short pause determined by the second For/Next loop.

```
\Sub Beeper (NumBeeps As Integer)
Dim I As Integer, J As Integer
For I = 1 To NumBeeps
 Beep
 For J = 1 To 10000      'Delay Loop
 Next J                  'Delay Loop
Next I
End Sub
```

See also   None

S Call

Purpose The Call statement passes control to a Sub procedure or external DLL procedure.

Syntax **Call** *routinename* [(*arglist*)]

or

routinename [*arglist*]

Arguments *routinename*—the name of the Sub procedure or DLL procedure to execut⋅.

arglist—the argument list for the called procedure. This is a comma-delimited list of variables, formulas, or constants, as required by the called function.

Description The Call statement executes a Sub procedure or a procedure in an external Dynamic Link Library (DLL). The Call keyword is not used in most Visual Basic programs, but is included for compatibility with other software. If the Call keyword is used, place the argument list within parentheses. If the Call keyword is not used, the argument list must not be within parrentheses.

The arguments to the called procedure are passed by reference; that is, only the address of the argument is passed to the procedure, and not the value of the variable itself. If an argument in the argument list is a formula, Visual Basic creates a temporary copy of the variable and passes the address of the copy. You can force a variable to be passed as a copy rather than as the original variable by enclosing it in parentheses. This protects a variable passed to a called procedure. If the procedure changes the value of the variable, it actually changes the value of the copy and not that of the original variable.

Another way to protect a variable passed to a called procedure is to include the ByVal keyword in the heading of the Sub procedure or the Declare statement for the DLL procedure. The ByVal keyword causes the value of an argument to be passed rather than the actual value itself. DLL procedures generally require that they be passed values instead of references.

For example The SumIt procedure has three arguments. The following two statements both call the SumIt procedure with the same arguments. In both cases, only a copy of the variable B is passed, so the original value remains unchanged.

```
Call SumIt(A, (B), C)
SumIt A, (B), C
```

See also Sub statement
Declare statement

 CCur

Purpose The CCur() function converts a number of any numeric type to the Currency type.

Syntax CCur(*number*)

Arguments *number*—a number of any type, or a formula that evaluates to a number.

Description The CCur() function converts a number in any numeric type to the Currency type. This function is not needed if you assign a number to a Currency type variable, because Visual Basic automatically does the conversion in such cases. This function is useful to force a calculation to be done in Currency type if the calculation contains other numeric types.

If every number used in a calculation is of the same numeric type, the entire calculation is done in that type. If a calculation contains different numeric types, Visual Basic converts everything to the most precise type before doing the calculation.

Returns The result is *number* converted to the Currency data type.

For example The following Sub procedure contains a simple formula involving two different numeric types. Applying the CCur() function to theRate forces it to the Currency data type, so the entire formula now is in the Currency data type.

Be careful when you do this to values with more than four characters to the right of the decimal, as anything beyond four is rounded off.

```
Function SalesTax (theCash As Currency,
    theRate As Single) As Currency
SalesTax = theCash * CCur(theRate)
End Function
```

See also   CDbl function
          CInt function
          CLng function
          CSng function

 **CDbl**

Purpose   The CDbl() function converts a number of any numeric type to the Double type.

Syntax   **CDbl(***number***)**

Arguments   *number*—a number of any type, or a formula that evaluates to a number.

Description   The CDbl() function converts a number in any numeric type to the Double type. This function is not needed if you assign a number to a Double type variable, because Visual Basic automatically does the conversion in such cases. This function is useful to force a calculation to be done in Double type if the calculation contains other numeric types.

If every number used in a calculation is of the same numeric type, the entire calculation is done in that type. If a calculation contains different numeric types, Visual Basic converts everything to the most precise type before doing the calculation.

Returns   The result is *number* converted to the Double data type.

For example   The following Sub procedure contains a simple formula involving two different numeric types. Applying the CDbl() function to Value2 forces it to the Double data type, so the entire formula now is in the Double data type.

```
Function MultiplyEm (value1 As Double,
    Value2 As Integer) As Double
MultiplyEm = Value1*CDbl(Value2)
End Function
```

See also   CCCur function
          CInt function
          CLng function
          CSng function

 **ChDir**

Purpose   The ChDir statement sets the default directory for a drive.

Syntax   ChDir *path$*

Arguments   *path$*—a string containing the directory path, including the disk letter, with the following syntax:

[*drive:*][\]*directory*[*directory*]...

where *drive* is the drive letter and *directory* is a directory name. Omit the drive argument to use the current drive. If the first backslash is omitted, the path is assumed to start in the default directory of the specified drive. The string must be less than 128 bytes long.

Description   The default directory on the current drive is where disk operations that do not specify a directory take place. The ChDir statement changes the default directory on a disk drive. Most commands that manipulate the directory system or open or create files can take a complete path and directory as an argument. By using this command first, they need only specify the file name. If no disk drive is specified in the path$ argument, the statement changes the default directory on the current drive. If a drive is specified in the path$ argument, the default directory is changed on that drive. Even if an alternate drive is specified, this statement does not change the current drive. Use the ChDrive statement to change the current drive.

For example   The first statement below changes the default directory on the C drive to \TOOLS\UTILITIES. The second statement changes the default directory relative to the old default directory. That is, if the current default directory is

C:\TOOLS\UTILITIES

the second command would change it to:

C:\TOOLS\UTILITIES\PROGRAMS\C.

```
ChDir "C:\TOOLS\UTILITIES"
ChDir "PROGRAMS\C"
```

See also   ChDrive statement
Kill statement
MkDir statement

Name statement
RmDir statement
CurDir$ function
Dir$ function

 ChDrive

Purpose	The ChDrive statement changes the current drive.
Syntax	**ChDrive** *drive$*
Arguments	*drive$*—a string containing the letter of the drive to make the current drive. The drive letter must be the first character in the string; any other characters in the string are ignored.
Description	The default directory on the current drive is where disk operations take place when the directory isn't explicitly defined. Each disk has a default directory set with the ChDir statement, and the current disk is set with the ChDrive statement.
For example	The first statement below changes the current drive to the A drive. The second statement changes the current drive to the C drive. The balance of the argument string is ignored.

```
ChDrive "A"
ChDrive "C:\TOOLS"
```

See also	ChDir statement
	Kill statement
	MkDir statement
	Name statement
	RmDir statement
	CurDir$ function
	Dir$ function

F Chr$

Purpose	The Chr$() function returns the character defined by the ASCII code.

Syntax	Chr$(*code*)

Arguments   *code*—an ASCII code. This must be an integer between 0 and 255.

Description   The ASCII character set consists of 128 standard characters, plus a second 128 characters defined in the ANSI standard. Each character has a code between 0 and 255. The Chr$() function returns the character defined by the ASCII code number used as its argument. Use the Asc() function to convert characters back to ASCII codes.

> The second 128 characters are different in DOS and Windows applications.

Returns   The result is a single character string containing the ASCII character defined by *code*.

For example   The following procedure prints a table of ASCII codes and characters on the Immediate window. It skips the first 32 characters (0 through 31) which are the control characters such as Enter, and Backspace.

```
Sub CodeTable
For I = 32 To 255
   Debug.Print I, Chr$(I)
Next I
End Sub
```

See also   Asc() function

 # CInt

Purpose   The CInt() function converts a number of any numeric type to the Integer type by rounding.

Syntax	CInt(*number*)

Arguments   *number*—a number of any type, or a formula that evaluates to a number.

Description   The CInt() function converts a number in any numeric type to the Integer type. This function is not needed if you assign number to an Integer type variable, because Visual Basic automatically does the conversion in that

case. This function is useful to force a calculation to be done in Integer type if the calculation contains other numeric types. If every number used in a calculation is of the same numeric type, the entire calculation is done in that type. If a calculation contains different numeric types, Visual Basic converts everything to the most precise type before doing the calculation.

CInt() is most useful for converting floating point numbers to integers by rounding instead of truncation, as is done by the Int and Fix functions.

Returns   The result is *number* converted to the Integer data type.

For example   The following statements show how CInt(), Int(), and Fix() convert different values.

n	*CInt(n)*	*Int(n)*	*Fix(n)*
3.7	4	3	3
3.4	3	3	3
−3.7	−4	−4	−3
−3.4	−3	−4	−3

See also   CCur function
CLng function
CSng function
Int function
Fix function

 # Circle

Purpose   The Circle method draws circles, ellipses, filled circles, filled ellipses, arcs, pie slices, and filled pie slices on Forms, Picture boxes, and the Printer object.

Syntax   [*object.*]**Circle** [Step]*(xc!,yc!)*, *radius!*
[,[*color&*][,[*startang!*][,[*endang!*]
[,*aspect!*]]]]

Arguments   *object*—the name of the object to draw on, a Form, Picture box, or the keyword Printer. Omit this argument to use the Form containing the statement.

Step —a keyword that specifies that the coordinates specifying the center of the circle are relative to the current position specified by the CurrentX and CurrentY properties.

xc!,yc!—the *x,y* coordinates of the center of the circle. See the ScaleMode property in Chapter 16, "Properties," for a discussion of drawing measurement units.

radius!—the radius of the circle.

color&—an RGB color number specifying the color to use for the circle's outline. Omit it to use the current ForeColor. If the object is closed (a circle, ellipse, or pie slice) it is filled with the current FillColor using the current FillStyle. See the RGB() function for more information on colors.

startang!, *endang!*—the starting and ending angles of an arc or pie slice, measured in radians. The 0 angle is at 3:00, and angles increase counterclockwise. If a negative value is used for an angle, its absolute value defines the end of the arc and another line is drawn from the center of the circle to that end of the arc.

aspect!—the aspect ratio of the circle. If the aspect ratio is 1.0, a circle is drawn. If the aspect ratio is less than 1, an ellipse is drawn with the long axis horizontal. If the aspect ratio is greater than 1, an ellipse is drawn with the long axis vertical.

Description The Circle method produces circles, filled circles, ellipses, filled ellipses, arcs, pie slices, and filled pie slices on Forms, Picture boxes, and the Printer object. Only completely closed figures are filled; these are circles, ellipses, and pie slices. To make a pie slice instead of an arc, use negative angles for the starting and ending angles of the arc. This forces the drawing of lines from the center of the circle to the ends of the arc.

The drawing is affected by the settings of all the drawing properties: CurrentX, CurrentY, DrawMode, DrawWidth, FillColor, FillStyle, and ForeColor.

There is a bug in this method that makes a Visual Basic program crash when drawing a pie slice if the combination of radius and aspect ratio makes the line length from the center of the circle to the end of an arc on the order of the size of a pixel.

For example   The statement below draws a circle on the Picture1 Picture box. Assuming that the default ScaleMode is in effect, the center is 2000 twips from the left side of the box and 1000 twips down from the top, and the radius is 800 twips. (See the ScaleMode property in Chapter 16 for a description of measurement units such as twips.) The circle is outlined in red—&HFF is the color number for red—and filled with the current FillColor using the current FillStyle.

```
Picture1.Circle (2000, 1000), 800, &HFF&
```

The following statement creates an elliptical, filled pie slice with an aspect ratio of 0.8 on the current Form. The *x, y* location and the radius of the circle are the same as for the preceding statement. This time the object is outlined in the current ForeColor because no color is specified. The arc ranges from 1 to 2 radians (57 to 114 degrees) and lines are drawn from the center to the ends of the slice.

```
Circle (2000, 1000), 800, , -1, -2, .8
```

See also   Line method
RGB() function
QBColor() function
CurrentX property
CurrentY property
DrawMode property
DrawWidth property
FillColor property
FillStyle property
ForeColor property

 Clear

Purpose   The Clear method deletes the current contents of the Clipboard.

Syntax   **Clipboard.Clear**

Arguments   None

Description   The Clear method clears the contents of the Clipboard.

For example   The following statement clears the contents of the Clipboard.

```
Clipboard.Clear
```

See also   SetData method
GetData method
GetFormat method

 CLng

Purpose   The CLng() function converts a number of any numeric type to the Long integer type by rounding.

Syntax   **CLng(** *number* **)**

Arguments   *number*—a number of any type, or a formula that evaluates to a number.

Description   The CLng() function converts a number in any numeric type to the Long integer type. This function is not needed if you assign *number* to a Long type variable, because Visual Basic automatically does the conversion in that case. CLng() is useful to force a calculation to be done in Long type if the calculation contains other numeric types. If every number used in a calculation is of the same numeric type, then the entire calculation is done in that type. If a calculation contains different numeric types, Visual Basic converts everything to the most precise type before doing the calculation.

Returns   The result is *number* converted to the Long integer data type.

For example   The following Function procedure contains a simple formula involving two different numeric types. Applying the CInt() function to Value2 forces it to the Long data type, so the entire formula now is in the Long data type.

```
Function MultiplyEm (Value1 As Long,
    Value2 As Double) As Long
MultiplyEm = Value1*CInt(Value2)
End Function
```

See also   CCCur function
CDbl function
CInt function
CSng function
Int function
Fix function

 Close

Purpose   The Close statement closes open disk files.

Syntax   **Close** *[[#]filenum][,[#]filenum]...*

Arguments   *filenum*—the file number used when the file was opened with the Open
                   statement. Omitting the # symbol has no effect. Omit all file numbers to
                   close all open files.

Description   The Close statement closes one or more open disk files, and releases the file
                   number for reuse. The file numbers assigned to each disk file to be closed
                   are listed in the arguments. If no arguments are used, all open disk files are
                   closed.

For example   The first example closes file numbers 1 and 2. The second example closes
                   only file number 1. The third example closes all open files.

```
Close #1, #2
Close 1
Close
```

See also   Open statement

M Cls

Purpose   The Cls method clears text and graphics from a Form or Picture box.

Syntax   *[object.]***Cls**

Arguments   *object*—the name of the object to draw on, a Form, or Picture box. Omit
                   this argument to use the Form containing the statement.

Description   The Cls method clears text and graphics drawn on a Form at run time.
                   Pictures stored in the Picture property at design time are not affected.
                   Drawing that occurs at run time is not affected if AutoRedraw was True and
                   if the drawing was set to False before Cls was executed. The values of the
                   CurrentX and CurrentY properties are set to 0.

For example   The following statement clears the contents of the Picture1 Picture box.

Picture1.Cls

See also   AutoRedraw property

 Command$

Purpose   The Command$ function returns the command-line arguments used to launch Visual Basic or a Visual Basic application.

Syntax   Command$

Arguments   None

Description   The Command$ function returns everything after the /cmd option in the command line used to launch Visual Basic, or everything after the program name in the command line used to launch a Visual Basic application. Command lines are set in the File Manager for applications launched from windows, and are typed at the command line for applications launched from DOS. You can change the contents of the command line when running in interpreted mode by executing the **M**odify Command$ command on the **R**un menu.

Returns   The result is a string containing the command-line arguments.

For example   The following assignment statement assigns the contents of the command line to the string theLine$.

theLine$ = Command$

See also   None

 Const

Purpose   The Const statement defines constants for use in Visual Basic programs.

Syntax   [**Global.**] **Const** *name* = *value*,*[name = value]...*

Arguments Global—a keyword that must precede the word Const when used in the Global module. Makes the defined constants available throughout a program.

name—the name of the constant value, a legal Visual Basic variable name.

value—the value to give the constant. This is usually only literals, but it may include other constants and simple arithmetic (+, -, *, /) or logical (=, <, >, <>, <=, >=) operators.

Description The Const statement defines constants for use in a program. Constants usually are defined in the Global module, and thus need the Global keyword. Constants make a program much more readable by allowing you to use words such as True and False instead of –1 and 0 in program. The words are much easier to understand than the raw numeric codes they stand for. Once defined, a constant cannot be redefined in a program.

For example The following statement defines the constants RED, and BLUE as the Long integer color numbers that produce those colors.

```
Global Const RED = &HFF&, BLUE = &HFF0000&
```

See also Dim statement
Global statement

Control

Purpose The data type Control matches any control name passed to a Sub or Function procedure.

Syntax *variable* **As Control**

Arguments *variable*—a variable name.

Description The data type Control is used in Sub and Function procedure headings to declare a variable as type control so that a control name may be passed to a procedure. The variable may then be used as a control name. To see what kind of a control has been passed to a procedure, use the TypeOf   Is expression in an If statement.

For example The following procedure defines Pic as a Control type and then uses an If statement to see if it is a Picture box. If it is, it sets the ScaleMode to 0 and defines a user-defined scale using the global variables Xmin, Xmax, Ymin, Ymax.

```
Sub ScaleIt (Pic As Control)
If TypeOf Pic Is PictureBox Then
    Pic.ScaleMode = 0   ' User-defined scale
    Pic.Scale (Xmin, Ymax)-(Xmax, Ymin)
End If
End Sub
```

See also   Declare statement
If statement
Type statement
Any data type
Currency date type
Double date type
Form date type
Integer data type
Long date type
Single data type
String data type

Cos

Purpose   The Cos() function calculates and returns the cosine of an angle in radians.

Syntax   **Cos(***angle***)**

Arguments   *angle*—an angle in radians expressed as a number, or a formula that evaluates to a number of any numeric type.

Description   The Cos() function calculates the cosine of an angle expressed in radians. Use the following to calculate the cosine of an angle expressed in degrees.

π = 3.141592654
theCosine = Cos(*dangle**π/180))

where *dangle* is measured in degrees.

Returns   The result is the cosine of *angle*, a number between −1 and +1.

For example   The following two assignment statements calculate the cosine of two angles, one in radians and one in degrees.

```
A = Cos(3.25)                'Assigns the cosine of 3.25
                             'radians to A = -0.99413.
π = 3.141592654
B = Cos(27.8*Pi/180)         'Assigns the cosine of 27.8
                             'degrees to B = 0.88458.
```

See also   Atn() function
                Sin() function
                Tan() function

 # CSng

Purpose   The CSng() function converts a number of any numeric type to the Single precision floating point type.

Syntax   **CSng(***number***)**

Arguments   *number*—a number of any type, or a formula that evaluates to a number.

Description   The CSng() function converts a number in any numeric type to the Single type. Numbers are rounded, if necessary, during the conversion. This function is not needed if you assign *number* to a Single type variable because Visual Basic automatically does the conversion in that case. This function is useful to force a calculation to be done in Single type if the calculation contains other numeric types. If every number used in a calculation is of the same numeric type, the entire calculation is done in that type. If a calculation contains different numeric types, Visual Basic converts everything to the most precise type before doing the calculation.

Returns   The result is *number* converted to the Single data type.

For example   The following Sub procedure contains a simple formula involving two different numeric types. Applying the CSng() function to Value2 forces it to the Single data type, so the entire formula now is in the Single data type.

```
Function MultiplyEm (value1 As Single, Value2 As Double)
    As Integer
MultiplyEm = Value1*CSng(Value2)
End Function
```

See also   CCCur function
CInt function
CLng function
CDbl function
Int function
Fix function

CurDir$

Purpose   The CurDir$ function returns the default directory on the specified drive.

Syntax   **CurDir$[(***drive$***)]**

Arguments   *drive$*—a string containing the letter of the drive to examine. The drive letter must be the first character in the string; any other characters in the string are ignored. Omit this argument to use the current drive.

Description   The default directory on the current drive is where disk operations take place when the directory isn't explicitly defined. Each disk has a default directory set with the ChDir statement. The current disk is set with the ChDrive statement. Use the CurDir$ function to get the current default path for a drive.

Returns   The result is a string containing the directory path, including the disk letter with the following syntax:

drive:*directory**directory*

where *drive* is the drive letter and *directory* is a directory name.

For example   If the current directory on the C drive is \TOOLS\UTILITIES, then thePath$ contains C:\TOOLS\UTILITIES.

```
thePath$ = CurDir$("c")
```

See also   ChDir
ChDrive statement
Kill statement
MkDir statement
Name statement
RmDir statement
Dir$ function

D Currency

Purpose The data type Currency matches or defines currency type variables.

Syntax *variable* **As Currency**

Arguments *variable*—a variable name.

Description The data type Currency is used in Sub and Function procedure headings to declare a variable as Currency type so that Visual Basic can check values passed to the procedure. The data type Currency is used also in a Dim, Global, or Static statement to define a variable as Currency type. The Currency data type is an eight-byte, fixed point number, with fifteen digits to the left of the decimal and four digits to the right, that ranges from –922,337,203,685,477.5808 to 922,337,203,685,477.5807. The Currency type is optimized for calculations where numeric accuracy is important, such as in money transactions.

For example The following Function procedure defines theCash as Currency type in the function heading so that Visual Basic can check the type of values passed to it. It then calculates and returns the amount of sales tax as a Currency type value.

```
Function SalesTax (theCash As Currency, theRate As Single)
    As Currency
SalesTax = theCash * CCur(theRate)
End Function
```

See also Dim statement
Static statement
Global statement
Type statement
Any data type
Control data type
Double data type
Form data type
Integer data type
Long data type
Single data type
String data type

 Date$

Purpose	The Date$ function gets and returns the current date from the system clock.
Syntax	`Date$`
Arguments	None
Description	The Date$ function gets the system date in a string. Use the Date$ statement to set the date. To get the current date as a date number, use the Now function or apply the DateValue() function to the string returned by Date$.
Returns	The result is a string containing the system date in the format: *mm-dd-yyyy* where *mm* is the month, *dd* is the day and *yyyy* is the year.
For example	The following assignment statement assigns the current date to the string variable A$.

```
A$ = Date$     'Assign the current date to A$
```

See also
DateSerial() function
DateValue() function
Day() function
Hour() function
Minute() function
Month() function
Now function
Second() function
Time$ function
Timer function
TimeSerial() function
TimeValue() function
Weekday() function
Year() function
Date$ statement
Time$ statement

15

S Date$

Purpose   The Date$ statement sets the system clock.

Syntax   **Date$** = *datestring$*

Arguments   *datestring$*—a string containing the date to which to set the clock, in one of the following formats:

mm-dd-yyyy
mm-dd-yy
mm/dd/yy
mm/dd/yyyy

where *mm* is the month, *dd* is the day and *yy* or *yyyy* is the year. The year must be between 1980 and 2099.

Description   The Date$ statement sets the date in the system clock. Depending on your system, you also may have to run a setup program to make the date change permanent.

For example   The following statement sets the system date to January 1, 1992.

```
Date$ = "1/1/1992"
```

You could also use:

```
Date$ = "01/01/1992"
```

See also   Date$ function
DateSerial() function
DateValue() function
Day() function
Hour() function
Minute() function
Month() function
Now function
Second() function
Time$ function
Timer function
TimeSerial() function
TimeValue() function
Weekday() function
Year() function
Time$ statement

F DateSerial

Purpose The DateSerial function calculates a serial date number from the month, day and year.

Syntax **DateSerial(**_year%,month%,day%_**)**

Arguments _year%_—the year as a numeric value between 1753 and 2078, or a formula that evaluates to a number in that range. The last two digits of the date may be used for dates after 1900.

month%—the month as a number from 1 to 12, or a formula that evaluates to a number in that range.

day%—the day as a number from 1 to 31, or a formula that evaluates to a number in that range.

Description The DateSerial() function converts numeric expressions representing the month, day, and year to a serial date number. The month, day, and year are integer values depicting the date. The serial date number is a double-precision, floating point number rather than Integer or Long, because it also stores the time to the right of the decimal. Using serial date numbers, you quickly can figure out the number of days between two events by simply subtracting the serial date numbers. Serial date numbers containing the time can be added to serial date numbers containing the date to store both the date and time in the same number.

Returns The result is the serial date number. A serial date number is a double-precision number containing the date, represented as the number of days since December 30, 1899. Negative serial date numbers represent dates from January 1, 1753 to December 30, 1899. Times are represented as fractions of a day. Years after 1900 are represented by the same serial date numbers used in several popular spreadsheet programs.

For example The following statement stores the serial date number (31853.0) for March 17, 1987 in the variable theDate.

```
theDate = DateSerial(1987,3,17)    'the date number
                                   'for 3/17/87
```

See also Date$ function
DateValue() function
Day() function
Hour() function

383

```
Minute() function
Month() function
Now function
Second() funtion
Time$ function
Timer function
TimeSerial() function
TimeValue() function
Weekday() function
Year() function
Date$ statement
Time$ statement
```

DateValue

Purpose   The `DateValue` function calculates a serial date number from a string containing a date.

Syntax   `DateValue(date$)`

Arguments   *date$*—a string containing the date to which to set the clock, in one of the following formats:

mm-dd-yyyy
mm-dd-yy
mm/dd/yy
mm/dd/yyyy

where *mm* is the month, *dd* is the day and *yy* or *yyyy* is the year. It also can recognize the month as a word or abbreviation, such as

```
March 18, 1990
Dec. 21, 1982
24-July-1985
16-Nov-1988
```

Description   The `DateValue()` function converts a string containing the date to a serial date number. The serial date number is a double-precision, floating point number that stores the date to the left of the decimal and the time to the right. Using serial date numbers, you quickly can figure out the number of days between two events by simply subtracting the serial date numbers.

Serial date numbers containing the time can be added to serial date numbers containing the date to store both the date and time in the same number.

Returns　　DateValue—the result is the serial date number. A serial date number is a double-precision number containing the date represented as the number of days since December 30, 1899. Negative serial date numbers represent dates from January 1, 1753 to December 30, 1899. Times are represented as fractions of a day. Years after 1900 are represented by the same serial date numbers used in several popular spreadsheet programs.

For example　　The following statement stores the serial date number (31853.0) for March 17, 1987 in the variable theDate.

```
theDate = DateValue("March 17, 1987")    'the date number
                                         'for 3/17/87
```

See also　　Date$ function
DateSerial() function
Day() function
Hour() function
Minute() function
Now function
Second() function
Time$ function
Timer function
TimeSerial() function
TimeValue() function
Weekday() function
Year() function
Date$ statement
Time$ statement

Day

Purpose　　The Day function calculates the day of the month from a serial date number.

Syntax　　Day(*serialdate#*)

Arguments　　*serialdate#*—a serial date number. A serial date number is a double-precision number containing the date, represented as the number of days

since December 30, 1899. Negative serial date numbers represent dates from January 1, 1753 to December 30, 1899. Times are represented as fractions of a day. Years after 1900 are represented by the same serial date numbers used in several popular spreadsheet programs.

Description   The Day() function takes a serial date number and returns the day of the month represented by that number. Use the Month() and Year() functions to extract the month and year. To extract the time, use the Hour(), Minute(), and Second() functions.

Returns   Day—the result is the day of the month as an integer from 1 to 31.

For example   The following statement extracts the day of the month from the serial date number for March 17, 1987.

```
theDay = Day(318530)    'Extracts the day (17)
                        'from the date number
```

See also   Date$ function
DateSerial() function
DateValue() function
Hour() function
Minute() function
Month() function
Now function
Second() function
Time$ function
Timer function
TimeSerial() function
TimeValue() function
Weekday() function
Year() function
Date$ statement
Time$ statement

Declare

Purpose   The Declare statement defines the interface to a procedure in an external Dynamic Link Library (DLL) or to an internal, parameterless function.

Syntax   For external procedures:

```
Declare Sub procname Lib libname$ [Alias procalias$]
   [([arglist])]
Declare Function procname Lib libname$ [Alias procalias$]
   [([arglist])] [As type]
```

For internal, parameterless functions:

```
Declare Function procname [Alias procalias$][([arglist])]
   [As type]
```

Arguments   Sub—indicates the procedure is a Sub procedure and does not return a value.

Function—indicates the procedure is a Function and does return a value.

procname—the name the procedure is to have in the program as literal text, not a quoted string or variable.

libname$—the name and path to the DLL library containing the procedure.

procalias$—the name of the procedure in the DLL library if different from *procname*. Use this to change the name of a procedure if it conflicts with a name in Visual Basic.

arglist—the argument list to be passed to the external procedure. This argument list has the following syntax.

```
[ByVal] arg[()][As type][,[ByVal]arg[()][As type]]...
```

ByVal—indicates the following argument is to be passed as a value instead of as an address that points to the variable containing the value. Numbers are passed as the type indicated in the statement. Strings are passed as an address to a null-terminated string.

arg—a variable name; only the type has meaning here. Follow array variables with empty parentheses.

type—one of the following Visual Basic types: Any, Control, Currency, Form, Integer, Long, Single, Double, or String. Use the As *type* clause or a character prefix symbol, but not both, to declare the type of the variable. (See the Introduction to Part III for information on prefix symbols.) The Any type is not allowed as the type of a function.

Description   The Declare statement defines the interface to an external DLL procedure so that a Visual Basic program can call it in the same manner as any internally defined procedure (a normal, user-defined procedure in a program). Declare also is used to declare an internal function with no

arguments. Internal functions must have parentheses even if they have no arguments. To use an internal function without parentheses, define it in a `Declare` statement. This last capability is largely for compatibility with other versions of BASIC.

For example The following declares the interface to the DLL function `InvertRect` in the library `User.DLL`. It has two arguments: `hdc`, which is passed by value, and a user defined type, `lpRect`, passed by address.

```
Declare Function InvertRect Lib "User" (ByVal hdc, lpRect As RECT)
```

See also `Call statement`
`Function statement`
`Sub statement`

S DefType

Purpose The six `DefType` statements declare default types for variables beginning with specific letters.

Syntax
`DefCur` *range*[,*range*]...	Currency type
`DefInt` *range*[,*range*]...	Integer type
`DefLng` *range*[,*range*]...	Long type
`DefSng` *range*[,*range*]...	Single type
`DefDbl` *range*[,*range*]...	Double type
`DefStr` *range*[,*range*]...	String type

Arguments *range*—a single letter, or a range of letters. Ranges of letters are separated by a hyphen. The statements are not case sensitive, so A-D is the same as a-d. The range A-Z is special in that it defines all variables as the specified type, including the extended characters with ASCII codes beyond 128 (see `Chr$()`).

Description The `DefType` statements define the default variable types for all variables beginning with a specific letter. Other forms of character typing (such as the character type prefix symbols), `Dim` statements, and `Global` statements override any definitions made by these statements. Each `DefType` statement defines the letters or ranges of letters in its arguments as a specific type. Use these in the declarations section of a Form or module, or in the Global module. The `DefType` statements do not follow the rules of scope, but apply only to the module or Form in which they are used. If you use them in the Global module, they apply only to variables in the Global module.

For example   The first statement below defines all variables beginning with A, C, R, S, T, W, X, Y, and Z as the integer data type. The second statement defines all variables beginning with B, D, G, H, I, and J as the `Double` data type.

```
DefInt A,C,R-T,W-Z
DefDbl b,d,g-j
```

See also   `Dim` statement
`Global` statement
`Static` statement

 **Dim**

Purpose   The `Dim` statement defines variables and declares their type in Forms and modules.

Syntax   **Dim** [**Shared**] *variable* [([*subscripts*])]
[**As** *type*][,*variable* [([subscripts])] [**As** *type*]]...

Arguments   `Shared`—included for compatibility with other BASICs so you don't have to rewrite imported programs; otherwise it does nothing.

variable—a variable name. Array names are followed by parentheses and the subscript range. There can be up to 60 subscripts. Omit subscripts to define a dynamic array whose subscripts and size are defined later in a program with a `ReDim` statement. The syntax of the subscript ranges is

[*lower*% **To**]*upper*%[,[*lower*% **To**]*upper*%]...

lower%—the lower limit for the array subscripts. If this argument is omitted, 0 is assumed unless the `Option Base` statement has been executed. (See the `Option Base` statement for more information.)

upper%—the upper limit for array subscripts.

type—one of the following Visual Basic types: `Control`, `Currency`, `Form`, `Integer`, `Long`, `Single`, `Double`, `String`, `String`*length*, or any user type defined with the `Type` statement. *Length* is the length of a fixed length string. Use the `As` *type* clause or a character prefix symbol, but not both, to declare the type of the variable. (See the Introduction to Part III for information on prefix symbols.)

15

Description   The Dim statement declares the type of variables and sets the dimensions of array type variables. When defined, all arrays are initialized to 0. Use Dim at the Form or Module level to define variables available to the entire Form or module. Alternatively, use Dim at the procedure level to define variables only available in a procedure. Use the Global statement to define global variables in the Global module.

There are two types of arrays in Visual Basic: static and dynamic. Static arrays are defined with a fixed number of elements and thus have a fixed length. They can be redimensioned, but the new total size in bytes must be the same or less than the old size.

A dynamic array is initially defined at the Global or module level with no dimensions. The size and dimensions are determined later, at the procedure level, with a ReDim statement. Memory is allocated for the array when the dimensions are added. Use the Erase statement to deallocate the memory of dynamic arrays.

For example   The following statement defines the variable myFile as a string variable, then defines anArray as a two dimensional array of integers. The first dimension of the array ranges from 3 to 6 and the second ranges from 0 to 10, giving a total of 44 elements in the array.

```
Dim myFile As String, anArray(3 To 6,10) As Integer
```

See also   Const statement
Erase statement
Global statement
Option Base statement
ReDim statement
Static statement

Dir$

Purpose   The Dir$ function returns a matched file name.

Syntax   **Dir$**[(*filespec$*)]

Arguments   *filespec$*—a string containing a file name, or a path and file name. A path specifies the location of a file in the directory system and has the following syntax:

[*drive*:][\]*directory*[*directory*]

where *drive* is the drive letter and *directory* is a directory name. Omit this argument to use the current drive. If the first backslash is omitted, the path is assumed to start in the default directory of the specified drive. The file name in the file specification may contain the wildcard characters * and ?, where * matches any number of any characters and ? matches any single character. The *filespec$* argument must be specified the first time *Dir$* is called. After the first time, if this argument is omitted, the name of the next file that matches the previous *filespec$* is returned.

Description   The Dir$() function returns the file name of any file that matches the *filespec$* argument. To match multiple files in the same directory, omit the *filespec$* argument after the first call; the function returns the next matching file with each call. If no files match, the function returns the null string. Dir$() is particularly useful for testing for the existence of a file before trying to open it with the Open statement, because trying to Open a nonexistent file for input causes an error.

Returns   The result is a string containing the file name that matched the *filespec%* argument.

For example   The following code fragment tests for the existence of a file before trying to open it. If the file doesn't exist, the fragment displays a message box instead of trying to open the file.

```
If Dir$(FileName$) <> "" Then
    Open FileName$ For Input As #1
Else
    MsgBox "The File doesn't exist"
End If
```

See also   ChDir statement
ChDrive statement
Kill statement
MkDir statement
Name statement
RmDir statement
Dir$ function

S Do/Loop

Purpose   The Do/Loop statement iterates a block of statements until a condition is true.

Syntax
```
Do [{While|Until}] condition]
   [statements]
   [Exit Do]
   [statements]
Loop
```
or
```
Do
   [statements]
   [Exit Do]
   [statements]
Loop [{While|Until} condition]
```

Arguments   While—a keyword that indicates to iterate the loop while the condition is True.

Until—a keyword that indicates to iterate the loop until the condition becomes True.

condition—a logical expression or value.

Exit Do—a statement that causes immediate termination of the innermost loop and continuation of the program after the Loop statement.

statements—a block of executable statements to be iterated.

Description   The Do/Loop statement iterates a block of code until a condition changes. If you use the While keyword, the block of statements is executed as long as the condition is True. If you use the Until keyword, the block of statements is iterated until the condition becomes True. Use the Exit Do statement to prematurely exit a loop.

For example   The following code fragment calculates the factorial of A by multiplying A times factorial, then reducing A by 1. As long as A is greater than 1, the loop continues.

```
factorial = 1
Do While A>1
   factorial = A*factorial
   A = A - 1
Loop
```

See also   For/Next statement
            While/Wend statement

DoEvents

Purpose   The DoEvents function passes control to the Windows operating system so that Windows can process system events.

Syntax   `DoEvents()`

Arguments   None

Description The DoEvents function passes control back to the Windows operating system so that Windows can process system events, such as updating Windows and handling user input. Visual Basic passes control back to the system automatically when it waits for an event to occur, such as a button being pressed; if you have a section of code that runs for a long time, you may want to pass control back to the system occasionally.

> Be careful of passing control back during a Click event handler. You might get a second click on the object during the system update period, which would start a second copy of the procedure before the first one is done with what it was doing.

Returns   The result is the number of Forms that Visual Basic has loaded.

For example The following assignment statement executes the DoEvents function and stores the value returned in the variable A.

    A = DoEvents()

See also   None

Double

Purpose   The data type Double matches or defines double-precision floating point variables.

Syntax *variable* **As Double**

Arguments *variable*—a variable name.

Description The data type Double is used in Sub and Function procedure headings to declare a variable as a double-precision, floating point type so that Visual Basic can check values passed to the procedure. It also is used in a Dim, Global, or Static statement to define a variable as double-precision floating point. The Double data type is an eight-byte, floating point number that ranges from $-1.797693134862315 \times 10^{308}$ to $-4.94066 \times 10^{-324}$ for negative numbers and 4.94066×10^{-324} to $1.797693134862315 \times 10^{308}$ for positive numbers. The Double data type also can be defined by appending the # character to the variable name. Double precision constants are written with a D between the mantissa and the exponent (for example, $1.23456789 \times 10^{56}$ = 1.23456789D56.)

For example The following procedure defines ANumber as a double-precision type in the function heading so that Visual Basic can check the type of values passed to it. The procedure then scales the value by dividing by 10,000.

```
Sub ScaleIt (ANumber As Double)
ANumber = ANumber/10000#
End Sub
```

See also Dim statement
Static statement
Global statement
Type statement
Any data type
Control data type
Currency data type
Form data type
Integer data type
Long data type
Single data type
String data type

 Drag

Purpose The Drag method controls the dragging of controls on a Form.

Syntax [*form.*][*control.*]**Drag** [*action%*]

Arguments *control*—the name of a control on a Form. If the control is on another Form, include the name of the Form as well. If the name of the Form isn't included, this argument defaults to the control on the Form containing the method.

action%—a code indicating the action to take concerning the dragging of a control.

0—Cancel the drag operation.

1—Begin the drag operation.

2—End the drag operation and drop the control.

Description The Drag method controls the dragging of controls. This is needed only when the controls DragMode property is set to manual. You normally would execute a Drag 1 when you get a MouseDown event in the Control, then do a Drag 2 when you get a DragDrop event in the Form or Picture box that the control is being dragged over. The mouse controls where an outline of a control is dragged, but you must move the control with your code if you want it to move and stay there. When you drag over a control and then execute a Drag 2, the Form or control you are over gets a FormDrop event.

For example The following two procedures drag a control button across a Form, and then move the control to the new position when the mouse button is released.

```
Sub Command1_MouseDown ( Button As Integer, Shift As
    Integer, X as Single, Y as Single)
Command1.Drag 1
End Sub


Sub Form_DragDrop (Source As Control, X As Single,
    Y As Single)
Source.Drag 2
Source.Move X, Y
End Sub
```

See also Move method
DragMode property
DragOver property
DragIcon property

 End

Purpose	The End statement closes all files and ends a program.
Syntax	**End**
Arguments	None
Description	When executed, the End statement closes all open files and ends a program. To pause a program, use the Stop statement instead of End.
For example	The following procedure is attached to the Exit command on a **File** menu. When Exit is executed, this procedure is called to end the program.

```
Sub ExitCmd_Click ()
End
End Sub
```

See also	Stop procedure

M **EndDoc**

Purpose	The EndDoc method tells the Printer to start printing a document.
Syntax	**Printer.EndDoc**
Arguments	None
Description	The EndDoc method applies only to the Printer object. When printing a document, the document is spooled to the Print Manager. Executing EndDoc releases the document to be printed.
For example	The following procedure prints a big Something and then releases the page for printing.

```
Sub PrintSomething
Printer.FontName = "Roman"
Printer.FontSize = 60
Printer.Print "Something"
Printer.EndDoc
End Sub
```

See also	NewPage method

 Environ$

Purpose	The Environ$() function reads an environment variable from the operating system.
Syntax	Environ$({*name$*¦*number%*})
Arguments	*name$*—a string containing the name of the environment variable to return.
	number%—the number of the environment variable to return, counting from the top of the table.
Description	The DOS operating system contains a table of strings, known as the environment. Several different DOS commands write into this table, including PATH and SET. Most entries consist of a variable name, an equals sign, and a string of information. Applications also can leave messages in this table for later applications. The function is case sensitive, so the string in *name$* must be all uppercase.
Returns	The resulting string contains the requested environment variable. The Environ$() function returns the contents of one entry in this string table. If you call the function with a number as the argument, it returns that string from the table, including the variable name and the equals sign. If you call the function with the variable name, it returns only the string to the right of the equals sign.
For example	The following prints the contents of the Path variable on the **Immediate** window using the Debug object.

```
Debug.Print Environ$("PATH")
```

See also	Command$() function

 EOF

Purpose	The EOF() function returns True if the next item to be read from a disk file is the end-of-file mark.
Syntax	EOF(*filenumber%*)
Arguments	*filenumber%*—the file number used when the file was opened.

Description   When reading from a disk file, you will generate an error if you attempt to read beyond the end-of-file mark. To prevent this, execute the EOF() function before each read operation.

Returns   The resulting value is True (–1) or False (0), depending on whether the end-of-file has been read.

For example   The following code fragment reads a file, until it reads the end-of-file mark.

```
Do Until EOF(1)
Line Input #1,A$
Printer.Print A$
Loop
```

See also   None

 # Eqv Operator

Purpose   The Eqv operator combines two logical expressions or all the bits in two numeric values using the logical equivalence operation.

Syntax   *express1* **Eqv** *express2*

Arguments   *express1, express2*—a logical expression, numeric expression, or numeric value.

Description   The Eqv operator combines two logical values according to the following truth table. If two numeric values are combined, the operator is applied bit by bit to the corresponding bits in the two values. That is, each bit in the result is equal to the logical equivalence of the corresponding bits in the two values.

A	*B*	*A Eqv B*
True	True	True
True	False	False
False	True	False
False	False	True

Returns   The logical Eqv of the two expressions equals True (–1) or False (0) if *express1* and *express2* are logical expressions. If *express1* and *express2* are numeric expressions, the result is the bitwise logical Eqv of the same bits in each of the two expressions.

For example   The following If statement causes a beep if both A and B are True, or if both A and B are False.

```
If A Eqv B then  Beep
```

See also   And operator
Imp operator
Not operator
Or operator
Xor operator

S Erase

Purpose   The Erase statement zeroes static arrays and deallocates dynamic arrays.

Syntax   `Erase array [,array]...`

Arguments   *array*—an array variable to erase.

Description   The Erase statement performs two different functions, depending on the array type. There are two types of arrays in Visual Basic: static and dynamic. Static arrays are defined with a fixed number of elements and thus have a fixed length. They can be redimensioned, but the new total size in bytes must be the same or less than the old size. Erase zeroes all the elements of a static array.

A dynamic array is initially defined with no elements. The size is determined later, with a ReDim statement. Memory is allocated for the array when the dimensions are added. Erase deallocates the memory of dynamic arrays and returns it to the system. When a dynamic array is erased, you must give it dimensions again before you can use it.

For example   The first statement defines anArray as an 11-element array. The next three statements fill each element with the number 0. The last line performs exactly the same function using the Erase statement.

```
Dim anArray(10)
For I = 0 to 10
   anArray(i) = 0
Next I
Erase anArray
```

See also   Const statement
            Dim statement
            Global statement
            Option Base statement
            ReDim statement
            Static statement

 Erl

Purpose   The Erl function returns the closest line number to a line that generated the last error.

Syntax   **Erl**

Arguments   None

Description   The Erl function, along with the Err function, usually is used in an error trap created with the On Error Goto statement. They are both zeroed by the Resume statement, a Sub or Function call within an error handler, or another On Error statement, so save the values if you want to use them. Because most modern programs do not have line numbers, this statement isn't much use. If you need to know which line in your code is having an error, number the lines in that part of the code and use the Erl function in your error procedure.

Returns   The result is the line number. If all lines are numbered, this is the number of the line that had the last error. If not all lines are numbered, it is the closest numbered line before the statement with the error. It returns 0 if there are no line numbers in a procedure.

For example   The following statement would go in an error trap to print the error using Err, the Error$ function, and the line number with Erl.

```
MsgBox Error$(Err) + " At line number:" + Str$(Erl)
```

See also   Err function
            Error$() function
            Err statement
            Error statement
            On Error Goto statement

 Err

Purpose	The Err function returns the error number of the last error.
Syntax	`Err`
Arguments	None
Description	The Err function, along with the Erl function, usually is used in an error trap created with the On Error Goto statement. They both are zeroed by the Resume statement, a Sub or Function call, or another On Error statement, so save the values if you want to use them. Use the Error$() function to get the text of the error from the error number.
Returns	The result is the error number of the last error. See Table 13.1 in Part II for a list of errors and error numbers.
For example	The following statement would go in an error trap to print the error using Err, the Error$ function, and the line number with Erl.

```
MsgBox Error$(Err) + " At line number:" + Str$(Erl)
```

See also	Erl function
	Error$() function
	Err statement
	Error statement
	On Error Goto statement

 Err

Purpose	The Err statement sets the value of Err.
Syntax	`Err =value%`
Arguments	*value%*—the error number to which to set Err in the range 0 to 32,767. See Table 13.1 for a list of Visual Basic error numbers.
Description	The Err function, along with the Erl function, usually is used in an error trap created with the On Error Goto statement. They both are zeroed by the Resume statement, a Sub or Function call, or another On Error statement, so save the values if you want to use them. Use the Err statement to set a Visual

401

Basic or user-defined error type to communicate error information between procedures. Setting `Err` does not cause an error condition; use the `Error` statement to initiate a user-defined error or to simulate a Basic error.

A possible use for a user-defined error code is to reuse an existing error handler for a user-defined error or condition, such as "parameter out of range."

For example   The following statement sets `Err` to 36, one of Visual Basic's unused error codes.

```
Err = 36
```

See also   `Erl` function
`Err` function
`Error$()` function
`Error` statement
`On Error Goto` statement

 Error

Purpose   The `Error` statement initiates an error condition in Visual Basic.

Syntax   **Error** *errornumber%*

Arguments   *errornumber%*—an error number; either one of Visual Basic error numbers from Table 13.1, or one of the unused codes as a user-defined error.

Description   The `Error` statement either simulates a Visual Basic error condition or initiates a user-defined error condition. If an error trap is in place, it is called when this statement is executed. If an error trap is not active, Visual Basic displays an error message and ends the program.

A possible use for a user-defined error code is to reuse an existing error handler for a user-defined error or condition, such as "parameter out of range."

For example   The following statement simulates an overflow error (error code 6).

```
Error 6
```

See also   Erl function
Err function
Error$() function
Err statement
On Error Goto statement

F Error$

Purpose   The Error$() function returns the text description of an error number.

Syntax   **Error$(***errornumber%***)**

Arguments   *errornumber%*—an error number of any type, or a formula that evaluates to a number.

Description   The Error$() function gets a text description of an error condition. If the description is to contain a file name, a hole is left for it with two single quotation marks.

Returns   The result is a string describing the error number.

For example   The following procedure prints a table of all the Visual Basic error codes and their descriptions in the Immediate window.

```
Sub Form_Click ()
For I = 1 To 1000
  If Error$(I) <> "User-defined error" Then
     Debug.Print I, Error$(I)
  End If
Next I
End Sub
```

See also   Erl function
Err function
Error statement
Err statement
On Error Goto statement

 Exp

Purpose	The Exp() function calculates and returns the exponential of a number.
Syntax	**Exp(*number*)**
Arguments	*number*—a number of any type, or a formula that evaluates to a number.
Description	The Exp() function calculates the exponential of a number. The exponential is the number **e** (2.71828...), the base of the natural logarithms, raised to the power number.
Returns	The result is the numeric value of **e** raised to the power *number*.
For example	The following two assignment statements calculate the exponential of 1, which returns the value of **e** (2.71828...), and the exponential of 4.7 (109.947).

```
A = Exp(1)      'Assigns the value of e to A
B = Exp(4.7)    'Assigns the exponential of 4.7 to B
```

See also	Log() function

 FileAttr

Purpose	The FileAttr function returns information about an open file.
Syntax	**FileAttr(*filenumber%, attribute%*)**
Arguments	*filenumber%*—the file number used in the Open statement when the file was opened.
	attribute%—a code (1 or 2) indicating the attribute to return.
Description	The FileAttr function returns either the mode of an open file or the operating system's handle for the file. The handle is an address of an address that points to a block of memory containing a file's buffers and other file information.
Returns	The resulting numeric value is the file mode if *attribute%* is 1, or the operating system's handle to the file if *attribute* is 2. The modes returned are

```
1—Input
2—Output
4—Random
8—Append
32—Binary
```

See the Open statement for a description of the modes.

For example The following statement stores the mode of file number 1 in the variable A.

```
A = FileAttr(1,1)
```

See also Open statement

 **Fix**

Purpose The Fix() function converts a number of any numeric type to an integer by truncation of the fractional part.

Syntax **Fix(*number*)**

Arguments *number*—a number of any type, or a formula that evaluates to a number.

Description The Fix() function converts a number in any numeric type to an integer by truncation of the fractional part.

Returns The result is *number* converted to an integer.

For example The following statements show how CInt(), Int(), and Fix() convert different values.

n	*CInt(n)*	*Int(n)*	*Fix(n)*
3.7	4	3	3
3.4	3	3	3
−3.7	−4	−4	−3
−3.4	−3	−4	−3

See also CCCur function
CLng function
CSng function
CDbl function
Int function

For/Next

Purpose   The For/Next statement iterates a block of statements a specified number of times.

Syntax
```
For counter = start To end [Step increment]
    [statements]
    [Exit For]
    [statements]
Next[counter,[counter]...]
```

Arguments   *counter*—a variable to store the number of iterations of the loop.

start—the starting value of *counter*.

end—the ending value of *counter*.

increment—the amount to increment *counter* each time the loop iterates. If this argument is omitted, 1 is assumed. This value may be negative if *end* is less than *start*, in which case the loop counts down rather than up.

Exit For—a statement that causes immediate termination of the innermost loop and continuation of the program after the Next statement.

statements—a block of executable statements to be iterated.

Description   The For/Next statement iterates a block of code a specified number of times counted with a counter. Each time the loop iterates, the counter is incremented either by 1 or by the Step value, if specified, and then compared to the ending value. If the counter is greater than the ending value, the loop terminates and execution continues with the statement after the Next statement. For/Next loops can be nested, and a single Next statement can terminate several loops by including the counters of each variable with the Next keyword. Use the Exit For statement to prematurely exit a loop.

For example   The following code fragment calculates the factorial of A by looping A times with a For/Next loop and multiplying the counter, B, times factorial.

```
factorial = 1
For B = 1 to A
    factorial = B*factorial
Next B
```

See also   Do/Loop statement
While/Wend statement

406

 Form

Purpose   The data type Form matches any Form name passed to a Sub or Function procedure.

Syntax   *variable* **As Form**

Arguments   *variable*—a variable name.

Description The data type Form is used in Sub and Function procedure headings to declare a variable as type Form so that a Form name can be passed to a procedure. The variable then can be used as a Form name.

For example The following procedure defines aForm as a Form type and adds the item Program One to the List1 List box on that Form.

```
Sub AddProgram (aForm As Form)
aForm.List1.AddItem "Program One"
End Sub
```

See also   Declare statement
If statement
Type statement
Any data type
Control data type
Currency data type
Double data type
Integer data type
Long data type
Single data type
String data type

 Format$

Purpose   The Format$ function converts numbers into formatted text.

Syntax   **Format$(***number*[*,theformat$*]**)**

Arguments   *number*—a number of any type, or a formula that evaluates to a number.

*theformat$*—a string containing the formatting commands. If this argument is omitted, it formats numbers in the same manner as the Str$() function. The formatting string has up to three sections delimited by semicolons. The format is

`"section1[;section2[;section3]]"`

If you include only *section1*, it applies to all numbers. If you have only two sections, *section1* applies to positive values and zeroes, and *section2* applies to negative values. If you include all three sections, *section1* applies to positive values, *section2* to negative values, and *section3* to zeroes.

Description The Format$() function converts numbers to text using a specific format. Create a formatting string with symbols placed wherever you want numbers in the resulting string. The symbols usable in the Format$ function are shown in "Formatting Commands," at the end of this command entry.

Returns The resulting string contains the number formatted according to the designated format.

For example Using the Format$() function and formatting strings often is confusing and difficult to figure out. The best way to set up a formatting string is to experiment with it using the Immediate window. Start any program, including a blank one, and immediately execute the Break command. Open the Immediate window and start typing Print statements into it, trying different variations of the Format$() function. The following is a listing of different values and variations of the formatting string.

n	Format$(n,"0.00")	Format$(n,"#.##")
.023	0.02	.02
38	38.00	38.
27.999	28.00	28.

n	Format$(n,"0.000")	Format$("#.###")
27.999	27.999	27.999

n	Format$(n,"$0.00;($0.00)")
15.35	$15.35
–15.35	($15.35)

408

n	*Format\$(n,"mm/dd/yy")*	*Format\$(n,"hh:mm:ss")*
34359.6	01/25/94	14:24:00

n	*Format\$(n,"dd mmm yyyy")*	*Format\$(n,"mmmm yyyy")*
34359.6	25 Jan 1994	January 1994

n	*Format\$(n,"mm/dd/yy hh:mmAM/PM")*
34459.6 05/05/94	02:24PM

n	*Format\$(n,"+0.000E+00")*	*Format\$(n,"0.000E-00")*
34459.6	+3.446E+04	3.446E04

n	*Format\$(n,"#,###,###.0")*	*Format\$(n,"#,###,.")*
1000000	1,000,000.0	1,000.

See also   Hex\$() function
Oct\$() function
Str\$() function

Formatting Commands:

#—a nonrequired digit. This is a place holder for a digit. If a number has more digits to the left of the decimal than there are formatting characters, the extra digits are printed anyway. If there are more digits to the right of the decimal than there are formatting characters, the number is rounded to the number of formatting characters. Essentially, you're placing a formatting character everywhere you want a character to appear in the converted number.

0—a required digit. This is place holder for a digit. This is the same as the # place holder except that leading and trailing zeroes are included. If the converted number does not have a digit in this position, a zero is inserted. For example, numbers formatted with "0.00" always have a leading zero if there are no characters to the left of the decimal and always have two characters to the right of the decimal.

.—a place holder for the decimal point. Place this in the string of place holders where you want the decimal point to appear.

%—a place holder for a percent sign. This character multiplies the number being formatted by 100.

,—a place holder for a comma to separate thousands. Placing two commas adjacent to each other causes Format$ to omit the three digits that would have appeared between them. Placing a comma immediately to the left of the decimal causes Format$ to omit the first three characters to the left of the decimal.

E+, E–, e+, e–—puts the number in scientific format (a number times a power of 10, the exponent) by following the number with an E or e and then the power of 10. If you follow the E with a minus sign, negative exponents will have a minus sign. If you follow the E with a plus sign, positive exponents will have plus signs and negative numbers have minus signs.

:—the time separator for converting a serial date number into a time. Insert a colon between hours and minutes and between minutes and seconds.

( )—surrounding a number, causes negative numbers to be surrounded by parentheses.

$—inserted as a literal character.

+,–—inserted where they appear in the formatting string.

\—displays the following character as a literal.

""—any characters between the double quotes are inserted as literal characters. To insert a double quote, use the Chr$(34) function.

/—separator for converting a serial date number into a printed date. Use it to separate the day from the month, and the day and the year.

d—displays the day without a leading 0.

dd—displays the day with a leading 0.

ddd—displays the abbreviated name of a day of the week (e.g., Mon, Tue).

dddd—displays the full text of the day of the week (e.g., Monday).

ddddd—displays a complete date in the format mm/dd/yy.

m—displays the month without a leading 0.

mm—displays the month with a leading 0.

mmm—displays the abbreviation for the month.

mmmm—displays the full text of the month's name.

yy—displays the year as a two-digit number.

yyyy—displays the day as a complete year.

h—displays the hour.

hh—displays the hour with a leading 0.

m—displays the minutes.

mm—displays the minutes with a leading 0.

s—displays the seconds.

ss—displays the seconds with a leading zero.

tttt—displays a complete time in the format h:mm:ss (a.m.).

AM/PM—convert a time to a 12-hour clock and use a.m. and p.m.

am/pm—convert a time to a 12-hour clock and use a.m. and p.m.

A/P—convert a time to a 12-hour clock and use A and P to specify morning and afternoon.

a/p—convert time to a 12-hour clock and use a and p to specify morning and afternoon.

AMPM or **ampm**—use the Windows default format set in the WIN.INI file.

F FreeFile

Purpose	The `FreeFile` function gets a valid file number for use with an `Open` statment.
Syntax	`FreeFile`
Arguments	None
Description	When opening and closing many files, you can become confused about which files are open and what file numbers they are using. Since you cannot have more than one file open with the same file number, use this function to supply an available file number.
Returns	The result is the next available file number.

For example The following assignment statement assigns the first available file number to the variable *FileNum%*.

```
FileNum% = FreeFile
```

See also Open statement

 Function

Purpose The Function statement declares the interface to a function procedure.

Syntax [**Static**] **Function** *procname* [(*arglist*)][**As** type]
[*statements*]
[*procname = expression*]
[**Exit Function**]
[*statements*]
[*procname = expression*]
End Function

Arguments Static—indicates the variables of the procedure do not go away when the procedure exits.

procname—the name the procedure is to have in the program.

arglist—the argument list to be passed to the procedure. The argument list can have the following syntax.

[**ByVal**] *arg*[()][**As** type][,[**ByVal**]*arg*[()][**As** type]]...

ByVal—indicates the following argument is to be passed as a value instead of as an address that points to the variable containing the value. Numbers are passed as the type indicated in the statement. Strings are passed as an address to a null-terminated string.

arg—a variable name. Follow array variables with empty parentheses.

type—one of the following Visual Basic types: Control, Currency, Form, Integer, Long, Single, Double, String, or a user-defined type. Use the As *type* clause or a character prefix symbol, but not both, to declare the type of a variable or function. (See the Introduction to Part III for information on prefix symbols.)

Exit Function—statement to exit the function before reaching the end.

statements—some or no statements.

procname = expression—before exiting, the function may assign the return value to the function's name.

Description The Function statement defines the interface to an internal function procedure so that a Visual Basic program can call it. The interface contains the arguments and types, and the type of the value returned by the function. Internal functions must have parentheses even if they have no arguments. To use an internal function without parentheses, define it in a Declare statement.

Returns The result is whatever the function is programmed to return.

For example The following function calculates and returns the factorial of the number N. Because N is changed in the function and you don't want it changed in the calling procedure, it is passed ByVal, so that only the local copy is changed.

```
Function Factorial (ByVal N As Integer) As Long
Factorial = 1
While N>0
   Factorial = Factorial * N
   N = N - 1
Wend
End Function
```

See also Call statement
Declare statement
Sub statement

Get

Purpose The Get statement reads a record from a random access or binary disk file.

Syntax Get [#]*filenumber%*[,*recnum&*],*recvariable*

Arguments *filenumber%*—the file number used when the file was opened with the Open statement.

recnum&—the number of the record to get in a random access file. If this argument is omitted, the next record in the file is returned. File records are consecutively numbered with the first record as record number 1. If the file is opened as binary, this is the byte number at which to start reading.

recvariable—any variable whose length is less than or equal to the length of a record defined when the file is opened. This is usually a user-defined variable, defined with the Type statement.

Description The Get statement reads a record's worth of data from a random access or binary disk file into a record variable. The record variable may be any type of variable as long as its total length is less than the length of a record. For random access files, the length of a record is defined with the Len *reclen* clause of the Open statement. In most cases, you define a record type variable with the Type statement and use that variable to access the disk file. The default length is 128 bytes. For binary files, the record length is as many bytes as can fit into the record variable.

For example The following statements first define the record variable DayType in the Global module. They then define the variable aDay as type DayType, open a disk file whose name is stored in the variable FileName, and read the first 128-byte record into aDay.

In the Global module,

```
Type DayType        'Type declaration for the
TheDate As Double   'record DayType, 128 bytes
Flags As Integer    'long
Msg As String * 118
End Type
```

In a procedure,

```
Dim aDay As DayType
Open FileName For Random As #1 Len = 128
Get #1, 1, aDay
```

See also Open statement
Put statement

 GetData

Purpose The GetData method retrieves a picture from the Clipboard.

Syntax `Clipboard.GetData([dataformat%])`

Arguments   *dataformat%*—a code for the type of picture to retrieve. Visual Basic recognizes only bitmaps, metafiles, and DIBs (device independent bitmaps). CF_BITMAP is assumed if this argument is omitted. The following codes are available in the file CONSTANT.TXT included with Visual Basic.

Picture type	Code
CF_BITMAP	2
CF_METAFILE	3
CF_DIB	8

Description   The GetData method gets Get a picture from the operating system's Clipboard object. Use GetData as you would use a function. The argument of the method determines what type of picture to get from the Clipboard.

Returns   The result is a picture from the Clipboard. Use it as you would a function and equate a control's Picture property to it. If no picture of the specified type is on the Clipboard, a null picture is returned.

For example   The following assignment statement reads a metafile type picture from the clipboard into the Picture property of Form1. The constant CF_METAFILE must have been defined in the declarations part of the Form or in the Global module. The definition is available in the file CONSTANT.TXT included with Visual Basic.

```
Form1.Picture = Clipboard.GetData(CF_METAFILE)
```

See also   GetFormat method
GetText method
SetData method
SetText method

 # GetFormat

Purpose   The GetFormat method checks the Clipboard object to see if data of a specific type is available there.

Syntax   **Clipboard.GetFormat(***dataformat%***)**

Arguments   *dataformat%*—a code for the type of data for which to check. The following codes are available in the file CONSTANT.TXT.

Picture type	Code
CF_LINK	&HBF00
CF_TEXT	1
CF_BITMAP	2
CF_METAFILE	3
CF_DIB	8

Description The GetFormat method tests the Clipboard object to see what kind of data is available. Use GetFormat as you would use a function. The argument of the method determines what type of data to test for.

Returns GetFormat returns True (–1) if the specified data type is available on the Clipboard or False (0) if it is not.

For example The following block If statement tests the Clipboard to see if it contains a metafile type picture before trying to extract it with the GetData method.

```
If Clipboard.GetFormat(CF_METAFILE) Then
    Form1.Picture = Clipboard.GetData(CF_METAFILE)
End If
```

See also GetData method
GetText method
SetData method
SetText method

 # GetText

Purpose The GetText method retrieves a text string from the Clipboard object.

Syntax `Clipboard.GetText([`*dataformat%*`])`

Arguments *dataformat%*—a code for the type of data to check for. The following codes are available in the file CONSTANT.TXT. If this is omitted, CF_TEXT is assumed.

Picture type	Code
CF_LINK	&HBF00
CF_TEXT	1

Description The GetText method gets a text string from the Clipboard object. Use GetText as you would use a function. The argument of the method determines what type of data to get. If the application the data was copied from supports linking, linking information is included along with text or a picture on the Clipboard. The linking information is in the following format.

Application¦LinkTopic¦LinkItem

Returns GetText returns a text string or Dynamic Data Exchange link information.

For example The following assignment statement retrieves any text on the Clipboard and stores it in the Text property of the Text1 Text box.

```
Text1.Text = Clipboard.GetText()
```

See also GetData method
GetFormat method
SetData method
SetText method

Global

Purpose The Global statement defines variables and declares their type in the Global module.

Syntax **Global** *variable* [([*subscripts*])]
  [**As** *type*][,*variable* [([*subscripts*])]
  [**As** *type*]]...

Arguments *variable*—a variable name. Array names are followed by parentheses and the subscript range. There can be up to 60 subscripts. If subscripts are omitted, a dynamic array is defined. The subscripts of the dynamic array are defined later in a program with a ReDim statement. The syntax of the subscript ranges is

[*lower%* **To**] *upper%*[,[*lower%* **To**] *upper%*]...

lower%—the lower limit for the array subscripts. If this argument is omitted, 0 is assumed unless the Option Base statement has been executed. (See the Option Base statement for more information.)

upper%—the upper limit for array subscripts.

type—one of the following Visual Basic types: Control, Currency, Form, Integer, Long, Single, Double, String, String*length*, or any user type defined with the Type statement. *Length* is the length of a fixed length string. Use the As *type* clause or a character prefix symbol, but not both, to declare the type of a variable or function. (See the Introduction to Part III for information on prefix symbols.)

Description   The Global statement declares the type of variables, and to set the dimensions of array type variables in the Global module. The syntax is nearly identical to the Dim statement, which is used at the Form and module level to define variables. Variables defined in the Global module are available throughout a program. When defined, all arrays are initialized to 0.

There are two types of arrays in Visual Basic: static and dynamic. Static arrays are defined with a fixed number of elements and thus have a fixed length. They can be redimensioned, but the new total size in bytes must be the same or less than the old size.

A dynamic array is initially defined at the Global or module level with no dimensions. The size and dimensions are determined later at the procedure level with a ReDim statement. Memory is allocated for the array when the dimensions are added. Use the Erase statement to deallocate the memory of dynamic arrays.

For example   The following statement defines the variable myFile as a string variable and then defines anArray as a two-dimensional array of Integers. The first dimension of the array ranges from 3 to 6 and the second ranges from 0 to 10, giving a total of 44 elements in the array.

```
Global myFile As String, anArray(3 To 6,10) As Integer
```

See also   Const statement
Dim statement
Erase statement
Option Base statement
ReDim statement
Static statement

GoSub/Return

Purpose   The GoSub statement transfers control to a subroutine within a procedure. A Return statement transfers it back.

Syntax	`GoSub {`*line*`\`*label*`}` `Return`
Arguments	*line*—a line number to which to branch if the program lines are numbered.
	label—a Label to which to branch.
Description	The `GoSub` statement works with the `Return` statement to implement a subroutine call within a procedure. When a program branches to a subroutine, execution begins there and continues until a `Return` statement is reached. When the `Return` statement is reached, the program branches back to the statement immediately following the `GoSub` statement. Both the `GoSub` statement and the subroutine it calls must be within the same procedure.
	Subroutines have the same uses as `Sub` procedures; that is, they allow the reuse of blocks of code. However, there are no local variables in subroutines as there are in `Sub` procedures. This statement is available largely for compatibility with older versions of BASIC because the newer `Sub` procedures are far superior to subroutine calls.
For example	The following do-nothing procedure illustrates calling a subroutine within a procedure.

```
Sub someprocedure ()
some lines of code
branch to the subroutine
GoSub SubA
SubA returns here
more statements
Exit Sub
SubA:
the subroutine's statements
Return
End Sub
```

See also	`Function` statement `GoTo` statement `If` statement `On/GoSub` statment `On/GoTo` statement `Select` statement `Sub` statement

S GoTo

Purpose The GoTo statement transfers control to a different location within a procedure.

Syntax GoTo {*line¦label*}

Arguments *line*—a line number to which to branch if the program lines are numbered.

label—a Label to which to branch.

Description The GoTo statement causes an unconditional branch to another location in a procedure. That location is marked either by a line number (if the lines are numbered) or a Label. Both the GoTo statement and the Label it branches to must be in the same procedure. Most well-structured code rarely needs GoTo statements; block If, Select Case, For/Next, Do/Loop, and While/Wend structures should cover most applications, so avoid using GoTo if possible. When you must use a GoTo statement, make sure that the location to which it branches is nearby; if not, document the branch with a remark.

For example The following do-nothing procedure illustrates branching within a procedure. As you can see, it can become confusing.

```
Sub someprocedure ()
some lines of code
branch to somewhere else
GoTo somewhere
label2:
more statements
GoTo done
somewhere:
some statements
GoTo label2
done:
End Sub
```

See Also Function statement
GoSub/Return statement
If statement
On/GoSub statment
On/GoTo statement
Select statement
Sub statement

 Hex$

Purpose	The Hex$() function converts a number into a string of hexadecimal characters.
Syntax	Hex$(*number*)
Arguments	*number*—a number of any type, or a formula that evaluates to a number.
Description	The Hex$ function converts numbers into a string of hexadecimal numbers, just as the Str$() function converts numbers into a string of decimal numbers. Hexadecimal numbers are base 16, and use the characters 0 through 9 and A through F to represent the numbers 0 through 15. Thus, &H0A in hexadecimal is 10 in decimal. The &H, which designates this as a hexadecimal string, is not returned by this function. Floating point numbers are rounded to an integer before conversion to a hexadecimal string.
Returns	The result is the number converted into hexadecimal number.
For example	The following is a listing of the results of most of the Hex$() statements.

n	Hex$(n)
135	87
135.2	87
135.7	88
255	FF
256	100
257	101
15	F
16	10
17	11
9	9
10	A
11	B
252	FC

n	Hex$(n)
253	FD
254	FE
5533	FFFD
65534	FFFE
65535	FFFF
65536	10000

See also   Format$() function
Oct$() function
Str$() function

Hide

Purpose   The Hide method hides a Form without unloading it from memory.

Syntax   [*form.*]**Hide**

Arguments   *form*—the name of a Form to hide. If this argument is omitted, the Form this
command resides on is assumed.

Description The Hide method hides a Form without unloading it by setting the Form's
Visible property to False. Since it isn't unloaded, all the controls on it can
be accessed by the running program or by a DDL-linked external program,
and the properties read or changed. If the Form isn't loaded when the
command is executed, it is loaded first and then hidden.

For example The **Cancel** command button on a file open dialog is an obvious use for the
Hide method. The example below hides the file open dialog box and returns
control to the main Form, without changing any of the variables.

```
Sub CancelCmd_Click ()
OpenDialog.Hide
End Sub
```

See also   Show method
Load statement
Unload statement
Visible property

 **Hour**

Purpose   The Hour function calculates the hour of the day from a serial date number.

Syntax   **Hour(** *serialdate#* **)**

Arguments   *serialdate#*—a serial date number. A serial date number is a double-precision number containing the date represented as the number of days since December 30, 1899. Negative serial date numbers represent dates from January 1, 1753 to December 30, 1899. Times are represented as fractions of a day. Years after 1900 are represented by the same serial date numbers used in several popular spreadsheet programs.

Description   The Hour() function takes a serial date number and returns the hour of the day represented by that number. Use the Day(), Month(), and Year() functions to extract the day, month, and year. To extract the time, use the Minute(), and Second() functions.

Returns   The result is the hour of the day as an integer from 1 to 24.

For example   The following statement extracts the hour (12) from a serial date number for noon on March 17, 1987.

```
theHour = Hour(31853.5)        'Extracts the hour (12)
                               'from the date number
```

See also   Date$ function
DateSerial function
DateValue function
Day function
Minute function
Month function
Now function
Second function
Time$ function
Timer function
TimeSerial function
TimeValue function
Weekday function
Year function
Date$ statement
Time$ statement

S If

Purpose	The If statement makes a decision based on a condition and executes different code depending on that decision.
Syntax	**If** *condition* **Then** *tstatements* [**Else** *fstatements*]

or

If *condition1* **Then**
  [statements]
[**ElseIf** *condition2* Then
  statements]
[**Else**
  statements]
End If

Arguments *condition, condition1, condition2*—logical formulas that result in a value of True (–1) or False (0). It also may be a TypeOf clause to test the type of an object. The TypeOf clause has the following syntax.

TypeOf *object* **Is** *type*

where *object* is a variable containing a reference to an object and *type* is the type of control from the following list.

CheckBox	Label
ComboBox	ListBox
CommandButton	Menu
DirListBox	OptionButton
DriveList Box	PictureBox
FileListBox	TextBox
Frame	Timer
HScrollBar	VScrollBar

statements—any number of statements to execute.
tstatements—statements to execute when the condition is True.
fstatements—statements to execute when the condition is False.
ElseIf—a clause to test for another condition.
Else—a clause to receive all other instances that don't invoke the If or ElseIf clauses.

424

Description The simple If statement executes the *tstatements* if the condition is True and *fstatements* if the condition is False. The block If statement executes the first block of statements if *condition1* is True. If not, it tests *condition2* and executes the second block of statements if *condition2* is True. There can be as many ElseIf statements as you need, and they are evaluated in order. If none of the If or ElseIf clauses is True, then the Else clause is executed.

For example The procedure uses the block If statement to either save the file or to create and save it with the Save dialog.

```
Sub SaveCmd_Click ()
If FileName <> "" Then
    SaveIt
Else
    SaveDialog.Show 1
End If
End Sub
```

See also GoTo statement
Select statement

Imp

Purpose The Imp operator combines two logical expressions or all the bits in two numeric values using the logical Implies operation.

Syntax *express1* **Imp** *express2*

Arguments *express1, express2*—a logical expression, numeric expression, or numeric value.

Description The Imp operator combines two logical values according to the following truth table. If two numeric values are being combined, the operator is applied bit by bit to the corresponding bits in the two values. That is, each bit in the result is equal to the logical Implies of the corresponding bits in the two values being combined.

A	B	A Imp B
True	True	True
True	False	False
False	True	True
False	False	True

425

Returns   The logical Implies of the two expressions equals True (–1) or False (0) if *express1* and *express2* are logical expressions. If *express1* and *express2* are numeric expressions, the result is the bitwise logical Implies of the same bits in each of the two expressions.

For example   The following If statement doesn't cause a beep if A is False and B is True.

```
If A Imp B then Beep
```

See also   And operator
Eqv operator
Not operator
Or operator
Xor operator

Input

Purpose   The Input # statement reads data from a sequential file.

Syntax   Input [#]*filenumber%,arglist*

Arguments   *filenumber%*—the file number used when the file was opened with the Open statement.

arglist—a list of variables to receive the data from the file.

Description   The Input # statement reads data from a sequential data file into its arguments. Leading spaces are ignored when reading a file. For a number, the first nonblank character is assumed to be the start of the number and the first blank, comma, or the end of the line terminates it. For a string, the first nonblank character starts the string and a comma or the end of the line terminates it. If the string is quoted, everything between the quotes is included in the string, including commas. Thus, data written with the Write # statement is more accurately read than data written with Print #.

For example   A disk file written with the following statements,

```
A1 = 5.355
B1 = 4.788
Print #1, "Values, are: ", A1, B1, " units"
Write #1, "Values, are: ", A1, B1, " units"
```

produces

```
Values, are: 5.355          4.788              units
"Values, are: ",5.355,4.788," units"
```

Reading those values with the following `Input #` statements,

```
Input #1, A$, B, C, D$
Input #1, E$, F, G, H$
```

stores the following data in these variables.

```
A$ = "Values"
B = 0
C = 5.355
D$ = "4.788          units"
E$ = "Values, are: "
F = 5.355
G = 4.788
H$ = " units"
```

Note how the first `Input #` statement stopped reading the string into `A$` at the first comma, so that the first numeric input, `B`, reads text instead of a number and gets a value of zero. Then the second numeric input, `C`, reads the first number, and the remaining number and string end up in `D$`.

See also   Get statement
Line Input # statement
Open statement
Print # statement
Put statement
Write # statement
Input$ function

F Input$

Purpose   The `Input$()` function reads a string of characters from a disk file.

Syntax   `Input$(num% [#] filenumber%)`

Arguments   *num%*—the number of characters to read from the file.

filenumber%—the file number used when the file was opened with the Open statement.

Description The Input$() function reads a specified number of characters from a disk file. Unlike the Input # statement, no characters are ignored by this function. It reads the disk file byte by byte, including carriage returns, line feeds, and other control characters. Use this function when you need access to every byte of a file.

Returns The resulting string contains *num%* characters read from the disk file.

For example If a disk file opened with file number 1 contains the following data.

```
Values, are: 5.355        4.788           units
"Values, are: ",5.355,4.788," units"
```

reading those values with the following Input$() function,

```
A$ = Input$(65, #1)
```

would store the following data in A$.

```
A =
Values, are: 5.355        4.788           units
"Values, are: "
```

Note how A$ contains not only the text, but also the carriage return and line feed at the end of the line, both of which count towards the 65 characters read.

See also Get statement
Input # statement
Line Input # statement
Open statement
Print # statement
Put statement
Write # statement

InputBox$

Purpose The InputBox$() function displays a dialog box and waits for user input.

Syntax **InputBox$(***prompt$*[, *title$*[, *default$*[,*x%*, *y%*]]]**)**

Arguments   *prompt$*—a prompt string of up to 255 characters. The string automatically wraps the words to fit in the dialog box.

title$—a string to use as the title of the dialog box. If this argument is omitted, nothing is placed in the title of the box.

default$—a string to place in the input box for the user to accept or change (about 40 characters.) If this argument is omitted, the input box is empty.

x%,y%—the *x,y* position of the upper-left corner of the box, measured down from the top of the screen and right from the left side of the screen. If these arguments are omitted, the box is in the upper-middle of the screen.

Description   The InputBox$() function gets a small amounts of data from the user. The function displays a dialog box with an instruction area, an input area, an **OK** button, and a **Cancel** button. The instructions are limited to 255 characters and the response is limited to about 40 characters. You can insert a default response by including the default argument.

Returns   If the user pressed **OK** or **Return**, the resulting string contains the contents of the input box. If the user pressed **Cancel**, the result is a blank string (" "). The input box can hold about 40 characters.

For example   The following statement creates a simple dialog box and places the text typed by the user in the string variable A$.

```
A$ = InputBox$("Type the number below and press OK")
```

See also   MsgBox statement
MsgBox function

InStr

Purpose   The InStr() function locates a substring within a string.

Syntax   **InStr(**[*start&,*]*searched$,find$***)**

Arguments   *start&*—the character position at which to start searching in *searched$*. A number of any type, or a formula that evaluates to a number. If this argument is omitted, 1 is assumed.

searched$—the string to search.

find$—the substring to search for.

Description   The `InStr()` function locates a substring within another, longer string. Only the first occurrence of a substring is located. Use the *start&* argument to locate other occurrences of the substring.

Returns   The resulting numeric value is the character position of the first character of the first occurrence of the *find$* string in *searched$* string. The first character of the string is character number 1. If the substring isn't found, this function returns 0. If the *find$* string is empty, this function returns *start&*.

For example   The following lists the results from various searches within a string.

```
A$ = "This is the string, to be searched for a substring"
```

InStr	*Result*
`InStr(A$,"string")`	13
`InStr(14,A$,"string")`	45
`InStr(A$,",")`	19
`InStr(20,A$,",")`	0

See also   Len function

Int

Purpose   The `Int()` function converts a number of any numeric type to the largest integer less than or equal to the number.

Syntax   `Int(`*number*`)`

Arguments   *number*—a number of any type, or a formula that evaluates to a number.

Description   The `Int()` function converts a number of any numeric type to the largest integer that is less than or equal to the number. This function is not needed if you assign number to an `Integer` type variable because Visual Basic automatically does the conversion in such cases. This function is useful to force a calculation to be done in `Integer` type if the calculation contains other numeric types. If every number used in a calculation is of the same numeric type, then the entire calculation is done in that type. If a calculation contains different numeric types, Visual Basic converts everything to the most precise type before doing the calculation.

Returns The result is the largest integer less than or equal to *number*.

For example The following lines from the Immediate window show how CInt(), Int(), and Fix() convert different values.

n	*CInt(n)*	*Int(n)*	*Fix(n)*
3.7	4	3	3
3.4	3	3	3
–3.7	–4	–4	–3
–3.4	–3	–4	–3

See also CCCur function
CLng function
CSng function
CDbl() function
Fix function

D | Integer

Purpose The data type Integer matches or defines two-byte integer variables.

Syntax *variable* **As Integer**

Arguments *variable*—a variable name.

Description The data type Integer is used in Sub and Function procedure headings to declare a variable as a two-byte integer so that Visual Basic can check values passed to the procedure. It also is used in a Dim, Global, or Static statement to define a variable as a two-byte integer. The Integer data type is a two-byte integer number that ranges from 32,768 to –32,767. The Integer data type also can be defined by appending the % character to the variable name.

For example The following procedure defines ANumber and I as Integers and AddEmUp as an Integer function. The function adds up and returns all the integers from 1 to ANumber.

```
Function AddEmUp (ANumber As Integer) As Integer
Dim I As Integer
AddEmUp = 0
For I = 1 to ANumber
```

continues

```
        AddEmUp = AddEmUp + I
    Next I
    End Function
```

See also   Dim statement
Static statement
Global statement
Type statement
Any data type
Control data type
Currency data type
Form data type
Double data type
Long data type
Single data type
String data type

 Kill

Purpose   The Kill statement deletes a disk file.

Syntax   **Kill** *filename$*

Arguments   *filename$*—a string containing the file name, and an optional directory path if the file isn't in the current directory. The file name may contain the * and ? wildcard characters, where * matches any number of any characters and ? matches any single character. The path, including the disk letter has the following syntax.

[*drive*:][[\]*directory*[*directory*...\]]*filename*

where *drive* is the drive letter, *directory* is a directory name, and *filename* is the file to delete. Omit this argument to use the current drive. If the first backslash is omitted, the path is assumed to start in the default directory of the specified drive. Use ChDir and ChDrive to change the current directory.

Description   The Kill statement deletes any file. It does not delete directories (use RmDir to do that). The file name may contain wildcard characters to select multiple files for deletion.

For example   The first statement below deletes the file myfile.doc in the current directory. The second statement deletes all executable files (.EXE files) in the Apps directory on disk C.

```
Kill "myfile.doc"
Kill "c:\apps\*.exe"
```

See also   ChDir statement
ChDrive statement
MkDir statement
Name statement
RmDir statement
CurDir$ function
Dir$ function

 # LBound

Purpose   The LBound function returns the smallest allowed array subscript.

Syntax   **LBound(***array*[*,dimension%*]**)**

Arguments   *array*—an array type variable.

dimension%—for multidimensional arrays, this number specifies the dimension to examine. The first dimension is number 1.

Description   The LBound function works with the UBound function to examine the lower and upper index values for an arrays dimensions.

Returns   The resulting numeric value is the lowest allowed subscript available for the array dimension.

For example   The first line below is from the general procedure of a Form, and defines the array variable anArray. The table shows the results of the operation of LBound and UBound for different arguments.

```
Dim anArray(4 To 23,-6 To 5,8) As Integer
```

Function	Result
LBound(anArray,1)	4
UBound(anArray,1)	23
LBound(anArray,2)	-6
UBound(anArray,2)	5
LBound(anArray,3)	0
UBound(anArray,3)	8

See also   Dim statement
Global statement
Static statement
UBound function

 LCase$

Purpose	The LCase$() function converts all the characters in a string to lowercase.
Syntax	**LCase$(**_string$_**)**
Arguments	_string$_—a string, or a formula that results in a string, to be converted.
Description	The LCase$() function converts all the characters in a string to lowercase. This is useful when you want to compare two strings and the case of the characters in unimportant.
Returns	The contents of _string$_ with each character converted to lowercase.
For example	The following lines demonstrate the use of LCase$ and UCase$.

```
A$ = "This Is a StRinG to ConVeRt"
```

Function	*Result*
LCase$(A$)	this is a string to convert
UCase$(A$)	THIS IS A STRING TO CONVERT

See also   UCase$() function

 Left$

Purpose	The Left$() function extracts a substring from the left side of a string.
Syntax	**Left$(**_string$_,_numchar&_**)**
Arguments	_string$_—a string, or a formula that results in a string.
	numchar&—the number of characters to extract from the string.
Description	The Left$() function extracts a substring from the left side of a string. Use it with the Right$() and Mid$() functions to extract different substrings.

Returns   The resulting string contains the leftmost *numchar&* characters from *string$*

For example   The following is from the Immediate window and compares the Left$(), Right$(), and Mid$() functions.

```
A$ = "This is a string to examine"
```

Function	*Result*
Left$(A$,6)	This i
Right$(A$,5)	amine
Mid$(A$,9,5)	a str

See also   Mid$ function
Right$ function
Mid$ statement

Len

Purpose   The Len() function returns the number of characters in a string or the number of bytes in a variable.

Syntax   **Len(***variable***)**

Arguments   *variable*—a string, or a formula that results in a string, or a variable name.

Description   The Len() function returns the number of characters in a string, or the number of bytes necessary to store a variable. This works for all variable types, including user-defined record variables defined with the Type statement.

Returns   The result is the number of characters in a string or the number of bytes in a variable.

For example   The Type definition statements and Global statement are from the Global module. The remaining lines are from the Immediate window, and demonstrate using Len to get the length of a user-defined type and a string.

```
Type DayType              'Type declaration for the
TheDate As Double         'record DayType, 128 bytes
Flags As Integer          'long
Msg As String * 118
End Type
Global ChangeDate As DayType   'Serial date being changed
```

continues

435

```
Print Len(ChangeDate)
128
A$ = "A string to examine"
Print Len(A$)
19
```

See also   InStr function

 Let

Purpose   The Let statement is an assignment statement.

Syntax   **[Let]** *variable* = *formula*

Arguments   *variable*—a variable name to receive the value generated by *formula*. For numeric types, if the type of value generated by *formula* is different from that of *variable*, the number is converted by rounding and truncation to the type of *variable*.

formula—a formula or constant value to assign to *variable*.

Description   The assignment statement assigns values to variables. The Let keyword is not needed, and is available only for compatibility with older versions of BASIC.

For example   The following are all assignment statements.

```
A = 1
Let B = 3
aVal = 3 * A + B
aString$ = "This is a string"
aString2$ = Left$(aString$,9) + " dumb" +
    Right$(aString$,7)
```

See also   LSet statement
RSet statement

 Line

Purpose The Line method draws lines, rectangles, and filled rectangles on Forms, Picture boxes, and the Printer object.

Syntax [*object.*]**Line** [[**Step**](*x1!,y1!*)]
⮡ -[**Step**](*x2!,y2!*)[,[*color&*],**B[F]**]]

Arguments *object*—the name of the object to draw on, a Form, a Picture box, or the keyword Printer. Omit this argument to use the Form containing this statement.

Step—a keyword that specifies that the coordinates following it are relative to the current position specified by the CurrentX and CurrentY properties.

x1!,y1!, x2!,y2!—the *x, y* coordinates of the ends of a line, or the upper-left corner and lower-right corner of a rectangle. The coordinates are measured in the current coordinate system for the object being drawn on. If the first pair of coordinates is omitted, they are assumed to be the current position specified by the CurrentX and CurrentY properties.

color&—an RGB color number specifying the color to use for the line or the rectangles outline. Omit this argument to use the current ForeColor. If the object is closed (a circle, an ellipse, or a pie slice) it is filled with the current FillColor using the current FillStyle. See the RGB() function for more information on colors.

B—an option indicating that a box is to be drawn. If this option is omitted, a line is drawn.

F—an option indicating that the box is to be filled with the color specified by the *color&* argument or, if *color&* is omitted, with the current FillColor and FillStyle of the object being drawn on.

Description The Line method draws lines, boxes, and filled boxes on Forms, Picture boxes and the Printer object. The drawing is affected by the settings of all the drawing properties: CurrentX, CurrentY, DrawMode, DrawWidth, FillColor, FillStyle, and ForeColor.

For example The first statement below draws a rectangle on the Picture1 Picture box. Assuming that the default ScaleMode is in effect, one corner is 2000 twips from the left side of the box and 1000 twips down from the top, while the

opposite corner is 5000 twips down and 3000 twips from the left. The box is outlined in red—&HFF is the color number for red—and filled with the current FillColor using the current FillStyle. The second statement draws a line on the current Form from the current location specified by the CurrentX and CurrentY properties to the point (2000,1000). This time the rectangle is outlined in the current ForeColor because no color is specified.

```
Picture1.Line (2000, 1000)-(3000,5000), &HFF&, BF
Line -(2000, 1000)
```

See also   Circle method
RGB function
QBColor function
CurrentX property
CurrentY property
DrawMode property
DrawWidth property
FillColor property
FillStyle property
ForeColor property

Line Input

Purpose   The Line Input # statement reads complete lines of data from a sequential file.

Syntax   **Line Input #***filenumber%,string$*

Arguments   *filenumber%*—the file number used when the file was opened with the Open statement.

string$—a string variable to receive the contents of the line read from the file.

Description   The Line Input # statement reads a line of data from a sequential data file into a string variable. When reading a file, all the characters in the line are placed into the string, including any leading spaces and up to, but not including, the carriage return-line feed at the end of the line.

For example   A disk file written with the following statements,

```
A1 = 5.355
B1 = 4.788
Print #1, "The values, are: ", A1, B1, " units"
Write #1, "The values, are: ", A1, B1, " units"
```

produces

```
Values, are: 5.355          4.788          units
"Values, are: ",5.355,4.788," units"
```

Reading those values with the following Input # statements,

```
Line Input #1, A$
Line Input #1, E$
```

stores the following data in these variables.

```
A$ = Values, are: 5.355          4.788          units
E$ = "Values, are: ",5.355,4.788," units"
```

See also   Get statement
              Input # statement
              Open statement
              Print # statement
              Put statement
              Write # statement
              Input$ function

 LinkExecute

Purpose   The LinkExecute method sends a command string to the other application
             in a DDE link.

Syntax   *object*.**LinkExecute** *cmds$*

Arguments   *object*—the name of the object involved in the DDE link, a Text box, a
             Picture box, or a Label.

             cmds$—a string containing the commands for the other application. The
             contents of the string depends on the application receiving the message.
             Microsoft Word and Excel both accept their own macro commands sur-
             rounded by square brackets.

Description   When a Visual Basic object and an external application are linked in a Dynamic Data Exchange (DDE), the LinkExecute method sends a command string to the connected application.

For example   The following three procedures set up a DDE link between the Text1 Text box and a Microsoft Excel worksheet. The Command1_Click procedure sets the LinkTopic, LinkItem, and LinkMode of the Text box. The link topic is the name of the application followed by a vertical bar and the name of the worksheet. The link item is the row and column number of the cell of interest. The link mode is cold, indicating that this link is to be updated only on request.

The Command2_Click procedure initiates a request to Excel to update the contents of the Text1 Text box with the contents of cell B2 (row 2, column 2) on the Sheet1 worksheet. The Command3_Click procedure sends three Excel macro commands to Excel. Since the macro commands contain double quotation marks, the commands have to be assembled with string fragments and the Chr$() functions (Chr$(34) is a double quotation mark). The first command asks Excel to activate Sheet1. The second command selects cell R3C2 (row 2 column 2). The third command sets the contents of the cell to the text From VB.

To run this, have Excel running with Sheet1.XLS open. Click **Command1** to set up the link, then **Command2** to get the contents of cell B2. Click **Command3** to change the contents of cell B2, and then **Command2** again to see the change.

```
Sub Command1_Click ()
Text1.LinkTopic = "Excel¦Sheet1.XLS"
Text1.LinkItem = "R2C2"
Text1.LinkMode = 2
End Sub

Sub Command2_Click ()
Text1.LinkRequest
End Sub

Sub Command3_Click ()
'Send the command: [ACTIVATE("SHEET1.XLS")]
Text1.LinkExecute "[ACTIVATE(" + Chr$(34) + "SHEET1.XLS"
   + Chr$(34) + ")]"
 'Send the command: [SELECT( "R2C2" )]
Text1.LinkExecute "[SELECT(" + Chr$(34) + "R2C2"
   + Chr$(34) + ")]"
```

```
'Send the command: [FORMULA(" From VB")]
Text1.LinkExecute "[FORMULA(" + Chr$(34) + "From VB"
   + Chr$(34) + ")]"
End Sub
```

See also   LinkPoke method
LinkRequest method
LinkSend method
LinkItem property
LinkMode property
LinkTimeout property
LinkTopic property

M LinkPoke

Purpose   The LinkPoke method sends the contents of a control to the server application in a DDE link.

Syntax   *object*.**LinkPoke**

Arguments   *object*—the name of the object involved in the DDE link, a Text box, a Picture box, or a Label.

Description   When a Visual Basic object is the client and an external application is the server in a Dynamic Data Exchange (DDE), the LinkPoke method sends the contents of the control to the server application. Not all applications operating in DDE server mode accept data from the client, and cause an error if this occurs.

For example   The following three procedures set up a DDE link between the Text1 Text box and a Microsoft Excel worksheet. The Command1_Click procedure sets the LinkTopic, LinkItem, and LinkMode of the Text box. The link topic is the name of the application followed by a vertical bar and the name of the worksheet. The link item is the row and column number of the cell of interest. The link mode indicates that this link is to be updated only on request.

The Command2_Click procedure initiates a request to Excel to update the contents of the Text1 Text box with the contents of cell B2 (row 2, column 2) on the Sheet1 worksheet. The Command4_Click procedure sends the contents of the Text1 Text box to Excel.

To run this, have Excel running with Sheet1.XLS open. Click **Command1** to set up the link, then **Command2** to get the contents of cell B2. Type something in the Text1 Text box and click **Command4** to send it to cell B2 on the worksheet, and then **Command2** again to see the change.

```
Sub Command1_Click ()
Text1.LinkTopic = "Excel¦Sheet1.XLS"
Text1.LinkItem = "R2C2"
Text1.LinkMode = 2
End Sub

Sub Command2_Click ()
Text1.LinkRequest
End Sub

Sub Command4_Click ()
Text1.LinkPoke
End Sub
```

See also   LinkExecute method
LinkRequest method
LinkSend method
LinkItem property
LinkMode property
LinkTimeout property
LinkTopic property

 # LinkRequest

Purpose   The LinkRequest method sends an update request to the other application in a DDE link.

Syntax   *object*.**LinkRequest**

Arguments   *object*—the name of the object involved in the DDE link, a Text box, a Picture box, or a Label.

Description   When a Visual Basic object is the client and an external application is the server in a Dynamic Data Exchange (DDE), the LinkRequest method sends a request to the connected application to update the linked data. This is only needed if the LinkMode property of the control is set to 2-Cold link, which needs manual updating. If the `LinkMode` is set to `1`-`Hot`, the linked data is automatically updated whenever the data changes.

For example   The following three procedures set up a DDE link between the `Text1` Text box and a Microsoft Excel worksheet. The `Command1_Click` procedure sets the `LinkTopic`, `LinkItem`, and `LinkMode` of the Text box. The link topic is the name of the application followed by a vertical bar and the name of the worksheet. The link item is the row and column number of the cell of interest. The link mode indicates that this link is to be updated only on request.

The `Command2_Click` procedure initiates a request to Excel to update the contents of the `Text1` Text box with the contents of cell `B2` (row 2, column 2) on the `Sheet1` worksheet. The `Command3_Click` procedure sends three Excel macro commands to Excel. Since the macro commands contain double quotation marks, the commands have to be assembled with string fragments and the `Chr$()` functions (`Chr$(34)` is a double quotation mark.) The first command asks Excel to activate `Sheet1`, the second selects cell `R3C2` (row 2 column 2), and the third sets the contents of the cell to the text `From VB`.

To run this, have Excel running with Sheet1.XLS open. Click **Command1** to set up the link, then **Command2** to get the contents of cell `B2`. Click **Command3** to change the contents of cell `B2`, and then **Command2** again to see the change.

```
Sub Command1_Click ()
Text1.LinkTopic = "Excel¦Sheet1.XLS"
Text1.LinkItem = "R2C2"
Text1.LinkMode = 2
End Sub


Sub Command2_Click ()
Text1.LinkRequest
End Sub


Sub Command3_Click ()
'Send the command: [ACTIVATE("SHEET1.XLS")]
Text1.LinkExecute "[ACTIVATE(" + Chr$(34) + "SHEET1.XLS"
    + Chr$(34) + ")]"
'Send the command: [SELECT( "R2C2" )]
Text1.LinkExecute "[SELECT(" + Chr$(34) + "R2C2"
    + Chr$(34) + ")]"
'Send the command: [FORMULA(" From VB")]
```

continues

443

```
Text1.LinkExecute "[FORMULA(" + Chr$(34) + "From VB"
    + Chr$(34) + ")]"
End Sub
```

See also   LinkExecute method
LinkPoke method
LinkSend method
LinkItem property
LinkMode property
LinkTimeout property
LinkTopic property

LinkSend

Purpose   The LinkSend method sends an update of a linked Picture box to a client application.

Syntax   *object*.**LinkSend**

Arguments   *object*—the name of the Picture box involved in the DDE link.

Description   When a Visual Basic object is the server and an external application is the client in a Dynamic Data Exchange (DDE), changes in linked Text properties are automatically sent to the client whenever they change. Picture properties, on the other hand, are not sent automatically because of the large amount of data involved. To send an updated Picture property to a linked client, use the LinkSend method.

For example   The following statement sends the contents of the Picture1 Picture box to the linked client application.

```
Picture1.LinkSend
```

See also   LinkExecute method
LinkPoke method
LinkRequest method
LinkItem property
LinkMode property
LinkTimeout property
LinkTopic property

 # Load

Purpose The Load statement loads a Form or control array element into memory.

Syntax `Load object`

Arguments *object*—the name of a Form or control array element to load. The Form's `Visible` property determines if it is visible or not.

Description The `Load` statement loads a Form or control array element into memory at run time. A Form is visible or not depending on its `Visible` property. Use the `Hide` method to load a Form but not display it. Use the `Show` method to load a Form and display it. The `Load` method can also be used to add elements to a control array. The first element of the control array must be on the Form already but subsequent elements can be loaded and attached to the Form.

For example The following statement loads element number 2 of an Option button control array. Element number 0 must already be on the Form.

```
Load Option1(2)
```

See also Hide method
Show method
Unload statement
Visible property

 # LoadPicture

Purpose The LoadPicture function loads a picture into a Form or Picture box.

Syntax `LoadPicture([filename$])`

Arguments *filename$*—a string containing the picture file name, and an optional directory path if the file isn't in the current directory. The path, including the disk letter, has the following syntax.

`[drive:][[\]directory[\directory...\]]filename`

where *drive* is the drive letter, *directory* is a directory name, and *filename* is the file to load. Omit this argument to use the current drive. If the first

backslash is omitted, the path is assumed to start in the default directory of the specified drive. Use ChDir and ChDrive to change the current directory.

Description The LoadPicture function loads a picture file into the Picture property of a Form or Picture box at run time. At design time, the Picture property can be loaded directly. Visual Basic recognizes Bitmaps (.BMP), Icons (.ICO), and Windows metafile (.WMF) type pictures. The LoadPicture function also can load icons into the Icon and DragIcon properties of controls.

Returns The result is a picture that can be assigned to the Picture property of a Form or Picture box.

For example The following statement loads the bitmap file BEAR.BMP into the Picture property of the Picture1 Picture box.

```
Picture1.Picture = LoadPicture("BEAR.BMP")
```

See also SavePicture statement
SetData method
DragIcon property
Icon property
Picture property

Loc

Purpose The Loc() function returns the current record or byte position in an open file.

Syntax **Loc(** *filenumber%* **)**

Arguments *filenumber%*—the file number used when the file was opened with the Open statement.

Description The Loc() function returns the current record or byte position in a file being read or written by Visual Basic.

Returns The result is the current location in an open disk file. If the file was opened as a random access file, the number of the last record accessed is returned. For a sequential file, the result is the byte location of the last byte accessed in the file, divided by 128. For binary files, the result is the byte location of the last byte accessed.

For example The following statement assigns the current location in file number 1 to the variable theLocation.

theLocation = Loc(1)

See also EOF function
LOF function
Open statement

S Lock/Unlock

Purpose For networked files, the Lock and Unlock statements control access to an open file.

Syntax Lock [#]*filenumber%*[,*startrec&* [To *endrec&*]]
Unlock [#]*filenumber%*[,*startrec&* [To *endrec&*]]

Arguments *filenumber%*—the file number used when the file was opened with the Open statement.

startrec&—the first record number of a file to lock, or the single record to lock if *endrec%* is omitted. For binary mode files, this is measured in bytes from the beginning of the file. The first record is number 1. This is ignored in a sequential access file. If this argument is omitted, the entire file is locked or unlocked.

endrec&—the ending record of a range of records to lock.

Description Networked files can be accessed by more than one application at the same time. To prevent two applications from trying to change the same record at the same time, the Lock statement reserves the indicated records for the use of this application only. The Unlock statement then releases it again. The SHARE.EXE program must have been run in DOS versions 3.1 and later to enable locking. Earlier versions of DOS cannot be locked. When locking and unlocking a block of records, the arguments of Lock and Unlock must match exactly. Individual records cannot be locked in a file opened in sequential mode; the entire file must be locked.

Be sure to unlock all locked records before closing a file or unpredictable results may occur.

For example   The following lines first lock, then unlock records 27 through 95 of file number 1.

```
Lock #1,27 To 95
'other statements that change these records
Unlock #1, 27 To 95
```

See also   Open statement

Purpose   The LOF() function returns the length of an open file.

Syntax   **LOF(** *filenumber%* **)**

Arguments   *filenumber%*—the file number used when the file was opened with the Open statement.

Description   The LOF() function returns the length of the file in bytes. If it is a random access file, divide by the length of a record to get the number of records in the file.

Returns   The result is the length of the file, in bytes.

For example   The following statement assigns the length of file number 1 to the variable theLength.

```
theLength = LOF(1)
```

See also   EOF function
Loc function
Open statement

Purpose   The Log() function calculates and returns the natural logarithm of a number.

Syntax   **Log(** *number* **)**

Arguments *number*—a number of any type, or a formula that evaluates to a number.

Description The Log() function calculates the natural logarithm of a number. The base of the natural logarithms is the number **e** (2.71828...). To get the common (base 10) logarithm of a number, use the following construction.

```
Log10 = Log(number)/Log(10)
```

Returns The resulting numeric value is the natural logarithm of *number*.

For example The following three assignment statements calculate the Log of 10 (2.30259), the log of 4.7 (1.54756), and the common logarithm of 4.7 (0.672098).

```
A = Log(10)
B = Log(4.7)
C = Log(4.7)/Log(10)
```

See also Exp() function

 # Long

Purpose The data type Long matches or defines four-byte integer variables.

Syntax *variable* **As Long**

Arguments *variable*—a variable name.

Description The data type Long is used in Sub and Function procedure headings to declare a variable as a four-byte integer, so that Visual Basic can check values passed to the procedure. It is also used in a Dim, Global, or Static statement to define a variable as a four-byte integer. The Long data type is a four-byte integer number that ranges from –2,147,483,648 to 2,147,483,647. The Long data type can also be defined by appending the & character to the variable name.

For example The following procedure defines ANumber and I as Long integers, and AddEmUp as an Long integer function. The function adds up and returns all the integers from 1 to ANumber.

```
Function AddEmUp (ANumber As Long) As Long
Dim I As Long
AddEmUp = 0
For I = 1 to ANumber
```

continues

```
        AddEmUp = AddEmUp + I
    Next I
End Function
```

See also   Dim statement
             Static statement
             Global statement
             Type statement
             Any data type
             Control data type
             Currency data type
             Form data type
             Double data type
             Integer data type
             Single data type
             String data type

LSet

Purpose   The LSet statement left-justifies strings and copies record variables.

Syntax   **LSet** *fixedstring$* = *string$*
                 Lset *recvar1* = *recvar2*

Arguments   *fixedstring$*—a fixed-length string.

                 string$—a string or a formula that results in a string to be left-justified in
                 the fixed-length string.

                 recvar1—a user-defined record variable.

                 recvar2—another user-defined variable.

Description The LSet statement left-justifies a string in a fixed-length string or copies
                 user-defined record variables. When left-justifying a string into a fixed-
                 length string, only as much of the left side of the string as fits in the fixed-
                 length string is copied. If the string is shorter than the fixed-length string,
                 the remainder of the right side of the fixed-length string is filled with blanks.
                 Use RSet to right-justify strings.

> When copying record-type variables of different types, interesting results may occur. Do this at your own risk.

For example   The following lines define a fixed-length string and left-justifies the word Welcome into it.

```
Dim anFString As String *10
LSet anFString = "Welcome"
```

The variable anFString now contains "Welcome   ".

See also   Let statement
RSet statement

 # LTrim$

Purpose   The LTrim$ function removes leading blanks from the left side of a string.

Syntax   **LTrim$(***string$***)**

Arguments   *string$*—a string or a formula that results in a string.

Description   The LTrim$() function removes leading spaces from strings. Use the RTrim$() function to remove trailing spaces.

Returns   The result is the argument string with the blanks removed from the left side.

For example   The following line trims the blanks from the left side of a string and stores it in A$.

```
A$ = LTrim$("    234.45    ")
```

A$ now contains the string "234.45   ".

See also   RTrim function

 # Mid$

Purpose   The Mid$() function extracts a substring from within a string.

Syntax	`Mid$(string$,start&[,numchar&])`
Arguments	*string$*—a string, or a formula that results in a string.
	start&—the number of the first character in the string to extract. The first character in the string is number 1.
	numchar&—the number of characters to extract from the string. If this argument is omitted, the right side of the string is extracted.
Description	The `Mid$()` function extracts a substring from within another string. Use it with the `Left$()` and `Right$()` functions to extract different substrings.
Returns	The resulting string contains *numchar&* characters from *string$* starting at character number *start&*.
For example	The following is from the Immediate window and compares the `Left$()`, `Right$()` and `Mid$()` functions.

```
A$ = "This is a string to examine"
Print Left$(A$,6)
This i
Print Right$(A$,5)
amine
Print Mid$(A$,9,5)
a str
```

See also	`Left$` function
	`Right$` function
	`Mid$` statement

Mid$

Purpose	The `Mid$` statement replaces a substring within a string.
Syntax	`Mid$(string$,start&[,numchar&]) = substring$`
Arguments	*string$*—a string to have its substring replaced.
	start&—the number of the first character to replace. The first character in the string is number 1.
	numchar&—the number of characters to replace. Omit this argument to use all of *substring$*.

substring$*—a string or formula that results in a string to replace the substring in *string$.

Description   The Mid$ statement replaces a substring within a string. The replacement is done character by character, so the resulting string does not change length. It is not possible to insert a longer or shorter substring within a string with this function.

For example   The following is from the Immediate window and shows the operation of the Mid$ statement.

```
A$ = "This is a string to examine"
Mid$(A$,11,6) = "  dog  "
Print A$
"This is a  dog  to examine"
```

To replace a substring in *string$* with a longer or shorter *substring$*, use something like the following.

```
A$ = Left$(string$,start& - 1) + substring$ +
    Mid$(string$, start& + numchar& - 1)
```

See also   Left$ function
Mid$ function
Right$ function

 # Minute

Purpose   The Minute function extracts the minute of the hour from a serial date number.

Syntax   `Minute(serialdate#)`

Arguments   *serialdate#*—a serial date number. A serial date number is a double-precision number containing the date represented as the number of days since December 30, 1899. Negative serial date numbers represent dates from January 1, 1753 to December 30, 1899. Times are represented as fractions of a day. Years after 1900 are represented by the same serial date numbers used in several popular spreadsheet programs.

Description   The Minute() function takes a serial date number and returns the minute of the hour represented by that number. Use the Hour() and Second() functions to extract the hour and second. To extract the date, use the Day(), Month(), and Year() functions.

453

Returns The result is the minute of the hour as an integer from 1 to 60.

For example The following statement extracts the Minute (0) from a serial date number for noon on March 17, 1987.

```
theMinute = Minute(31853.5)   'Extracts the minute (0)
                              'from the date number
```

See also Date$ function
DateSerial function
DateValue function
Day function
Hour function
Month function
Now function
Second function
Time$ function
Timer function
TimeSerial function
TimeValue function
Weekday function
Year function
Date$ statement
Time$ statement

MkDir

Purpose The MkDir statement creates a new directory in the file system.

Syntax **MkDir** *path$*

Arguments *path$*—a string containing the new directory path, including the disk letter, with the following syntax.

[*drive*:][\]*directory*[*directory*]

where *drive* is the drive letter and *directory* is a directory name. Omit *drive* to use the current drive. If the first backslash is omitted, the path is assumed to start in the default directory of the specified drive. The string must be less than 128 bytes long.

Description The MkDir statement creates a new directory in the file system in the same manner as the DOS command of the same name. To use the current drive, omit the disk drive specification in the *path$* argument. If the first backslash is omitted, the path is assumed to be relative to the default directory on either the current drive (if no drive is specified) or on the specified drive.

> It is possible with this function to create directories with blanks embedded in their names that cannot be accessed with the DOS file system commands.

For example The first statement creates the UTIL directory in the TOOLS directory on the C drive. The second statement creates the C directory in the PROGRAMS directory, which is in the current default directory. That is, if the current directory was D:\APPS, the PROGRAMS directory must be in the APPS directory and the new C directory is created in the PROGRAMS directory.

```
MkDir "C:\TOOLS\UTIL"
MkDir "PROGRAMS\C"
```

See also ChDir statement
ChDrive statement
Kill statement
Name statement
RmDir statements
CurDir$ function
Dir$ function

Mod

Purpose The Mod operator performs modulus arithmetic on two integers.

Syntax *express1* **Mod** *express2*

Arguments *express1, express2*—integer values or expressions that result in integer values.

Description The Mod operator combines two integer expressions using modulo arithmetic. For two integer values, modulo arithmetic returns the remainder from an integer division. That is, 6 Mod 4 is 2, the remainder of the integer division of 6 by 4. Integer division is performed with the \ operator. The modulus operator is useful for things such as determining the actual angle

455

from angles larger than 360 degrees, or figuring feet and inches from inches.

Returns The resulting integer value is equal to *express1* modulo *express2*, which is the remainder of the integer division of *express1* by *express2*.

For example The following lists the results from several Mod operations.

Operation	Result
6\4	1
6 Mod 4	2
370 Mod 360	10
1300 Mod 360	220
Str$(75\12)+ " feet "	6 feet
Str$(75 Mod 12)" inches"	3 inches

See also None

 **Month**

Purpose The Month function calculates the month of the year from a serial date number.

Syntax `Month(serialdate#)`

Arguments *serialdate#*—a serial date number. A serial date number is a double-precision number containing the date represented as the number of days since December 30, 1899. Negative serial date numbers represent dates from January 1, 1753 to December 30, 1899. Times are represented as fractions of a day. Years after 1900 are represented by the same serial date numbers used in several popular spreadsheet programs.

Description The Month() function takes a serial date number and returns the month of the year represented by that number. Use the Day(), Weekday(), and Year() functions to extract the day, weekday, and year. Use the Hour(), Minute(), and Second() functions to extract the time.

Returns The result is the month of the year as an integer from 1 to 31.

For example The following statement extracts the month of the year from the serial date number for March 17, 1987.

```
theMonth = Day(31853)    'Extracts the month (3)
                         'from the date number
```

See also   Date$ function
DateSerial function
DateValue function
Day function
Hour function
Minute function
Now function
Second function
Time$ function
Timer function
TimeSerial function
TimeValue function
Weekday function
Year function
Date$ statement
Time$ statement

 Move

Purpose   The Move method moves or resizes a Form or control at run time.

Syntax   [*object.*]**Move** *left!*[,*top!*[,*width!*[,*height!*]]]

Arguments   *object*—the object to move; any Form or control except Timers and menus.

left!—the distance from the left edge of the drawing area to the left edge of the object.

top!—the distance from the top of the drawing area to the top of the object.

width!—the width of the object.

height!—the height of the object.

Description   The Move method moves or scales an object while a program is running. The drawing area is the screen, Form, or frame that the object lies on. Forms lie on the screen so the measure is from the top-left corner of the screen. Controls that lie on a Form measure from the top-left corner of the Form, excluding the Title bar. Controls on a frame measure from the top-left corner of the frame.

The coordinate system used is that of the object that the Form or control lies on. Forms always lie on the screen so the measure is in twips. Controls on Frames are also measured in twips. Everything else depends on the value of the ScaleHeight, ScaleWidth, ScaleLeft, and ScaleRight properties. If these have not been changed, the default is twips.

For example   The following moves the **Command1** command button to the location 2000 twips down and 1000 twips left of the upper left corner of the Form.

```
Command1.Move 1000,2000
```

See also   Scale method
Height property
Width property
Left property
Top property
ScaleHeight property
ScaleWidth property
ScaleLeft property
ScaleRight property

# MsgBox

Purpose   The MsgBox() function displays a dialog box containing a message and waits for the user to press a button.

Syntax   **MsgBox(***message$*[, *type%*[, *title$*]])

Arguments   *message$*—a string message up to 255 characters long. The string automatically word wraps to fit in the dialog box.

title$—a string to use as the title of the dialog box. If this this argument is omitted, Microsoft Visual Basic is used.

type%—a code number that determines the type of dialog box to display, and the number and type of buttons. Add the codes together to come up with the code for the box you want. The codes are

Buttons		*Icon*	
0	**OK**	16	Critical Message
1	**OK** and **Cancel**	32	Warning Query
2	**Abort**, **Retry**,	48	Warning Message
	and **Ignore**	64	Information Message
3	**Yes**, **No**, **Cancel**		
4	**Yes**, **No**		
5	**Retry** and **Cancel**		

Default button

0	First
256	Second
512	Third

Description   The MsgBox() function sends a message to the user, or asks a question that can be answered by pressing some buttons. The number and type of buttons, the icon, and the default button are determined by a type code. Create the type code by combining the codes in the table above. Add the code for the buttons you want to the code for the Icon and the code for the default button. The default button is the one selected when you press Enter. The Esc key always selects the **Cancel** button.

Returns   The resulting numeric code determines which button was pressed by the user. The codes are

1 **OK**	5 **Ignore**
2 **Cancel**	6 **Yes**
3 **Abort**	7 **No**
4 **Retry**	

For example   The following statement creates a simple message box with **OK** and **Cancel** buttons and the Critical Message icon. The **OK** button is active. The code consists of 1 + 16 + 0 = 17 for the options listed. A receives a 1 or 2, depending on which button was pressed.

```
A = MsgBox$("Kiss the Cook!",17)
```

See also   MsgBox statement
InputBox$ function

S MsgBox

Purpose   The MsgBox statement displays a dialog box containing a message and waits for the user to press a button.

Syntax   **MsgBox** *message$*[, *type%*[, *title$*]]

Arguments   *message$* — a string message up to 255 characters long. The string automatically word wraps to fit in the dialog box.

title$ — a string to use as the title of the dialog box. If this argument is omitted, Microsoft Visual Basic is used.

type% — a code number that determines the type of dialog box to display, and the number and type of buttons. Add the codes together to come up with the code for the box you want. Note that since this box does not return a value, the codes for multiple buttons serve no purpose. The codes are

Buttons		*Icon*	
0	**OK**	16	Critical Message
1	**OK** and **Cancel**	32	Warning Query
2	**Abort**, **Retry**,	48	Warning Message
	and **Ignore**	64	Information Message
3	**Yes**, **No**, **Cancel**		
4	**Yes**, **No**		
5	**Retry** and **Cancel**		

Default button

0	First
256	Second
512	Third

Description   The MsgBox statement is nearly identical to the MsgBox() function, except that it does not return a value. MsgBox sends a message to the user. The number and type of buttons, the icon, and the default button are determined by a type code, although any of the combinations with more than one button serve no purpose because the box does not return a value. Create the type code by combining the codes in the table above. Add the code for the buttons you want to the code for the Icon and the code for the default button. The default button is the one selected when you press Enter. The Esc key always selects the **Cancel** button.

For example   The following statement creates a simple message box, with the **OK** button and the Critical message icon. The **OK** button is active. The code consists of $0 + 16 + 0 = 16$ for the options listed.

```
MsgBox$("Kiss the Cook!",16)
```

See also   MsgBox function
InputBox$ function

 # Name

Purpose   The Name statement moves and changes the name of a disk file.

Syntax   **Name** *oldfile$* **As** *newfile$*

Arguments   *oldfile$* — the old file name in a string and an optional directory path if the file isn't in the current directory. The file name may contain the * and ? wildcard characters, where * matches any number of any characters and ? matches any single character. The path, including the disk letter has the following syntax,

[*drive*:][[\]*directory*[*directory*...\]]*filename*

where *drive* is the drive letter, *directory* is a directory name, and *filename* is the name of the file. Omit the *drive* argument to use the current drive. If the first backslash is omitted, the path is assumed to start in the default directory of the specified drive. Use ChDir and ChDrive to change the current directory.

newfile$ — the new file name in a string and an optional path.

Description   The Name statement moves and renames files. If only the file names are different, Name changes the name. If the directory paths are different, Name moves the file to the new directory and, optionally, changes the name.

For example   The following changes the name of MYFILE.DOC to YOURFILE.DOC in the default directory.

```
Name "myfile.doc" As "yourfile.doc"
```

See also   ChDir statement
ChDrive statement
Kill statement
MkDir statement

461

RmDir statement
CurDir$ function
Dir$ function

 NewPage

Purpose	The NewPage method advances the page on the printer.
Syntax	`Printer.NewPage`
Arguments	None
Description	The NewPage method advances the page on the printer. The printer automatically advances a page when text is printed beyond the bottom, and also when the EndDoc method is executed. NewPage advances an unfilled page within a document.
For example	The following line advances the page on the printer.
	`Printer.NewPage`
See also	EndDoc method Page property

 Not

Purpose	The Not operator reverses the logical value of a logical expression, or each of the bits in a numeric value.
Syntax	`Not express1`
Arguments	*express1*—a logical expression, numeric expression, or numeric value.
Description	The Not operator converts a logical value according to the following truth table. If it is applied to a numeric value, the operator is applied bit by bit to each bit in the value. That is, each bit in the result is equal to the logical Not of the corresponding bit in the value.

A	*Not A*
True	False
False	True

Returns The logical Not of an expression equals True (–1) or False (0) if *express1* is a logical expression. If *express1* is a numeric expression, the result is the bitwise logical inverse of the bits in the argument.

For example The following If statement causes a beep only if A is False.

```
If Not A then Beep
```

See also And operator
Eqv operator
Imp operator
Or operator
Xor operator

 **Now**

Purpose The Now function gets and returns the current date and time from the system clock as a serial date number.

Syntax **Now**

Arguments None

Description The Now function gets the current date and time as a serial date number. To find the difference in days, subtract the later serial date number from the earlier one. Use the Date$ or Time$ functions to get the current date or time as a string.

Returns The result is the serial date number for the current date and time. A serial date number is a double-precision number containing the date represented as the number of days since December 30, 1899. Negative serial date numbers represent dates from January 1, 1753 to December 30, 1899. Times are represented as fractions of a day. Years after 1900 are represented by the same serial date numbers used in several popular spreadsheet programs.

For example The following assignment statement assigns the current date and time to the double-precision variable A#.

```
A# = Now     'Assign the current date to A#
```

See also
Date$ function
DateSerial function
DateValue function
Day function
Hour function
Minute function
Month function
Second function
Time$ function
Timer function
TimeSerial function
TimeValue function
Weekday function
Year function
Date$ statement
Time$ statement

F Oct$

Purpose The Oct$() function converts a number into a string of octal characters.

Syntax **Oct$(***number***)**

Arguments *number*—a number of any type, or a formula that evaluates to a number.

Description The Oct$() function converts numbers into octal numbers in a string, just as the Str$() function converts numbers into decimal numbers in a string. Octal numbers are base 8, and use the characters 0 through 7. Thus, &O12 in octal is 10 in decimal. The &O, which designates this as an octal string, is not returned by this function. Floating point numbers are rounded to an integer before conversion to an octal string.

Returns The resulting string is the number converted into an octal number.

For example The following lists the results from several Oct$ functions.

Oct$ Function	Result
Oct$(135)	207
Oct$(135.2)	207
Oct$(135.7)	210

Oct$(6)	6
Oct$(7)	7
Oct$(8)	10
Oct$(9)	11
Oct$(10)	12
Oct$(11)	13
Oct$(63)	77
Oct$(64)	100
Oct$(65)	101
Oct$(511)	777
Oct$(512)	1000
Oct$(513)	1001
Oct$(65534)	177776
Oct$(65535)	177777
Oct$(65536)	200000

See also   Format$ function
Hex$ function
Str$ function

S On Error/Resume

Purpose   The On Error/Resume statements enable and return from an error handling routine.

Syntax   **On [Local] Error {Goto *line*¦Resume Next¦Goto 0}**
Resume {[0]¦Next¦*line*}

Arguments   Local—does nothing; included for compatibility with other versions of BASIC.

GoTo *line*—enables the error handling routine that starts at *line*, where *line* is a line number or Label. The line must be in the same procedure as the On Error statement.

Resume Next—when used with the On Error statement, this option ignores any errors and resumes processing at the next statement after the error.

> Be careful with this argument; use it to store an error for handling a short time later.

Goto 0—disable the error handler.

[0]—resume at the statement that caused the error after correcting the problem in the error handler.

Next—resume at the statement after the one that caused the error.

line— resume execution at line, where *line* is a line number or a Label.

Description   The On Error/Resume statement traps all the run-time errors listed in Table 13.1 in Chapter 13, "Debugging and Error Trapping," and sends control to the error handler at the indicated line when an error occurs. The error handler then handles the error if it can, or sends a message and quits the application if it cannot. The error number of the last error is returned by the Err function and, if the lines are numbered, the line number where the error occurred is returned by the Erl function. The text of the error message is returned by the Error$() function. The error handler must end with a Resume statement.

For example   The following procedure contains an outline of a function to calculate the sine integral, and an error handler to trap the possible divide-by-zero error (error number 11). At (xint) = 0, Sin(xint) is also 0, but the quotient is 1 even though Visual Basic gives a divide-by-zero error. If the error isn't a divide-by-zero error, the error handler displays a message box containing the error message and then ends the application.

```
Function Si(x As Single) As Single
'function to calculate the sine integral
'statements to integrate sin(x)/x from x to infinity
On Error GoTo FixSin     'turn the error handler on
.
.
.
Integrand = Sin(xint)/xint
.
.
.Exit Function
FixSin:
If Err = 11 Then
   Integrand = 1
Else
   MsgBox Error$(Err)
```

```
        Stop
    End If
    Resume Next
    End Function
```

See also   Err function
Erl function
Error$() function

On...GoSub

Purpose   The On...Gosub statement is a computed branch to one of several sub routines.

Syntax   **On** *number* **GoSub** *label*[,*label*[,*label*]]...

Arguments   *number*—a number of any type, or a formula that evaluates to a number between 0 and 255.

label—a line number or a Label of a subroutine.

Description   The On...Gosub statement causes a branch to one of several subroutines in the same procedure. This procedure is largely for compatibility with older versions of Basic. Sub procedures and the Select Case statement are much more powerful than On...Gosub. The subroutine is selected according to the value of the *number* argument. The value of *number* is rounded to an integer that identifies the Label to be selected. That is, if *number* rounds to 1, the subroutine at the first Label is branched to; if *number* rounds to 2, the subroutine at the second Label is branched to, and so forth. If *number* rounds to 0 or to a value larger than the number of Labels in the list, control drops through to the next statement after the On...Gosub statement. If *number* is negative or greater than 255, an error results. Subroutine procedures end with a Return statement and control passes to the line after the On...Gosub statement. See GoSub for a discussion of subroutine procedures.

For example   The following do-nothing procedure demonstrates the On...Gosub statement. If A equals 1, the statement branches to Label lab1 and does something. The Return at the end of that subroutine returns control to the statement after the On...GoSub statement. If A equals 2, the statement branches to lab2. If A = 3, the statement branches to lab3. The subroutines are placed after the Exit *procedure* statement so they are not executed accidently during the procedure's normal operation.

```
On A GoSub lab1,lab2,lab3
other statements
Exit procedure
lab1:
'do something
Return
lab2:
'do something different
Return
lab3:
'do a third thing
Return
End procedure
```

See also   GoSub/Return statement
GoTo statement
On GoTo statement
Select Case statement

 # On...GoTo

Purpose   The On...GoTo statement is a computed branch to one of several Labels.

Syntax   **On** *number* **GoTo** *label*[*,label*[*,label*]]...

Arguments   *number*—a number of any type, or a formula that evaluates to a number between 0 and 255.

label—a line number or a Label.

Description   The On...GoTo statement causes a branch to one of several statements in the same procedure. This procedure is largely for compatibility with older versions of Basic. Sub procedures and the Select Case statement are much more powerful than On...GoTo. The statement is selected according to the value of the *number* argument. The value of *number* is rounded to an integer that identifies the Label to be selected. That is, if *number* rounds to 1, control branches to the first Label, if *number* rounds to 2, it branches to the second Label and so forth. If *number* rounds to 0 or to a value larger than the number of Labels in the list, control drops through to the next statement after the On...GoTo statement. If *number* is negative or greater than 255, an error results.

For example   The following do-nothing procedure demonstrates the On...GoTo statement. If A equals 1, the statement branches to Label lab1. If A equals 2, the
statement branches to lab2. If A = 3, the statement branches to lab3. When
each of the blocks of code that were branched to is complete, a GoTo
statement is needed to skip over the intervening blocks of code. A Select
Case statement would work much simpler here.

```
On A GoSub lab1,lab2,lab3
other statements
lab1:
'do something
GoTo done
lab2:
'do something different
GoTo done
lab3:
'do a third thing
done:
End procedure
```

See also   GoSub/Return statement
GoTo statement
On GoSub statement
Select Case statement

S Open

Purpose   The Open statement establishes a connection to a disk file.

Syntax   Open *filename$* [For *mode*] [Access *access*] [*lock*]
As [#]*filenumber%* [Len = *rlen%*]

Arguments   *filename$*—a string containing the file name, and an optional directory
path if the file isn't in the current directory. The path, including the disk
letter, has the following syntax,

[*drive*:][[\]*directory*[*directory*...\]]*filename*

where *drive* is the drive letter, *directory* is a directory name, and *filename*
is the file to name. Omit the *drive* argument to use the current drive. If the
first backslash is omitted, the path is assumed to start in the default

directory of the specified drive. Use ChDir and ChDrive to change the current directory.

mode — the *mode* of the file is either Append, Binary, Input, Output, or Random. For sequential files, the allowed modes are Input, Output, or Append. When a file is opened For Input, the file must already exist and you only may read data from it. When a file is opened For Output, it is opened if it exists, or created if it does not, and you only may write data to it. When an existing file is opened For Output, writing starts at the first record, overwriting any old data in the file. The Append mode is a variation of Output in which, when the file is opened, writing starts at the end, preserving the old data. Random creates a random access file where each record can be read or written in any order. Binary files are similar to Random, but they access the file byte by byte instead of by record.

access — the *access* argument controls the file access type and is either Read, Write, or Read Write. The *access* argument applies to networked environments, where multiple users may have access to the same file. The *access* argument controls what access you want for the file in case someone else already has it open.

lock — the *lock* argument has the value Shared, Lock Read, or Lock Write, and controls access to a file by other processes. The *lock* argument also applies only to networked environments. *Lock* controls what access to the file you allow others if you are the first to open it. Shared allows everyone access. Lock Read prevents anyone from reading it. Lock Write prevents anyone from writing to it. Use the Lock statement to lock individual records instead of the entire file.

filenumber% — the *filenumber%* is a unique number that identifies the open file to all the other file access commands. The *filenumber* argument must be included with every Open statement, and used with every command that accesses the file. Since you may have more than one file open at any one time, this number uniquely identifies that file. Usually, the first file you open is file number 1, the second is 2, and so forth. If you close a file, you can reuse its file number. If you know how many files you have open, you can assign a constant for the file number. However, if you have a situation where you don't know how many files you have open, such as a word processor having multiple files open at the same time, use the FreeFile function to give you the next available file number.

rlen% — the record length, in bytes, to use with random access files. The default record length is 128 bytes.

Description The Open statement creates an access path between an application and a disk file. The access path is identified with the file number, which is assigned to the file with the Open statement. Once defined, all statements that access the file use the file number to identify what file they want to access.

There are three types of disk files: sequential access, random access and binary. Sequential access files are standard text files. Everything written to them is readable with a word processor or printable with the DOS TYPE command. They get their name from the fact that they are sequentially read or written to, in order from the beginning to the end. Random access files are also text files, but have fixed-length records set with the Len option on the Open statement. Any record can be read or written in any order without disturbing the rest of the file. Binary files can read or write randomly any single byte in the file.

When you are done with any file, close it with the Close statement. The Close statement also releases the file number for reuse by another file.

For example The following lines demonstrate opening and then closing the file MYFILE.DBK as a random access file, with file number 1 and a record length of 128 bytes. The record length isn't really needed here because 128 is the default length, but including it makes what you're doing more clear.

```
Open "MYFILE.DBK" For Random As #1 Len = 128
'some statements
Close #1
```

See also Get statement
Put statement
Close statement
Print statement
Write statement
Input statement
Line Input statement
Input$ function

S Option Base

Purpose The Option Base statement changes the default lower limit for array variables.

Syntax	`Option Base` *number%*
Arguments	*number%*—the number 0 or 1, which becomes the default lower limit for arrays.
Description	When an array variable is defined with the `Dim`, `Global`, or `Static` statement and the lower limit isn't explicitly given in the definition, the default value is 0. The `Option Base` statement can change that default to 1. I can't think of any use for this statement.
For example	The following changes the default lower limit to 1. `Option Base 1`
See also	`Dim` statement `Global` statement `Static` statement

 Or

Purpose	The `Or` operator combines two logical expressions, or all the bits in two numeric values, using the logical `OR` operation.
Syntax	*express1* `Or` *express2*
Arguments	*express1*, *express2*—a logical expression, numeric expression, or numeric value.
Description	The `Or` operator combines two logical values according to the following truth table. If two numeric values are combined, the operator is applied bit by bit to the corresponding bits in the two values. That is, each bit in the result is equal to the logical `OR` of the corresponding bits in the two values.

A	*B*	*A Or B*
True	True	True
True	False	True
False	True	True
False	False	False

Returns	The logical `OR` of the two expression equals `True` (–1) or `False` (0) if *express1* and *express2* are logical expressions. If *express1* and *express2* are numeric expressions, the result is the bitwise Logical `OR` of the same bits in each of the two expressions.

For example The following If statement causes a beep when either A or B are True.

```
If A Or B then Beep
```

See also And operator
Eqv operator
Imp operator
Not operator
Xor operator

 Point

Purpose The Point method gets the color of a point on a Form or Picture box.

Syntax [*object*.]**Point**(*x!, y!*)

Arguments *object*—the name of the object to examine, a Form, or a Picture box. If this argument is omitted, the Form containing the statement is used.

x!, y!—the *x,y* coordinates of the point to examine on the object in object's coordinate system.

Description The Point method gets the color of a point on a Form or Picture box. The location of the point is in the coordinate system of the object being examined, and is determined by the objects ScaleMode, ScaleHeight, ScaleWidth, ScaleTop, and ScaleLeft properties. See the RGB function for a discussion of colors.

Returns The result is the color of the selected point as a Long integer color number (see the RGB function).

For example The following gets the color of the point 200 twips from the left and 500 twips down from the top of the Picture1 Picture box, and stores it as a Long integer in the variable theColor.

```
theColor& = Picture1.Point(200,500)
```

See also Circle method
Line method
Print method
PSet methods
RGB function
QBColor function

 PrintForm

Purpose	The `PrintForm` method sends a copy of the Form to the printer.
Syntax	`[form.]PrintForm`
Arguments	*form*—the name of a Form. If this argument is omitted, the Form this statement is on is assumed.
Description	The `PrintForm` method sends a pixel-by-pixel image of the Form to the printer. To print any pictures or graphics added at run time, the `AutoRedraw` property must be set to `True` before the graphics are drawn.
For example	The following statement prints the `InputDialog` Form.

```
InputDialog.PrintForm
```

See also	`Print` method
	`AutoRedraw` property

S Print

Purpose	The `Print #` statement prints data to a disk file.
Syntax	`Print #filenumber%,arglist[{;¦,}]`
Arguments	*filenumber%*—the file number used when the file was opened with the `Open` statement.

arglist—a list of variables and expressions to print. Numeric variables are converted automatically to strings. Commas between arguments print the next argument at the next tab stop (there is a tab stop every 14 characters). A semicolon between arguments prints the next argument immediately after the last one, with no added spaces between them. Normally, a carriage return-line feed is placed in the file after the *arglist* is printed; if a comma is placed at the end, the insertion point is moved to the next tab field. A semicolon at the end leaves the insertion point at the right side of the last character printed.

Description   The Print # statement prints data in a disk file in exactly the same manner as the Print method prints on the screen. This statement is primarily used to create files that are read with the DOS TYPE command or by a word processor. If you plan to read the data back into a BASIC program, consider the Write # statement instead.

For example   A disk file written with the following statements,

```
A1 = 5.355
B1 = 4.788
Print #1, "Values, are: ", A1, B1, " units"
Write #1, "Values, are: ", A1, B1, " units"
```

produces

```
Values, are: 5.355          4.788              units
"Values, are: ",5.355,4.788," units"
```

Reading those values with the following Input # statements,

```
Input #1, A$, B, C, D$
Input #1, E$, F, G, H$
```

stores the following data in these variables

```
A$ = "The values"
B = 0
C = 5.355
D$ = "4.788          units"
E$ = "The values, are: "
F = 5.355
G = 4.788
H$ = " units"
```

Note how the first Input # statement stopped reading the string into A$ at the first comma, so that the first numeric input, B, sees text instead of a number and gets a value of zero. Then the second numeric input, C, reads the first number, and the remaining number and string ends up in D$.

See also   Get statement
Input # statement
Line Input # statement
Open statement
Put statement
Write # statement
Input$ function
Print method

M Print

Purpose The `Print` method writes data on a Form, a Picture box, or the Printer object.

Syntax `[object.]Print arglist[{;¦,}]`

Arguments *object*—the name of the object to draw on, a Form, a Picture box, or the keyword `Printer`. Omit this argument to use the Form containing this statement.

arglist—a list of variables and expressions to print. Numeric variables are converted automatically to strings. Commas between arguments print the next argument at the next tab stop (one every 14 characters). A semicolon between arguments prints the next argument immediately after the last one, with no added spaces between them. Normally, a carriage return-line feed is printed after the *arglist* is printed; if a comma is placed at the end, the insertion point moves to the next tab field. A semicolon at the end leaves the insertion point at the right side of the last character printed.

Description The `Print` method prints text and numbers on a Form, a Picture box, or the `Printer` object. The text font, size, color, and style are determined by the object's current font properties. Printing starts at the position indicated by the `CurrentX` and `CurrentY` properties.

For example The following statements,

```
A1 = 5.355
B1 = 4.788
Picture1.Print, "Values, are: ", A1, B1, " units"
```

produce

```
Values, are: 5.355        4.788          units
```

on the `Picture1` Picture box.

See also Get statement
Input # statement
Line Input # statement
Open statement
Put statement
Write # statement
Input$ function
Print method

 PSet

Purpose   The PSet method sets the color of a point on a Form or Picture box.

Syntax   [*object*.]**PSet** [Step](*x!, y!*)[*color&*]

Arguments   *object*—the name of the object to draw on, a Form, a Picture box, or the keyword Printer. If the argument is omitted, the Form containing this statement is used.

Step—a keyword that specifies that the following coordinates are relative to the current position specified by the CurrentX and CurrentY properties.

x!, y!—the *x,y* coordinate of the point to set, in the coordinate system of the object contained in the ScaleMode, ScaleHeight, ScaleWidth, ScaleLeft, and ScaleTop properties.

color&—a Long integer color value. (See the RGB() function for a discussion of colors.)

Description   The PSet method sets the color of a point on a Form, a Picture box, or the Printer object according to the DrawMode property. The location of the point is in the coordinate system of the object being set, and is determined by the objects ScaleMode, ScaleHeight, ScaleWidth, ScaleTop, and ScaleLeft properties. The size of the point is determined by the DrawWidth property.

For example   The following statement sets the color of the point on the Picture1 Picture box that is 700 twips down and 200 twips from the left side of the Picture box. The color is set to red with the color number &HFF. The definitions of several common colors are available in the file CONSTANT.TXT, included with Visual Basic.

```
Picture1.PSet (200,700), &HFF
```

See also   Point function
RGB function
QBColor function
CurrentX property
CurrentY property
DrawMode property
DrawWidth property

S Put

Purpose The Put statement stores a record in a random access or binary disk file.

Syntax **Put** [#]*filenumber%*[*,recnum&*]*,recvariable*

Arguments *filenumber%*—the file number used when the file was opened with the Open statement.

recnum&—the number of the record to store in a random access file. Omit this argument to use the next record in the file. File records are consecutively numbered with the first record as record number 1. If the file is opened as binary, this is the byte number at which to start writing.

recvariable—any variable whose length is less than or equal to the length of a record defined when the file is opened. This is usually a user-defined variable defined with the Type statement.

Description The Put statement writes a records worth of data to a random access or binary disk file. The record variable may be any type of variable as long as its total length is less than the length of a record. For random access files, the length of a record is defined with the Len *reclen* clause of the Open statement. In most cases, you define a record type variable with the Type statement and use that to access the disk file. The default length is 128 bytes. For binary files, the record length is as many bytes as can fit into the record variable.

For example The following statements first define the record variable DayType in the Global module. They then define the variable aDay as type DayType, open a disk file whose name is stored in the variable FileName, load aDay with data, and write it to the first record in the file.

In the Global module,

```
Type DayType              'Type declaration for the
   TheDate As Double      'record DayType, 128 bytes
   Flags As Integer       'long
   Msg As String * 118
End Type
```

In a procedure,

```
Dim aDay As DayType
Open FileName For Random As #1 Len = 128
```

```
aDay.TheDate = Now
aDay.Flags = 1
aDay.Msg = ""
Put #1, 1, aDay
```

See also   Open statement
Get statement

QBColor

Purpose   The QBColor() function returns the RGB color number for the standard BASIC colors.

Syntax   QBColor(*colorcode%*)

Arguments   *colorcode%*—a code number ranging from 0 to 15, representing one of the following 16 standard colors.

Code	Color	Code	Color
0	Black	8	Gray
1	Blue	9	Light Blue
2	Green	10	Light Green
3	Cyan	11	Light Cyan
4	Red	12	Light Red
5	Magenta	13	Light Magenta
6	Yellow or Brown	14	Light Yellow
7	White	15	Bright White

Description   Most older BASICs, including BASICA, GW-BASIC, and QuickBasic, used a set of 16 standard colors for most applications. Those colors are selected with a color attribute, which is a number ranging from 0 to 15. The QBColor() function is a translator between those color attributes and the Visual Basic color numbers. While this function is primarily for compatibility with those older versions of BASIC, I find it quite useful when I want to select a color under program control. To go beyond the 16 standard colors, use the RGB() function, which generates the color numbers for more than sixteen million colors.

A Visual Basic color number is a single Long integer. Within that integer are four one-byte codes. The rightmost three bytes contain the color in RGB

479

format. The rightmost byte contains the intensity of red. The second byte from the right contains the the intensity of green. The third byte from the right contains the intensity of blue. Each byte holds a value that ranges from 0 to 255, where 0 is no color, or black, and 255 is the brightest.

The simplest way to represent these values is as hexadecimal numbers (see the Hex$() function) where each byte is represented by a pair of hexadecimal digits. The following list of colors is from the file CONSTANT.TXT, included with Visual Basic. Use one of these constants as an alternative to using the two color functions QBColor() and RGB(). To use them, copy them from CONSTANT.TXT into the Global module.

Color	Hexadecimal Value
BLACK	&H000000
RED	&H0000FF
GREEN	&H00FF00
YELLOW	&H00FFFF
BLUE	&HFF0000
MAGENTA	&HFF00FF
CYAN	&HFFFF00
WHITE	&HFFFFFF

The leftmost byte is 0 for normal RGB colors. If the byte has a value of &H80, the color number becomes a code for one of the default system colors shown below. The default system colors are those set in the Windows control panel.

System Color	Hexadecimal value
Gray area on Scroll bars	&H80000000
Desktop background	&H80000001
Caption of an active window	&H80000002
Caption of an inactive window	&H80000003
Menu background	&H80000004
Window background	&H80000005
Window frame	&H80000006
Menu text	&H80000007
Window text	&H80000008
Caption text	&H80000009
Border of an active window	&H8000000A
Border of an inactive window	&H8000000B
Background of MDI applications	&H8000000C
Selected items	&H8000000D
Selected text	&H8000000E

Command button	&H8000000F
Command button edge	&H80000010
Disabled text	&H80000011
Push buttons	&H80000012

Returns The result is a Long integer containing an RGB color number usable by all Visual Basic functions that handle color.

For example The following assignment statement assigns the color number for light red to the variable theColor.

```
theColor = QBColor(12)
```

See also Hex$ function
RGB function

S Randomize

Purpose The Randomize statement initializes the seed of the random number generator.

Syntax Randomize [*number%*]

Arguments *number%*—a number of any type, or a formula that evaluates to a number. Omit *number%* to use the current value of the Timer() function.

Description Random numbers in computer programs aren't truly random, but are pseudo random numbers generated by a function whose output distribution is reasonably random. As a consequence, every time you run a Visual Basic program, you get the same sequence of random numbers from the Rnd() function. There are cases where this is desirable (debugging, for example), but usually you would want a different set of numbers every time you run a code.

Random number generators have a seed value that initializes the function that generates the random numbers, and the Randomize statement sets that value. If you don't use the Randomize statement, or always use the same seed value when you run a program, you'll get the same sequence of random numbers every time.

A convenient way to get around that is to omit the *number%* argument on the `Randomize` statement, which forces `Randomize` to use the value of the `Timer()` function. The `Timer()` function returns the number of seconds since midnight, so it is highly unlikely that you would get the same sequence of numbers with each run.

Use the `Randomize` function once near the beginning of your program, before you use any of the `Rnd()` functions. In most cases, it is unnecessary to run `Randomize` more than once in any program.

For example   The following lines initialize the random number generator and then generate two random numbers: `val1`, between 0 and 10, and `val2`, between 5 and 10.

```
Randomize
val1 = Rnd * 10
val2 = Rnd *5 + 5
```

See also   `Rnd` function
`Timer` function

 ReDim

Purpose   The `ReDim` statement declares the elements of dynamic arrays, or reallocates static arrays, at the procedure level.

Syntax   **ReDim** [**Shared**] *variable* (*subscripts*) [**As** *type*] [, *variable* (*subscripts*) [**As** *type*]]...

Arguments   `Shared`—Included for compatibility with other BASICs so you don't have to rewrite imported programs; otherwise does nothing.

variable—a variable name. Array names are followed by parentheses and the subscript range. There can be up to 60 subscripts for static arrays or eight for dynamic arrays. The syntax of the subscript ranges is

[*lower%* To]*upper%*[, [*lower%* To]*upper%*]...

lower%—the lower limit for the array subscripts. If omitted, 0 is assumed unless the `Option Base` statement has been executed. (See the `Option Base` statement.)

upper%—the upper limit for array subscripts.

type—one of the following Visual Basic types: Control, Currency, Form, Integer, Long, Single, Double, String, String*length*, or any user type defined with the Type statement. *Length* is the length of a fixed-length string. Use the As *type* clause or a character prefix symbol, but not both, to declare the type of the variable. (See the Introduction to Part III for information on character prefix symbols.) You may not change the type of a static array.

Description   The ReDim statement changes the number of elements in each dimension of a static array, or to set the number of elements in a dynamic array. When defined, all arrays are initialized to 0. ReDim is used only at the procedure level.

There are two types of arrays in Visual Basic: static and dynamic. Static arrays are defined with a fixed number of elements and thus have a fixed length. They can be redimensioned, but the new total size in bytes must be the same or less than the old size. You may change only the number of elements in each dimension; you may not change the number of dimensions or the numeric type of the array.

A dynamic array is initially defined at the Global or module level with no dimensions. The size and dimensions are determined later at the procedure level with a ReDim statement. Memory is allocated for the array when the dimensions are added. Use the Erase statement to deallocate the memory of dynamic arrays.

For example   Assuming anArray was defined in the Global module as

```
Global anArray(10,3) as Integer
```

The following statement redefines anArray with the first dimension of the array ranging from 3 to 6 and the second from 0 to 10. Note that this has the same number of dimensions and elements as the array defined in the Global module; they simply are arranged differently.

```
ReDim anArray(3 To 6,10) As Integer
```

See also   Const statement
Dim statement
Erase statement
Global statement
Option Base statement
Static statement

 Refresh

Purpose   The Refresh method updates the contents of a control after some changes.

Syntax   [*object*.]**Refresh**

Arguments   *object*—the name of the object to refresh; a Form or control. Omit this argument to use the Form containing the statement.

Description   Most Visual Basic objects are refreshed whenever a program is waiting for an event to occur. Use the Refresh method, however, if you are making changes to a control and want to refresh its contents without exiting a procedure. The DoEvents() function also refreshes the controls, but, additionally, takes care of any events waiting to be handled. Refresh updates the objects without handling any other pending events. Refresh also updates the list of file names in a File List box after adding or deleting some.

> If you are drawing on a Picture box and the AutoRedraw property is set to True, you won't see the results on the screen until the Picture box is updated. This is because you are drawing on the persistent bitmap (referenced with the Image property) rather than the Picture. If you are doing a lot of drawing and want to see the drawing as it occurs rather than waiting until it is done, use the Refresh method at appropriate moments.

Note that using Refresh or DoEvents() significantly slows down a drawing program.

For example   The following procedure draws 100 circles on the BlackBoard Picture box. Because we want the system to take care of redrawing the Picture box if it is covered and uncovered, the AutoRedraw property is set to True. Because drawing 100 circles takes a few seconds (and we don't want to sit staring at a blank screen), use the Refresh method after each circle is drawn.

```
Sub CirclesCmd_Click ()
'Draw 100 random circles
Dim Color As Long, I As Integer
BlackBoard.ScaleMode = 1 ' - Twips
```

```
BlackBoard.DrawStyle = 0 ' - Solid
BlackBoard.FillStyle = 0 ' - Solid
BlackBoard.AutoRedraw = True
BlackBoard.Cls
For I = 1 To 100
    XC = Rnd(1) * BlackBoard.ScaleWidth
    YC = Rnd(1) * BlackBoard.ScaleHeight
    Radius = Rnd(1) * BlackBoard.ScaleHeight / 2
    Color = QBColor(Rnd(1) * 15)
    BlackBoard.FillColor = Color
    BlackBoard.Circle (XC, YC), Radius, Color
    BlackBoard.Refresh
Next I
End Sub
```

See also   DoEvents function

 Rem

Purpose   The Rem statement sets the balance of the line as a remark.

Syntax   **Rem** *anything*
or
[*statement*]   '*anything*

Arguments   *anything*—as it says, anything can go here. This argument is ignored by the running program.

statement—any programming line.

Description   The Rem, or remark, statement documents the operation of a program. Any line that begins with the Rem keyword, or any text that follows a single quote (') is ignored by a running program. Put any text here you wish to explain what you're doing, define variables, and so forth.

Use remarks liberally in a program. They make it much easier to understand and debug. They quickly pay for the time spent typing them by reducing the time required to modify or debug a program. Though they are ignored by a running program, they can be branched to by GoTo or GoSub statements if your program lines are numbered.

For example   The following three lines contain remarks. The first two are all remarks, the last one has an executable statement at the beginning of a line and a remark at the end.

```
Rem This is a remark, anything can go here.
'This is also a remark,
aVal = Abs(1)    'but not the beginning of this line.
```

See also   None

 # RemoveItem

Purpose   The RemoveItem method removes an entry from a List or Combo box.

Syntax   *control*.**RemoveItem** *index*%

Arguments   *control*—the name of a List or Combo box. If the control is on another Form, include the name of the Form with the name of the control as follows: *form.control*. If the name of the Form isn't included, this argument defaults to the control on the Form containing the method.

index%—the number of the item in the List or Combo box to remove. The first item is number 0, the second is 1, and so forth. Use the ListCount property to determine the largest number that *index*% can be. The last item in the list is number ListCount - 1.

Description   The RemoveItem method removes items from the List in a List or Combo box.

For Example   The following code fragment repeatedly removes the first item of the List1 List box on Form2 until the list is empty.

```
While Form2.List1.ListCount >0
Form2.List1.RemoveItem 0
Wend
```

See also   AddItem method
List property
ListCount property
ListIndex property

 Reset

Purpose	The Reset statement flushes all file buffers and then closes all disk files.
Syntax	**Reset**
Arguments	None
Description	The Reset statement empties all file buffers and closes all files. When a program writes to a disk file, it doesn't really write to the disk but to a buffer in memory. When the buffer is full, the buffer is written to disk as a block. The primary use of Reset is to assure that any buffers that are linked to files on removable media are written to disk, even if they aren't full. The media then can be safely removed. Otherwise, a file on a removed disk may be incomplete. Ending an executable program or the Visual Basic program has the same effect. Ending an interpreted program running within Visual Basic may not close the files completely until you end Visual Basic.

If your program does not open any disk files, there is no reason to execute Reset.

For example	The following procedure is for an Exit command that ends a program. Before executing the End statement, it executes Reset to ensure that all disk files have been closed and the file buffers have been flushed to the files.

```
Sub ExitCmd_Click ()
'End the program
Reset
End
End Sub
```

See also	DoEvents function

 RGB

Purpose	The RGB() function creates an RGB color number from three color intensities.
Syntax	**RGB** (*red%,green%,blue%*)

Arguments   *red%*—the intensity of red as an integer ranging from 0 (black) to 255 (bright red).

green%—the intensity of green as an integer ranging from 0 (black) to 255 (bright green).

blue%—the intensity of blue as an integer ranging from 0 (black) to 255 (bright blue).

Description   The RGB() function converts three color intensities (red, green, and blue) into one of over sixteen million color numbers. To generate the 16 standard basic colors, see the QBColor() function.

A Visual Basic color number is a single Long integer. Within that integer are four one-byte codes. The rightmost three bytes contain the color in RGB format. The rightmost byte contains the intensity of red. The second byte from the right contains the intensity of green. The third byte from the right contains the intensity of blue. Each byte holds a value that ranges from 0 to 255, where 0 is no color, or black, and 255 is the brightest.

The simplest way to represent these values is as hexadecimal numbers (see the Hex$() function), where each byte is represented by a pair of hexadecimal digits. The following list of colors is from the file CONSTANT.TXT, included with Visual Basic. Use one of these constants as an alternative to using the two color functions QBColor() and RGB(). To use them, copy them from CONSTANT.TXT into the Global module.

Color	*Hexadecimal Value*
BLACK	&H000000
RED	&H0000FF
GREEN	&H00FF00
YELLOW	&H00FFFF
BLUE	&HFF0000
MAGENTA	&HFF00FF
CYAN	&HFFFF00
WHITE	&HFFFFFF

The leftmost byte is 0 for normal RGB colors. If it has a value of &H80, the color number becomes a code for one of the default system colors shown below. The default system colors are those set in the Windows control panel.

System Color	Hexadecimal Value
Gray area on Scroll bars	&H80000000
Desktop background	&H80000001
Caption of an active window	&H80000002
Caption of an inactive window	&H80000003
Menu background	&H80000004
Window background	&H80000005
Window frame	&H80000006
Menu text	&H80000007
Window text	&H80000008
Caption text	&H80000009
Border of an active window	&H8000000A
Border of an inactive window	&H8000000B
Background of MDI applications	&H8000000C
Selected items	&H8000000D
Selected text	&H8000000E
Command button	&H8000000F
Command button edge	&H80000010
Disabled text	&H80000011
Push buttons	&H80000012

Returns The result is a Long integer containing an RGB color number usable by all Visual Basic functions that handle color.

For example The following assignment statement assigns the color number for light red to the variable theColor.

```
theColor = RGB(255,0,0)
```

See also Hex$ function
QBColor function

 **Right$**

Purpose The Right$() function extracts a substring from the right side of a string.

Syntax **Right$(***string$*,*numchar&***)**

Arguments *string$*—a string, or a formula that results in a string.

numchar&—the number of characters to extract from the string.

Description The Right$() function extracts a substring from the right side of a string. Use it with the Left$() and the Mid$() functions to extract different substrings.

Returns The resulting string contains the rightmost *numchar&* characters from *string$*.

For example The following is from the Immediate window and compares the Left$(), Right$(), and Mid$() functions.

```
A$ = "This is a string to examine"
Print Left$(A$,6)
This i
Print Right$(A$,5)
amine
Print Mid$(A$,9,5)
a str
```

 **RmDir**

Purpose The RmDir statement removes a subdirectory from the file system.

Syntax **RmDir***path$*

Arguments *path$*—a string containing the path to the directory to be removed, including the disk letter, with the following syntax,

[*drive*:][\]*directory*[*directory*]

where *drive* is the drive letter and *directory* is a directory name. Omit the *drive* argument to use the current drive. If the first backslash is omitted, the path is assumed to start in the default directory of the specified drive. The string must be less than 128 characters long.

Description The RmDir statement deletes a directory in the file system in the same manner as the DOS command with the same name. The directory to delete must be empty or an error results. If no disk drive is specified in the *path$* argument, RmDir uses the current drive. If the first backslash is omitted, the path is assumed to be relative to the default directory on either the current drive (if no drive is specified) or on the specified drive.

For example   The first statement below deletes the UTILITIES directory in the TOOLS directory on the C drive. The second statement below deletes the C directory within the PROGRAMS directory within the current default directory. That is, if the current directory is D:\APPS, the command deletes the D:\APPS\PROGRAMS\C directory.

```
RmDir "C:\TOOLS\UTILITIES"
RmDir "PROGRAMS\C"
```

The code fragment below uses the Dir$() function to see if the directory in the Path$ variable is empty before trying to delete it.

```
If Dir$(thePath$) = "" Then
   RmDir thePath$
Else
   MsgBox "The directory isn't empty"
End If
```

See also   ChDir statement
ChDrive statement
Kill statement
MkDir statement
Name statement
CurDir$ function
Dir$ function

Rnd

Purpose   The Rnd() function returns a random number between 0 and 1.

Syntax   **Rnd[(*number#*)]**

Arguments   *number#*—a number of any type, or a formula that evaluates to a number. If *number#* is a negative number, Rnd() returns the same number every time. If *number#* is 0, it returns the previous number again. If *number#* is positive or omitted, the next random number in the sequence is returned.

Description   Random numbers in computer programs aren't truly random, but are pseudo random numbers generated by a function whose output distribution is reasonably random. As a consequence, every time you run a Visual

Basic program, you get the same sequence of random numbers from the Rnd() function. There are cases where this is desirable, debugging for example, but usually you would want a different set of numbers every time you run a code. Random number generators have a seed value that initializes the function that generates the random numbers, and the Randomize statement sets that value. The Rnd() function returns the next number in the random number sequence, or, if the argument is negative or zero, a specific random number.

Returns　The result is a random number between 0 and 1. To get a random number with a different range, Multiply Rnd by the width of the range and add the value of the lower limit.

For example　The following lines initialize the random number generator and then generate two random numbers: val1, between 0 and 10, and val2, between 5 and 10.

```
Randomize
val1 = Rnd * 10
val2 = Rnd *5 + 5
```

See also　Randomize function
Timer function

 # RSet

Purpose　The RSet statement right-justifies strings.

Syntax　**RSet** *fixedstring$ = string$*

Arguments　*fixedstring$*—a fixed-length string.

string$—a string to be right-justified in the fixed-length string, or a formula that results in a string to be right-justified in the fixed-length string.

Description　The RSet statement right-justifies a string in a fixed-length string. When right-justifying a string into a fixed-length string, only as much of the right side of the string as will fit in the fixed-length string is copied. If the string is shorter than the fixed-length string, the remainder of the left side of the fixed-length string is filled with blanks. To left-justify strings, use LSet.

For example　The following lines define a fixed-length string and right justifies the word Welcome into it.

```
Dim anFString As String *10
RSet anFString = "Welcome"
```

The variable anFString now contains "Welcome".

See also   Let statement
LSet statement

F RTrim$

Purpose   The RTrim$() function removes trailing blanks from the right side of a string.

Syntax   **RTrim$(*string$*)**

Arguments   *string$*—a string, or a formula that results in a string.

Description   The RTrim$ function removes trailing spaces from strings. To remove leading spaces use the LTrim$() function.

Returns   The result is the argument string with the blanks removed from the right side.

For example   The following line trims the blanks from the right side of a string and stores it in A$.

```
A$ = RTrim$("    234.45      ")
```

A$ now contains the string "   234.45".

See also   LTrim function

S SavePicture

Purpose   The SavePicture statement saves the contents of a Picture property of a Form or Picture box into a disk file.

Syntax   **SavePicture *object*, *filename$***

Arguments   *object*—the Picture or Image property of a Form or Picture box to be saved.

filename$—a string containing this picture file name, and an optional directory path if the file doesn't go in the current directory. The path, including the disk letter has the following syntax,

[*drive*:][[\]*directory*[*directory*...\]]*filename*

where *drive* is the drive letter, *directory* is a directory name, and *filename* is the file name. Omit the *drive* argument to use the current drive. If the first backslash is omitted, the path is assumed to start in the default directory of the specified drive. See ChDir and ChDrive to change the current directory and the current drive.

Description The SavePicture function saves the contents of the Picture or Image property of a Form or Picture box into a disk file. Image property files are always bitmaps. Picture property files for pictures previously loaded from a disk file are the same type as the original file. The Image property is a system resource where the contents of a Form or control are stored when the AutoRedraw property is set to True.

For example The following statement saves the contents of the Picture property of the Picture1 Picture Box into the bitmap file BEAR.BMP.

SavePicture Picture1.Picture, "BEAR.BMP"

See also LoadPicture function
SetData method
DragIcon property
Icon property
Picture property

 # Scale

Purpose The Scale method sets all the scale properties of a Form, Picture box, or the Printer object.

Syntax [*object.*]**Scale** [(*x1!*, *y1!*) - (*x2!*, *y2!*)]

Arguments *object*—the name of the object to scale, a Form, Picture box, or the keyword Printer. Omit this argument to use the Form containing the statement.

x1!, y1!—the *x, y* coordinates of the upper-left corner of the object. If both sets of coordinates are omitted, the scale is reset to the default scale (twips), with the origin in the upper-left corner of the object.

x2!, y2!—the *x, y* coordinates of the lower-right corner of the object.

Description Forms, Picture boxes, and the `Printer` object have a default scale with the origin in the upper-left corner. The horizontal scale increases from left to right and the vertical scale increases from the top down. The `ScaleMode` property sets one of six standard scales (twips, points, pixels, characters, inches, millimeters, or centimeters). The `Scale` method defines an arbitrary scale for the object. The `Scale` method changes the `ScaleMode` property to `0 - User defined` and sets the values of the `ScaleWidth`, `ScaleHeight`, `ScaleTop`, and `ScaleLeft` properties to achieve the requested scale. This is a convenient way to set all these properties with a single statement.

For example The following procedure receives the name of a control and the requested minimum and maximum values for the horizontal and vertical scales. It then tests the control to be sure it is a Picture box and uses the `Scale` method to scale the object.

```
Sub ScaleIt (Xmin As Single, Xmax As Single,
    Ymin As Single, Ymax As Single Pic As Control)
        If TypeOf Pic Is PictureBox Then
            Pic.Scale (Xmin, Ymax)-(Xmax, Ymin)
        End If
    End Sub
```

See also `ScaleWidth` property
`ScaleHeight` property
`ScaleTop` property
`ScaleLeft` property
`ScaleMode` property

 Second

Purpose The `Second` function calculates the second of the minute from a serial date number.

Syntax **Second(*serialdate#*)**

Arguments   *serialdate#*—a serial date number. A serial date number is a double-precision number containing the date represented as the number of days since December 30, 1899. Negative serial date numbers represent dates from January 1, 1753 to December 30, 1899. Times are represented as fractions of a day. Years after 1900 are represented by the same serial date numbers used in several popular spreadsheet programs.

Description   The Second() function takes a serial date number and returns the second of the minute represented by that number. To extract the day, month, and year, use the Day(), Month(), and Year() functions. To extract the time, use the Minute(), and Hour() functions.

Returns   The result is the second of the minute as an integer from 1 to 59.

For example   The following statement extracts the second (0) from a serial date number for noon on March 17, 1987.

```
theSecond = Second(31853.5)
```

See also   Date$ function
DateSerial function
DateValue function
Day function
Minute function
Month function
Now function
Time$ function
Timer function
TimeSerial function
TimeValue function
Weekday function
Year function
Date$ statement
Time$ statement

 Seek

Purpose   The Seek() function returns the current read/write location in a disk file.

Syntax   **Seek(***filenumber%***)**

Arguments   *filenumber%*—the file number assigned to a file when it was opened with the Open statement.

Description	The Seek() function gets the number of the next record or byte in a file following the last one accessed. The first byte or record in a file is number 1, the second is number 2, and so forth. This complements the Loc() function, which returns the last record or byte accessed. To set the position in a file, use the Seek statement.

Returns The result is the current position in the open file. For random access files, this is the number of the record following the last one accessed. For sequential files, this is the number of the next byte to be read or written. For binary files, this is the number of the byte following the last one accessed.

For example The following line stores the current read/write position for file number 1 in the variable A&.

```
A& = Seek(1)
```

See also EOF function
Loc function
LOF function
Open statement
Seek statement

S Seek

Purpose The Seek statement sets the current read/write position in a disk file.

Syntax **Seek** [#]*filenumber%, location&*

Arguments *filenumber%*—the file number assigned to a file when it was opened with the Open statement.

location&—the location where the next read or write operation is to occur. This must be a Long integer greater than zero. For random access files, this is the record number. For sequential access and binary files, this is the byte number. Both bytes and records number the first record as 1, the second as 2, and so forth.

Description The Seek statement sets the current position in a file for read/write operations. This is largely for sequential access and binary files, because the record number used with Get and Put statements overrides the settings of this statement.

For example   The following statement moves the current position in file number 1 to the
25th byte if it is a sequential or binary file, or the 25th record if it is a random
access file.

```
Seek #1, 25
```

See also   EOF function
Loc function
LOF function
Seek function
Get statement
Open statement
Put statement

S Select Case

Purpose   The Select Case statement selects one of a group of blocks of code to
execute according to the value of an expression.

Syntax   `Select Case` *expression*

```
[Case {val1¦val1 To val2¦Is operator val3}
    [,{val1¦val1 To val2¦Is operator val3}]...
    [block1]]
[Case {val1¦val1 To val2¦Is operator val3}
    [,{val1¦val1 To val2¦Is operator val3}]...
    [block2]]
[Case Else]
    [blockelse]
End Select
```

Arguments   *expression*—any text or numeric expression.

Case—a Case statement. If the value of *expression* matches one of the values
or ranges that follow the Case keyword, the block of code following that
Case statement is executed. There can be as many Case statements as are
needed.

val1, val2, val3—string or numeric values to compare to the value of
expression, to select which code block to execute. If only a single value is

used, it must match *expression* exactly to select a block. If the To clause is used, the expression must be within the specified range. If the Is clause is used, the expression must fit the relationship given.

operator—a logical operator (>, <, >=, <=, =, <>.)

block1, *block2*, *blockelse*—blocks of code to execute if *expression* matches a Case statement. Only the first block whose Case statement matches *expression* is executed.

Case Else—the block of code following this statement is executed if none of the other Case statements match.

Description   The Select Case statement is a powerful way to select among several blocks of code using the value of an expression as a selector. Only one of the blocks of code within the Select Case statement is executed. When the Select Case statement is encountered, the value of *expression* is calculated and compared to the values and ranges on the first Case statement. If a match is found, the block of code following that statement is executed and then execution jumps to the statement following the End Select statement. If a match isn't found, the next Case statement is checked. This continues until a match is found, or, if no match is found, the code block after the Case Else statement is executed. If there is no match and no Case Else statement, execution continues after the End Select statement.

The comparisons done in the Case statements must match exactly. If *expression* is text, it must match both character and case. If a range is given, then the ASCII codes of the characters determines the extent of the range (see Chr$( ) and Appendix B).

For example   The following code block prints text strings to the Immediate window according to the value of the variable Action. If Action equals 5, then the first Case statement is activated and Action = 5 is printed. Note that the second Case statement won't be activated, even though Action is in its range. If Action is in the range 2 to 6, but not equal to 5, the second Case statement is activated and 2 < Action < 6 but not 5 is printed. If Action is 9 or greater than 10, the third Case statement is activated and Action = 9, or is greater than 10 is printed. If action does not fit any of these ranges, the last Case statement is activated, and Action did not fit anything is printed.

```
Select Case Action
   Case 5
      Debug.Print "Action = 5"
   Case 2 To 6
      Debug.Print " 2 < Action < 6 but not 5"
```

continues

```
                     Case Is > 10, 9
                        Debug.Print "Action = 9, or is greater than 10"
                     Case Else
                        Debug.Print "Action did not fit anything'
                  End Select
```

See also   If...Then statement
              On...GoSub statement
              On...GoTo statement

S SendKeys

Purpose   The SendKeys statement sends keystrokes to the active window as if they had been typed at the keyboard.

Syntax   **SendKeys** *string$*[,*wait%*]

Arguments   *string$*—a string containing the keystrokes to send to the active window. Normal keyboard keys stand for themselves, special keys use the codes that follow. To include a Shift, Control, or Alt modifier key, precede each character with +, ^, and %. To hold down a modifier key while several keys are pressed, enclose the keys with parentheses preceded by the modifier. To repeat a key, insert a number between the name and the right curly bracket.

For example: {x 4} = press x four times.
                  ^(ab) = hold down control and press a then b.
                  %g = hold down Alt and press g.
                  {LEFT 5} = press left arrow five times.

Key	*Code*
Backspace	{BACKSPACE} or {BS} or {BKSP}
Break	{BREAK}
Caps Lock	{CAPSLOCK}
Clear	{CLEAR}
Delete	{DELETE} or {DEL}
Down arrow	{DOWN}
End	{END}
Enter (return)	{ENTER}

Esc	{ESCAPE} or {ESC}
Help	{HELP}
Home	{HOME}
Insert	{INSERT}
Left arrow	{LEFT}
Num Lock	{NUMLOCK}
Page down	{PGDN}
Page up	{PGUP}
Print screen	{PRTSC}
Right arrow	{RIGHT}
Scroll Lock	{SCROLLLOCK}
Tab	{TAB}
Up arrow	{UP}
F1 through F16	{F1} through {F16}
+	{+}
^	{^}
%	{%}
{	{{}
}	{}}

wait%—a logical value or expression. If True, SendKeys waits for the keys to be accepted before returning. If False, SendKeys passes the keys to the window and returns immediately.

Description   The SendKeys statement sends keystrokes to the active window. It usually is used to send keystrokes to another application activated with the AppActivate statement.

For example   The following Sub procedure activates the Timer program created in Part II, Chapter 13 and presses the **On/Off** button. The Timer program must be running already.

```
Sub ActivateTimer
AppActivate "The Timer"
SendKeys "{Enter}", -1
End Sub
```

See also   DoEvents function
AppActivate statement

 SetData

Purpose The SetData method stores a picture on the Clipboard using the specified format.

Syntax `Clipboard.SetData Picture%, [dataformat%]`

Arguments *picture%*—the picture to send to the Clipboard: The `Picture` or `Image` property of a Picture box or Form.

dataformat%—a code for the picture format to use. Visual Basic only recognizes bitmaps, metafiles and dib (device independent bitmap). `CF_BITMAP` is assumed if this is omitted. The following codes are available in the file CONSTANT.TXT included with Visual Basic.

Picture type	Code
CF_BITMAP	2
CF_METAFILE	3
CF_DIB	8

Description The SetData method stores a picture on the operating systems Clipboard object. The first argument is the picture to send, and it is the `Picture` or `Image` property of a Form or Picture box. The second argument determines what format to use to encode the picture when it is sent to the Clipboard.

For example The following statement sends a metafile type picture to the clipboard from the `Picture` property of Form1. The constant `CF_METAFILE` must have been defined in the declarations part of the Form or in the Global module.

`Clipboard.SetData Form1.Picture, CF_METAFILE`

See also GetData method
GetFormat method
GetText method
SetText method

 SetFocus

Purpose The SetFocus method moves the focus to the specified control.

Syntax	*object*.**SetFocus**
Arguments	*object*—the name of the object to which to move the focus. The object must be available to receive the focus.
Description	The SetFocus method moves the focus to the specified object.
For example	The following moves the focus to the **Command1** command button.

Command1.SetFocus

See also	ActiveControl property

 **SetText**

Purpose	The SetText method puts a text string onto the Clipboard object.
Syntax	**Clipboard.SetText** *text$[, dataformat%]*
Arguments	*text$*—the text string to put on the Clipboard object.

dataformat%—a code for the type of data to put on the clipboard. The following codes are available in the file CONSTANT.TXT. If this argument is omitted, CF_Text is assumed.

Text type	*Code*
CF_LINK	&HBF00
CF_TEXT	1

Description The SetText method puts a text string onto the Clipboard object. The argument of the method determines what type of data to put onto the Clipboard. If the application that is to receive the data from the Clipboard supports Dynamic Data Linking, you may put link information on the Clipboard using the CF_LINK data format. The linking information is in the following format,

Application¦LinkTopic¦LinkItem

where *Application* is the name of the project without the .MAK extension if you are running the Visual Basic interpreter. If you are running a complied application, *Application* is the name of the Visual Basic application without the .EXE extension. *LinkTopic* is the name of the Form and *LinkItem* is the name of the Text box, Label, or Picture box whose contents you want to link to the foreign application. The foreign application then

establishes a DDE connection to that Text box, Label, or Picture box, and requests its contents. Visual Basic handles the connection and data transfer automatically. See the `LinkTopic`, `LinkItem`, and `LinkMode` properties for more information.

For example   The following statement puts the contents of the `Text` property of the `Text1` Text box onto the clipboard.

```
Clipboard.SetText Text1.Text
```

See also   GetData method
GetFormat method
GetText method
SetData method
LinkTopic property
LinkItem property
LinkMode property

 Sgn

Purpose   The `Sgn()` function returns the sign of a number.

Syntax   **Sgn(***number***)**

Arguments   *number*—a number of any type, or a formula that evaluates to a number.

Description   The `Sgn()` function gets the sign of a numeric value.

Returns   The result is the sign of *number*. If *number* is greater than 0 it returns 1, if *number* is less than 0 it returns –1, and if *number* equals 0 it returns 0.

For example   The following lines assign –1 to A, 0 to B, and +1 to C.

```
A = Sgn(-376)
B = Sgn(0)
C = Sgn(476.98)
```

See also   Abs function

 Shell

Purpose   The Shell() function launches another application.

Syntax   **Shell(**_program$_[, _window%_]**)**

Arguments   _program$_—a string containing the program name, including the path if the program isn't in the current directory, and any command-line switches.

window%—a code indicating the type of window to use. Can be one of the following codes.

Code	Window
1	Normal front window with focus
2	Minimized with focus (default)
3	Maximized with focus
4	Normal without focus
5	Minimized without focus

Description   The Shell() function is used to launch another application in a window. It can then be activated with AppActivate, and have keystrokes sent to it with SendKeys.

Returns   The result is the Windows task ID for the successfully launched application. The Task ID uniquely identifies the application to Windows. If the launch isn't successful, an error occurs. Use the On/Error statement to trap this error (a File-Not-Found error.)

For example   The following lines run the Timer program developed in Part II, Chapter 13 and press its button. By running the PIF file, the program does not need to know where Timer is on the disk. That information is in the PIF file.

```
A = Shell("Timer.pif")
SendKeys "{Enter}", -1
```

See also   AppActivate statement
SendKeys statement

505

 Show

Purpose   The Show method makes a Form visible.

Syntax   [*form*.]**Show** [*modal%*]

Arguments   *form*—the name of a Form to show. If this argument is omitted, the Form this command resides on is assumed.

modal%—If the *modal%* argument is 1, the Form is modal, and no other Form in the program can be made active until this Form is hidden or unloaded. If this argument is 0 then the Form is modeless and may be covered by another Form by simply clicking the other window.

Description   The Show method displays a Form. If the Form hasn't been loaded yet, it is loaded first. To load a Form so you can access its properties, yet keep the form visible, use the Hide method. A Form that has been made visible with this method can be modal or modeless. Modal Forms must be handled and closed before any other Forms in a program can be accessed. Making a Form modal prevents any other Form in the program from being made active, although other programs can be made active. Also, the code after the line containing the Show method is not executed until the modal Form is closed or hidden. Use modal Forms for dialog boxes whose questions must be answered before a program can continue. Nonmodal Forms can be sent to the background by simply clicking some other Form.

For example   The Save command on the File menu is an obvious place to use the Show method. In this procedure, the variable FileName is checked to see if it contains a file name. If it does, then call SaveIt procedure to save the file, otherwise, call the SaveDialog dialog box to get a file name. Nothing else can be done until the Save Dialog dialog box is closed.

```
Sub SaveCmd_Click ()
If FileName <> "" Then
    SaveIt
Else
    SaveDialog.Show 1
End If
End Sub
```

See also   Hide method
Load method
Unload method
Visible property

 Sin

Purpose The Sin() function calculates and returns the sine of an angle in radians.

Syntax **Sin***(angle)*

Arguments *angle*—an angle in radians as a number or a formula that evaluates to a number of any numeric type.

Description The Sin() function calculates the sine of an angle expressed in radians. To calculate the sine of an angle expressed in degrees, use the following,

```
Pi = 3.141592654
theSine = Sin(dangle*Pi/180))
```

where dangle is measured in degrees.

Returns The result is the sine of *angle*, a number between –1 and +1.

For example The following two assignment statements calculate the sine of two angles, one in radians and one in degrees.

```
A = Sin(3.25)        'Assigns the sine of 3.25 radians
                     'to A = -0.108195.
Pi = 3.141592654
B = Sin(27.8*Pi/180)   'Assigns the sine of 27.8
                       'degrees to B = 0.466387.
```

See also Atn function
Cos function
Tan function

 Single

Purpose The data type Single matches or defines single-precision, floating point variables.

Syntax *variable* **As Single**

Arguments *variable*—a variable name.

Description The data type Single is used in Sub and Function procedure headings to declare a variable as a single-precision, floating point type so that Visual Basic can check values passed to the procedure. It also is used in a Dim, Global, or Static statement to define a variable as single-precision, floating point. The Single data type is a four-byte floating point number that ranges from -3.402823×10^{38} to $-1.401298 \times 10^{-45}$ for negative numbers and 1.401298×10^{-45} to 3.402823×10^{38} for positive numbers. The Single data type can also be defined by appending the ! character to the variable name. Single precision constants are written with an E between the mantissa and the exponent (that is, $1.234 \times 10^{56} = 1.234E56$).

For example The following procedure defines ANumber as a Single precision type in the function heading so that Visual Basic can check the type of values passed to it. The function then scales the value by dividing by 10,000.

```
Sub ScaleIt (ANumber As Double)
ANumber = ANumber/10000!
End Sub
```

See also Dim statement
Static statement
Global statement
Type statement
Any data type
Control data type
Currency data type
Form data type
Integer data type
Long data type
Double data type
String data type

 # Space$

Purpose The Space$() function returns a string of spaces.

Syntax **Space$(***number***)**

Arguments *number*—a number of any type, or a formula that evaluates to a number.

Description The Space$() function generates a string of spaces. It is often used to space printed text, or to initialize a string variable.

Returns   The result is a string of *number* spaces.

For example   The following statement fills A$ with 10 spaces.

```
A$ = Space$(10)
```

See also   Spc function
String$ function

 **Spc**

Purpose   The Spc function skips a specified number of spaces in a Print # statement or Print method.

Syntax   **Spc(***number%***)**

Arguments   *number%*—a number of any type, or a formula that evaluates to a number.

Description   The Spc() function is only usable in a Print # statement or the Print method. It causes the print position to move right the indicated number of spaces.

For example   The following is from the Immediate window of an application in Break mode. This is a useful way to test the operation of functions and methods.

```
Print Spc(5);"h";Spc(5); "h"
   h
   h
Print Spc(10);"H"
   H
```

See also   Space$ function
Tab function

 **Sqr**

Purpose   The Sqr() function calculates the square root of a number.

Syntax   **Sqr(***number***)**

Arguments   *number*—a number of any type, or a formula that evaluates to a number greater than or equal to zero. Negative values of *number* cause an error.

Description   The Sqr() function calculates the square root of a number.

Returns   The result is the square root of *number*.

For example   The following line stores the square root of 16 (4) in A.

```
A = Sqr(16)
```

See also   None

 # Static

Purpose   The Static statement defines variables and declares their type at the procedure level and makes their values persist from one call of the procedure to the next.

Syntax

```
Static variable [([subscripts])]
    [As type][,variable [([subscripts])]
    [As type]]...
```

Arguments   *variable*—a variable name. Array names are followed by parentheses and the subscript range. There can be up to 60 subscripts.

```
[lower% To]upper%[,[lower% To]upper%]...
```

lower%—the lower limit for the array subscripts. If it is omitted, 0 is assumed unless the Option Base statement has been executed. (See the Option Base statement.)

upper%—the upper limit for array subscripts.

type—one of the following Visual Basic types: Control, Currency, Form, Integer, Long, single, Double, String, String*length, or any user type defined with the Type statement. *Length* is the length of a fixed-length string. Use the As *type* clause or a character prefix symbol, but not both, to declare the type of the variable. (See the Introduction to Part III for information on character prefix symbols.)

Description   The Static statement is used at the procedure level to declare the type of variables, and to set the dimensions of array type variables. Using Static at the procedure level is nearly identical to using Dim, except that the variables persist from one call of the procedure to another. Variables defined with Dim are redefined and zeroed each time the procedure is called. Use Dim to define variables at the form or module level and Global at the Global module level.

If the entire procedure is declared Static with the Sub or Function statement, you can use either Static or Dim to define variables because everything is static.

For example   The following statement defines the variable myFile as a string variable, then defines anArray as a two dimensional array of integers. The first dimension of the array ranges from 3 to 6 and the second ranges from 0 to 10, giving a total of 44 elements in the array.

```
Static myFile As String, anArray(3 To 6,10) As Integer
```

See also   Const statement
Dim statement
Erase statement
Function statement
Global statement
Option Base statement
ReDim statement
Sub statement

Stop

Purpose   The Stop statement pauses a program running in the Visual Basic environment, or ends a compiled program.

Syntax   **Stop**

Arguments   None

Description   The Stop statement is primarily for debugging purposes. Stop pauses the operation of a code so that its variables can be examined. Use the Continue command on the **Run** menu to continue running the program. In a compiled application, Stop behaves the same as the End statement. Breakpoints set with the Toggle **B**reakpoint command on the **Run** menu have the same effect as Stop, except that they go away when the file is closed.

For example In the following procedure the Stop statement stops execution at that point every time the For/Next loop is iterated. When stopped, the values of the variables can be examined using Print statements in the Immediate window. Restart the program using the Continue command.

```
Sub DrawStripes (C As FlagType, Pic As Control)
'Draw stripes
Dim I As Integer, Color As Double
'Calculate the position of the stripes, and
'alternate the colors between RED and WHITE.
Color = WHITE
For I = 1 To 13
If Color = WHITE Then Color = RED Else Color = WHITE
  Pic.Line (C.Xmin, (I - 1) * C.Stripe)-(C.Xmax, I
    * C.Stripe), Color, BF
  Stop
Next I
End Sub
```

See also End statement

 # Str$

Purpose The Str$() function converts a number into a string of decimal characters.

Syntax **Str$(**_number_**)**

Arguments _number_—a number of any type, or a formula that evaluates to a number.

Description The Str$() function converts a number into a string of text. The string returned preserves the accuracy of the original number in the most compact form. To convert a number using a specific format, use the Format$() function.

Returns The resulting string is the number converted into a decimal number. The conversion displays all significant digits in the most compact format.

For example The following lists the results of various Str$(0) commands.

Str$()	*Result*
Str$(135)	135
Str$(135.4)	135.4
Str$(135.7)	135.7
Str$(12345678901234567890)	1.23456789012346D+19
Str$(0.12345678901234567890)	.123456789012346
Str$(123456789000000)	123456789000000
Str$(0.00000000001)	.00000000001
Str$(12345678900000000)	1.23456789D+16
Str$(0.000000000000000001)	1D-18

See also Format$ function
Hex$ function
Oct$ function

String$

Purpose The String$() function returns a string of characters.

Syntax **String$(*number&*,{*code%¦string$*})**

Arguments *number&*—a number of any type, or a formula that evaluates to a number. This is the number of copies of the character to make.

code%—the ASCII code (see Chr$()) of the character to be repeated.

string$—a string. The first character in the string is used as the character to be repeated.

Description The String$() function produces a string containing a character repeated *number&* times. For a string of spaces, use the Space$() function.

Returns The resulting string contains *number&* copies of the character whose ASCII code is *code%*, or which is the first character in *string$*.

For example The following assignment statements set A$ to ggggg, and B$ to 10 carriage returns. Note that only the "g" in "ghi" is repeated.

```
A$ = String$(5,"ghi")
B$ = String$(10,13)
```

See also Space$ function

D String

Purpose   The data type String matches or defines string variables.

Syntax   *variable* **As String** [**len*]

Arguments   *variable*—a variable name.

len—the integer length of a fixed-length string.

Description   The data type String is used in Sub and Function procedure headings to declare a variable as a string type so that Visual Basic can check values passed to the procedure. String also is used in a Dim, Global, or Static statement to define a variable as a string. The String data type normally has a variable length and uses one byte per character. Fixed-length strings primarily are used in user-defined variable types used with random access disk files. The String data type also can be defined by appending the $ character to the variable name. String constants are defined by surrounding them with double quotation marks.

For example   The following Function procedure defines tstString as a String variable, then uses a While/Wend loop and the InStr() function to count and return the number of commas in tstString.

```
Function NCommas (tstString As String) As Integer
Dim counter As Integer, start As Integer
counter = 0
start = 1
While InStr(start, tstString, ",")>0
    start = InStr(start, tstString, ",") + 1
    counter = counter + 1
Wend
NCommas = counter
End Function
```

See also   Dim statement
Static statement
Global statement
Type statement
Any data type
Control data type
Currency data type
Double data type

Form data type
Integer data type
Long data type
Single data type

 Sub

Purpose   The Sub statement declares the interface to a Sub procedure.

Syntax   [**Static**] **Sub** *procname* [(*arglist*)]
[*statements*]
[**Exit Sub**]
[*statements*]
End Sub

Arguments   Static—indicates that the variables of the procedure do not go away when the procedure exits.

procname—the name the procedure has in the program.

arglist—the argument list passed to the procedure. The argument list can have the following syntax.

[**ByVal**] *arg*[()][**As** *type*][,[**ByVal**]*arg*[()][**As** *type*]]

ByVal—indicates the following argument is passed as a value instead of as an address that points to the variable containing the value. Numbers are passed as the type indicated in the statement. Strings are passed as an address to a null-terminated string.

arg—a variable name; only the type has meaning here. Follow array variables with empty parentheses.

type—one of the following Visual Basic types: Control, Currency, Form, Integer, Long, Single, Double, String, or a user-defined type. Use the As *type* clause or a character prefix symbol, but not both, to declare the type of the variable. (See the Introduction to Part III for information on character prefix symbols.) You may not change the type of a static array.

Exit Sub—a statement to terminate the procedure before reaching the end.

statements—Some or no statements.

Description   The Sub statement defines the interface to a Sub procedure so that a Visual Basic program can call the procedure. The interface contains the names of the arguments and their types. The interface can also declare the procedure as Static, which makes all the local variables persist from one execution to the next.

For example   The following Sub procedure calculates and returns the factorial of the number N in the variable theFact. Because N is changed in the function and we don't want it changed in the calling procedure, N is passed to this procedure by the value ByVal so that only the local copy is changed.

```
Sub Factorial (ByVal N As Integer, theFact As Long)
theFact = 1
While N>0
   theFact = theFact * N
   N = N - 1
Wend
End Sub
```

Sub procedures also can be called recursively, with a procedure even calling itself. Each time the procedure is called, it gets a new set of local variables so the *fvalues* won't conflict with each other. You cannot do this if the procedure uses Global variables or is declared Static. The following procedure also calculates the factorial by recursively calling itself to calculate the factorial of N-1 until N equals 1.

```
Sub Factorial (N As Integer, theFact As Long)
If N <= 1 Then
theFact = 1
Exit Sub
End If
Factorial N - 1, theFact
   theFact = theFact * N
End Sub
```

See also   Call statement
Declare statement
Function statement

 Tab

Purpose	The Tab function skips to a specified column number in a Print # statement or Print method.
Syntax	**Tab(** *column%* **)**
Arguments	*column%*—the column number (character position) to which to skip. If you are already past that column, the insertion point moves down one line and then skips to the column. If *column%* is greater than the width of a line in a file set with the Width statement, Tab moves to the *column%* Mod *width* column. The width of a column is determined by the average width of the currently selected font.
Description	The Tab() function is usable only in a Print # statement or the Print method. It causes the print position to move to the indicated column.
For example	The following is from the Immediate window of an application in Break mode. This is a useful way to test the operation of functions and methods.

```
Print Tab(10);"H";Tab(10);"H"
         H
         H
```

```
Print "This contains more than 12 characters";
    Tab(12);"More text"
This contains more than 12 characters
            More text
```

See also	Space$ function
	Spc function

 Tan

Purpose	The Tan() function calculates and returns the tangent of an angle in radians.
Syntax	**Tan(** *angle* **)**
Arguments	*angle*—an angle in radians as a number or a formula that evaluates to a number of any numeric type.

15

Description   The Tan() function calculates the tangent of an angle expressed in radians. Note that the tangent has poles at [+[–π/2, [+[–3π/2, and so on. The Tan() function generates an overflow error at those values. To calculate the tangent of an angle expressed in degrees, use the following,

```
π= 3.141592654
theTangent = Tan(dangle*π/180))
```

where dangle is measured in degrees.

For example   The following two assignment statements calculate the tangent of two angles, one in radians and one in degrees.

```
A = Tan(3.25)
'Assigns the tangent of 3.25 radians to A = 0.108834
π = 3.141592654
B = Tan(27.8*Pi/180)
'Assigns the tangent of 27.8 degrees to B = 0.527240
```

Returns   The result is the tangent of *angle*, a number between $-\infty$ and $+\infty$.

See also   Atn function
Cos function
Sin function

 # TextHeight

Purpose   The TextHeight method returns the height some text will occupy.

Syntax   [*object.*]**TextHeight**(*string$*)

Arguments   *object*—the name of the object to print on, a Form, a Picture box, or the keyword Printer. Omit this argument to use the Form containing the statement.

string$—a string of text.

Description   Used as you would use a function, the TextHeight method uses the current values of the Font and Scale properties of the object to determine how much vertical space is needed to print the text.

Returns   The result is the height used by the text in *string$* if it were printed on the indicated object. The scale used is whatever is in place in the object being printed on.

For example   The following line determines how much vertical space is required to print the string "This is a short string" on Form1 and stores it in A.

```
A = Form1.TextHeight("This is a short string")
```

See also   FontName property
FontSize property
ScaleHeight property
ScaleMode property

 # TextWidth

Purpose   The TextWidth method returns the width some text will occupy.

Syntax   [*object*.]**TextWidth**(*string$*)

Arguments   *object*—the name of the object to print on, a Form, a Picture box, or the keyword Printer. Omit this argument to use the Form containing the statement.

string$—a string of text.

Description   Used as you would use a function, the TextWidth method uses the current values of the Font and Scale properties of the object to determine how much horizontal space is needed to print the text.

Returns   The result is the width used by the text in *string$* if it were printed on the indicated object. The scale used is whatever is in place in the object being printed on.

For example   The following line determines how much horizontal space is required to print the string "This is a short string" on Form1 and stores it in A.

```
A = Form1.TextWidth("This is a short string")
```

See also   FontName property
FontSize property
ScaleWidth property
ScaleMode property

F Time$

Purpose   The Time$ function gets and returns the current time from the system clock.

Syntax   `Time$`

Arguments   None

Description   The Time$ function gets the system time in a string. Use the Time$ statement to set the time. Use the Now function to get the current time as a serial date number.

Returns   The result is an 8-character string containing the system date in the format:

hh:*mm*:*ss*

where *hh* is the hour, *mm* is the minute and *ss* is the second.

For example   The following assignment statement assigns the current time to the string variable A$.

```
A$ = Time$      'Assign the current time to A$
```

See also   Date$ function
DateSerial function
DateValue function
Day function
Hour function
Minute function
Month function
Now function
Second function
Timer function
TimeSerial function
TimeValue function
Weekday function
Year function
Date$ statement
Time$ statement

S Time$

Purpose   The Time$ statement sets the system time.

Syntax   **Time$** = *timestring$*

Arguments   *timestring$*—a string containing the time to which to set the clock in one of the following formats.

hh
hh:mm
hh:mm:ss

Use a 24-hour clock for times after noon.

Description   The Time$ statement sets the time in the system clock. Depending on your system, you may also have to run a setup program to make the date change permanent.

For example   The following statement sets the system time to 1:27 p.m.

Time$ = "13:27"

See also   Date$ function
DateSerial function
DateValue function
Day function
Hour function
Minute function
Month function
Now function
Second function
Time$ function
Timer function
TimeSerial function
TimeValue function
Weekday function
Year function
Date$ statement

F Timer

Purpose The `Timer` function returns the number of seconds since midnight.

Syntax `Timer`

Arguments None

Description The `Timer` function returns the number of seconds since midnight as a double-precision number. Use `Timer` to time operations. `Timer` also initializes the random number generator with the `Randomize` statement.

Returns The resulting `Double` numeric value is the number of seconds since midnight.

For example The following lists results from using the `Timer` functions in the Immediate window.

```
Print Timer
   60847.71875
Print Timer
   60852.828125
for i = 1 to 10:print timer:next i
   60911.48828125
   60911.6015625
   60911.76171875
   60911.98046875
   60912.1484375
   60912.37109375
   60912.58984375
   60912.75
   60912.96875
   60913.19140625
```

See also Randomize statement
Timer event
Timer control

F TimeSerial

Purpose   The TimeSerial function calculates a serial date number from the hour, minute, and second.

Syntax   `TimeSerial(`*hour%*`,`*minute%*`,`*second%*`)`

Arguments   *hour%*—the hour as a numeric value between 0 and 23, or a formula that results in a number in that range.

minute%—the minute as a number from 0 to 59, or a formula that results in a number in that range.

second%—the second as a number from 0 to 59, or a formula that results in a number in that range.

Description   The TimeSerial() function converts numeric expressions representing the hour, minute, and second to a serial date number. The hour, minute, and second are integer values depicting the time. The serial date number is a double-precision, floating point number, which stores the time to the right of the decimal and the date to the left. Serial date numbers containing the time may be added to serial date numbers containing the date to store both the date and time in the same number.

Returns   The result is the serial date number. A serial date number is a double-precision number containing the date represented as the number of days since December 30, 1899. Negative serial date numbers represent dates from January 1, 1753 to December 30, 1899. Times are represented as fractions of a day. Years after 1900 are represented by the same serial date numbers used in several popular spreadsheet programs.

For example   The following statement stores the serial date number (0.5) for 12:00 noon in the variable theTime.

```
theTime = TimeSerial(12,0,0)
'the date number for noon
```

See also   Date$ function
DateSerial function
DateValue function
Day function

Hour function
Minute function
Month function
Now function
Second function
Time$ function
Timer function
TimeValue function
Weekday function
Year function
Date$ statement
Time$ statement

 TimeValue

Purpose The TimeValue function calculates a serial date number from a string containing a time.

Syntax **TimeValue(** *time$* **)**

Arguments *time$*—a string containing the time to which to set the clock in one of the following formats,

hh:*mm*:*ss*
hh:*mm*
hh:*mm*:*ss*PM
hh:*mm*PM

where *hh* is the hour between 0 and 23, *mm* is the minute between 0 and 59, *ss* is the second between 0 and 59, and PM can be AM, a.m., or p.m. If you don't use the a.m. and p.m., you must use a 24-hour clock.

Description The TimeValue() function converts a string containing the time to a serial date number. The serial date number is a double-precision, floating point number that stores the date to the left of the decimal and the time to the right. Serial date numbers containing the time may be added to serial date numbers containing the date to store both the date and time in the same number.

Returns The result is the serial date number. A serial date number is a double-precision number containing the date represented as the number of days since December 30, 1899. Negative serial date numbers represent dates from January 1, 1753 to December 30, 1899. Times are represented as fractions of a day. For years after 1900, these are the same serial date numbers used in several popular spreadsheet programs.

For example   The following statement stores the serial date number (31853.0) for 1:24 p.m. in the variable `theTime`.

```
theTime = TimeValue("1:24PM")
'the date number for 1:24 PM
```

See also   Date$ function
DateSerial function
DateValue function
Day function
Hour function
Minute function
Now function
Second function
Time$ function
Timer function
TimeSerial function
Weekday function
Year function
Date$ statement
Time$ statement

 Type

Purpose   The `Type` statement is used in the Global module to combine several variable types into a user defined type.

Syntax   **Type** *newtypename*

elementname **As** *typename*
[*elementname* **As** *typename*
   .
   .
   .]
End Type

525

Arguments   *newtypename*—the name for the new type definition.

elementname—the name for the element that is going to be a part of this new type.

typename—the type of variable that *elementname* is. *Typename* may be any of the built-in types: Integer, Long, Single, Double, Currency , or String, or some other user-defined type.

Description   In addition to built-in variable types such as Integer and String, you can define your own variable types made up of a combination of the built-in types. Record type variables are used like any other variable, and passed to Function or Sub procedures using a single name to pass the entire contents of the record. To create a record type variable you must first define the record type with a Type statement, then define a variable with that type. The Type statement defines which variables make up the record, and in what order.

Once a type is defined, a variable must be defined as that type using a Dim, Global, or Static statement. This record variable now has all the parts defined in the Type statement. To access the contents of a record variable, type the record variable name followed by a dot, and then the *elementname*.

For example   The following Type definition would be in the Global module, and defines the variable type DayType, which consists of three elements. The first is theDate, which is a double-precision, floating point number for storing a date. The second is an Integer named Flags. The third is a fixed-length String named Msg.

```
Type DayType
    theDate As Double
    Flags As Integer
    Msg As String * 118
End Type
```

The next statements define variables with the new type. The first line defines aLine as a string variable and Today as the new variable type DayType. The second line defines an array named Month of 31 DayType variables.

```
Dim aLine As String, Today as DayType
Global theMonth(1 To 31) As DayType
```

Finally, in a procedure, the elements of the user-defined type are accessed by combining the variable name and the element names of the type. The first line stores a 2 in the Flags element of Today (the Integer). The second inserts a string in the Msg element of the fifth element of Month. The third line uses the function Now to insert today's date and time into the theDay element of Today.

526

```
Today.Flags = 2
Month(5).Msg = "Some interesting message"
Today.theDay = Now
```

See also   LSet statement
Dim statement
Global statement
Static statement

 UBound

Purpose   The UBound function returns the largest allowed array subscript.

Syntax   **UBound(***array*[,dimension%]**)**

Arguments   *array*—an array type variable.

dimension%—for multidimensional arrays, this number specifies the dimension to examine. The first dimension is number 1.

Description   The UBound() function works with the LBound() function to examine the upper and lower index values for an array's dimensions.

Returns   The resulting numeric value is the largest allowed subscript available for the array dimension.

For example   The first line below is from the general procedure of a Form, and defines the array variable anArray. The following lines list the results of various LBound and UBound functions.

```
Dim anArray(4 To 23,-6 To 5,8) As Integer
```

Function	Result
LBound(anArray,1)	4
UBound(anArray,1)	23
LBound(anArray,2)	–6
UBound(anArray,2)	5
LBound(anArray,3)	0
UBound(anArray,3)	8

See also   Dim statement
Global statement
Static statement
LBound function

 **UCase$**

Purpose	The UCase$() function converts all the characters in a string to uppercase.
Syntax	**UCase$(***string$***)**
Arguments	*string$*—a string, or a formula that results in a string, to be converted.
Description	The UCase$() function converts all the characters in a string to uppercase. This is useful when you want to compare two strings and the case of the characters in unimportant.
Returns	The resulting string is all uppercase.
For example	The following lines are from the Immediate window and demonstrate using LCase$() and UCase$():

```
A$ = "This Is a StRinG to ConVeRt"
Print LCase$(A$)
this is a string to convert
Print UCase$(A$)
THIS IS A STRING TO CONVERT
```

See also	LCase$ function

 **Unload**

Purpose	The Unload statement unloads a Form or control array element from memory.
Syntax	**Unload** *object*
Arguments	*object*—the name of a Form or control array element to unload.
Description	The Unload statement unloads a Form or control array element from memory. To simply hide the Form without unloading it, use the Hide method. The unload method can also be used to remove elements from a control array. Only elements attached to a control array at run time with the Load statement can be unloaded.

For example   The following statement unloads element number 2 of an Option button control array.

```
UnLoad Option1(2)
```

See also   Hide method
Show method
Load statement
Visible property

 Val

Purpose   The Val() function converts a number in a text string into a value.

Syntax   **Val(***string$***)**

Arguments   *string$*—a string containing a number in the leftmost character positions. Val() ignores any leading blanks, tabs, and linefeeds when looking for a number. Val() continues reading numbers until it encounters a character that it cannot interpret as a number, such as a comma, a letter other than D or E, or a carriage return. Val() does not recognize dollar signs, percent signs, or commas as a part of a number.

Description   The Val() function converts a number in a string to a value. This is the inverse of the Str$() and Format$() functions. If the numbers to be converted contain formatted characters, such as dollar signs and commas, you have to remove them first using the InStr() function to locate them and the Mid$() function to extract them.

Returns   The result is the numeric value of the number in *string$*.

For example   The following lists the results from applying Val to various strings.

Function	Result
Val(" -1234.56 ")	−1234.56
Val(" 1.23E22,")	1.23D+22
Val(" $123.34")	0
Val(" -1,234,567.99")	−1
Val(" abc 123.45")	0

See also   Str$ function
Format$ function

Weekday()

Purpose   The Weekday() function calculates the day of the week from a serial date number.

Syntax   `Weekday(`*serialdate#*`)`

Arguments   *serialdate#*—a serial date number. A serial date number is a double-precision number containing the date represented as the number of days since December 30, 1899. Negative serial date numbers represent dates from January 1, 1753 to December 30, 1899. Times are represented as fractions of a day. For years after 1900, these are the same serial date numbers used in several popular spreadsheet programs.

Description   The Weekday() function takes a serial date number and returns the day of the week represented by that number. Weekday() uses 1 for Sunday and 7 for Saturday. Use the Day(), Month(), and Year() functions to extract the day, month, and year. To extract the time, use the Hour(), Minute(), and Second() functions.

Returns   The result is the day of the week, with Sunday as number 1 and Saturday as number 7.

For example   The following statement extracts the day of the week (3 - Tuesday) from the serial date number for March 17, 1987.

```
theWeek = Weekday(31853)
'Extracts the weekday (3) from the date number
```

See also   Date$ function
DateSerial function
DateValue function
Day function
Hour function
Minute function
Month function
Now function
Second function
Time$ function
Timer function
TimeSerial function

TimeValue function
Year function
Date$ statement
Time$ statement

While/Wend

Purpose   The While/Wend statement iterates a block of statements until a condition is False.

Syntax

```
While condition
    statements
Wend
```

Arguments   *condition*—a logical expression or value.

statements—a block of executable statements to be iterated

Description   The While/Wend statement iterates a block of code until a condition changes to False.

For example   The following code fragment calculates the factorial of A by multiplying A times factorial, and then reducing A by 1. As long as A is greater than 1, the loop continues.

```
factorial = 1
While A>1
    factorial = A*factorial
    A = A - 1
Wend
```

See also   For/Next statement
Do/Loop statement

Width

Purpose   The Width # statement assigns a line width to a disk file.

Syntax	`Width #`*`filenumber%`*`, `*`width%`*
Arguments	*filenumber%*—the file number assigned to the file when it was opened with the Open statement.
	width%—the width, in characters, of a line in a disk file. Printing beyond this width causes a carriage return line feed, and printing continues on the next line down. This argument must be an integer in the range 0 to 255. A width of 0 indicates infinite width.
Description	The Width # statement specifies a width for a disk file, because disk files don't have a physical width to limit where printing must stop. Use a width of 0 to not check the width of printed text. This statement is useful when creating print files, when the program does not keep track of how many characters are printed on each line.
For example	The following line sets the width of file number 1 to 80 characters.
	`Width #1, 80`
See also	Open statement
	Print statement
	Width property

S Write

Purpose	The Write # statement prints delimited data to a disk file.
Syntax	`Write #`*`filenumber%`*`,`*`arglist`*
Arguments	*filenumber%*—the file number used when the file was opened with the Open statement.
	arglist—a list of variables and expressions to print. Numeric variables are automatically converted to strings before being printed. Arguments are separated with commas, and printed strings are surrounded with quotation marks.
Description	The Write # statement prints data in a disk file and delimits that data so that it can read accurately with the Input # statement. Each argument is separated with a comma, and string arguments are surrounded with

quotation marks. If you are creating a file to be read by a word processor, or to be printed with the DOS TYPE command, consider the Print # statement instead.

For example A disk file written with the following statements,

```
A1 = 5.355
B1 = 4.788
Print #1, "Values, are: ", A1, B1, " units"
Write #1, "Values, are: ", A1, B1, " units"
```

would produce:

```
Values, are: 5.355          4.788          units
"Values, are: ",5.355,4.788," units"
```

Reading those values with the following Input # statements,

```
Input #1, A$, B, C, D$
Input #1, E$, F, G, H$
```

would store the following data in these variables,

```
A$ = "Values"
B = 0
C = 5.355
D$ = "4.788          units"
E$ = "Values, are: "
F = 5.355
G = 4.788
H$ = " units"
```

Note how the first Input # statement stopped reading the string into A$ at the first comma, so that the first numeric input, B, sees text instead of a number and gets a value of zero. Then the second numeric input, C, reads the first number, and the remaining number and string ends up in D$.

See also Get statement
Input # statement
Line Input # statement
Open statement
Print # statement
Put statement
Input$ function

O XOR

Purpose   The Xor operator combines two logical expressions or all the bits in two numeric values using the logical Exclusive OR operation.

Syntax   *express1* **Xor** *express2*

Arguments   *express1, express2*—a logical expression, numeric expression or numeric value.

Description   The Xor operator combines two logical values according to the following truth table. If two numeric values are combined, the operator is applied bit by bit to the corresponding bits in the two values. That is, each bit in the result is equal to the logical Exclusive Or of the corresponding bits in the two values being combined.

A	B	A Xor B
True	True	False
True	False	True
False	True	True
False	False	False

Returns   The logical Exclusive Or of the two expressions equals True (−1) or False (0) if *express1* and *express2* are logical expressions. If *express1* and *express2* are numeric expressions, the result is the bitwise logical Exclusive Or of the same bits in each of the two expressions.

For example   The following If statement causes a beep when A or B are True, but not both.

```
If A Xor B then Beep
```

See also   And operator
Eqv operator
Imp operator
Not operator
Or operator

 Year

Purpose	The Year function extracts the year from a serial date number.
Syntax	`Year(serialdate#)`
Arguments	*serialdate#*—a serial date number. A serial date number is a double-precision number containing the date represented as the number of days since December 30, 1899. Negative serial date numbers represent dates from January 1, 1753 to December 30, 1899. Times are represented as fractions of a day. For years after 1900, these are the same serial date numbers used in several popular spreadsheet programs.
Description	The `Year()` function takes a serial date number and returns the year represented by that number. Use the `Day()`, `Month()`, and `Year()` functions to extract the day, and month. To extract the time, use the `Hour()`, `Minute()`, and `Second()` functions.
Returns	The result is the year as a number from 1753 to 2078.
For example	The following statement extracts the year from the serial date number for March 17, 1987.

```
theYear = Year(31853)
'Extracts the Year (1987) from the date number
```

See also   Date$ function
DateSerial function
DateValue function
Day function
Hour function
Minute function
Month function
Now function
Second function
Time$ function
Timer function
TimeSerial function
TimeValue function
Weekday function
Date$ statement
Time$ statement

Properties

This section deals with the properties of objects. Properties are those attributes of an object that control what the object looks like and how it reacts to different events. For each property in this section, the following items are listed:

Purpose A brief description of what the property contains, plus any caveats or special requirements for the property.

Objects Which controls have that property

Type What type of variable the property expects. If the type is listed as `Boolean`, it is actually an `Integer`, with two allowed values: –1 for `True`, and 0 for `False`.

Available Design Time—Can the value of this property be changed at design time?

Run-Time Read—Can the value of this property be determined at run time?

Run-Time Write—Can the value of this property be changed at run time?

See Also A listing of related, and complimentary, properties and functions.

Accessing Properties

Properties available at design time are set by selecting the object, selecting the property in the Properties List box, and setting its value in the Settings box. Properties available at run time are accessed by name. To get the value of a property at run time, use a statement with the following syntax. Optional elements are in [brackets]. Place holders for variables, objects, and property names are in *monospace italics*. For example,

```
variable = [form.][control[(index)].]property
```

Here, *variable* is some variable with the correct type to receive the value of the property. *Form* is the name of the Form the control is on, and if this is omitted, the current Form is assumed. *Control* is the name of the control, and if it is omitted, the current Form is assumed to have the *property*. *Index* is the index number for the particular control in a control array, and *property* is the name of the property. If *property* is a numeric type, *variable* can be of any type, and the value of *property* is coerced to that type by truncation and rounding. Note that you can lose data if the type of variable is less precise than the type of *property*. If *property* is a String type, *variable* must be of type String, or an error results.

To set a property at run time, just reverse the assignment statement above.

```
[form.][control[(index)].]property = variable
```

The arguments are the same as for reading the property, except that *variable* can be an expression that evaluates to a value the property expects.

All properties are accessed in the manner described above, and generally can be used like any other variable. Only the properties that contain pictures need slightly different treatment. The Picture, Image, Icon, and DragIcon properties contain pictures, and pictures cannot be stored in a normal variable. Picture-type properties must be equated to other picture-type properties. An Icon property of one control, for instance, can be equated to another control's Picture property. Picture-type properties also can be used in the SavePicture statement, and the LoadPicture function, to save or load a picture from a disk file, and in the SetData and GetData methods to pass pictures to and from the Clipboard.

ActiveControl

Purpose	The `ActiveControl` property of the `Screen` contains a reference to the control that currently has the focus. It is used to access the properties of that control at run time. The control's properties are accessed by using the `ActiveControl` property, rather than using the control's name. For example to access the `CtlName` property of the active control, use

```
Screen.ActiveControl.CtlName
```

Objects	Screen
Type	Control
Available	Design Time: No
	Run-Time Read: Yes
	Run-Time Write: No
See Also	`ActiveForm` property

ActiveForm

Purpose	The `ActiveForm` property of the `Screen` contains a reference to the currently active Form. It is used to access the properties of the active Form at run time. The properties are accessed in a manner similar to that used here to get the `CtlName` property.
Usage	**`Screen.ActiveForm.`**`FormName`
Objects	Screen
Type	Form
Available	Design Time: No
	Run-Time Read: Yes
	Run-Time Write: No
See Also	`ActiveControl` property

Alignment

Purpose	The Alignment property controls the alignment of the text in a Label.
Objects	Label
Type	Integer code
	0—Left-Justify (default)
	1—Right-Justify
	2—Center
Available	Design Time: Yes
	Run-Time Read: Yes
	Run-Time Write: Yes
See Also	None

Archive

Purpose	The Archive, Hidden, Normal, ReadOnly, and System properties apply to a File List box and control the display of files with these attributes.
Objects	File List box
Type	Boolean
	True (–1)—Display files with this attribute (default for Archive, Normal, ReadOnly).
	False (0)—Don't display files with this attribute (default for Hidden, System).
Available	Design Time: Yes
	Run-Time Read: Yes
	Run-Time Write: Yes

16

See Also   Hidden property
Normal property
Pattern property
ReadOnly property
System property

AutoRedraw

Purpose   The AutoRedraw property controls whether drawing performed on a Form or Picture box is stored on the persistent bitmap. If AutoRedraw is enabled, the system takes care of redrawing the object if it is covered by another window and then uncovered. This applies only to graphics drawn on the object and text printed on the object at run time, not to anything drawn at design time. AutoRedraw must be True for the PrintForm to work.

Objects   Form, Picture box

Type   Boolean

True (–1)—Enables redrawing of the object by the system.

False (0)—Disables redrawing by the system. The application must redraw the window when it receives a Paint event (or not).

Available   Design Time: Yes

Run-Time Read: Yes

Run-Time Write: Yes

See Also   Paint event
PrintForm method

AutoSize

Purpose   The AutoSize property controls whether a control is sized automatically to fit its contents.

Objects   Label, Picture box

Type   Boolean

True (−1)—Automatically resize to fit the contents.

False (0)—Don't change the size of the control (default).

Available   Design Time: Yes

Run-Time Read: Yes

Run-Time Write: Yes

See Also   None

BackColor

Purpose   The BackColor property controls the background color of an object. The background of an object includes any graphics loaded into the object's Picture property. Setting the background color of a control erases all drawing and graphics drawn on the control and all text printed on the control. It does not erase the text and the graphics associated with the control. Although a Command button has a BackColor property, it does not appear to do anything.

Objects   Check box, Combo box, Command button, Directory List box, Drive List box, Form, Frame, Label, List box, Option button, Picture box, Text box

Type   Long, containing an RGB color number (see the RGB() function).

Available   Design Time: Yes

Run-Time Read: Yes

Run-Time Write: Yes

See Also   ForeColor property
RGB() function

BorderStyle

Purpose The BorderStyle property sets the type of border an object has. Borders are thick or thin and are resizable or not. You can change the shape of a resizeable object at run time by dragging its borders.

Objects Form, Label, Picture box, Text box

Type Integer code for a Form:

0—None.

1—Fixed Single, cannot be resized by dragging, optional Control box, **Minimize** button, and **Maximize** button.

2—Sizable, resizable by dragging the borders, optional Control box, **Maximize** button, and **Minimize** button (default).

3—Fixed Double, cannot be resized by dragging, optional Control box, no **Minimize** button or **Maximize** button.

Integer code for a control:

0—None (default for Label).

1—Fixed Single (default for Picture box and Text box).

Available Design time: Yes

Run-Time Read: Yes

Run-Time Write: No

See Also Controlbox property
Minbutton property
Maxbutton property

Cancel

Purpose The Cancel property controls whether a Command button is the **Cancel** button. If it is, pressing Esc automatically clicks it. It is also the default button on the Form, if no other button has been designated so with the

Default property. The default button is selected by pressing the Enter key. Only one Command button on a Form can be the **Cancel** button.

Objects   Command button

Type   Boolean

True (–1)—The Command button is the **Cancel** button. Esc presses it. Enter presses it if no other button has the Default property set.

False (0)—The Command button is not the **Cancel** button (default).

Available   Design Time: Yes

Run-Time Read: Yes

Run-Time Write: Yes

See Also   Default property

Caption

Purpose   The Caption property contains the title of an object or the contents of a Label. The Caption is the text displayed in the title bar of a Form, in a Label, on the front of a button, or on the Labels of Option buttons and Check boxes. This text is different from the control name in the CtlName property, although they have the same default strings. To set an Access key for a control, place an & character immediately before the letter you want to press to move the focus to that control. The letter appears underlined when it is displayed. Because Labels cannot receive the focus, giving them an Access key causes the focus to move to the next control after the Label in the tab order set with the TabIndex property. To give Access keys to controls that don't have a Caption, such as Text and Picture boxes, place a Label with an access key just before the control.

Objects   Form, Check box, Command button, Frame, Label, Menu, Option button

Type   String

Available   Design Time: Yes

Run-Time Read: Yes

Run-Time Write: Yes

See Also   AutoSize property
CtlName property
TabIndex property

Checked

Purpose   The Checked property controls whether a menu item is checked.

Objects   Menu

Type   Boolean

True (–1)—The menu item is checked.

False (0)—The menu item is not checked (default).

Available   Design Time: Yes

Run-Time Read: Yes

Run-Time Write: Yes

See Also   Enabled property

ControlBox

Purpose   The ControlBox property controls whether a Form has a Control box in the upper-left corner. A Control box has a menu that contains the commands **Move**, **Minimize**, **Maximize**, **Switch**, **Close**, **Restore**, and **Size**. Other commands automatically disable different entries in the Control box's menu.

Objects   Form

Type   Boolean

True (–1)—The Form has a Control box (default).

False (0)—The Form does not have a Control box.

Available   Design Time: Yes

Run-Time Read: Yes

Run-Time Write: No

See Also   BorderStyle property
Minbutton property
Maxbutton property

CtlName

Purpose   The CtlName property sets the name the object is known as in the code windows. The control name must be a valid Visual Basic identifier (a variable name). The CtlName has to be less than 40 characters long, start with an alphabetic character, and contain alphabetic characters numbers, and the underscore (_). In a control array, all the controls have the same CtlName.

Objects   Check box, Combo box, Command button, Directory List box, Drive List box, File List box, Frame, Horizontal Scroll bar, Label, List box, Menu Item, Option button, Picture box, Timer, Vertical Scroll bar

Type   String

Available   Design Time: Yes

Run-Time Read: Yes

Run-Time Write: No

See Also   FormName property

CurrentX

Purpose   The CurrentX and CurrentY properties are determined by the last thing drawn or printed on a Form. These properties identify the location on an object where printing or drawing will start. CurrentX controls the horizontal coordinate of the point. Drawing commands move the location to the last point drawn, or, for a circle, to the center. Cls and NewPage reset CurrentX and CurrentY to the origin (usually the upper-left corner of the object. The scale used for CurrentX is the scale defined on the object it is attached to. Changing the Scale of an object also changes CurrentX so that it points to the same physical location on the screen as it did before the scale was changed. Drawing or printing on the screen moves CurrentX.

Objects   Form, Picture box, Printer

Type   Single, the *x* location of the drawing point.

Available   Design Time: Yes

Run-Time Read: Yes

Run-Time Write: Yes

See Also   CurrentY property
ScaleMode method

CurrentY

Purpose   The CurrentX and CurrentY properties are determined by the last thing printed or drawn on a Form. They identify the location on an object where printing or drawing will start. CurrentX controls the horizontal coordinate of the point. Drawing commands move the location to the last point drawn, or, for a circle, to the center. Cls and NewPage reset CurrentX and CurrentY to the origin (usually the upper-left corner of the object). The scale used for CurrentY is the scale defined on the object it is attached to. Changing the Scale of an object also changes CurrentY so that it still points to the same physical location on the screen as it did before the scale was changed. Drawing or printing on the screen moves CurrentY.

Objects   Form, Picture box, Printer

Type   Single, the *y* location of the drawing point.

Available   Design Time: Yes

Run-Time Read: Yes

Run-Time Write: Yes

See Also   CurrentX property
ScaleMode method

Default

Purpose	The Default property controls which Command button is the default. The default Command button gets pressed anytime you press Enter instead of using the mouse. Only one button on a Form can be the default button, and setting one to the default button disables that property in all the other Command buttons.
Objects	Command button
Type	Boolean
	True (–1)—Make this Command button the default button.
	False (0)—Do not make this Command button the default button (default).
Available	Design Time: Yes
	Run-Time Read: Yes
	Run-Time Write: Yes
See Also	Cancel property

DragIcon

Purpose	The DragIcon property controls the shape of the cursor when it drags an object. The default is a pointer on a rectangle the size of the control. Using this property, you can change that default to any icon. The DragIcon property is loaded by placing shells within it.
Objects	Check box, Combo box, Command button, Directory List box, Drive List box, File List box, Frame, Horizontal Scroll bar, Label, List box, Option button, Picture box, Text box, Vertical Scroll bar
Type	Integer, but cannot be stored in an integer. Icons must be assigned by directly equating one control's icon property to another, or to the LoadPicture() function.
Available	Design Time: Yes

Run-Time Read: Yes

Run-Time Write: Yes

See Also   DragMode property
LoadPicture() function

DragMode

Purpose   The DragMode property controls automatic or manual dragging of the control. Use the Drag method to manually drag a control and the Move method to make the move.

Objects   Check box, Combo box, Command button, Directory List box, Drive List box, File List box, Frame, Horizontal Scroll bar, Label, List box, Option button, Picture box, Text box, Vertical Scroll bar

Type   Integer code

0—Manual dragging; use the Drag method (default).

1—Automatic dragging; press the mouse over the object to drag it. The object does not respond to click events.

Available   Design Time: Yes

Run-Time Read: Yes

Run-Time Write: Yes

See Also   None

DrawMode

Purpose   The DrawMode controls how drawing combines with graphics already on the screen. The modes are a Boolean combination of the color of the drawing pen and any graphics already on the object. The effects of many of the modes are not obvious, so experiment if you want to use them.

Objects   Form, Picture box, Printer

Type   Integer code

The color numbers for the pen's color and the existing screen colors are combined using the logical formulas given here.

Code	Definition	Description
1	Black	Black
2	Not Merge Pen	NOT (Pen AND Screen)
3	Mask Not Pen	NOT Pen OR Screen
4	Not Copy Pen	NOT Pen
5	Mask Pen Not	Pen OR NOT Screen
6	Invert	NOT Screen
7	Xor Pen	Pen XOR Screen
8	Not Mask Pen	NOT (Pen OR Screen)
9	Mask Pen	Pen OR Screen
10	Not Xor Pen	NOT (Pen XOR Screen)
11	Transparent	Screen
12	Merge Not Pen	NOT Pen AND Screen
13	Copy Pen (Default)	Pen
14	Merge Pen Not	Pen AND NOT Screen
15	Merge Pen	Pen AND Screen
16	White	White

Of the 16 possible modes shown, only the following six give results that are easily predictable.

1—Black, draw with a black pen

6—Invert, draw with the inverse of whatever is already there

7—Xor Pen, draw with the colors that are not common to both the pen and screen. Drawing with this mode twice returns the screen to its original condition.

11—Transparent, don't draw anything

13—Copy Pen, draw with the current ForeColor (default)

16—White, draw with a white pen

Available   Design Time: Yes

Run-Time Read: Yes

Run-Time Write: Yes

See Also   DrawStyle property
            DrawWidth property
            Circle method
            Line method
            Pset method

DrawStyle

Purpose   The DrawStyle property controls the line style for the graphics methods as
            long as DrawWidth is 1. If DrawWidth is greater than 1, all the DrawStyles
            produce solid lines except styles 5 and 6.

Objects   Form, Picture box, Printer

Type   Integer code

            0   Solid (Default)

            1   Dashed line

            2   Dotted line

            3   Dash-dot

            4   Dash-dot-dot

            5   Invisible

            6   Inside solid

Available   Design Time: Yes

            Run-Time Read: Yes

            Run-Time Write: Yes

See Also   DrawMode property
            DrawWidth property
            Circle method
            Line method
            Pset method

DrawWidth

Purpose The DrawWidth property controls the width of lines drawn with the drawing methods. The value is the width of a line in pixels. For values of DrawWidth greater than 1, the DrawStyle property gives only solid lines.

Objects Form, Picture box, Printer

Type Integer, width of a line in pixels.

Available Design Time: Yes

Run-Time Read: Yes

Run-Time Write: Yes

See Also DrawMode property
DrawStyle property
Line method
Circle method

Drive

Purpose The Drive property sets or returns the drive selected in a Drive List box. Setting it also regenerates the Drive list.

Objects Drive List box

Type String, only the first character is significant when setting it, and is assumed to be the drive letter.

Available Design Time: No

Run-Time Read: Yes

Run-Time Write: Yes

See Also FileName property
Path property
Pattern property

Enabled

Purpose   The Enabled property controls whether a control can respond to user input.

Objects   Check box, Combo box, Command button, Directory List box, Drive List box, File List box, Frame, Horizontal Scroll bar, Label, List box, Menu, Option button, Picture box, Text box, Timer, Vertical Scroll bar

Type   Boolean

True (–1)—The object can respond to events, the Timer is counting.

False (0)—The object does not respond to events, the Timer is not counting.

Available   Design Time: Yes

Run-Time Read: Yes

Run-Time Write: Yes

See Also   Checked property

FileName

Purpose   The FileName property sets or returns the selected file name in a File List box. A path can be included when setting it to change the directory or disk as well.

Objects   File List box

Type   String, containing the file name. When setting this property, a path and drive letter can be included, and wild-card characters can be used in the file name. Including the path and drive letter here changes the Path and Drive properties as well. Including wild-card characters in the file name changes the Pattern property. The wild-card characters are *, which matches any number of characters, and ?, which matches any single character. The syntax of a path is

```
[drive:][[\][directory][\directory]...\]filename
```

Available   Design Time: No

Run-Time Read: Yes

Run-Time Write: Yes

See Also   Drive property
Path property
Pattern property

FillColor

Purpose   The FillColor and FillStyle properties control how circles and boxes created with the Circle and Line methods are filled.

Objects   Form, Picture box, Printer

Type   Long integer containing an RGB color number (see the RGB() function). The default is black.

Available   Design Time: Yes

Run-Time Read: Yes

Run-Time Write: Yes

See Also   FillStyle property
Circle method
Line method

FillStyle

Purpose   The FillColor and FillStyle properties control how circles and boxes created with the Circle and Line methods are filled.

Objects   Form, Picture box, Printer

Type   Integer code

0   Solid

1   Transparent (default)

2 Horizontal line

3 Vertical line

4 Upward diagonal (\\\)

5 Downward diagonal (///)

6 Cross

7 Diagonal cross

Available Design Time: Yes

Run-Time Read: Yes

Run-Time Write: Yes

See Also FillColor property
Circle method
Line method

FontBold

Purpose The FontBold property makes the font style bold on the object. For most objects, this applies to all text contained in the object, such as the text in a Label or List box. For printed output on a Form, a Picture box, or the Printer, this applies only to new printing and not to old.

Objects Check box, Combo box, Command button, Directory List box, Drive List box, File List box, Form, Frame, Label, List box, Option button, Picture box, Text box, Printer

Type Boolean

True (–1)—Format text in bold (default).

False (0)—Do not format text as bold.

Available Design Time: Yes

Run-Time Read: Yes

Run-Time Write: Yes

See Also FontItalic property
FontStrikethru property

FontTransparent property
FontUnderline property

FontCount

Purpose The FontCount property returns the number of fonts available for use on the screen or the Printer.

Objects Printer, Screen

Type Integer, the number of fonts.

Available Design Time: No

Run-Time Read: Yes

Run-Time Write: No

See Also Fonts property

FontItalic

Purpose The FontItalic property makes the font style italic on this object. For most objects, this applies to all text contained in the object, such as the text in a Label or List box. For printed output on a Form, a Picture box, or the Printer, this applies only to new printing and not to old.

Objects Check box, Combo box, Command button, Directory List box, Drive List box, File List box, Form, Frame, Label, List box, Option button, Picture box, Text box, Printer

Type Boolean

True (–1)—Format text in italic.

False (0)—Do not format text in italic (default).

Available Design Time: Yes

Run-Time Read: Yes

Run-Time Write: Yes

See Also   FontBold property
FontStrikethru property
FontTransparent property
FontUnderline property

FontName

Purpose   The FontName property sets or returns the font used for text printed on objects. For most objects, this applies to all text contained in the object, such as the text in a Label or List box. For printed output on a Form, a Picture box, or the Printer, this applies only to new printing and not to old.

Objects   Check box, Combo box, Command button, Directory List box, Drive List box, File List box, Form, Frame, Label, List box, Option button, Picture box, Text box, Printer

Type   String, containing the font name.

Available   Design Time: Yes

Run-Time Read: Yes

Run-Time Write: Yes

See Also   FontCount property
Fonts property
FontSize property

Fonts

Purpose   The Fonts property returns the names of all the fonts available for use on the Screen or Printer.

Objects   Printer, Screen

Type   String array, containing all the font names. Use FontCount to get the number of elements in the array.

Available   Design Time: No

Run-Time Read: Yes

Run-Time Write: No

See Also   FontCount property
FontName property
FontSize property

FontSize

Purpose   The FontSize property sets or returns the font size in points used for text printed on objects. For most objects, this applies to all text contained in the object, such as the text in a Label or List box. For printed output on a Form, a Picture box, or the Printer, this applies only to new printing and not to old.

Objects   Check box, Combo box, Command button, Directory List box, Drive List box, File List box, Form, Frame, Label, List box, Option button, Picture box, Text box, Printer

Type   Single, containing the size in points. (A point is 1/72 of an inch.)

Available   Design Time: Yes

Run-Time Read: Yes

Run-Time Write: Yes

See Also   FontCount property
FontName property
Fonts property

FontStrikethru

Purpose   The FontStrikethru property makes the font style strikethru on this object. For most objects, this applies to all text contained in the object, such as the text in a Label or List box. For printed output on a Form, a Picture box, or the `Printer`, this applies only to new printing and not to old.

Objects Check box, Combo box, Command button, Directory List box, Drive List box, File List box, Form, Frame, Label, List box, Option button, Picture box, Text box, Printer

Type `Boolean`

`True` (–1)—Format text in strikethru style.

`False` (0)—Do not format text in strikethru style (default).

Available Design Time: Yes

Run-Time Read: Yes

Run-Time Write: Yes

See Also `FontBold` property
`FontItalic` property
`FontTransparent` property
`FontUnderline` property

FontTransparent

Purpose The `FontTransparent` property makes the font style transparent on this object. Normally, printed text has white space surrounding the characters that covers up anything already there. Setting this property to `True` makes the white space transparent so existing text and graphics show between the newly printed characters. (Only the black part of the text is printed.)

Objects Form, Picture box, Printer

Type `Boolean`

`True` (–1)—Format text as transparent (default).

`False` (0)—Do not format text as transparent.

Available Design Time: Yes

Run-Time Read: Yes

Run-Time Write: Yes

See Also   FontBold property
                FontItalic property
                FontStrikethru property
                FontUnderline property

FontUnderline

Purpose   The FontUnderline property makes the font style underlined on this object. For most objects, this applies to all text contained in the object, such as the text in a Label or List box. For printed output on a Form, a Picture box, or the Printer, this applies only to new printing and not to old.

Objects   Check box, Combo box, Command button, Directory List box, Drive List box, File List box, Form, Frame, Label, List box, Option button, Picture box, Text box, Printer

Type   Boolean

                True (–1)—Format text as underlined.

                False(0)—Do not format text as underlined (default).

Available   Design Time: Yes

                Run-Time Read: Yes

                Run-Time Write: Yes

See Also   FontBold property
                FontItalic property
                FontStrikethru property
                FontTransparent property

ForeColor

Purpose   The ForeColor property controls the Foreground color of an object. The foreground color is the color used for text and for graphics drawn on an object.

Objects	Check box, Combo box, Directory List box, Drive List box, Form, Frame, Label, List box, Option button, Picture box, Printer, Text box
Type	Long, containing an RGB color number (see the RGB() function).
Available	Design Time: Yes
	Run-Time Read: Yes
	Run-Time Write: Yes
See Also	BackColor property
	RGB() function

FormName

Purpose	The FormName property sets the name the Form is known as in the code windows. The Form name must be a valid Visual Basic identifier. A valid identifier consists of alphabetic and numeric characters and the underscore (_) in less than 40 characters. The first character has to be alphabetic as well.
Objects	Form
Type	String
Available	Design Time: Yes
	Run-Time Read: Yes
	Run-Time Write: No
See Also	CtlName property

hDC

Purpose	The hDC property returns a handle to the device context of the object. The Windows operating system identifies an object with a handle, and this handle is needed by some external functions in Dynamic Link Libraries that operate on the object. The description of the function in the libraries manual indicates if it needs the hDC handle. External functions are defined

with the `Define` statement. Note that the value of `hDC` can change while a program is running, so don't store it in a variable. If `AutoRedraw` is set to `True`, the `hDC` property of a Form or Picture box points to the device context of the persistent bitmap. If `AutoRedraw` is `False`, `hDC` points to the device context of the Form window or Picture box window.

Objects Form, Picture box, Printer

Type `Integer`

Available Design Time: No

Run-Time Read: Yes

Run-Time Write: No

See Also `hWind` property
`Define` statement

Height

Purpose The `Height` property sets or returns the height of a Form or control, or returns the length of a sheet of paper for the `Printer`, or the height of the `Screen`. The `Screen`, `Printer`, and Form are measured in twips. The controls are measured in the units defined by the `ScaleMode` of the underlying Form. As a control or Form is resized, the value of this property changes.

Objects Check box, Combo box, Command button, Directory List box, Drive List box, File List box, Form, Frame, Horizontal Scroll bar, Label, List box, Option button, Picture box, Printer, Text box, Screen, Vertical Scroll bar

Type `Single`

Available Design Time:
Yes: Controls
No: `Screen`, `Printer`

Run-Time Read: Yes

Run-Time Write:
Yes: Controls
No: `Screen`, `Printer`

See Also `Width` property

Hidden

Purpose   The `Archive`, `Hidden`, `Normal`, `ReadOnly`, and `System` properties apply to a File List box and control the display of files with these attributes.

Objects   File List box

Type   `Boolean`

`True`—Display files with this attribute (default for `Archive`, `Normal`, `ReadOnly`).

`False`—Don't display files with this attribute (default for `Hidden`, `System`).

Available   Design Time: Yes

Run-Time Read: Yes

Run-Time Write: Yes

See Also   `Archive` property
`Normal` property
`Pattern` property
`ReadOnly` property
`System` property

hWind

Purpose   The `hWind` property returns a handle to a Form. Note that the value of `hWind` can change while a program is running, so don't store it in a variable. The Windows operating system identifies a Form's window with a handle. This identification is needed for some external Dynamic Link Library functions. The description of the Library functions indicates if this handle is needed. External functions are defined with the `Define` statement.

Objects   Form

Type   `Integer`

Available   Design Time: No

Run-Time Read: Yes

Run-Time Write: No

See Also   hDC property
Define statement

Icon

Purpose   The Icon property contains the Icon a Form displays when it is minimized. The property can be loaded with an icon file at design time and read or written at run time. Many useful icons are included with Visual Basic and the Icon editor is included as a sample application.

Objects   Form

Type   Integer, but cannot be stored in an integer. Icons must be assigned by directly equating one control's Icon or DragIcon property to another, or to the LoadPicture() function or to the SavePicture statement.

Available   Design Time: Yes

Run-Time Read: Yes

Run-Time Write: Yes

See Also   DragIcon property
LoadPicture() function
SavePicture statement

Image

Purpose   The Image property is a handle to the operating system's persistent bitmap for a Form or Picture box. When AutoRedraw is True, any graphics written on a Form or Picture box also are stored on the persistent bitmap. Actually, drawing occurs on the persistent bitmap, and then the system copies it to the screen. When the Form or Picture box needs redrawing because it has been covered by another Form and uncovered, the system copies the picture from the persistent bitmap to the screen. If AutoRedraw is False, graphics are drawn directly on the screen and are not stored in the persistent bitmap. When Forms or Picture boxes need redrawing, your application must redraw them in response to Paint events. Use the Image property to save a copy of the persistent bitmap.

Objects   Form, Picture box

Type   Integer handle, but this cannot be stored in an integer variable. To copy an image, it must be directly equated to another image type property, such as the Picture property. The Image also can be saved to disk with the SavePicture() function. The Image property always is saved as a bitmap (.BMP) file.

Available   Design Time: Yes

Run-Time Read: Yes

Run-Time Write: No

See Also   Picture property
SavePicture property

Index

Purpose   The Index property identifies an element in a control array. A control array is created at design time by making several objects' CtlName the same. In run mode, additional elements can be added to the control array using the Load statement.

Objects   Check box, Combo box, Command button, Directory List box, Drive List box, File List box, Form, Frame, Horizontal Scroll bar, Label, List box, Menu, Option button, Picture box, Text box, Timer, Vertical Scroll bar

Type   Integer

Available   Design Time: Yes

Run-Time Read: Yes

Run-Time Write: No

See Also   Load statement
Unload statement

Interval

Purpose	The Interval property sets or returns the amount of time a Timer has to wait before issuing a Timer event. Only 16 Timers are available in Windows for all applications requesting them. If a Timer is unavailable, an error results. A Timer event is issued by the Timer whenever an Interval property's worth of time has passed. The timing can be turned on and off with the Enabled property.
Objects	Timer
Type	Long, the number of milliseconds to count.
Available	Design Time: Yes
	Run-Time Read: Yes
	Run-Time Write: Yes
See Also	Timer event

LargeChange

Purpose	The LargeChange property of a Scroll bar controls how much the Scroll bar's value changes whenever the gray area above or below the Thumb is clicked. A Thumb is a white triangle on a Scroll bar that moves up and down.
Objects	Horizontal Scroll bar, Vertical Scroll bar
Type	Integer
Available	Design Time: Yes
	Run-Time Read: Yes
	Run-Time Write: Yes
See Also	Min property
	Max property
	SmallChange property

Left

Purpose	The Left property sets or returns the horizontal position of an object. It is the distance between the left edge of an object and the left edge of the object it's drawn upon. The Form is measured in twips, and the controls are measured in the units defined by the ScaleMode of the underlying object. As a control or Form is moved, the value of this property changes.
Objects	Check box, Combo box, Command button, Directory List box, Drive List box, File List box, Form, Frame, Horizontal Scroll bar, Label, List box, Option button, Picture box, Text box, Vertical Scroll bar
Type	Single, distance from the left.
Available	Design Time: Yes
	Run-Time Read: Yes
	Run-Time Write: Yes
See Also	Height property Top property Width property

LinkItem

Purpose	The LinkItem property contains the text of the item property to be passed to the other application in a Dynamic Data Exchange (DDE) conversation. A DDE conversation consists of three parts, the application name, the topic, and the item. For a spreadsheet like Microsoft Excel, the application name is Excel, the topic is the worksheet name, and the item is the cell reference. For Visual Basic, the application name is either the project name without the .MAK extension or the executable file name without the .EXE extension, the topic is the Form name, and the item is the control name. The application and topic are set with the LinkTopic property.
Objects	Label, Picture box, Text box
Type	String, the DDE item.

Available   Design Time: Yes

Run-Time Read: Yes

Run-Time Write: Yes

See Also   `LinkMode` property
`LinkTimeout` property
`LinkTopic` property
`LinkExecute` method
`LinkPoke` method
`LinkRequest` method
`LinkSend` method

LinkMode

Purpose   The `LinkMode` property contains a code that enables or disables Dynamic Data Exchange (DDE) linking with another program using Visual Basic. The `LinkTopic` and `LinkItem` properties contain the application, topic, and item needed to establish the link. For controls, the `LinkMode` property enables or disables them as clients in a DDE conversation. That is, it enables them to ask another application for information. For a Form, the `LinkMode` property enables it to be a server so that other programs can ask it for the contents of one of its controls (Label, Text box, or Picture box).

Objects   Form, Label, Picture box, Text box

Type   `Integer` code for controls:

0—No DDE interaction allowed (default).

1—Hot; the control is updated whenever the data on the server changes.

2—Cold; the control is updated only when a LinkRequest is executed for the control.

`Integer` code for server Forms:

0—No DDE interaction allowed.

1—Server. Any control on the Form can become a server for some other client application (default).

Available   Design Time: Yes

                 Run-Time Read: Yes

                 Run-Time Write: Yes

See Also   `LinkItem` method
                 `LinkTimeout` method
                 `LinkTopic` method
                 `LinkExecute` statement
                 `LinkPoke` statement
                 `LinkRequest` statement
                 `LinkSend` statement

LinkTimeout

Purpose   The `LinkTimeout` property sets the amount of time you should wait for an external application to respond to a request. The `LinkTopic` and `LinkItem` properties contain the application, topic, and item needed to establish the link.

Objects   Label, Picture box, Text box

Type   `Integer` amount of time to wait in tenths of a second. the default is 50, or 5 seconds.

Available   Design Time: Yes

                 Run-Time Read: Yes

                 Run-Time Write: Yes

See Also   `LinkItem` method
                 `LinkMode` method
                 `LinkTopic` method
                 `LinkExecute` statement
                 `LinkPoke` statement
                 `LinkRequest` statement
                 `LinkSend` statement

LinkTopic

Purpose   The LinkTopic property contains the application name and the topic of a Dynamic Data Exchange (DDE) conversation. A DDE conversation consists of three parts: the application name, the topic, and the item. For a spreadsheet like Microsoft Excel, the application name is Excel, the topic is the worksheet name, and the item is the cell reference. For Visual Basic, the application name is either the project name without the .MAK extension or the executable file name without the .EXE extension, the topic is the Form name, and the item is the control name. The item of a DDE is set with the LinkItem property. The LinkTopic property contains the program name and the topic in a string with the following format:

appname¦*topic*

in which *appname* is the name of the application, and *topic* is the object in the server application that is to supply the data, separated by the piping (¦) symbol.

Objects   Form, Label, Picture box, Text box

Type   String, the application and topic of a DDE conversation.

Available   Design Time: Yes

Run-Time Read: Yes

Run-Time Write: Yes

See Also   LinkItem property
LinkTimeout property
LinkMode property
LinkExecute method
LinkPoke method
LinkRequest method
LinkSend method

List

Purpose   The List() property is a string array that contains the contents of List boxes with one list item in each element of the array. Lists can be set or read only at run time. New items are added to the list with the AddItem method and removed with the RemoveItem method. After an item has been added to a list, it can be read or changed by reading or changing an element of the List array. The Drive, Directory, and File List boxes are read only at run time; they are written by the system.

Objects Combo box, Directory List box, Drive List box, File List box, List box

Type String array, with one list item in each element of the array. The first item is in element 0 of the array. The ListCount property contains the number of elements in the array.

Available Design Time: No

Run-Time Read: Yes

Run-Time Write: Yes (Combo and List boxes only)

See Also ListCount property
ListIndex property
AddItem method
RemoveItem method

ListCount

Purpose The ListCount property contains the number of elements in a list. To add or remove items, use the AddItem and RemoveItem methods.

Objects Combo box, Directory List box, Drive List box, File List box, List box

Type Integer

Available Design Time: No

Run-Time Read: Yes

Run-Time Write: No

See Also List property
ListIndex property
AddItem method
RemoveItem method

ListIndex

Purpose	The ListIndex property contains the item number of the currently selected item in a list. The first item in a list is number 0. Use the element number from ListIndex to select the array element in the List property to get the text of the currently selected item. Change the value of ListIndex to change the selected item in a List box. For Combo boxes, the item selected with ListIndex might not be the same as the Text property, because the Text property can be edited by the user.
Objects	Combo box, Directory List box, Drive List box, File List box, List box
Type	Integer, equals –1 if no item is selected. The first item in the list is item number 0.
Available	Design Time: No
	Run-Time Read: Yes
	Run-Time Write: Yes
See Also	List property ListCount property AddItem method RemoveItem method

Max

Purpose	The Max property controls the value of a Scroll bar when the thumb is all the way right for a Horizontal Scroll bar, or all the way down for a Vertical Scroll bar. Use it with the Min property to define the complete range of Scroll bar movement. Note that Max can be less than Min, which reverses the sense of a Scroll bar.
Objects	Horizontal Scroll bar, Vertical Scroll bar
Type	Integer, the maximum value of a Scroll bar.
Available	Design Time: Yes
	Run-Time Read: Yes

Run-Time Write: Yes

See Also   Min property
LargeChange property
SmallChange property

Maxbutton

Purpose   The Maxbutton property controls whether there is a **Maximize** button on the upper-right corner of a Form. The **Maximize** button enables the Form to be enlarged to full screen. The BorderStyle property of the Form must be 1 - Fixed single or 2 - Sizable.

Objects   Form

Type   Boolean

True (–1)—Include a **Maximize** button (default).

False (0)—No **Maximize** button.

Available   Design Time: Yes

Run-Time Read: Yes

Run-Time Write: No

See Also   BorderStyle property
Controlbox property
Minbutton property

Min

Purpose   The Min property controls the value of a Scroll bar when the Thumb is all the way left for a Horizontal Scroll bar, or all the way up for a Vertical Scroll bar. Use it with the Max property to define the complete range of Scroll bar movement. Note that Max can be less than Min, which reverses the sense of a Scroll bar.

Objects   Horizontal Scroll bar, Vertical Scroll bar

Type   `Integer`, the minimum value of a Scroll bar.

Available   Design Time: Yes

             Run-Time Read: Yes

             Run-Time Write: Yes

See Also   `Max` property
`LargeChange` property
`SmallChange` property

Minbutton

Purpose   The `Minbutton` property controls whether there is a **Minimize** button on the upper-right corner of a Form. The **Minimize** button enables a Form to be collapsed to an icon. The `BorderStyle` property of the Form must be `1 - Fixed single` or `2 - Sizable`.

Objects   Form

Type   `Boolean`

             `True` (–1)—Include a **Minimize** button (default).

             `False` (0)—No **Minimize** button.

Available   Design Time: Yes

             Run-Time Read: Yes

             Run-Time Write: No

See Also   `BorderStyle` property
`Controlbox` property
`Minbutton` property

MousePointer

Purpose   The `MousePointer` property controls the icon displayed as the mouse pointer when it is over an object.

16

Objects	Check box, Combo box, Command button, Directory List box, Drive List box, File List box, Form, Frame, Horizontal Scroll bar, Label, List box, Option button, Picture box, Screen, Text box, Vertical Scroll bar
Type	Integer code:

0—Shape determined by the control (default)

1—Arrow

2—Cross

3—I-Beam

4—Icon, small square within a square

5—Size, two crossed double arrows

6—Size NE SW, double arrow diagonal from lower left to upper right

7—Size NS, double arrow pointing up and down

8—Size NW SE, double arrow, diagonal from lower right to upper left

9—Size WE, double arrow pointing left and right

10—Up arrow

11—Wait, hourglass

12—No drop, square with slashed circle

Available	Design Time: Yes
	Run-Time Read: Yes
	Run-Time Write: Yes
See Also	DragIcon property

MultiLine

Purpose   The MultiLine property enables a Text box to contain more than one line. If you are typing in a Text box on a Form with no default button (a button with its Default property set to True), pressing Enter moves down a line if the MultiLine property is True. If there is a default button, pressing Enter presses the button instead, so use Ctrl-Enter to move down a line.

Objects	Text box
Type	`Boolean`
	`True` (–1)—Allow multiple lines of text.
	`False` (0)—Single lines of text even if the string contains a carriage return (default).
Available	Design Time: Yes
	Run-Time Read: Yes
	Run-Time Write: No
See Also	`Default` property

Normal

Purpose	The `Archive`, `Hidden`, `Normal`, `ReadOnly`, and `System` properties apply to a File List box and control the display of files with these attributes.
Objects	File List box
Type	`Boolean`
	`True` (–1)—Display files with this attribute (default for `Archive`, `Normal`, `ReadOnly`).
	`False` 0—Don't display files with this attribute (default for `Hidden`, `System`).
Available	Design Time: Yes
	Run-Time Read: Yes
	Run-Time Write: Yes
See Also	`Archive` property `Hidden` property `Pattern` property `ReadOnly` property `System` property

Page

Purpose The Page property returns the current page being drawn on or printed for the Printer. Printing beyond the bottom of a page or executing the NewPage method increments the page number by 1. Executing the EndDoc method resets the page number to 1.

Objects Printer

Type Integer, page number.

Available Design Time: No

Run-Time Read: Yes

Run-Time Write: No

See Also EndDoc statement
NewPage statement

Parent

Purpose The Parent property contains the name of the Form this control lies on. Use this property like the Form name with methods and other properties. To get the Form name, examine the FormName property with Parent as the Form.

Parent.FormName

Objects Check box, Combo box, Command button, Directory List box, Drive List box, File List box, Frame, Horizontal Scroll bar, Label, List box, Option button, Picture box, Text box, Timer, Vertical Scroll bar

Type Form

Available Design Time: No

Run-Time Read: Yes

Run-Time Write: No

See Also ActiveForm property
ActiveControl property

Path

Purpose   The Path property controls the current path in a Directory or File List box. The Path contains the complete absolute path to the directory displayed in the Directory and File List boxes. Changing the Path property changes the directory the boxes display. In the File List box, Path does not contain the file name; use the FileName property to get it. To create a complete path to a file, combine the Path property with a backslash and the Filename property. The syntax of a path is

    `[drive:][[\][directory][\directory]...]`

Objects   Directory List box, File List box

Type   String, containing the path to the displayed directory.

Available   Design Time: No

    Run-Time Read: Yes

    Run-Time Write: Yes

See Also   FileName property
Drive property
Pattern property

Pattern

Purpose   The Pattern property controls the files displayed in a File List box. The Archive, Hidden, Normal, ReadOnly, and System properties control the type of file displayed, and the Pattern property controls the names of displayed files. Use the * and ? wild-card characters to select a set of files to display.

Objects   File List box

Type   String, containing a DOS type pattern to match to file names. Use the wild-card characters: * to match any number of characters, and ? to match any single character. The default is *.* (all files).

Available   Design Time: Yes

Run-Time Read: Yes

Run-Time Write: Yes

See Also Archive property
Hidden property
Normal property
Path property
ReadOnly property
System property

Picture

Purpose The Picture property provides a means to read or write the graphic content of a Form or Picture box. If AutoRedraw is True, the contents also are stored in the Image property. The Picture property is loaded by equating it to another object's Picture or Image property, or by using the LoadPicture() or GetData() functions. It is read by assigning it to another Form's Picture property, or with the SavePicture() and SetData() functions.

Objects Form, Picture box

Type Integer handle, but this cannot be stored in an integer variable. To copy an image, it must be directly equated to another image type property, such as the Picture property.

Available Design Time: Yes

Run-Time Read: Yes

Run-Time Write: Yes

See Also Image property
SetData() function
GetData() function

ReadOnly

Purpose The `Archive`, `Hidden`, `Normal`, `ReadOnly`, and `System` properties apply to a File List box and control the display of files with these attributes.

Objects File List box

Type `Boolean`

True (−1)—Display files with this attribute (default for `Archive`, `Normal`, `ReadOnly`).

False (0)—Don't display files with this attribute (default for `Hidden`, `System`).

Available Design Time: Yes

Run-Time Read: Yes

Run-Time Write: Yes

See Also `Archive` property
`Hidden` property
`Normal` property
`Pattern` property
`System` property

ScaleHeight

Purpose The `ScaleHeight` property works with the `ScaleWidth`, `ScaleLeft`, and `ScaleTop` properties to define a scale to use for drawing on a Form, a Picture box, or the `Printer`. All four of these are setable with the `Scale` method. The normal vertical scale increases as you go downward, so setting a negative value for `ScaleHeight` makes the scale increase as you go upward, and setting `ScaleTop` to the absolute value of `ScaleHeight` moves the origin to the lower-left corner. Setting any of the four scale properties changes the `ScaleMode` property to `0 - User Defined`. Changing the `ScaleMode` to any of the standard scales changes all the scale properties to reflect that standard scale. The size of a unit on a scaled axis is fixed when the scale is defined.

If you later resize the object, the scale properties also are changed to keep the scale unit the same.

Objects   Form, Picture box, Printer

Type   `Single`, the height of the object.

Available   Design Time: Yes

Run-Time Read: Yes

Run-Time Write: Yes

See Also   `ScaleWidth` property
`ScaleLeft` property
`ScaleTop` property
`Scale` method

ScaleLeft

Purpose   The `ScaleLeft` property works with the `ScaleWidth`, `ScaleHeight`, and `ScaleTop` properties to define a scale to use for drawing on a Form, a Picture box, or the `Printer`. All four of these are setable with the `Scale` method. Setting any of the four scale properties changes the `ScaleMode` property to `0 - User Defined`. Changing the `ScaleMode` to any of the standard scales changes all the scale properties to reflect that standard scale. The size of a unit on a scaled axis is fixed when the scale is defined. If you later resize the object, the scale properties also are changed to keep the scale unit the same.

Objects   Form, Picture box, Printer

Type   `Single`, the value of the scale at the left side of the object.

Available   Design Time: Yes

Run-Time Read: Yes

Run-Time Write: Yes

See Also   `ScaleWidth` property
`ScaleHeight` property
`ScaleTop` property
`Scale` method

Visual Basic • *Part III*

ScaleMode

Purpose The `ScaleMode` property defines one of several standard scales for a Form, a Picture box, or the Printer, or indicates a user-defined scale. The `ScaleMode` property is set to `0 - User Defined` if any scale properties are set by the user, either directly or with the `Scale` method. Setting the `ScaleMode` to any of the standard scales changes all the scale properties to fit that scale. For all the standard scales, the origin is at the upper-left corner of the object. The upper edge of a Form is just below the title bar.

Objects Form, Picture box, Printer

Type `Integer code`

0—User Defined

1—Twips

2—Points

3—Pixels

4—Characters

5—Inches

6—Millimeters

7—Centimeters

Available Design Time: Yes

Run-Time Read: Yes

Run-Time Write: Yes

See Also `ScaleHeight` property
`ScaleLeft` property
`ScaleTop` property
`ScaleWidth` property
`Scale` method

ScaleTop

Purpose The `ScaleTop` property works with the `ScaleWidth`, `ScaleLeft`, and `ScaleTop` properties to define a scale to use for drawing on a Form, a Picture box, or the Printer. All four of these are setable with the `Scale` method. The normal vertical scale increases as you go downward, so setting a negative value for `ScaleHeight` makes the scale increase as you go upward, and setting `ScaleTop` to the absolute value of `ScaleHeight` moves the origin to the lower-left corner. Setting any of the four scale properties changes the `ScaleMode` property to `0 - User Defined`. Changing the `ScaleMode` to any of the standard scales changes all the scale properties to reflect that standard scale. The size of a unit on a scaled axis is fixed when the scale is defined. If you later resize the object, the scale properties also are changed to keep the scale unit the same.

Objects Form, Picture box, Printer

Type `Single`, the value of the scale at the top of the object. The top of a Form is the top of the drawable area, just below the title bar.

Available Design Time: Yes

Run-Time Read: Yes

Run-Time Write: Yes

See Also `ScaleWidth` property
`ScaleLeft` property
`ScaleTop` property
`Scale` method

ScaleWidth

Purpose The `ScaleWidth` property works with the `ScaleHeight`, `ScaleLeft`, and `ScaleTop` properties to define a scale to use for drawing on a Form, a Picture box, or the Printer. All four of these are setable with the `Scale` method. Setting any of the four scale properties changes the `ScaleMode` property to `0 - User Defined`. Changing the `ScaleMode` to any of the standard scales changes all the scale properties to reflect that standard scale. The size of a

unit on a scaled axis is fixed when the scale is defined. If you later resize the object, the scale properties also are changed to keep the scale unit the same.

Objects Form, Picture box, Printer

Type `Single`, the width of the object.

Available Design Time: Yes

Run-Time Read: Yes

Run-Time Write: Yes

See Also `ScaleHeight` property
`ScaleLeft` property
`ScaleTop` property
`Scale` method

Scrollbars

Purpose The `Scrollbars` property enables Scroll bars on a multiline Text box. The `MultiLine` property must also be `True`.

Objects Text box

Type `Integer` code:

0—None (default)

1—Horizontal Scroll bars

2—Vertical Scroll bars

3—Both

Available Design Time: Yes

Run-Time Read: Yes

Run-Time Write: No

See Also `MultiLine` property

SelLength

Purpose   The SelLength property contains the number of selected characters in a Text or Combo box. It works with the SelStart and SelText properties to facilitate text editing in those boxes. When the user selects some text in a Text box, or in the Edit box portion of a Combo box, SelStart contains the character position of the first character selected, SelLength contains the number of characters selected, and SelText contains the actual text. Setting the value of SelLength or SelStart causes the indicated text to be selected in the box. Equating SelText to a string replaces the selected text with the string. Note that the length of the string and the length of the selected text do not have to be the same, which is useful for implementing Cut and Paste operations.

If you change any of these properties, change SelText first, because changing it resets SelLength to 0. Next change SelStart, because it also changes SelLength to 0. Finally change SelLength.

Objects   Combo box, Text box

Type   Integer, the length of the selected text in characters.

Available   Design Time: No

Run-Time Read: Yes

Run-Time Write: Yes

See Also   SelStart property
SelText property
Text property

SelStart

Purpose   The SelStart property contains the number of the first selected character in a Text or Combo box. It works with the SelLength and SelText properties to facilitate text editing in those boxes. When the user selects some text in a Text box, or in the Edit box portion of a Combo box, SelStart contains the character position of the first character selected, SelLength contains the number of characters selected, and SelText contains the actual text. Setting

the value of `SelLength` or `SelStart` causes the indicated text to be selected in the box. Equating `SelText` to a string replaces the selected text with the string. Note that the length of the string and the length of the selected text do not have to be the same, which is useful for implementing `Cut` and `Paste` operations.

If you change any of these properties, change `SelText` first, because changing it resets `SelLength` to 0. Next change `SelStart`, because it also changes `SelLength` to 0. Finally change `SelLength`.

Objects   Combo box, Text box

Type   `Long`, the character number of the first selected character, or the location of the insertion point if no characters are selected. The first character is character number 0, and the beginning of the string to the left of the first character is location number 0.

Available   Design Time: No

Run-Time Read: Yes

Run-Time Write: Yes

See Also   `SelLength` property
`SelText` property
`Text` property

SelText

Purpose   The `SelText` property contains the selected characters in a Text or Combo box. It works with the `SelLength` and `SelStart` properties to facilitate text editing in those boxes. When the user selects some text in a Text box, or in the Edit box portion of a Combo box, `SelStart` contains the character position of the first character selected, `SelLength` contains the number of characters selected, and `SelText` contains the actual text. Setting the value of `SelLength` or `SelStart` causes the indicated text to be selected in the box. Equating `SelText` to a string replaces the selected text with the string. Note that the length of the string and the length of the selected text do not have to be the same, which is useful for implementing `Cut` and `Paste` operations.

If you change any of these properties, change SelText first, because changing it resets SelLength to 0. Next change SelStart, because it also changes SelLength to 0. Finally change SelLength.

Objects   Combo box, Text box

Type   String, the selected text.

Available   Design Time: No

Run-Time Read: Yes

Run-Time Write: Yes

See Also   SelStart property
SelLength property
Text property

SmallChange

Purpose   The SmallChange property of a Scroll bar controls how much the Scroll bar's value changes whenever scroll arrows are clicked.

Objects   Horizontal Scroll bar, Vertical Scroll bar

Type   Integer, the amount to change the Value property when the scroll arrows are clicked.

Available   Design Time: Yes

Run-Time Read: Yes

Run-Time Write: Yes

See Also   LargeChange property
Min property
Max property

Sorted

Purpose The Sorted property controls whether items in a List or Combo box are sorted in alphabetical order. When new items are added to the list with the AddItem method, they automatically are inserted at the correct alphabetical location. If you specify a location with the AddItem method, strange results can occur. Note that the ListIndex for an item might change after the AddItem method has been executed, because Visual Basic might need to adjust the list to insert the new item at its correct location.

Objects Combo box, List box

Type Boolean

True (–1)—Sort the items alphabetically.

False (0)—Don't sort the items; place new items at the end (default).

Available Design Time: Yes

Run-Time Read: Yes

Run-Time Write: No

See Also List property
ListCount property
ListIndex property
AddItem method
RemoveItem method

Style

Purpose The Style property controls the type of Combo box displayed. If you want a user to be able to select from a list or type an entry, use styles 0 or 1. Style 0 saves some room on the Form by hiding the list until it is needed. Use style 2 when you want the user to be able to select from a list but not edit the entry.

Objects Combo box

Type   Integer code:

0—Dropdown Combo box. This box has an editable Text box and a Dropdown List.

1—Simple Combo. This box has an editable Text box and a List box.

2—Dropdown List. This box has only a Dropdown list. The entry cannot be edited.

Available   Design Time: Yes

Run-Time Read: Yes

Run-Time Write: No

See Also   SelLength property
SelStart property
SelText property

System

Purpose   The Archive, Hidden, Normal, ReadOnly, and System properties apply to a File List box and control the display of files with these attributes.

Objects   File List box

Type   Boolean

True (–1)—Display filcs with this attribute (default for Archive, Normal, ReadOnly).

False (0)—Don't display files with this attribute (default for Hidden, System).

Available   Design Time: Yes

Run-Time Read: Yes

Run-Time Write: Yes

See Also   Archive property
Hidden property
Normal property
ReadOnly property

TabIndex

Purpose   The TabIndex property indicates a control's location in the tab order. All controls on a Form are in the tab order, and pressing the Tab key moves to the next control in the tab order. The initial tab order is the same order that you drew the controls on the Form. Use the TabIndex property to read or change the tab order. When you change a control's TabIndex property, the TabIndex of all the other controls on the Form are adjusted to account for the change.

Disabled controls, Labels, and Frames are in the tab order but cannot receive the focus, so if you tab to one of them, the focus moves to the next control in the tab order. Use this feature to give an Access key to a Text box by placing a Label with an access key just before the Text box in the tab order. When the access key for the Label is pressed, the focus cannot move to the Label, so it moves to the next control, the Text box. The same can be done for any control that does not have a Caption property to specify an Access key.

Objects   Check box, Combo box, Command button, Directory List box, Drive List box, File List box, Frame, Horizontal Scroll bar, Label, List box, Option button, Picture box, Text box, Vertical Scroll bar

Type   Integer, the location of the control in the tab order. Valid numbers range from 0 to one less than the number of controls on the Form.

Available   Design Time: Yes

Run-Time Read: Yes

Run-Time Write: Yes

See Also   TabStop property

TabStop

Purpose   The TabStop property controls whether a Tab stops at a control. All controls on a Form are in the tab order, and pressing the Tab key moves to the next control in the tab order. The initial tab order is the same order in which you drew the controls on the Form. Use the TabIndex property to read or change the tab order. Use the TabStop property to skip a control when tabbing.

Objects Check box, Combo box, Command button, Directory List box, Drive List box, File List box, Horizontal Scroll bar, List box, Option button, Text box, Vertical Scroll bar

Type Boolean

True (–1)—The tab stops at this control (default).

False (0)—The tab does not stop at this control.

Available Design Time: Yes

Run-Time Read: Yes

Run-Time Write: Yes

See Also TabIndex property

Tag

Purpose The Tag property is a user-definable string property attached to a control. It usually is used for identification, but use it for whatever you want. It is useful for identifying a control that is passed to a procedure. You can also use it to share information that is carried along with the control's name, such as a previous location or a value to use with an Undo procedure.

Objects Check box, Combo box, Command button, Directory List box, Drive List box, File List box, Form, Frame, Horizontal Scroll bar, Label, List box, Menu, Option button, Picture box, Text box, Timer, Vertical Scroll bar

Type String, anything goes.

Available Design Time: Yes

Run-Time Read: Yes

Run-Time Write: Yes

See Also None

Text

Purpose	The Text property contains the contents of a Text box, the Text box part of a Combo box, or the selected item in a List or Dropdown List box.
Objects	Combo box, List box, Text box
Type	String, whatever is in the Text box.
Available	Design Time: Yes
	Run-Time Read: Yes
	Run-Time Write: Yes, except for List and Dropdown List Combo boxes
See Also	List property
	ListIndex property
	ListCount property
	SelLength property
	SelStart property
	SelText property

Top

Purpose	The Top property sets or returns the vertical position of an object. It is the distance from the top edge of an object and the top edge of the object it is drawn upon. The Form is measured in twips, and the controls are measured in the units defined by the ScaleMode of the underlying object. As a control or Form is moved, the value of this property changes.
Objects	Check box, Combo box, Command button, Directory List box, Drive List box, File List box, Form, Frame, Horizontal Scroll bar, Label, List box, Option button, Picture box, Text box, Vertical Scroll bar
Type	Single, the vertical position of an object
Available	Design Time: Yes
	Run-Time Read: Yes
	Run-Time Write: Yes

See Also   Height property
              Left property
              Width property

Value

16

Purpose   The Value property contains the current state of a control.

Objects   Check box, Command button, Horizontal Scroll bar, Option button, Vertical Scroll bar

Type   Check box, Integer code:

0—Off (default).

1—On.

2—Grayed.

Command button, Option button

Boolean:

True (–1)—The button is pressed. Only one Option button in a group can be pressed at any time.

False (0)—The button is not pressed (default).

Scroll bar, use:

Integer, the current location of the thumb, between the values of the Min and Max properties for the Scroll bar.

Available   Design Time: Yes for all but the Command button

Run-Time Read: Yes

Run-Time Write: Yes

See Also   Text property

Visible

Purpose
The Visible property controls whether a control or Form can be seen. An invisible control or Form cannot be interacted with by the user, but can be accessed by code. For a Form, the Show and Hide methods just set the Form's Visible property.

Objects
Check box, Combo box, Command button, Directory List box, Drive List box, File List box, Form, Frame, Horizontal Scroll bar, Label, List box, Menu, Option button, Picture box, Text box, Vertical Scroll bar

The Timer is always invisible.

Type
Boolean

True (–1)—The object is visible (default).

False (0)—The object is hidden.

Available
Design Time: Yes

Run-Time Read: Yes

Run-Time Write: Yes

See Also
WindowState property
Hide method
Show method

Width

Purpose
The Width property sets or returns the width of a Form, a control, a sheet of paper for the Printer, or the Screen. The Screen, Printer, and Form are measured in twips. Controls are measured in the units defined by the ScaleMode of the underlying object. As a control or Form is resized, the value of this property changes.

Objects
Check box, Combo box, Command button, Directory List box, Drive List box, File List box, Form, Frame, Horizontal Scroll bar, Label, List box, Option button, Picture box, Printer, Text box, Screen, Vertical Scroll bar

Type
Single

Available   Design Time: Yes—Controls

No—Screen, Printer

Run-Time Read: Yes

Run-Time Write:

Yes—Controls

No—Screen, Printer

See Also   Height property
Left property
Top property

WindowState

Purpose   The WindowState property controls whether a Form is normal, minimized, or maximized.

Objects   Form

Type   Integer code

0—Normal (default)

1—Minimized to an icon

2—Maximized to full screen

Available   Design Time: Yes, but does not take effect until run time

Run-Time Read: Yes

Run-Time Write: Yes

See Also   Visible property

Events

Events are messages from the Visual Basic objects indicating that some action has occurred to that object. When events are passed to a program, they trigger event procedures in that program. When any event occurs, such as pressing a key or clicking a button, it is placed in an event queue, which is simply a first-in-first-out list. As soon as one event is processed, the next one is taken from the queue and processed. Some events trigger others and add them to the queue. For example, pressing a key causes a KeyDown event, followed by a KeyUp event, and then a KeyPress event. If you were typing into a Text box, a Changed event would follow the KeyPress event, and so forth.

When a Form loads and is shown, the following events occur in order: Load, Resize, Paint, GotFocus.

When a key is pressed and the focus is in an editable item, the following events occur in order: KeyDown, KeyUp, KeyPress, Change. If the item with the focus is a Command button, an Option button, or a Check box, and the key is the Enter or Spacebar, a Click event replaces the Change event.

When the mouse is clicked, the following events occur in order: MouseDown, MouseUp, Click.

This chapter lists all the events, the event procedure headers, and a description of the arguments in the following format:

Event Name

Purpose Description of what causes this particular event to occur.

Procedure Header Header for the event procedure.

Arguments Arguments of the event procedure.

Objects Objects which this event happens to.

See Also Listing of related events.

Change

Purpose The Change event occurs when the contents of a control changes.

Procedure Header `Sub object_Change (Index As Integer)`

Arguments *object*—The object that changed.

Index—For a control array of the objects, Index is equal to the Index property of the changed object.

Objects Combo box, Directory List box, Drive List box, Horizontal Scroll bar, Label, Picture box, Text box, Vertical Scroll bar

See Also None

Click

Purpose   The `Click` event occurs when an object is clicked with the mouse. It also occurs when you press Enter or the Spacebar when a Command button, an Option button, or a Check box is selected. Pressing Esc causes a `Click` event to a Command button that has its `Cancel` property set to `True`. Pressing Enter causes a `Click` event to a Command button that has its `Default` property set to `True`. You also can trigger a `Click` event with code by changing the `Value` property of a Command button, an Option button, or a Check box to `True`.

Procedure
Header   `Sub` *object*`_Click (Index As Integer)`

Arguments   *object*—The object that was clicked.

Index—For a control array of the objects, `Index` is equal to the `Index` property of the clicked object.

Objects   Check box, Combo box, Command button, Directory List box, File List box, Form, Label, List box, Menu, Option button, Picture box

See Also   None

DblClick

Purpose   The `DblClick` event occurs when an object is rapidly clicked twice with the mouse. It also occurs when you use code to change the `Path` property of a Directory List box, or the `FileName` property of a File List box to a valid file name.

Procedure
Header   `Sub` *object*`_DblClick (Index As Integer)`

Arguments   *object*—The object that was double clicked.

Index—For a control array of the objects, `Index` is equal to the `Index` property of the double clicked object.

Objects   Check box, Combo box, Command button, Directory List box, File List box, Form, Label, List box, Menu, Option button, Picture box

See Also   None

DragDrop

Purpose The DragDrop event occurs when a control is dragged over a Form or control and released. A drag event can be performed with a mouse or with the Drag method.

Procedure Header

```
Sub object_DragDrop (Index As Integer,
    Source As Control, X As Single,
    . Y As Single)
```

Arguments *object*—The object that changed.

Index—For a control array of the objects, Index is equal to the Index property of the dropped-upon Form or object.

Source—The control that was dragged and dropped.

X, Y—The *x,y* position of the mouse pointer when the Source was dropped on the object.

Objects Check box, Combo box, Command button, Directory List box, Drive List box, File List box, Form, Frame, Horizontal Scroll bar, Label, List box, Option button, Picture box, Text box, Vertical Scroll bar

See Also None

DragOver

Purpose The DragOver event occurs when a control is dragged over an object. Events occur every time the mouse pointer is moved while dragging an object.

Procedure Header

```
Sub object_DragOver (Index As Integer,
    Source As Control, X As Single,
    Y As Single, State As Integer)
```

Arguments *object*—The object that was dragged over.

Index—For a control array of the objects, Index is equal to the Index property of the object which was dragged over.

Source—The control that was being dragged.

X, Y—The *x,y* position of the mouse pointer when the event occurred.

State—A code indicating:

0—Entering the object

1—Leaving the object

2—Over the object and moved

Objects   Check box, Combo box, Command button, Directory List box, Drive List box, File List box, Frame, Form, Horizontal Scroll bar, Label, List box, Option button, Picture box, Text box, Vertical Scroll bar

See Also   None

DropDown

Purpose   The DropDown event occurs when the list of a Dropdown List box is just about to drop down.

Procedure Header   `Sub object_Dropdown (Index As Integer)`

Arguments   *object*—The Combo box CtlName.

Index—For a control array of the objects, Index is equal to the Index property of the Combo box that is going to drop its list.

Objects   Combo box

See Also   None

GotFocus

Purpose   The GotFocus event occurs when an object gets the focus. The focus can be gotten either by user action, such as pressing Tab or clicking with the mouse, or with code using the SetFocus method.

**Procedure
Header**   `Sub` *object*`_GotFocus (Index As Integer)`

Arguments   *object*—The object that got the focus.

`Index`—For a control array of the objects, `Index` is equal to the `Index` property of the control that got the focus.

Objects   Check box, Combo box, Command button, Directory List box, Drive List box, File List box, Form, Horizontal Scroll bar, List box, Option button, Picture box, Text box, Vertical Scroll bar

See Also   `LostFocus` event

KeyDown

Purpose   The `KeyDown` event occurs when a control has the focus and a key is pressed down. The `KeyUp` and `KeyPress` events will occur when the key is released. The `KeyUp` and `KeyDown` events get key codes rather than characters from the system. Key codes are different from the ASCII character codes. Key codes refer to individual keys, and ASCII codes refer to characters. The key code for a key is the same whether the Shift key is down or up, but the ASCII code is different when the Shift key is down than when it is up. See Appendix C, "Key Code Chart," for a list of key codes, and Appendx B, "ASCII\ANSI Code Chart," for a list of ASCII and ANSI codes.

**Procedure
Header**   `Sub` *object*`_KeyDown (Index As Integer,`
       ↳   `KeyCode As Integer, Shift As Integer)`

Arguments   *object*—The object that had the focus when a key was pressed.

`Index`—For a control array of the objects, `Index` is equal to the `Index` property of the object that had the focus when the key was pressed.

`KeyCode`—The key's code number (see also Appendix C, "Key Code Chart," and the file CONSTANT.TXT included with Visual Basic for a list of key codes).

`Shift`—A code indicating which of the modifier keys was held down when the key was pressed. The value of this code is equal to the sum of the following codes for the modifier keys held down.

1—Shift

2—Ctrl

4—Alt

Objects   Check box, Combo box, Command button, Directory List box, Drive List box, File List box, Form, Horizontal Scroll bar, List box, Option button, Picture box, Text box, Vertical Scroll bar

See Also   KeyUp, KeyPress events

KeyPress

Purpose   The KeyPress event occurs when an object has the focus and a key is pressed and released. Because the KeyPress event occurs before a keystroke is given to the control, you can filter the input here if necessary. If you change the value of KeyAscii, the changed value is given to the control.

Procedure Header

```
Sub object_KeyPress (Index As Integer,
    KeyAscii As Integer)
```

Arguments   *object*—The object that had the focus when the key was pressed.

Index—For a control array of the objects, Index is equal to the Index property of the object that had the focus when the key was pressed.

KeyAscii—The ASCII code of the key that was pressed (see Appendix B, "ASCII\ANSI Code Chart"). Use Chr$() to convert the code to text.

Objects   Check box, Combo box, Command button, Directory List box, Drive List box, File List box, Form, Horizontal Scroll bar, List box, Option button, Picture box, Text box, Vertical Scroll bar

See Also   KeyUp, KeyDown events

KeyUp

Purpose   The KeyUp event occurs when a control has the focus and a pressed key is released. A KeyPress event will follow. The KeyUp and KeyDown events get key

codes rather than characters from the system. Key codes are different from ASCII codes. Key codes refer to individual keys, and ASCII codes refer to characters. The key code for some key is the same whether the Shift key is down or up, but the ASCII code is different when the Shift key is down than when it is up.

Procedure Header

```
Sub object_KeyUp (Index As Integer,
    KeyCode As Integer, Shift As Integer)
```

Arguments *object*—The object that had the focus when a key was released.

Index—For a control array of the objects, Index is equal to the Index property of the object that had the focus when the key was released.

KeyCode—The key's code number (see Appendix C, "Key Code Chart," and the file CONSTANT.TXT included with Visual Basic for a list of key codes).

Shift—A code indicating which of the modifier keys was held down when the key was pressed. The value of this code is equal to the sum of the following codes for the modifier keys held down.

> 1—Shift
>
> 2—Ctrl
>
> 4—Alt

Objects Check box, Combo box, Command button, Directory List box, Drive List box, File List box, Form, Horizontal Scroll bar, List box, Option button, Picture box, Text box, Vertical Scroll bar

See Also KeyDown, KeyPress events

LinkClose

Purpose The LinkClose event occurs when a Dynamic Data Exchange (DDE) link closes. A DDE Link is a dynamic connection between two different applications. Similar objects in both applications are linked so when the object in the server application changes, that change is transmitted to the client application.

Procedure Header

```
Sub object_LinkClose (Index As Integer)
```

Arguments   *object*—The Visual Basic object that had the DDE link.

Index—For a control array of the objects, Index is equal to the Index property of the object that had the link close.

Objects   Form, Label, Picture box, Text box

See Also   LinkError, LinkExecute, and LinkOpen events

LinkError

Purpose   The LinkError event occurs when an error occurs during a Dynamic Data Exchange (DDE) conversation. A DDE Link is a dynamic connection between two different applications. Similar objects in both applications are linked so when the object in the server application changes, that change is transmitted to the client application.

Procedure
Header
```
Sub object_LinkError (Index As Integer,
    LinkErr As Integer)
```

Arguments   *object*—The object that had the DDE conversation.

Index—For a control array of the objects, Index is equal to the Index property of the object that had the link error.

LinkErr—The error codes are things done to the Visual Basic end of a DDE link by the external application.

> 1—Data requested was in the wrong format.
>
> 2—Data was requested without opening a DDE conversation.
>
> 3—DDE was requested without opening a DDE conversation.
>
> 4—Attempted to change an item without opening a DDE conversation.
>
> 5—Attempted to poke data without opening a DDE conversation. A client *pokes* data when he or she sends data backward through the link to the server.
>
> 6—Attempted to continue DDE after the LinkMode was set to 0 - none.
>
> 7—Too many DDE links.

8—String too long for DDE transmission, truncated.

9—Invalid control array element specified as the link item.

10—Unexpected DDE message.

11—Not enough memory for DDE.

12—A server attempted client operations.

Objects   Form, Label, Picture box, Text box

See Also   `LinkClose`, `LinkExecute`, and `LinkOpen` events

LinkExecute

Purpose   The `LinkExecute` event occurs when your Visual Basic program is a Dynamic Data Exchange (DDE) server for an external client application, and the client sends the server a command string. The content of that string is up to you. You must define what commands your application will respond to and put them in a `Form_LinkExecute` procedure.

Procedure
Header
```
Sub Form_LinkExecute (CmdStr As Integer,
    Cancel As Integer)
```

Arguments   `CmdStr`—The command string from the client application.

`Cancel`—A message back to the client.

> `True` (–1)—Command rejected.

> `False` (0)—Command accepted (default).

Objects   Form

See Also   `LinkClose`, `LinkError`, and `LinkOpen` events

LinkOpen

Purpose   The `LinkOpen` event occurs when an external client application is initiating a Dynamic Data Exchange (DDE) conversation with a Form, or when a

Visual Basic control is initiating a DDE conversation with an external server. A DDE Link is a dynamic connection between two different applications. Similar objects in both applications are linked so when the object in the server application changes, that change is transmitted to the client application.

Procedure
Header

```
Sub object_LinkOpen (Index As Integer,
  Cancel As Integer)
```

Arguments   *object*—The object that is opening the DDE conversation (controls), or that is being asked to open a conversation (Forms).

Index—For a control array of the objects, Index is equal to the Index property of the affected object.

Cancel—Change the value of this argument to accept or reject the DDE conversation.

True (–1)—Reject the conversation.

False (0)—Accept the conversation (default).

Objects   Form, Label, Picture box, Text box

See Also   LinkClose, LinkError, and LinkExecute events

Load

Purpose   The Load event occurs when a Form is loaded. This is a good place to put start-up code for a program.

Procedure
Header   `Sub Form_Load ()`

Arguments   None

Objects   Form

See Also   Unload event

LostFocus

Purpose   The LostFocus event occurs when an object loses the focus. The focus can be lost either by user action, such as pressing Tab or clicking with the mouse, or with code using the SetFocus method.

**Procedure
Header**   **Sub** *object*_**LostFocus (Index As Integer)**

Arguments   *object*—The object that lost the focus.

Index—For a control array of the objects, Index is equal to the Index property of the object that lost the focus.

Objects   Check box, Combo box, Command button, Directory List box, Drive List box, File List box, Form, Horizontal Scroll bar, List box, Option button, Picture box, Text box, Vertical Scroll bar

See Also   GotFocus event

MouseDown

Purpose   The MouseDown event occurs when a mouse button is pressed and the mouse pointer is over an object. The MouseDown, MouseUp, and MouseMove events distinguish between the different buttons of the mouse and the state of the Shift, Ctrl, and Alt keys at the time. The Click event responds only to the left mouse button.

**Procedure
Header**

```
Sub object_MouseDown (Index As Integer,
   Button As Integer, Shift As Integer,
   X As Single, Y As Single)
```

Arguments   *object*—The object that the mouse pointer was on.

Index—For a control array of the objects, Index is equal to the Index property of the object under the mouse pointer.

Button—The mouse button pressed as a code.

> 1—Left Button
>
> 2—Right Button
>
> 4—Center Button

Shift—The state of the modifier keys when the button was pressed as a code. The codes for the different keys are added together if more than one key is held down. For example, if both the Alt and Ctrl keys were pressed, Shift would equal 6.

> 1—Shift
>
> 2—Ctrl
>
> 4—Alt

X, Y—The *x,y* location of the mouse pointer when the mouse button was pressed.

Objects   File List box, Form, Label, List box, Picture box

See Also   Click, MouseUp, and MouseMove events

MouseMove

Purpose   The MouseMove event occurs when a mouse pointer is moved over an object. The MouseDown, MouseUp, and MouseMove events distinguish between the different buttons of the mouse and the state of the Shift, Ctrl, and Alt keys at the time. The Click event responds only to the left mouse button.

Procedure Header

```
Sub object_MouseMove (Index As Integer,
    Button As Integer, Shift As Integer,
    X As Single, Y As Single)
```

Arguments   *object*—The object that the mouse pointer is over.

Index—For a control array of the objects, Index is equal to the Index property of the object under the mouse pointer.

Button—The mouse button that is down when the event occurs as a code. If more than one button is pressed, the codes are added together.

> 1—Left Button
>
> 2—Right Button
>
> 4—Center Button

Shift—The state of the modifier keys when the event occurs as a code. The codes for the different keys are added together if more than one key is held down.

> 1—Shift
>
> 2—Ctrl
>
> 4—Alt

X, Y—The *x,y* location of the mouse pointer when the event occurs.

Objects File List box, Form, Label, List box, Picture box

See Also Click, MouseDown, and MouseUp events

MouseUp

Purpose The MouseUp event occurs when a pressed mouse button is released while the mouse pointer is over an object. The MouseDown, MouseUp, and MouseMove events distinguish between the different buttons of the mouse and the state of the Shift, Ctrl, and Alt keys at the time. The Click event responds only to the left mouse button.

Procedure Header

```
Sub object_MouseUp (Index As Integer,
    Button As Integer, Shift As Integer,
    X As Single, Y As Single)
```

Arguments *object*—The object that the mouse pointer was on.

Index—For a control array of the objects, Index is equal to the Index property of the object under the mouse pointer.

Button—The mouse button released as a code.

> 1—Left Button
>
> 2—Right Button
>
> 4—Center Button

Shift—The state of the modifier keys when the button was released as a code. The codes for the different keys are added together if more than one key is held down.

1—Shift

2—Ctrl

4—Alt

X, Y—The *x,y* location of the mouse pointer when the mouse button was released.

Objects File List box, Form, Label, List box, Picture box

See Also Click, MouseDown, and MouseMove events

Paint

Purpose The Paint event occurs when the contents of a Form or Picture box are uncovered and need to be repainted. If AutoRedraw is set to True for the object, the system will take care of repainting it. Repainting applies only to text and graphics drawn on the objects at run time. The Refresh method also invokes a Paint event. Be careful with Paint event procedures; you can create a cascade of events (imagine what would happen if a Refresh method were placed within a Paint procedure).

**Procedure
Header** Sub *object*_**Paint (Index As Integer)**

Arguments *object*—The Form or Picture box that needs repainting.

Index—For a control array of the objects, Index is equal to the Index property of the object that needs redrawing.

Objects Form, Picture box

See Also None

PathChange

Purpose The PathChange event occurs when the Path or FileName properties of a control are changed.

Procedure Header	`Sub object_PathChange (Index As Integer)`
Arguments	*object*—The object whose `Path` or `FileName` properties changed.
	`Index`—For a control array of the objects, `Index` is equal to the `Index` property of the object whose `Path` or `FileName` properties have changed.
Objects	Directory List box, File List box
See Also	`PatternChange` event

PatternChange

Purpose	The `PatternChange` event occurs when the `Pattern` property of a File List box changes.
Procedure Header	`Sub object_PatternChange (Index As Integer)`
Arguments	*object*—The name of the File List box.
	`Index`—For a control array of the objects, `Index` is equal to the `Index` property of the affected File List box.
Objects	File List box
See Also	`PathChange` event

Resize

Purpose	The `Resize` event occurs when a Form is first displayed or is resized.
Procedure Header	`Sub Form_Resize ()`
Arguments	None
Objects	Form
See Also	None

Timer

Purpose	The Timer event occurs when a Timer's time interval has expired. When using a Timer like an alarm clock, use this procedure to take action when the alarm goes off. The Timer event does not stop a Timer; it continues to count down to the next Timer event.
Procedure Header	`Sub object_Timer (Index As Integer)`
Arguments	*object*—The name of the Timer.
	Index—For a control array of the objects, Index is equal to the Index property of the Timer that had an event.
Objects	Timer
See Also	None

Unload

Purpose	The Unload event occurs just before a Form is unloaded. Use it to save values and clean up any loose ends before the Form is removed from memory. When a Form is removed from memory, any data stored in its variables is lost unless those variables are defined in the Global module or put somewhere by the Unload event procedure.
Procedure Header	`Sub Form_Unload ()`
Arguments	None
Objects	Form
See Also	Load event

Objects

The Objects of Visual Basic consist primarily of Controls and the Form. These objects are the visual pieces that comprise an application. Other objects include the Clipboard, Debug, Printer, and Screen objects. These last four objects are used for interaction with the Windows Clipboard, debugging, controlling the printer, and receiving information about what is visible on the screen. The operation and use of the controls is covered in Part II of this book, so this chapter contains a brief description of each object and the Properties, Events, and Methods that apply to it in the following format:

Object Name

Purpose	Describes what the object is used for.
Properties	Lists the properties of the object.
Events	Lists the events that can happen to the object.
Methods	Lists the methods that affect this object.

Check Box

Purpose The Check box control is used to set nonexclusive options; therefore, any number of Check boxes in a group can be checked or unchecked. The Check box is a square box followed by a Label. When it is checked, there is an X in the box. The Check box is related to the Option buttons that are used to select exclusive options. The state of the Check box is given by the `Value` Property, which can have the following values: 0 for Unchecked, –1 for Checked, and 2 for Grayed (Disabled).

Properties

BackColor	Caption	CtlName
DragIcon	DragMode	Enabled
FontBold	FontItalic	FontName
FontSize	FontStrikethru	FontUnderline
ForeColor	Height	Index
Left	MousePointer	Parent
TabIndex	TabStop	Tag
Top	Value	Visible
Width		

Events

Click	DragDrop	DragOver
GotFocus	KeyDown	KeyPress
KeyUp	LostFocus	

Methods	Drag	Move	Refresh
	SetFocus		

Clipboard

Purpose	The Clipboard object is used to communicate with the Windows operating system's Clipboard. There is no visual control associated with the Clipboard object, and only Methods apply to it.

Properties	None
Events	None

Methods	Clear	GetData	GetFormat
	GetText	SetData	SetText

 # Combo Box

Purpose	The Combo box is a combination of a List box and a Text box. The Combo box allows a user to select a value from a list, or to type a value. The appearance of the Combo box is determined by the Style property. Variations include a Text box above a List box, a Text box above a drop-down List box, and a drop-down List box.

Properties	BackColor	CtlName	DragIcon
	DragMode	Enabled	FontBold
	FontItalic	FontName	FontSize
	FontStrikethru	FontUnderline	ForeColor
	Height	Index	Left
	List	ListCount	ListIndex
	MousePointer	Parent	SelLength
	SelStart	SelText	Style

	Sorted	TabIndex	TabStop
	Tag	Text	Top
	Visible	Width	

Events	Change	Click	DblClick
	DragDrop	DragOver	DropDown
	GotFocus	KeyDown	KeyPress
	KeyUp	LostFocus	

Methods	AddItem	Drag	Move
	Refresh	RemoveItem	SetFocus

Command Button

Purpose The Command button, along with the menus, is the primary method for initiating some action in a program. The Command button is a rounded-corner rectangle with a Caption across its face. Command buttons initiate events rather than set options like the Option buttons and Check boxes do.

Properties	BackColor	Cancel	Caption
	CtlName	Default	DragIcon
	DragMode	Enabled	FontBold
	FontItalic	FontName	FontSize
	FontStrikethru	FontUnderline	Height
	Index	Left	MousePointer
	Parent	TabIndex	TabStop
	Tag	Top	Value
	Visible	Width	

Events	Click	DragDrop	DragOver
	GotFocus	KeyDown	KeyPress
	KeyUp	LostFocus	
Methods	Drag	Move	Refresh
	SetFocus		

Debug

18

Purpose The Debug object creates a path from the running application to the Immediate window. Values within a running program are printed on the Immediate window with the Debug object and the Print method. There is no visual control associated with the Debug object.

Properties None

Events None

Methods Print

 # Directory List Box

Purpose The Directory List box is a special version of a List box that is linked to the DOS file system. It is designed to work with the File List box and the Drive List box to make a complete disk file access system. It appears as a list of file folders for a disk specified in the Path property. When the user clicks a directory, it reveals its subdirectories, and the path to the selected directory appears in the Path property.

Properties	BackColor	CtlName	DragIcon
	DragMode	Enabled	FontBold
	FontItalic	FontName	FontSize
	FontStrikethru	FontUnderline	ForeColor
	Height	Index	Left

	List	ListCount	ListIndex
	MousePointer	Parent	Path
	TabIndex	TabStop	Tag
	Top	Visible	Width
Events	Change	Click	DragDrop
	DragOver	GotFocus	KeyDown
	KeyPress	KeyUp	LostFocus
	MouseDown	MouseMove	MouseUp
Methods	Drag	Move	Refresh
	SetFocus		

Drive List Box

Purpose The Drive List box is a special version of a List box that is linked to the DOS file system. It is designed to work with the Directory List box and the File List box to make a complete disk file access system. It is a drop-down list of the disk drive and its name. Clicking a disk puts its letter in the Path property.

Properties	BackColor	CtlName	DragIcon
	DragMode	Drive	Enabled
	FontBold	FontItalic	FontName
	FontSize	FontStrikethru	FontUnderline
	ForeColor	Height	Index
	Left	List	ListCount
	ListIndex	MousePointer	Parent
	TabIndex	TabStop	Tag
	Top	Visible	Width

Events	Change	DragDrop	DragOver
	GotFocus	KeyDown	KeyPress
	KeyUp	LostFocus	
Methods	Drag	Move	Refresh
	SetFocus		

 File List Box

Purpose The File List box is a special version of a List box that is linked to the DOS file system. It is designed to work with the Directory List box and the Drive List box to make a complete disk file access system. The File List box contains a list of the files in the directory specified in its Path property. Clicking a file puts its name in the FileName property.

Properties	Archive	BackColor	CtlName
	DragIcon	DragMode	Enabled
	FileName	FontBold	FontItalic
	FontName	FontSize	FontStrikethru
	FontUnderline	ForeColor	Height
	Hidden	Index	Left
	List	ListCount	ListIndex
	MousePointer	Normal	Parent
	Path	Pattern	ReadOnly
	System	TabIndex	TabStop
	Tag	Top	Visible
	Width		
Events	Click	DblClick	DragDrop
	DragOver	GotFocus	KeyDown
	KeyPress	KeyUp	LostFocus

	MouseDown	MouseMove	MouseUp
	PathChange	PatternChange	
Methods	Drag	Move	Refresh
	SetFocus		

Form

Purpose   The Form object is the basis of all Visual Basic Applications. All the controls are attached to the Form window.

Properties

AutoRedraw	BackColor	BorderStyle
Caption	ControlBox	CurrentX
CurrentY	DrawMode	DrawStyle
DrawWidth	Enabled	FillColor
FillStyle	FontBold	FontItalic
FontName	FontSize	FontStrikethru
FontTransparent	FontUnderline	ForeColor
FormName	hDC	Height
hWnd	Icon	Image
Left	LinkMode	LinkTopic
MaxButton	MinButton	MousePointer
Picture	ScaleHeight	ScaleLeft
ScaleMode	ScaleTop	ScaleWidth
Tag	Top	Visible
Width	WindowState	

Events

Click	DblClick	DragDrop
DragOver	GotFocus	KeyDown
KeyPress	KeyUp	LinkClose

	LinkError	LinkExecute	LinkOpen
	Load	LostFocus	MouseDown
	MouseMove	MouseUp	Paint
	Resize	Unload	
Methods	Circle	Cls	Hide
	Line	Move	Point
	Print	PrintForm	PSet
	Refresh	Scale	SetFocus
	Show	TextHeight	TextWidth

 Frame

Purpose A Frame is a control for grouping other controls. It is a square box with a caption at the top. Any controls placed on a Frame move with the Frame when it is moved. Option buttons placed on a Frame form a single option-button group, separate from any other Option buttons on the Form.

Properties	BackColor	Caption	CtlName
	DragIcon	DragMode	Enabled
	FontBold	FontItalic	FontName
	FontSize	FontStrikethru	FontUnderline
	ForeColor	Height	Index
	Left	MousePointer	Parent
	TabIndex	Tag	Top
	Visible	Width	
Events	DragDrop	DragOver	
Methods	Drag	Move	Refresh

 # Horizontal Scroll Bar

Purpose   A Horizontal Scroll bar can scan quickly through a long list of numbers or items. Visually, it is the same as any Scroll bar at the side of a Windows window. (It is a long, thin rectangle with a slider in the middle, known as the Thumb.) The Thumb is dragged with the mouse, to quickly move from one end of the Scroll bar to the other. Clicking the gray area above or below the Thumb moves the Thumb in the direction and distance specified by the LargeChange property. Clicking the arrows at each end moves the Thumb in that direction by one SmallChange amount. Although a Scroll bar is usually associated with movement within a window, it is actually a control that either displays or returns an integer value according to the location of the thumb. Programmers have to create code that coordinates that value with a window or list. The Integer value is between the Min and Max properties.

Properties	CtlName	DragIcon	DragMode
	Enabled	Height	Index
	LargeChange	Left	Max
	Min	MousePointer	Parent
	SmallChange	TabIndex	TabStop
	Tag	Top	Value
	Visible	Width	
Events	Change	DragDrop	DragOver
	GotFocus	KeyDown	KeyPress
	KeyUp	LostFocus	
Methods	Drag	Move	Refresh

 # Label

Purpose   A Label contains text you want the user to read, but not change. A Label is a rectangular box filled with the text that is stored in its Caption property.

Properties	Alignment	AutoSize	BackColor
	BorderStyle	Caption	CtlName
	DragIcon	DragMode	Enabled
	FontBold	FontItalic	FontName
	FontSize	FontStrikethru	FontUnderline
	ForeColor	Height	Index
	Left	LinkItem	LinkMode
	LinkTimeout	LinkTopic	MousePointer
	Parent	TabIndex	Tag
	Top	Visible	Width
Events	Change	Click	DblClick
	DragDrop	DragOver	LinkClose
	LinkError	LinkOpen	MouseDown
	MouseMove	MouseUp	
Methods	Drag	LinkExecute	LinkPoke
	LinkRequest	Move	Refresh

 List Box

Purpose A List box contains a list of selectable items. It is a rectangular window filled with lines of text. Each line is a list item. If there are more items than can fit in the window, a Scroll bar appears to allow scrolling of the list. A list cannot be loaded at design time, but must be filled with data by a running program, using the AddItem method.

Properties	BackColor	CtlName	DragIcon
	DragMode	Enabled	FontBold
	FontItalic	FontName	FontSize
	FontStrikethru	FontUnderline	ForeColor

	Height	Index	Left
	List	ListCount	ListIndex
	MousePointer	Parent	Sorted
	TabIndex	TabStop	Tag
	Text	Top	Visible
	Width		

Events	Click	DblClick	DragDrop
	DragOver	GotFocus	KeyDown
	KeyPress	KeyUp	LostFocus
	MouseDown	MouseMove	MouseUp

Methods	AddItem	Drag	Move
	Refresh	RemoveItem	SetFocus

Menu

Purpose   A Menu is most closely related to the Command buttons because it is used to initiate events, although it can be used to set options as well. A menu is a pull-down list of items attached to the top of a Form. Each of the items is a separate command that initiates some piece of code. In addition, items can be checked to indicate selected options, or grayed to indicate unavailability.

Properties	Caption	Checked	CtlName
	Enabled	Index	Parent
	Tag	Visible	

Events   Click

Methods   None

Option Button

Purpose Option buttons are used to set exclusive options, therefore only one Option button in a group can be pressed. Option buttons are round circles with a Label to their right. When an option button is pressed, a black dot appears in the center. Option buttons are related to Check boxes, which set nonexclusive options. Option buttons are grouped by placing them on a Frame.

Properties

BackColor	Caption	CtlName
DragIcon	DragMode	Enabled
FontBold	FontItalic	FontName
FontSize	FontStrikethru	FontUnderline
ForeColor	Height	Index
Left	MousePointer	Parent
TabIndex	TabStop	Tag
Top	Value	Visible
Width		

Events

Click	DblClick	DragDrop
DragOver	GotFocus	KeyDown
KeyPress	KeyUp	LostFocus

Methods

Drag	Move	Refresh
SetFocus		

 # Picture Box

Purpose A Picture box is used to display graphics. The Form and the Picture box are the only objects that can display graphics on the screen. Along with the Printer, they are the only objects that can be drawn on or printed on. Other objects contain text, but text is printed or drawn on a Picture box. Text printed on a Picture box cannot be retrieved as text, only as graphics.

627

Properties	AutoRedraw	AutoSize	BackColor
	BorderStyle	CtlName	CurrentX
	CurrentY	DragIcon	DragMode
	DrawMode	DrawStyle	DrawWidth
	Enabled	FillColor	FillStyle
	FontBold	FontItalic	FontName
	FontSize	FontStrikethru	FontTransparent
	FontUnderline	ForeColor	hDC
	Height	Image	Index
	Left	LinkItem	LinkMode
	LinkTimeout	LinkTopic	MousePointer
	Parent	Picture	ScaleHeight
	ScaleLeft	ScaleMode	ScaleTop
	ScaleWidth	TabIndex	TabStop
	Tag	Top	Visible
	Width		
Events	Change	Click	DblClick
	DragDrop	DragOver	GotFocus
	KeyDown	KeyPress	KeyUp
	LinkClose	LinkError	LinkOpen
	LostFocus	MouseDown	MouseMove
	MouseUp	Paint	
Methods	Circle	Cls	Drag
	Line	LinkExecute	LinkPoke
	LinkRequest	LinkSend	Move
	Point	Print	PSet
	Refresh	Scale	SetFocus
	TextHeight	TextWidth	

Printer

Purpose	The Printer object is used to communicate with the printer. Draw or print on the printer exactly as you would on a Picture box or Form. When you issue the NewPage or EndDoc methods, the page is printed. The PrintForm method is also available to print a Form as it appears on the screen.

Properties

CurrentX	CurrentY	DrawMode
DrawStyle	DrawWidth	FillColor
FillStyle	FontBold	FontCount
FontItalic	FontName	Fonts
FontSize	FontStrikethru	FontTransparent
FontUnderline	ForeColor	hDC
Height	Page	ScaleHeight
ScaleLeft	ScaleMode	ScaleTop
ScaleWidth	Width	

Events None

Methods

Circle	EndDoc	Line
NewPage	Print	PSet
Scale	TextHeight	TextWidth

Screen

Purpose	The Screen object is used to access objects displayed on the screen.

Properties

ActiveControl	ActiveForm	FontCount
Fonts	Height	MousePointer
Width		

Events None

Methods None

629

 # Text Box

Purpose	A Text box is used to gather text from the user. A Text box is a rectangular box where text can be typed, selected, and edited with the keyboard. The Clipboard, and the **C**ut, **C**opy, and **P**aste commands are not supported without adding code.	

Properties	BackColor	BorderStyle	CtlName
	DragIcon	DragMode	Enabled
	FontBold	FontItalic	FontName
	FontSize	FontStrikethru	FontUnderline
	ForeColor	Height	Index
	Left	LinkItem	LinkMode
	LinkTimeout	LinkTopic	MousePointer
	MultiLine	Parent	ScrollBars
	SelLength	SelStart	SelText
	TabIndex	TabStop	Tag
	Text	Top	Visible
	Width		
Events	Change	DragDrop	DragOver
	GotFocus	KeyDown	KeyPress
	KeyUp	LinkClose	LinkError
	LinkOpen	LostFocus	
Methods	Drag	LinkExecute	LinkPoke
	LinkRequest	Move	Refresh
	SetFocus		

Timer

Purpose A Timer is a control that works like an alarm clock. You set its `Interval` property for a specific number of milliseconds, and it issues a `Timer` event whenever that time has passed. Note that there are a limited number of Timers available (16 total in Windows). A Timer is always invisible on a Form.

Properties

CtlName	Enabled	Index
Interval	Parent	Tag

Events Timer

Methods None

Vertical Scroll Bar

Purpose A Vertical Scroll bar is used for quickly scanning through a long list of numbers or items. Visually, it is the same as any Scroll bar at the side of a Windows window. (It is a long, thin rectangle with a slider in the middle, known as the Thumb.) The Thumb is dragged with the mouse, to quickly move from one end of the Scroll bar to the other. Clicking the gray area above or below the Thumb moves the Thumb in the direction and distance specified by the `LargeChange` property. Clicking the arrows at each end moves the Thumb in that direction by one `SmallChange` amount. Although a Scroll bar is usually associated with movement within a window, it is actually a control that either displays or returns an integer value according to the location of the Thumb. Programmers have to create code that coordinates that value with a window or list. The `Integer` value is between the `Min` and `Max` properties.

Properties

CtlName	DragIcon	DragMode
Enabled	Height	Index
LargeChange	Left	Max
Min	MousePointer	Parent

	SmallChange	TabIndex	TabStop
	Tag	Top	Value
	Visible	Width	
Events	Change	DragDrop	DragOver
	GotFocus	KeyDown	KeyPress
	KeyUp	LostFocus	
Methods	Drag	Move	Refresh

Part IV

Appendixes

Installing Visual Basic

Installing Visual Basic is relatively simple, with most the work done by the actual Visual Basic Setup program. Take care of the following few steps before doing the installation.

1. Check the hardware.

2. Write protect the distribution disks.

3. Copy the distribution disks.

4. Install Visual Basic.

5. Make the run-time library available.

Checking Your Hardware

Visual Basic requires some specific hardware and software to run, so before you open your Visual Basic package, be sure the machine you have runs the necessary equipment. You must have at least a 286 machine, with DOS 3.1

and Windows 3.0 running. A later version of the machine or software is better. You need at least 1 megabyte (1M) of memory, although 2–4M would be much better. You need a hard disk with about 5M free for the complete Visual Basic package. You can get away with about 2.5M if you leave out the icon library, the examples, and the tutorial. You need a graphics monitor and card such as the CGA, EGA, VGA, 8514, Hercules, or compatible. I don't recommend anything less than an EGA system if you want to take full advantage of the capabilities of Visual Basic. You need a Mouse. You may be able to get by without one, but don't try. It's much easier if you have a mouse, and they are not too expensive.

Hardware:

CPU: 286 or higher.

Monitor and card: CGA, EGA, VGA, 8514, or Hercules.

Mouse:

Memory: 1M or more.

Disk space: 5M for complete installation.
  2.5M for partial installation.

Software:

System: DOS 3.31 or later.

Windows: Version 3.0 or later.

If you are not sure what hardware you have, start your system, and see if it starts up in Windows. Windows 3.0 displays a large banner while it loads, so it's obvious if it is installed. If your system starts at the DOS prompt instead, type `win /s` to activate Windows. If you get an invalid command error, Windows is probably not installed. If Windows is installed, then you have the correct hardware to run Visual Basic. The only thing you must check is that you have enough disk space to hold the complete system. The installer will check this for you, and tell you if you don't have enough space before it tries to install Visual Basic.

Write Protecting the Distribution Disks

As soon as you take the distribution disks out of the box, protect them. To protect them, put write protect tabs on the 5 1/4-inch disks and slide open

636

the write protect tabs on the 3 1/2-inch disks. This not only protects the disks from accidental erasure and unwanted changes, but also protects them from virus attacks.

Making a Copy of the Distribution Disks

The second step is to copy the distribution disks with the DOS DISKCOPY command or the Windows File Manager. Both 5 1/4-inch and 3 1/2-inch disks come with Visual Basic, so copy the set that fits in your A drive.

You can copy the installation disks with either Windows or DOS. Use the method you prefer.

Copying the Disks with Windows

To copy disks with the Windows File Manager, use the following steps.

1. Open the File Manager.

2. Insert a distribution disk in drive A and click the A drive in the File Manager window.

3. On the **D**isk menu, select the **C**opy Diskette command.

4. If you have a second floppy disk drive of the same type as the A drive, select it when you are asked for the destination drive. If you don't have another matching drive, select the A drive as the destination drive.

5. Follow the instructions for inserting and removing source and destination disks. Note that the destination disk does not have to be blank or formatted.

6. When a disk is done, remove it and go back to step one to copy the next disk in the distribution.

A

Copying the Disks with DOS

There are two methods for copying the disks with DOS, depending on whether you have a second disk drive of the same type as the A drive. If you do have a second drive, then use the following steps. If you don't have a second drive, then use the steps in the next section. Note that to use the DISKCOPY command, your DOS system directory must be in your current path, or you must be in that directory. If you execute the DISKCOPY command, and get an invalid command error, try moving to the DOS directory using the CD (change directory) command, and then try executing DISKCOPY again. The following steps assume your DOS system directory is named DOS.

1. At the DOS prompt, type

   `C:\DOS>`**`DISKCOPY A: B:`**

2. When you are instructed to do so, put the locked distribution disk in drive A, the destination disk in drive B, and press Enter. Note that the destination disk does not have to be blank or formatted.

3. Remove the disks when each installation is done.

4. You are asked whether you want to copy another disk. Type **Y** and Enter, and copy the rest of the distribution disks. After copying the last disk, type **N** and hit Enter to quit.

   To copy disks using the DISKCOPY command and a single floppy disk drive, follow these steps.

1. At the DOS prompt, type

   `C:\DOS>`**`DISKCOPY A: A:`**

2. When instructed, insert the locked distribution disk in drive A, and press Enter.

3. When instructed, remove the distribution disk, place the destination disk in drive A, and press Enter. Note that the destination disk does not have to be blank or formatted.

4. Exchange the disks when requested until installation is completed.

5. You are asked whether you want to copy another disk. Type **Y** and enter, and copy the rest of the distribution disks. After copying the last disk, type **N** and hit Enter to quit.

Installing with Setup

Now that you have a copy of your distribution set, insert Disk 1 in drive A. Visual Basic must be installed from drive A. It cannot be installed from any other disk drive. (I tried, it doesn't work.) If your A drive is a 5 1/4-inch, 360K drive, you cannot install Visual Basic with the disks supplied. Microsoft does supply an exchange coupon for a set of 360K disks. If you have a 5 1/4-inch high-density disk, or 3 1/2-inch disk on your system and are technically inclined, you can rewire your system to change one of these disks into the A drive rather than the 360K disk. Warning: Don't do this unless you know what you are doing.

1. Insert Disk 1 of the distribution set in your A drive.

2. The SETUP program is a Windows program, so Windows must be running for SETUP to work. If Windows is running, execute the **Run** command on the **File** menu and type **A:SETUP** in the dialog box.

   If Windows isn't running, type

   ```
   C:\>A:
   A:\>WIN SETUP
   ```

3. A window appears, as shown in Figure A.1, asking you to personalize your copy of Visual Basic. Type your name or your company name and click **Continue**.

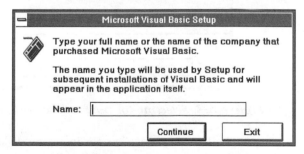

Figure A.1. *Personalizing Visual Basic.*

4. A second window appears, as shown in Figure A.2, asking you to specify the drive and directory in which you want to install Visual Basic. Make your choice and click **Continue**.

639

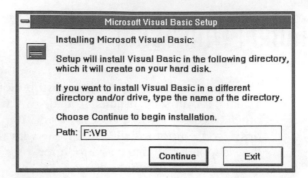

Figure A.2. Selecting the drive and path to install Visual Basic.

5. The next window asks what parts of Visual Basic you want installed—see Figure A.3. You have a choice of installing the entire
Visual Basic package, or installing certain parts. If you have limited
disk space, you can install part of the package, then install the
other parts at a later time. Eliminating the icon library, the sample
applications, and the tutorial saves 2.8M of disk space. Make your
selection and click **Continue**.

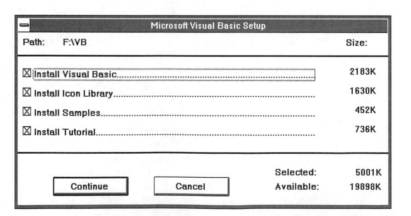

Figure A.3. Selecting the parts of the package to install.

6. Follow the directions for inserting disks until the window shown
in Figure A.4 appears. Click **Exit** and the installation is complete.

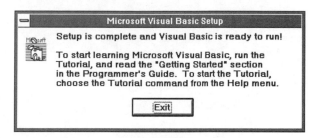

Figure A.4. Completing the Visual Basic installation.

Using the Run-Time Library

The file VBRUN100.DLL in the Visual Basic (\VB) directory is a run-time library needed by all compiled Visual Basic applications. This library must be accessible to the Visual Basic application, so it must be somewhere in the current path. If you have only one application, put a copy of the run-time library in the directory with the application. If you have several applications, you don't want several copies or the run-time library floating around, so put one copy in the \WINDOWS directory. If you give one of your compiled Visual Basic programs to someone else, include a copy of the run-time library with the application.

ASCII/ANSI Code Chart

This is the Windows/Visual Basic version of the ANSI chart. All character information in BASIC applications is stored as strings of codes. The most commonly used characters are the ASCII codes (American Standard Code for Information Interchange), which comprise the first 128 codes in this table. Windows applications actually support most of the 256 character ANSI (American National Standards Institute) code set, of which the ASCII codes are a subset. The following table contains the ANSI characters, and their ASCII/ANSI codes in both hexadecimal and decimal format. Missing codes are unsupported by Windows.

Character	Hex code	Decimal code
Backspace	&H08	8
Tab	&H09	9
Line feed	&H0A	10
Carriage return	&H0D	13
Space	&H20	32
!	&H21	33

Character	Hex code	Decimal code
"	&H22	34
#	&H23	35
$	&H24	36
%	&H25	37
&	&H26	38
'	&H27	39
(	&H28	40
)	&H29	41
*	&H2A	42
+	&H2B	43
,	&H2C	44
-	&H2D	45
.	&H2E	46
/	&H2F	47
0	&H30	48
1	&H31	49
2	&H32	50
3	&H33	51
4	&H34	52
5	&H35	53
6	&H36	54
7	&H37	55
8	&H38	56
9	&H39	57
:	&H3A	58
;	&H3B	59
<	&H3C	60

Character	Hex code	Decimal code
=	&H3D	61
>	&H3E	62
?	&H3F	63
@	&H40	64
A	&H41	65
B	&H42	66
C	&H43	67
D	&H44	68
E	&H45	69
F	&H46	70
G	&H47	71
H	&H48	72
I	&H49	73
J	&H4A	74
K	&H4B	75
L	&H4C	76
M	&H4D	77
N	&H4E	78
O	&H4F	79
P	&H50	80
Q	&H51	81
R	&H52	82
S	&H53	83
T	&H54	84
U	&H55	85
V	&H56	86
W	&H57	87

B

Character	Hex code	Decimal code
X	&H58	88
Y	&H59	89
Z	&H5A	90
[	&H5B	91
\	&H5C	92
]	&H5D	93
^	&H5E	94
_	&H5F	95
`	&H60	96
a	&H61	97
b	&H62	98
c	&H63	99
d	&H64	100
e	&H65	101
f	&H66	102
g	&H67	103
h	&H68	104
i	&H69	105
j	&H6A	106
k	&H6B	107
l	&H6C	108
m	&H6D	109
n	&H6E	110
o	&H6F	111
p	&H70	112
q	&H71	113
r	&H72	114

Character	Hex code	Decimal code
s	&H73	115
t	&H74	116
u	&H75	117
v	&H76	118
w	&H77	119
x	&H78	120
y	&H79	121
z	&H7A	122
{	&H7B	123
¦	&H7C	124
}	&H7D	125
~	&H7E	126
'	&H91	145
'	&H92	146
''	&H93	147
''	&H94	148
O	&H95	149
–	&H96	150
—	&H97	151
	&HA0	160
¡	&HA1	161
¢	&HA2	162
£	&HA3	163
⊗	&HA4	164
¥	&HA5	165
¦	&HA6	166
§	&HA7	167

B

Character	Hex code	Decimal code
"	&HA8	168
.	&HA9	169
ª	&HAA	170
«	&HAB	171
¬	&HAC	172
–	&HAD	173
.	&HAE	174
‾	&HAF	175
°	&HB0	176
±	&HB1	177
²	&HB2	178
.	&HB3	179
,	&HB4	180
μ	&HB5	181
.	&HB6	182
■	&HB7	183
,	&HB8	184
.	&HB9	185
º	&HBA	186
»	&HBB	187
¼	&HBC	188
½	&HBD	189
.	&HBE	190
¿	&HBF	191
À	&HC0	192
Á	&HC1	193
Â	&HC2	194

Character	Hex code	Decimal code
Ã	&HC3	195
Ä	&HC4	196
Å	&HC5	197
Æ	&HC6	198
Ç	&HC7	199
È	&HC8	200
É	&HC9	201
Ê	&HCA	202
Ë	&HCB	203
Ì	&HCC	204
Í	&HCD	205
Î	&HCE	206
'Ï	&HCF	207
Đ	&HD0	208
Ñ	&HD1	209
Ò	&HD2	210
Ó	&HD3	211
Ô	&HD4	212
Ǒ	&HD5	213
Ö	&HD6	214
·	&HD7	215
ø	&HD8	216
Ù	&HD9	217
Ú	&HDA	218
Û	&HDB	219
Ü	&HDC	220
Ÿ	&HDD	221

B

Character	Hex code	Decimal code
Þ	&HDE	222
ß	&HDF	223
à	&HE0	224
á	&HE1	225
â	&HE2	226
ã	&HE3	227
ä	&HE4	228
å	&HE5	229
æ	&HE6	230
ç	&HE7	231
è	&HE8	232
é	&HE9	233
ê	&HEA	234
ë	&HEB	235
ì	&HEC	236
í	&HED	237
î	&HEE	238
ï	&HEF	239
ð	&HF0	240
ñ	&HF1	241
ò	&HF2	242
ó	&HF3	243
ô	&HF4	244
õ	&HF5	245
ö	&HF6	246
·	&HF7	247
ø	&HF8	248

Character	Hex code	Decimal code
ù	&HF9	249
ú	&HFA	250
û	&HFB	251
ü	&HFC	252
`y	&HFD	253
þ	&HFE	254
ÿ	&HFF	255

Key Code Chart

The key codes given in the following chart are needed by the KeyUp and KeyDown event procedures. These key codes identify particular keys on the keyboard that are being pressed, rather than the characters that the keys represent. Thus, they don't differentiate between shifted and unshifted keys, and keys on the keypad return different key codes from the same keys on the main keyboard. Not every keyboard supports all of these codes.

Key	Hex code	Decimal code
LeftMouseButton	&H1	1
RightMouseButton	&H2	2
Cancel	&H3	3
MiddleMouseButton	&H4	4
Backspace	&H8	8
Tab	&H9	9
Clear	&HC	12
Return	&HD	13
Shift	&H10	16
Control	&H11	17
Menu	&H12	18

Key	Hex code	Decimal code
Pause	&H13	19
CapsLock	&H14	20
Esc	&H1B	27
Spacebar	&H20	32
PageUp	&H21	33
PageDown	&H22	34
End	&H23	35
Home	&H24	36
LeftArrow	&H25	37
UpArrow	&H26	38
RightArrow	&H27	39
DownArrow	&H28	40
Select	&H29	41
Print	&H2A	42
Execute	&H2B	43
SnapShot	&H2C	44
Insert	&H2D	45
Delete	&H2E	46
Help	&H2F	47
0	&H30	48
1	&H31	49
2	&H32	50
3	&H33	51
4	&H34	52
5	&H35	53
6	&H36	54
7	&H37	55
8	&H38	56
9	&H39	57
A	&H41	59
B	&H42	60
C	&H43	61
D	&H44	62
E	&H45	63
F	&H46	64
G	&H47	65
H	&H48	66
I	&H49	67
J	&H4A	68
K	&H4B	69

Key	Hex code	Decimal code
L	&H4C	70
M	&H4D	71
N	&H4E	72
O	&H4F	73
P	&H50	74
Q	&H51	75
R	&H52	76
S	&H53	77
T	&H54	78
U	&H55	79
V	&H56	80
W	&H57	81
X	&H58	82
Y	&H59	83
Z	&H5A	84
0	&H60	90
1	&H61	91
2	&H62	92
3	&H63	93
4	&H64	94
5	&H65	95
6	&H66	96
7	&H67	97
8	&H68	98
9	&H69	99
;	&HBA	186
=	&HBB	187
,	&HBC	188
-	&HBD	189
.	&HBE	190
/	&HBF	191
`	&HC0	192
[	&HDB	219
\	&HDC	220
]	&HDD	221
`	&HDE	222
ScrollLock	&H91	145

Key	Hex code	Decimal code
Keypad Keys		
*	&H6A	106
+	&H6B	107
Separator	&H6C	108
-	&H6D	109
.	&H6E	110
/	&H6F	111
NumLock	&H90	144
Function Keys		
F1	&H70	112
F2	&H71	113
F3	&H72	114
F4	&H73	115
F5	&H74	116
F6	&H75	117
F7	&H76	118
F8	&H77	119
F9	&H78	120
F10	&H79	121
F11	&H7A	122
F12	&H7B	123
F13	&H7C	124
F14	&H7D	125
F15	&H7E	126
F16	&H7F	127

Index

X

Y-Z

Sams' First Books Get You Started Fast!

"The First Book Series ... is intended to get the novice off to a good start, whether with computers in general or with particular programs ...."

The New York Times

The First Book of WordPerfect 5.1
Kate Miller Barnes
275 pages, 7³/8 x 9¹/4, $16.95 USA
0-672-27307-1

Look For These Books In Sams' First Book Series

The First Book of Excel 3 for the Mac
Christopher Van Buren
320 pages, 7³/8 x 9¹/4, $16.95 USA
0-672-27328-4

The First Book of Excel 3 for Windows
Chrisopher Van Buren
320 pages, 7³/8 x 9¹/4, $16.95 USA
0-672-27359-4

The First Book of Harvard Graphics
Jack Purdum
300 pages, 7³/8 x 9¹/4, $16.95 USA
0-672-27310-1

The First Book of Lotus 1-2-3 Release 2.3
Alan Simpson & Paul Lichtman
330 pages, 7³/8 x 9¹/4, $16.95 USA
0-672-27365-9

The First Book of Microsoft Windows 3
Jack Nimersheim
304 pages, 7³/8 x 9¹/4, $16.95 USA
0-672-27334-9

The First Book of Microsoft Word 5.5, Second Edition
Brent Heslop & David Angell
320 pages, 7³/8 x 9¹/4, $16.95 USA
0-672-27333-0

The First Book of Microsoft Word for Windows
Brent Heslop & David Angell
304 pages, 7³/8 x 9¹/4, $16.95 USA
0-672-27332-2

The First Book of Microsoft Works for the PC
Debbie Walkowski
304 pages, 7³/8 x 9¹/4, $16.95 USA
0-672-27360-8

The First Book of MS-DOS
Jack Nimersheim
272 pages, 7³/8 x 9¹/4, $16.95 USA
0-672-27312-8

The First Book of Norton Utilities 6
Joseph Wikert, Rev. by Lisa Bucki
275 pages, 7³/8 x 9¹/4, $16.95 USA
0-672-27384-5

The First Book of Paradox 3.5
Jonathan Kamin
320 pages, 7³/8 x 9¹/4, $16.95 USA
0-672-27370-5

The First Book of PC Paintbrush
Deke McClelland
289 pages, 7³/8 x 9¹/4, $16.95 USA
0-672-27324-1

The First Book of PC Tools 7
Gordon McComb
350 pages, 7³/8 x 9¹/4, $16.95 USA
0-672-27371-3

The First Book of Personal Computing Second Edition
W.E. Wang & Joe Kraynak
275 pages, 7³/8 x 9¹/4, $16.95 USA
0-672-27385-3

The First Book of PFS: First Publisher
Karen Brown & Robert Bixby
308 pages, 7³/8 x 9¹/4, $16.95 USA
0-672-27326-8

The First Book of PowerPoint for Windows
Douglas Snyder
330 pages, 7³/8 x 9¹/4, $16.95 USA
0-672-27356-X

The First Book of PROCOMM PLUS
Jack Nimersheim
250 pages, 7³/8 x 9¹/4, $16.95 USA
0-672-27309-8

The First Book of PS/1
Kate Barnes
300 pages, 7³/8 x 9¹/4, $16.95 USA
0-672-27346-2

The First Book of Q&A 4
Sandra E. Schnyder
272 pages, 7³/8 x 9¹/4, $16.95 USA
0-672-27311-X

The First Book of Quattro Pro 3
Patrick Burns
300 pages, 7³/8 x 9¹/4, $16.95 USA
0-672-27367-5

The First Book of Quicken in Business
Gordon McComb
300 pages, 7³/8 x 9¹/4, $16.95 USA
0-672-27331-4

The First Book of the Mac
Carla Rose & Jay Rose
350 pages, 7³/8 x 9¹/4, $16.95 USA
0-672-27355-1

The First Book of UNIX
Douglas Topham
300 pages, 7³/8 x 9¹/4, $16.95 USA
0-672-27299-7

The First Book of WordPerfect for Windows
Kate Barnes
400 pages, 7³/8 x 9¹/4, $16.95 USA
0-672-27343-8

SAMS

See your local retailer or call 1-800-428-5331.

Do It Yourself Visual Basic Examples Disk

If you want to use all the examples in this book, but don't want to type them yourself, you can obtain them on disk. Complete the following order form and return it to the address below with a check or money order for $20.00, US currency only. For countries outside of the United States and Canada, please add $1.00 for overseas shipping. For California orders, please add state sales tax (7.25%). The Visual Basic examples disk will be sent to you by first-class mail. Please specify the disk size.

William J. Orvis
226 Joyce St.
Livermore, CA 94550

Name: _____

Address: _____

City/State/Zip: _____

Disk Price $20.00

    Overseas shipping $1.00
    (outside of the U.S. and Canada)   _____

    State sales tax (7.25% = $1.45)   _____
    (California only)

Total   _____

Enclosed is my check or money order for $_____
(Make checks payable to William J. Orvis.)
Please send me the Visual Basic Examples Disk.

I prefer: ___5 1/4-inch disk

           ___3 1/2-inch disk